COLORS OF KYOTO:
THE SEIFŪ YOHEI CERAMIC STUDIO

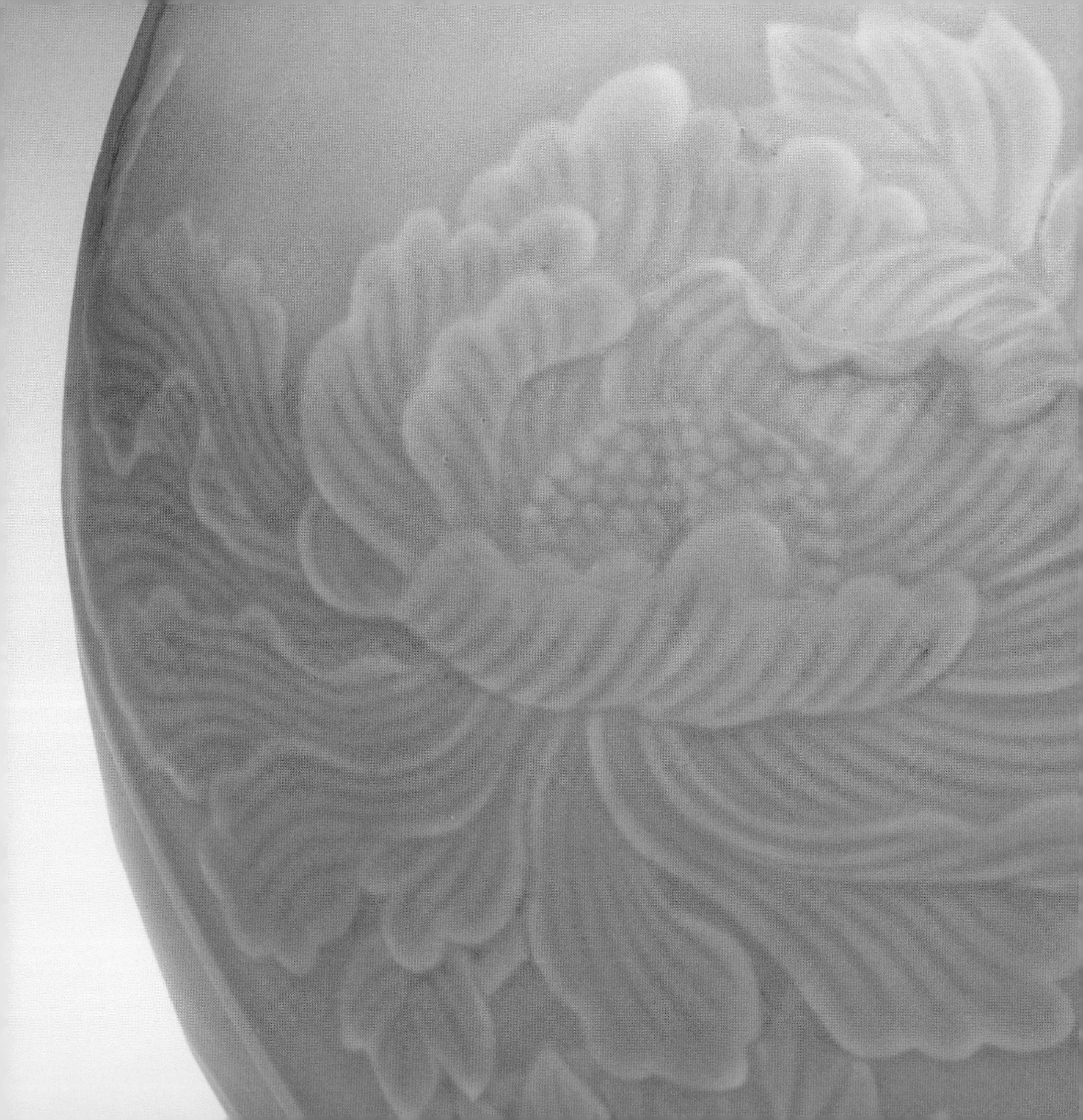

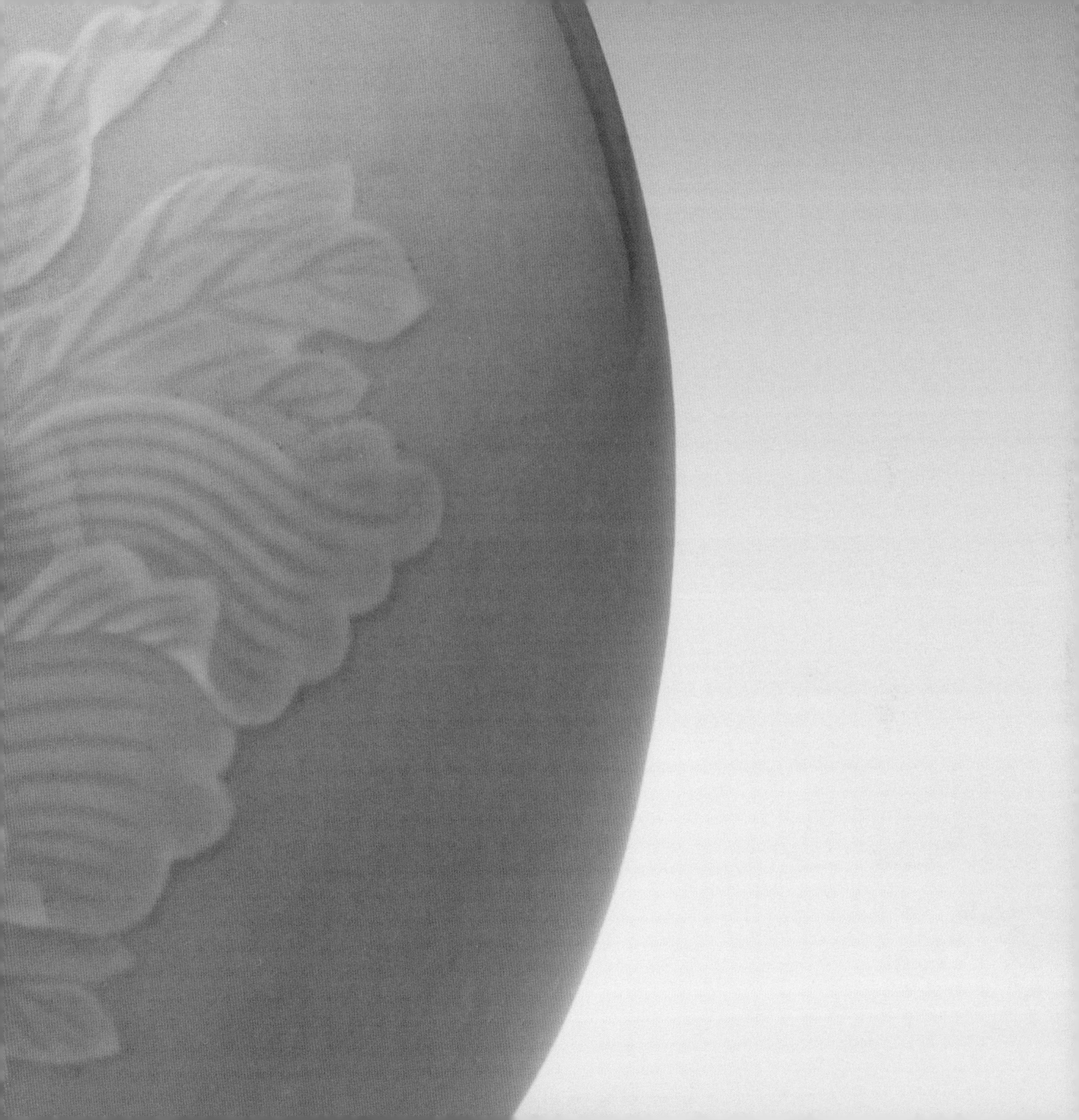

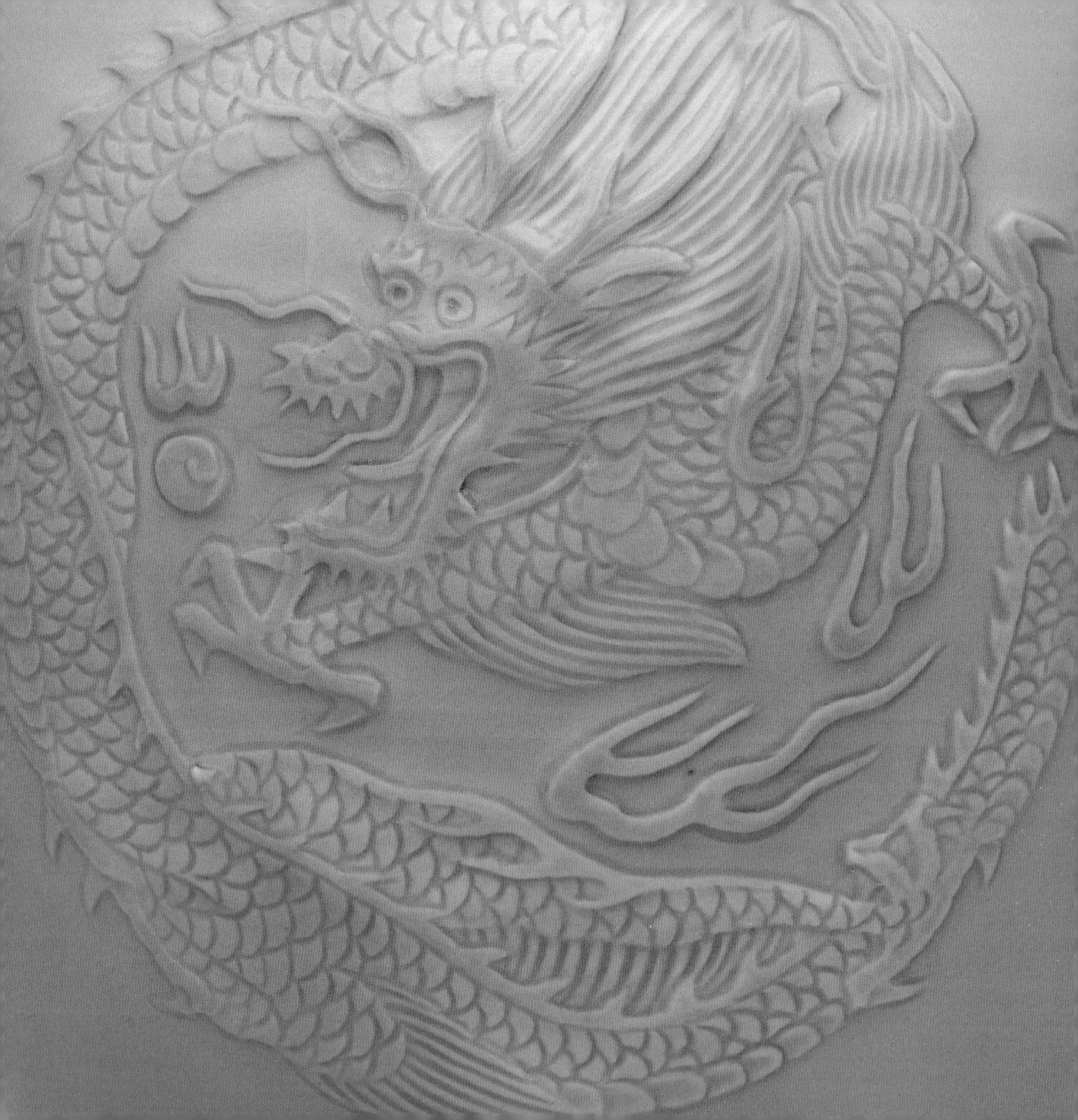

CLEVELAND MASTERWORK SERIES 7

COLORS OF KYOTO
THE SEIFŪ YOHEI CERAMIC STUDIO

SHINYA MAEZAKI

SINÉAD VILBAR

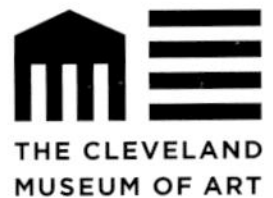

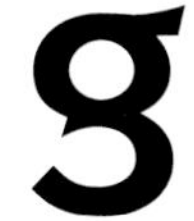

The Cleveland Museum of Art in association with D Giles Limited

THIS PUBLICATION IS MADE POSSIBLE IN PART BY
THE ANDREW W. MELLON FOUNDATION.

Published on the occasion of the exhibition *Colors of Kyoto: The Seifū Yohei Ceramic Studio*, on view at the Cleveland Museum of Art August 19, 2023–March 10, 2024.

All exhibitions at the Cleveland Museum of Art are underwritten by the CMA Fund for Exhibitions. Principal annual support is provided by the late Roy L. Williams. Generous annual support is provided by an anonymous supporter, the late Dick Blum and Harriet Warm, Gary and Katy Brahler, Cynthia and Dale Brogan, Dr. Ben and Julia Brouhard, Brenda and Marshall Brown, Richard and Dian Disantis, the Jeffery Wallace Ellis Trust in Memory of Lloyd H. Ellis Jr., Leigh and Andy Fabens, Janice Hammond and Edward Hemmelgarn, Cathy Lincoln, Eva and Rudolf Linnebach, William S. and Margaret F. Lipscomb, Bill and Joyce Litzler, Tim O'Brien and Breck Platner, William J. and Katherine T. O'Neill, the Kelvin and Eleanor Smith Foundation, and Margaret and Loyal Wilson.

The Cleveland Museum of Art is funded in part by residents of Cuyahoga County through a public grant from Cuyahoga Arts & Culture.

This exhibition was supported in part by the Ohio Arts Council, which receives support from the State of Ohio and the National Endowment for the Arts.

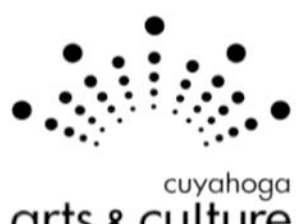

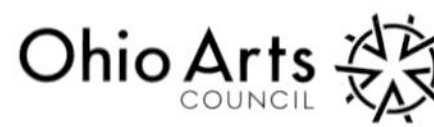

NOTES TO THE READER

All measurements are in centimeters; height precedes width precedes depth or diameter. Catalogue numbers appear in [brackets].

Japanese and Chinese names appear with the family name preceding the given name with the exception of author Shinya Maezaki.

J. indicates Japanese transliteration;
C. indicates Chinese transliteration.

Objects in the collection of the Cleveland Museum of Art were photographed by Gary Kirchenbauer. James Kohler prepared the digital files. The museum holds copyright to its images. When known, other copyright holders and photographers are acknowledged in the credits.

Library of Congress Control Number: 2023933031

ISBN: 978-1-913875-54-1

Designed by Thomas Barnard, Director of Publications

Emily Mears, Director of Exhibitions

Rachel Beamer, Publication Project Manager

Edited by Akiko Yamagata, Graphite Editing

Proofread by Kathleen Mills

The Cleveland Museum of Art
11150 East Boulevard
Cleveland, OH 44106-1797
www.clevelandart.org

First published in 2023 by GILES, an imprint of
D Giles Limited
66 High Street
Lewes, BN7 1XG, UK
gilesltd.com

Printed and bound by SYL L'Art Gràfic Premium, S.L. in Barcelona, Spain

FRONT COVER
[13]. *Dining Bowl with Clematis* (detail), 1893–97. Seifū Yohei III (Japanese, 1851–1914). Porcelain with underglaze color and molded and incised designs; h. 6.9 cm, diam. 19 cm. The Cleveland Museum of Art, Gift of James and Christine Heusinger 2022.156

PAGES 2–3
[53]. *Water Container with Peonies* (detail), 1900–14. Seifū Yohei III. Porcelain with molded and carved design and green glaze; h. with lid 17.8 cm, diam. 16 cm. The Cleveland Museum of Art, Gift of James and Christine Heusinger 2022.197

PAGE 4
[94]. *Vase with Dragon Roundels* (detail), 1900–14. Seifū Yohei III. Porcelain with molded and carved design and purple glaze; h. 15 cm, diam. 10 cm. The Cleveland Museum of Art, Gift of James and Christine Heusinger 2022.236

BACK COVER
[80]. *Rabbit with Jewel*, 1930s–90s. Shinkai Kanzan (Japanese, 1912–2011). Porcelain with underglaze pink and cream glaze; h. 16 cm, w. 9 cm, d. 12.5 cm. The Cleveland Museum of Art, Gift of James and Christine Heusinger 2022.220

In recent years, the Cleveland Museum of Art has systematically augmented its holdings of the ceramics of Japan, one of the world's great contributors to ceramic history. Following modest beginnings in the first half of the twentieth century, the bequest of the Severance and Greta Millikin Collection in 1964 ensured the museum had a selection of Japanese porcelain that represented some of the notable traditions of the Edo period (1615–1868), including Kakiemon and Nabeshima. In the second half of the 1960s and in the 1970s, the museum purchased fine examples of Shigaraki and Mino stoneware from the fifteenth to the early seventeenth century, in addition to an important work by Kyoto ceramist Nonomura Ninsei (active 1640s–90s). It was also during this period that the museum received its first gifts of contemporary Japanese ceramics: works by Bizen-ware ceramists Fujiwara Yū (1932–2001) and Kimura Kōzō (b. 1941). Acquisitions of archaeological earthenware followed in the 1980s, including a remarkable "flame-rim" vessel datable to about 2500 BCE. In the final decade of the twentieth century, a range of Japanese ceramics—from prehistoric to contemporary, in a wide variety of clays and made with diverse firing processes—entered the collection. A work gifted by eminent ceramist Kohyama Yasuhisa (b. 1936), titled *Hajibito*, or "Ceramist of Ancient Times," on the occasion of the museum's seventy-fifth anniversary, in 1992, spoke both to Japan's long history as a region of ceramics production and to the close relationship between the Cleveland Institute of Art, where Kohyama has taught, and the CMA.

Cleveland stepped into the twenty-first century with gifts of modern and contemporary Japanese ceramics from Dixon T. Long, which added the work of such famed ceramists associated with the *mingei* movement as Hamada Shōji (1894–1978) to our burgeoning holdings. Long's gift was complemented in 2015 with medieval stoneware bequeathed to the CMA by George Gund III; these objects not only enhanced our representation of works from historically important kilns, but also provided essential context for understanding the traditions from which contemporary artists, such as Tsujimura Shirō (b. 1947), have drawn for their own creations. Most recently, in 2020, Joseph P. and Nancy F. Keithley gave the museum masterpieces by top Japanese modern and contemporary ceramists, many of whom were not previously represented in the collection, guaranteeing that their finest efforts will be known to CMA audiences. At the same time, we have selectively acquired porcelains produced in northern Kyushu during the seventeenth century to add definition and nuance to our displays in the permanent collection galleries.

On this occasion, I wish to acknowledge the extraordinary generosity of James and Christine Heusinger, who with their transformative gift of works from Seifū Yohei III (1851–1914) and the other members of the Seifū studio, have allowed us to make outstanding works produced in Kyoto during a time of rapid change in Japan part of the transnational cultural narratives that we tell at the museum. In 1893, Seifū Yohei III became the first of only five Japanese ceramists to be designated an Imperial Household Artist. He took seriously not only his role in representing Japan at the turn of the last century, but also his place within a grand tradition of ceramists active across East Asia. Seifū Yohei III drew inspiration from the works of fellow artists past and present in China and Korea and wished to add his own voice, with great admiration, to their centuries-long dialogue. The Heusingers assembled their collection quietly and with the intention to honor the contributions of the Seifū studio to ceramics history. With their humble and serious approach, they managed to assemble a remarkably comprehensive collection of more than one hundred works representing most aspects of the Seifū studio's production. We are extremely grateful to be able to share their vision with our audiences now and in the future, as we continue to recognize the role that ceramics have served across the world as containers and embodiments of shared cultures and technologies.

William M. Griswold
Director
Sarah S. and Alexander M. Cutler Chair
The Cleveland Museum of Art

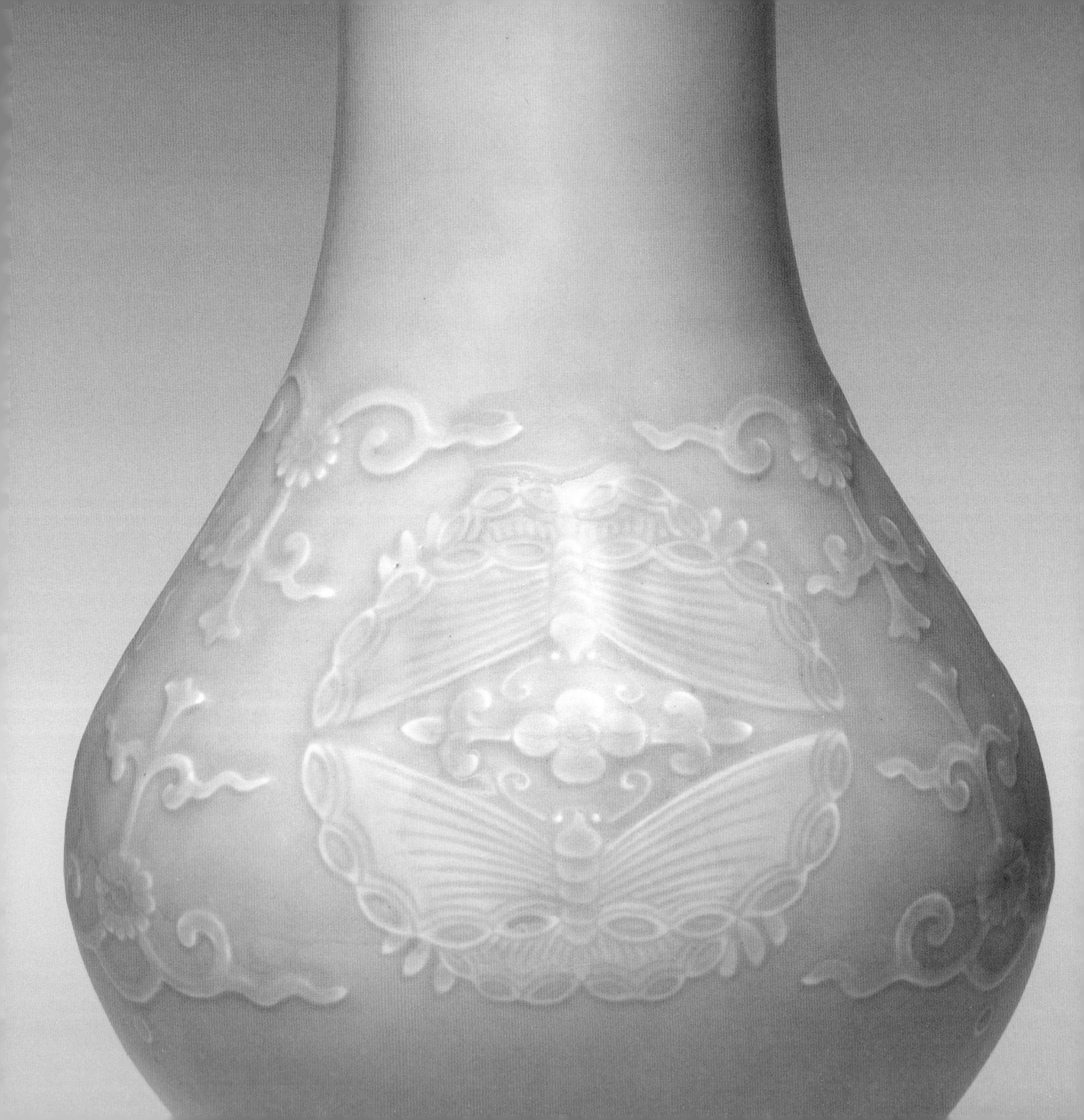

PURSUIT OF PERFECTION

Collector Jim Heusinger carefully untied the purple cord securing the lid of the wooden box and opened it to reveal an exquisite porcelain teapot by Seifū Yohei III (1851–1914). My first introduction to this ceramic artist was through viewings of the collection of works assembled over nearly three decades by Jim and Chris Heusinger; they gifted their collection to the Cleveland Museum of Art in December 2022. Each piece in the Heusingers' collection of over one hundred stoneware and porcelain works was shaped with precision, and many were decorated with innovative glazing techniques. Most pieces were also enclosed in wooden boxes called *tomobako*, literally "accompanying boxes," custom crafted to fit the height and width of each fragile ceramic and protect it. While carefully removing the fastening cord, or *kumihimo*, Jim explained, "I almost always purchased Seifū Yohei III's porcelains that were still in their original *tomobako*. The inscriptions and seals on the box help to authenticate the piece and explain its history." For example, Yohei III often inscribed or sealed the inside of the lid with the title "Imperial Household Artist," or *teishitsu gigei'in*, after it was bestowed on him in 1893. He was the first ceramist to be given this title.

As Jim placed the teapot back in its box and retied the cord, taking care to align it properly, he talked about this talented artist and his own interest in collecting Yohei III's works. "He was a Sinophile and a true genius!" he exclaimed. Highly regarded during his lifetime as the leader of the Seifū workshop in Kyoto, Yohei actually began his career apprenticed to a literati painter and studied Chinese painting and poetry. He then apprenticed in the Seifū studio and married into the family. Shortly after the untimely death of Seifū Yohei II (1845–1878), he became the third ceramist to use the Seifū Yohei name, becoming head of the studio. From the late 1880s to 1910, Yohei III's porcelains were featured in international expositions in Europe and the United States. Even with international recognition, Yohei maintained a very small workshop, producing porcelains primarily for the domestic market; both factors contributed to the rarity of his work. Yohei's engagement with Chinese culture and art continued throughout his lifetime, impacting his own porcelain creations. He was particularly influenced by Qing monochromatic porcelains. He experimented relentlessly with glazes, emulating those on Chinese porcelains and adding his own artistic nuances. "I really wanted to acquire porcelains illustrating all of

[92]. *Flower Vase with Butterflies* (detail), 1907–14. Seifū Yohei III. Porcelain with carved and molded designs and green glaze; h. 35.5 cm, diam. 16 cm. The Cleveland Museum of Art, Gift of James and Christine Heusinger, 2022.234

his glazes and even tried to find his glaze book," Jim said, "It probably doesn't exist anymore."

Jim discovered his first Yohei III porcelain in the 1990s on the internet and was immediately struck by the elegant aesthetic. He said of that work, "The simple shape and exquisite glaze—it was so very different. It was unlike any of the Japanese porcelains I had seen in museum collections and exhibitions." These, he explained, typically featured tea wares for *chanoyu*, or Japanese-style tea gatherings, blue-and-white porcelains, or decorative pieces from Arita in northern Kyushu.

Jim and Chris always sought out art experiences and frequented museums in the Midwest—the Albright-Knox Art Gallery (now the Buffalo AKG Art Museum) in their hometown of Buffalo, New York; the Toledo Museum of Art in Toledo, Ohio; the Detroit Institute of Arts, and, of course, the Cleveland Museum of Art: "Having the CMA at our back door was (and is) such an asset to our lives. We spent hours exploring the old Asian galleries and attended all the Japanese exhibitions. *Tsutsumu: The Art of the Japanese Package* (fig. 1) was a delightful show that impressed on us the importance of presentation and aesthetics in all levels of Japanese society. The sense of beauty was evident even when wrapping a

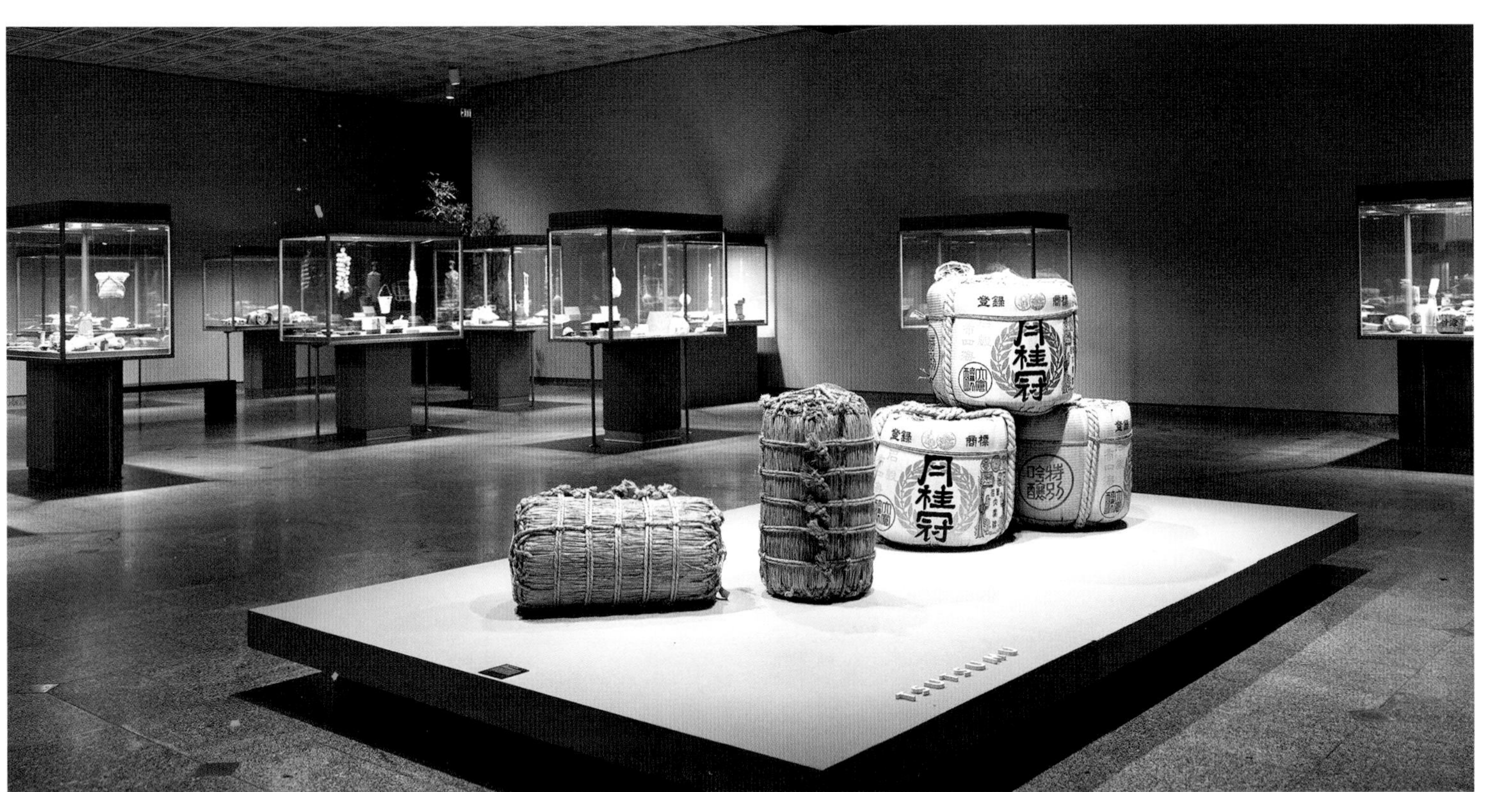

Figure 1. *Tsutsumu: The Art of the Japanese Package*, The Cleveland Museum of Art, 1977. Photo: Courtesy CMA Archives

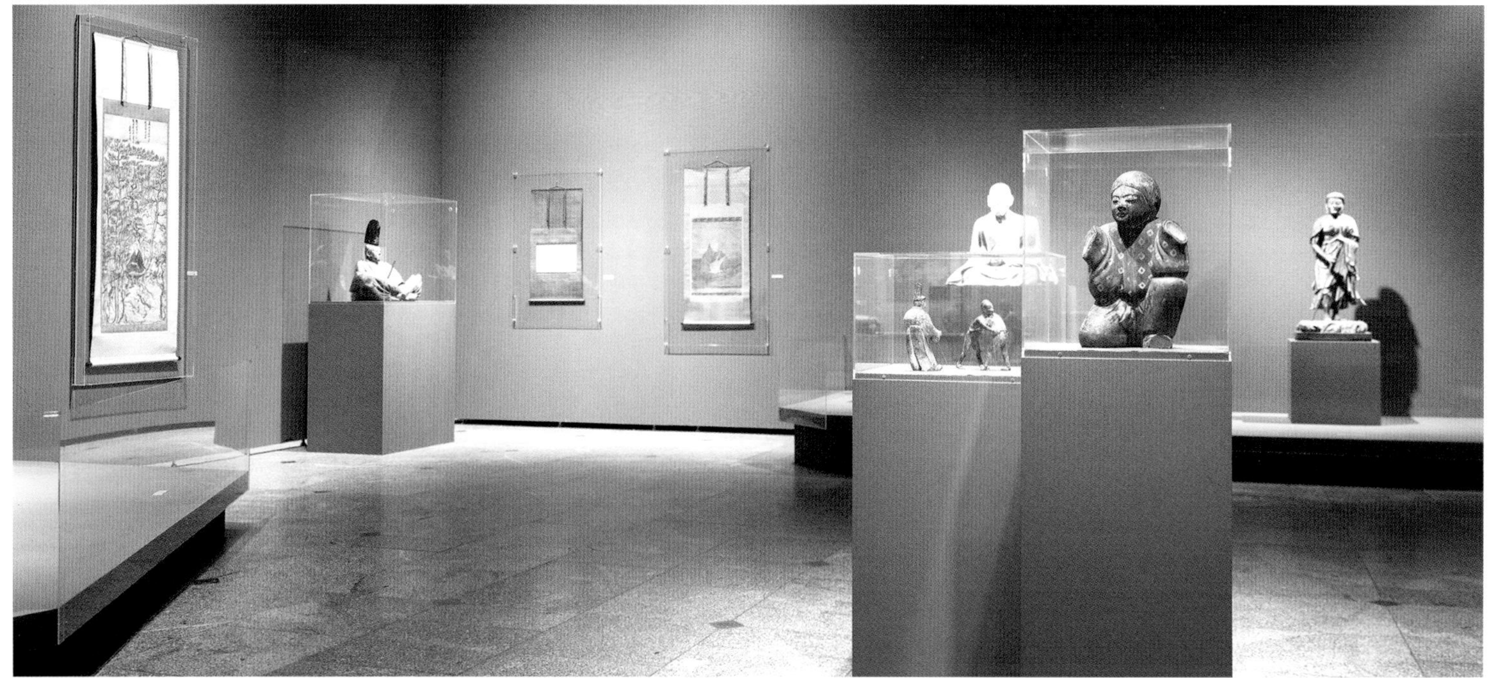

Figure 2. *Reflections of Reality in Japanese Art*, The Cleveland Museum of Art, 1983. Photo: Courtesy CMA Archives

mere five eggs." Based on the 1967 book by Oka Hideyuki, *How to Wrap Five Eggs: Traditional Japanese Packaging*, the 1977 exhibition was co-organized by Japan House (now Japan Society, New York) and the American Federation of Arts, with objects selected by Oka.

Also influential was CMA director Sherman Lee's 1983 retirement exhibition, *Reflections of Reality in Japanese Art* (fig. 2). "[It] was an eye-opener," Jim said. "The many National Treasures and Important Cultural Properties featured in the exhibition made it possible to experience rare masterpieces of painting and sculpture. These unique opportunities helped shape my understanding of Japanese aesthetics and helped me recognize the uniqueness of Yohei III's porcelains, even though we had not seen them exhibited before." The 1983 exhibition was co-organized by Japan's Agency for Cultural Affairs and the CMA, with the co-sponsorship of the Japan Foundation. It featured ten National Treasures and more than sixty Important Cultural Properties.

Jim was always interested in collecting, even as a child. As an adult, he has collected many things, including fountain pens: "They are portable so you can easily transport them to national conferences to share with other collectors." He also became interested in rare woods and acquired a collection from Yale University in the mid-1980s. It had been assembled to study the potential medicinal properties of wood. Jim's interest in exotic woods evolved into a business, Berea Hardwoods Company, that supplied wood to craftspeople and artists like

Sam Maloof (1916–2009), James Krenov (1920–2009), and George Nakashima (1905–1990). He even assisted in the renovation of then vice president George H. W. Bush's office by identifying wood similar to an extinct type of mahogany used to craft eighteenth-century furniture.

Over the years, he has also collected prints. When he acquired his first Japanese print, *Torii Gate* by Kawase Hasui (1883–1957), print specialist Michael Verne suggested that Jim and Chris join the Cleveland Museum of Art's Print Club. Jim's response: "Well, I don't really consider myself a print collector." By that time, however, he had already acquired about two hundred prints. The couple's long association with the club and friendships with many members and dealers further inspired them to continue visiting museums and galleries and to add to their collection.

Jim had already started collecting pieces of Japanese lacquer, blue-and-white porcelains, and Hirado ware by the time he acquired his first porcelain by Seifū Yohei III. To seriously collect Yohei III's work, Jim had to learn more about him, so he sought out dealers and collectors who had a similar passion for works by this extremely talented, yet little-known artist. Edward Kawanabe was a friend and mentor in his collecting journey.

A network of dealers in Japan worked with Jim to find other porcelains by Yohei III, including *Flower Vase with Phoenix in Paulownia* [55], purchased in 2005. "It's one of my favorite pieces," Jim said. "The phoenix in white relief is true perfection." This network also introduced him to works by other members of the Seifū Yohei studio, including those by Yohei III's son, Seifū Yohei IV (1871–1951). "The brilliant yellow *Prunus Vase with Amaranthus* [87] with the red and purple cockscomb motif was a stunning discovery," he added, of a vase by Yohei IV.

The only other significant private collection of Seifū Yohei III porcelains outside of Japan at the time was located in England. David Hyatt King (1946–2016), an administrator for the UK postal system, was inspired by Yohei III's work and assembled a collection through persistence and patience. Although competitors in the marketplace, David and Jim became friends, visiting each other to compare their collections. "We kept in touch throughout his life and even traded some Seifū porcelains," Jim said. "At his death, David gifted his collection to the National Museums Scotland."

Shinya Maezaki, a Japanese scholar and contributor to this catalogue, wrote the first serious English-language study of Seifū Yohei III and his workshop. Titled "Qing-Style Porcelain in Meiji Japan: The Ceramic Art of Seifū Yohei III," this was his 2009 doctoral dissertation for the School of Oriental and African Studies, University of London. When Shinya was conducting research, he made a trip to Cleveland to examine and photograph the Heusingers' collection, and he later illustrated selected works in his study. The exchange was rewarding for Jim and Chris as well: “It was a pleasure to share our collection with Shinya. We are indebted to him for deepening our understanding of the importance of Yohei and his impact on Japanese ceramic traditions during his lifetime.”

A particular goal for Jim and Chris was to assemble a collection that illustrates the great diversity of Yohei III’s glazes and sophisticated design processes: the works need to remain together to truly understand the scope of his accomplishments. In the museum, Yohei’s porcelains will be exhibited alongside Japanese ceramics and paintings also created during the Meiji period (1868–1912) so visitors can understand the time when he was working. Equally important, the museum’s collection of Qing dynasty (1644–1911) monochromatic porcelains on display in the Chinese galleries enables visitors to view the techniques that inspired Yohei in making his own forms and glazes.

“It is a great honor for Chris and me to gift our collection of works by the Seifū Yohei studio to the Cleveland Museum of Art” Jim said. “Seifū Yohei III is really a forgotten artist in his homeland and the rest of the world. His artistic genius can only be appreciated when you are able to experience the evolution of his work as he became the leading master of porcelains.” Now that the donated collection has been integrated into CMA’s permanent collection, visitors and scholars alike will be able to enjoy and study it. Hopefully their encounters with Seifū Yohei III’s works and those by the other generations of the studio will broaden their understanding of Japanese ceramic ware and its evolution in the late nineteenth and early twentieth centuries. It is so important that Yohei III’s extraordinary talents be understood and that his pursuit of perfection in the porcelain medium be recognized and admired today—just as it was during his lifetime.

Marjorie L. Williams

The project to present this stunning collection of works from the studio of Seifū Yohei has come together over the last ten years, but in truth, its origins lie in the more distant past. In 2007, a cohort of junior Japanese art scholars came together in Seattle, Washington, for the ninth iteration of a program known as JAWS, the Japan Art History Workshop. JAWS has served over the years as an important convening of scholars from around the world embarking on professional careers in the study and presentation of Japanese art. It was there that I met the author of the primary essay of this catalogue, Professor Shinya Maezaki; he was at the time a graduate student at the School of Oriental and African Studies, University of London, working on his dissertation on Seifū Yohei III. I was at the Princeton University Art Museum as the assistant curator of Asian art while writing my own dissertation on the "Illustrated Life and Acts of Hōnen," the National Treasure set of handscrolls belonging to the temple Chion'in in Kyoto. It was thanks to JAWS, organized that year by Dr. Shirahara Yukiko at the Seattle Art Museum with the faculty advisors Professors Kawai Masatomo of Keio University and Donohashi Akio of Kobe University, that Professor Maezaki and I had the chance to learn about each other's research and share our enthusiasm for connecting people with Japanese art. I am grateful for that encounter, which enables me to bring Professor Maezaki's groundbreaking scholarship on the Seifū Yohei studio to a wider audience through this book.

Soon after my arrival in Cleveland in January 2014, the Cleveland Museum of Art opened an exhibition of works of modern Japanese art from the Tokyo National Museum. As coordinating curator, I had the pleasure of installing with our team in the final room of the exhibition a vase by Seifū Yohei III that would be designated an Important Cultural Property by the Japanese government in 2017. Professor Maezaki had meanwhile continued to research and publish essays on this fascinating chapter in Japanese art and world ceramics history. In 2014, he also curated an important exhibition on Seifū Yohei III at the Shosha Art and Craft Museum in the city of Himeji in commemoration of the hundredth anniversary of the artist's death, the fruit of the joint efforts of the Ōisomachi Seifū Research Association, the Kyoto Ceramics Association, and the Ritsumeikan University Art Research Center.

During these very busy first few months in Cleveland, I had the opportunity, through the introduction of Marjorie L. Williams, to meet James and Christine Heusinger and to visit their home. Lucy Ruowan Yan, then a graduate student at Case Western Reserve University and a Cleveland Foundation Fellow, accompanied me on these visits. It was Lucy who photographed many of the Seifū Yohei studio pieces as we looked together with Mr. Heusinger and he explained why each was important in relation to the others in the collection.

In the spring of 2017, with the support of CMA director William Griswold and the chief officer of design, exhibitions, and publications Heidi Strean, our deputy director and chief curator, Heather Lemonedes Brown, visited the Heusingers to see their collection and make plans for a special installation in the summer of 2017. We aimed to display selected modern porcelains from the Heusingers' collection in our Japanese art galleries along with recently accessioned modern Japanese paintings and prints; the installation would serve as a complement to the concurrent special exhibition of the George Gund III bequest of medieval Japanese ink painting and stoneware. We also reached out to Professor Maezaki at that time to request his cooperation with our future exhibition project, and he agreed to write the primary essay for this book. Over the next couple of years, I was deeply focused on our 2019 *Shinto: Discovery of the Divine in Japanese Art* exhibition, and just as I was ready to turn my full attention to Seifū Yohei, the global pandemic took place, a time of disruption and irreparable losses. In the greater world and in my work related to this exhibition, the discovery of important connections was an unanticipated gift during this time. Even though I could not visit important exhibitions related to our work, thanks to Professor Meghan Jones and her team at Alfred University, I virtually attended a rich symposium on the concept of the teabowl at which Professor Maezaki, among others in multiple time zones, presented new research.

In the summer of 2021, the Heusingers allowed a small team, comprising art handler Tony Cisneros, registrar Jacob Emmett, and me, to set up shop in their home to photograph and measure numerous works in preparation for preliminary cataloguing. Using the information we gathered, alongside Lucy's photographs and Mr. Heusinger's comprehensive database, we began to lay the foundation for bringing the ceramics from the Heusingers' home to the CMA. This was done in the summer of 2022 with an expanded team, now including object conservator Beth Edelstein, environmental specialist Laura Gaylord, art handler Andrew Robinson, and collections manager Jennifer Cicero. In July 2022, I had the great pleasure of working with Warshawsky Fellow and Summer on the Cuyahoga Intern Vinnie Yiting Hua of Smith College to carefully examine each of the works in the collection. It was an amazing experience of object-centered learning for the two of us, as we took thousands of photographs and incrementally corrected our understanding of each piece and each set of works. In the process, we both studied the history of ceramics in East Asia and gained greater insights into the literati themes embraced by members of the Seifū studio. I cherish that experience as a once-in-a-lifetime chance to enjoy true intellectual and emotional growth with someone I hope will be a future colleague in the field.

I could not have produced my own essay and entries for the book without the sage advice of Professor Maezaki, who answered many questions about glazes and techniques. I also wish to acknowledge my colleagues here in Cleveland, Sooa Im McCormick and Clarissa von Spee, who enhanced my understanding of Korean and Chinese ceramics, as well as colleagues across the United States, including Patricia Graham, who shared generously of her knowledge of *sencha*; Morgan Pitelka, who read and commented on an early draft of my essay, offering crucial guidance; and Ai Fukunaga, who provided cutting-edge information on the state of the field and important advice on image selection. I am also extremely grateful for the insightful editing of the text by Akiko Yamagata of Graphite Editing, who pushed me to improve my explanations with her thoughtful questions and suggestions. At CMA, Rachel Beamer's excellent shepherding of the book and Tom Barnard's design were accompanied by many graciously given lessons about book production.

Imagining the book and, indeed, the exhibition would not have been possible without the wonderful exchanges with our photographer, Gary Kirchenbauer, who took on the daunting task of capturing not only hundreds of objects with subtle surface decoration under the most sympathetic lighting, but also their boxes, making sure that every inscription, seal, and inserted document will be available to scholars digitally on the CMA's website. Gary's attention to detail is perhaps matched only by that of Seifū Yohei III, who I believe would have approved of Gary's work. Asian Art Department curatorial assistant Katie Kilroy Blaser joined Gary and me in the photo studio for a week in the late fall of 2022 to take measurements of all the objects we had not measured in the summer of 2021 and entered all the data simultaneously as the three of us enjoyed the unexpected details we spied as we went about the work. The camaraderie and mutual delight in the objects helped me immensely in considering how I might reproduce that feeling for our exhibition visitors. Professor Maezaki's kind introduction to a private collector in the United States, Hermann Ferré, provided me with the chance to examine Seifū studio works that have brought another dimension to my knowledge and a new friend with whom to share my enthusiasm for modern ceramics. Of my other CMA colleagues who helped to bring this exhibition to life, I wish to thank, in particular, Jim Englemann in exhibition design, Rachel Arzuaga in interpretation, and Andrew Cappetta in programming, who have already done so much to shape my thoughts around the exhibition, as well as Emily Mears, director of exhibitions, who has kept us optimistic during this unusual era, and Elizabeth Saluk, registrar, for keeping us organized. Finally, I extend my gratitude to James and Christine Heusinger. It goes without saying that none of this would have been possible without their tremendous generosity. As always, I thank my husband, Dann Vilbar, for his love and patience.

Sinéad Vilbar
Janice Hammond and Edward Hemmelgarn Curator of Japanese Art
The Cleveland Museum of Art

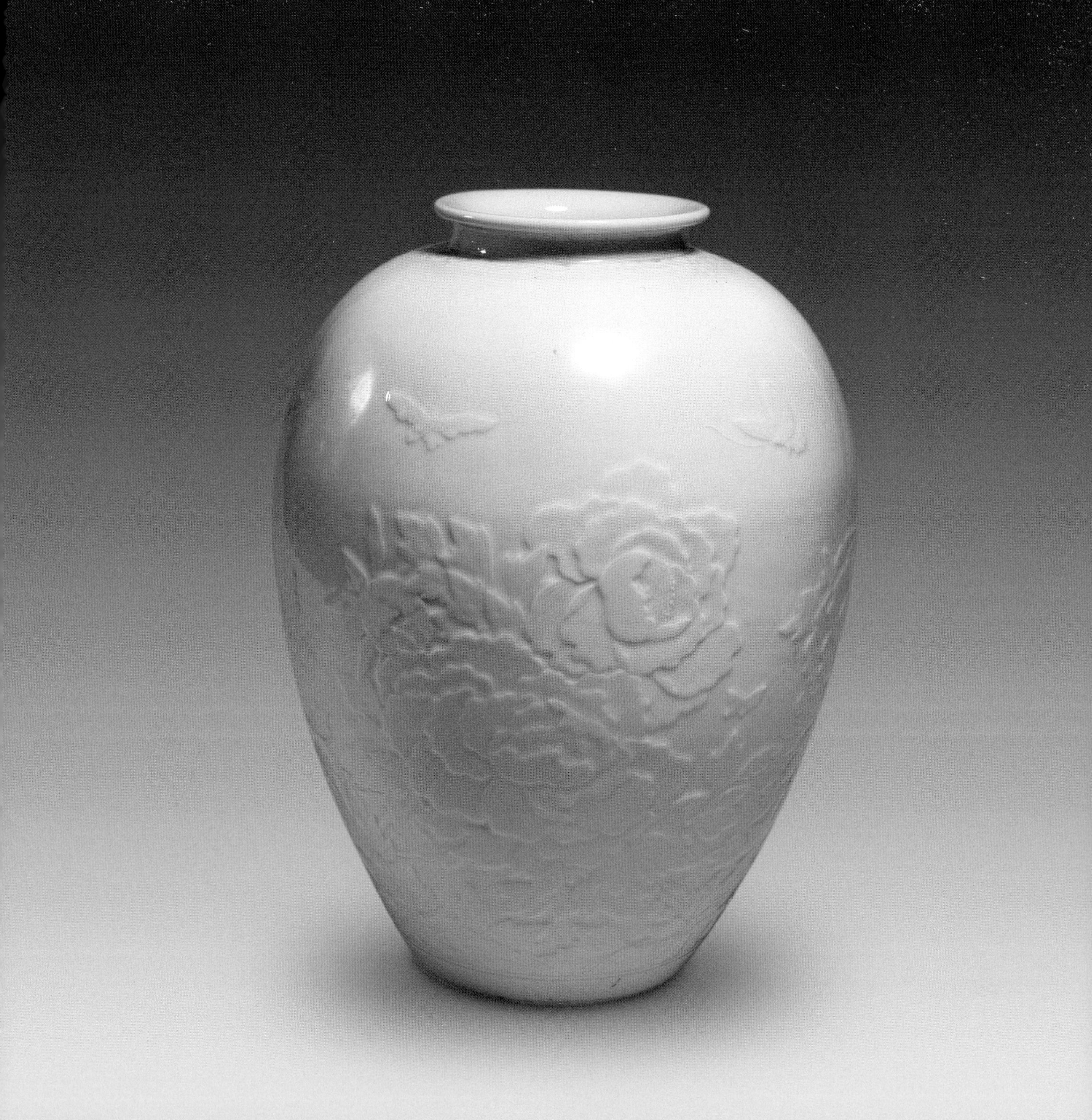

ESTABLISHING CERAMICS OF IMPERIAL JAPAN: THE LIFE AND ART OF SEIFŪ YOHEI III

SHINYA MAEZAKI

Seifū Yohei III 三代清風與平 (1851–1914), a leading Japanese ceramist of the Meiji period (1868–1912) (fig. 3), created elegant and delicate works that blended the best of Japanese and Chinese ceramics (fig. 4). He won much acclaim in exhibitions at home and abroad. His workshop was small and his output was limited.

Since the beginning of this millennium, Meiji-period arts have witnessed a gradual reassessment, and more and more galleries and museums in Japan are seeking out Yohei III works to own or exhibit. Yet because he produced few works, they are not easy to find. Moreover, because he was not keen to export his works, few can be found outside of Japan. Hence, the Cleveland Museum of Art's acquisition of Yohei works from the James and Christine Heusinger Collection is very welcome news for anyone interested in Japanese ceramic art of the Meiji period—although I am somewhat envious that this museum has beaten Japanese art museums to the punch.

From the seventeenth century, under the Tokugawa shogunate, the island country of Japan limited its contacts with the outside world. It was not until after 1853, when US Commodore Matthew C. Perry and his "black ships" sailed into Sagami Bay near present-day Yokohama to press Japan to establish trade relations, that the archipelago began to open up. The life of Yohei, who was born in 1851, coincided with the time of enormous change that followed, in the waning years of the shogunate and the early decades of the new Meiji government. Modernization was at the heart of these major shifts. After the shogun was overthrown and the emperor restored to power in 1868, a political revolution known as the Meiji Restoration, Japan promoted broad-scale modernization (including in the field of ceramics), with the West as its model, and underwent rapid growth. Any discussion of the artist's works thus entails not only appreciating their beauty, as well as that of Japanese ceramics as a whole, but also understanding them in the context of Japan's history, politics, and economy during the nineteenth century. Hence this essay introduces both nineteenth-century Japan and Yohei.

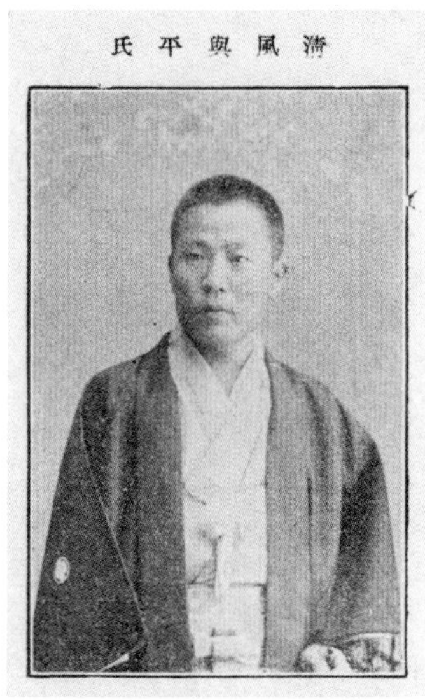

Figure 3. Photograph of Seifū Yohei III. Kuroda Tengai, "Seifū Yohei-shi," in vol. 1 of *Meika rekihō roku* (Kyoto: printed by the author, 1899). Photo: Private collection

OPPOSITE
Figure 4. *Large Vase with Butterflies and Peonies*, 1892. Seifū Yohei III. Porcelain; h. 38.2 cm, mouth diam. 13.6 cm, body diam. 29 cm. Tokyo National Museum, G-124. Important Cultural Property of Japan. Image: TNM Image Archives

Ceramics Production in Late Edo-Period Kyoto

Ceramics culture has been highly influential in Japan. In technical terms, Japan's ceramics are no match for those of neighboring China, but the range of its products is unrivaled. In the mid-nineteenth century, during the late Edo period (1615–1868), more than three hundred sites across the archipelago were producing a wide variety of ceramic products. The old capital of Kyoto today remains a leading area of ceramics production, along with Arita, Kutani, Satsuma, and Seto. The production system in Kyoto's ceramics industry, however, differed from that in many areas. Potteries generally emerge where good-quality clay, whether for stoneware or for porcelain, is found; but in Kyoto, raw materials produced elsewhere had to be imported. As overhead costs increased as a result, Kyoto ceramists focused on making high-quality works for an elite clientele.

Before discussing the life and work of Seifū Yohei III, let me briefly introduce nineteenth-century Kyoto, where he was active as a potter, and its ceramics industry. Ceramics production at the time took place in two areas: Awataguchi and Kiyomizu Gojōzaka, located on opposite sides of the famous Gion geisha district. On the north side was Awataguchi, and on the south side was Kiyomizu Gojōzaka. Awataguchi was the entrance to Kyoto from the historic Tōkaidō road, which ran from Nihonbashi in the capital of Edo (present-day Tokyo) to Kyoto. The fifty-three stations of the Tōkaidō are well known from the ukiyo-e woodblock prints by Utagawa Hiroshige (1797–1858). The final print in this famous

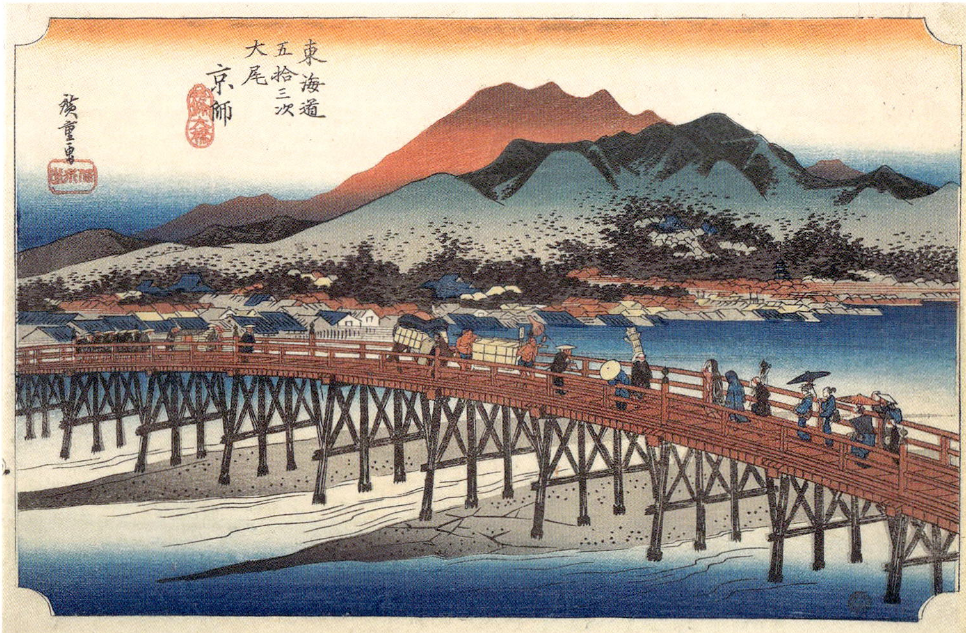

Figure 5. *The Great Bridge at Third Avenue in Kyoto*, from the series *Fifty-Three Stations of the Tōkaidō*, c. 1833–34. Utagawa Hiroshige (Japanese, 1797–1858). Woodblock print; 24.4 x 35.7 cm. The Metropolitan Museum of Art, Rogers Fund, 1918

series, number 55, portrays Sanjō Ōhashi (Third Avenue Bridge) in Kyoto (fig. 5). Continuing east from this bridge, the Tōkaidō was lined with pottery kilns and workshops. It was here that the ceramics with ornate decorations in gold and gorgeous colors known as Kyoto Satsuma ware—much of it exported to the West during the Meiji period—were produced (fig. 6).

The other ceramics-producing area in Kyoto was called Kiyomizu Gojōzaka (fig. 7). Originally, Kiyomizu (in the foothills below Kiyomizudera) and Gojōzaka (the Fifth Avenue hill leading up to Kiyomizudera) were regarded as separate districts. By Yohei III's day, however, the boundary between them had disappeared, and the whole neighborhood, which produced similar products, came to be known as Kiyomizu Gojōzaka. The production of ceramic wares started in the Kiyomizu district and later spread to Gojōzaka. At first, as in Awataguchi, pottery was produced, but after it became possible to fire porcelain in Kyoto at the end of the eighteenth century, both pottery and porcelain were made.

With the new porcelain kilns in this area and with the growing popularity of steeped green tea, or *sencha*, which was consumed using porcelain utensils, this area flourished. The history of the Seifū family of potters, founded in Kiyomizu Gojōzaka by Seifū Yohei I 初代清風與平 (1801–1861) and known for its production of *sencha* utensils—including teapots, teacups, and other implements—was linked to these developments in porcelain production and tea consumption.

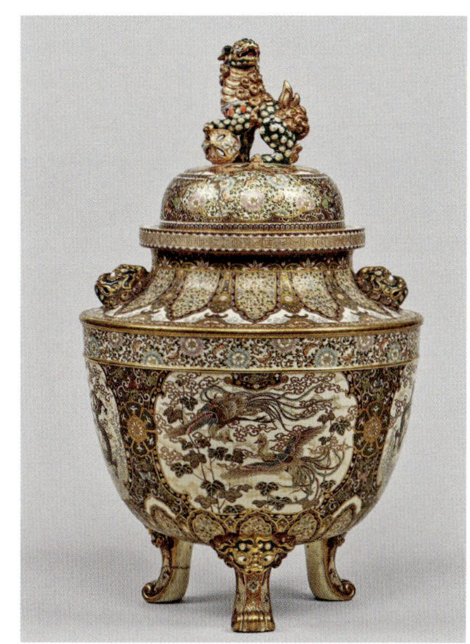

Figure 6. *Ornamental Jar with a Pair of Phoenixes*, c. 1900. Kinkōzan Sōbei VII (Japanese, 1868–1927). Stoneware with polychrome enamel decoration and gold (Kyō-satsuma ware); h. incl. cover 46.4 cm, mouth diam. 23.2 cm. The Tokyo National Museum, G-125. Image: TNM Image Archives

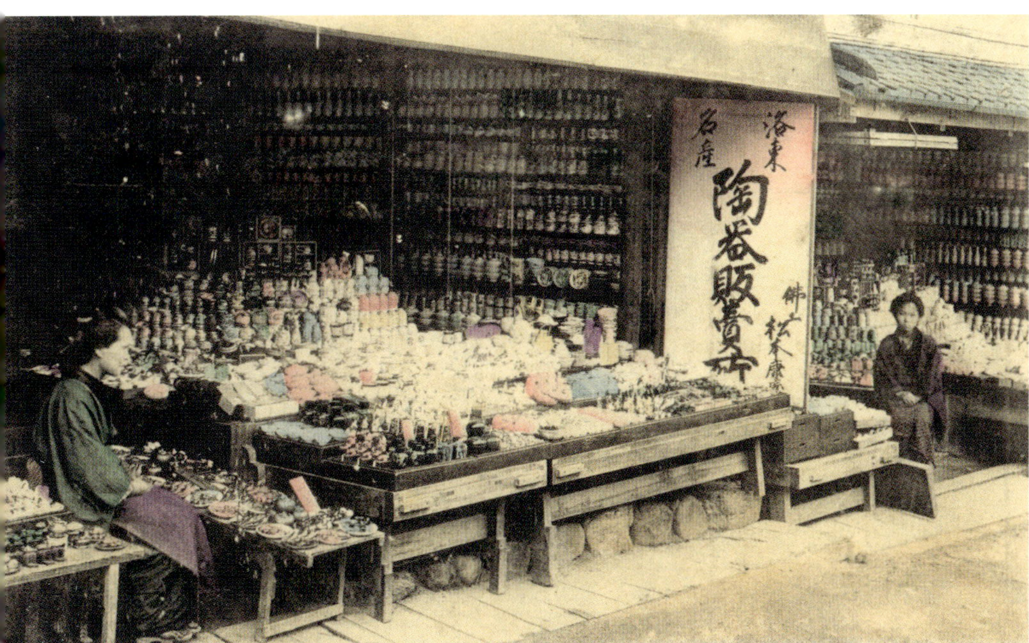

Figure 7. "Chawanzaka (Teabowl Street) in Kyoto," late 1800s–early 1900s. Postcard. Private collection

Kyoto Ware and Sencha

In contemporary Japan, "traditional" tea is associated with *chanoyu* (literally "hot water for tea"), often called the tea ceremony in English. Matcha is prepared by spooning green powder made from ground tea leaves into a ceramic bowl, pouring hot water over it, and then whisking the mixture. In the Edo period, *chanoyu* spread throughout Japan as a samurai accomplishment. By the end of the eighteenth century, however, this cultural pursuit had largely ceased to be practiced except among high-ranking samurai and Buddhist monks. It was replaced by another form of tea consumption that spread mainly among townspeople in Osaka and Kyoto. This was *sencha*, whereby tea leaves are placed in a teapot and boiled or steeped in hot water to produce a clear green tea (fig. 8). Its popularity ultimately spread throughout the archipelago, and this type of green tea became the most commonly drunk by Japanese. The widespread consumption of *sencha* continues today, with green tea sold in plastic bottles in convenience stores and vending machines across Japan.

The impetus for *sencha*'s popularization lay in a Buddhist temple south of the city of Kyoto. The person said to have introduced steeped green tea to Japan was Yinyuan Longqi (J. Ingen Ryūki; 1592–1673), a monk from China. Born in Fujian Province, Yinyuan came to Japan in 1654 to serve as chief priest at a temple for Chinese residents in Nagasaki, in northwestern Kyushu. At the time, trade between China and Japan was conducted mainly through the Chinese compound in that city. In 1660, the fourth Tokugawa shogun, Ietsuna (r. 1651–1680), granted Yinyuan land for a temple, and the following year the monk founded Manpukuji, an Ōbaku (C. Huangbo) Zen Buddhist temple, at its present site in

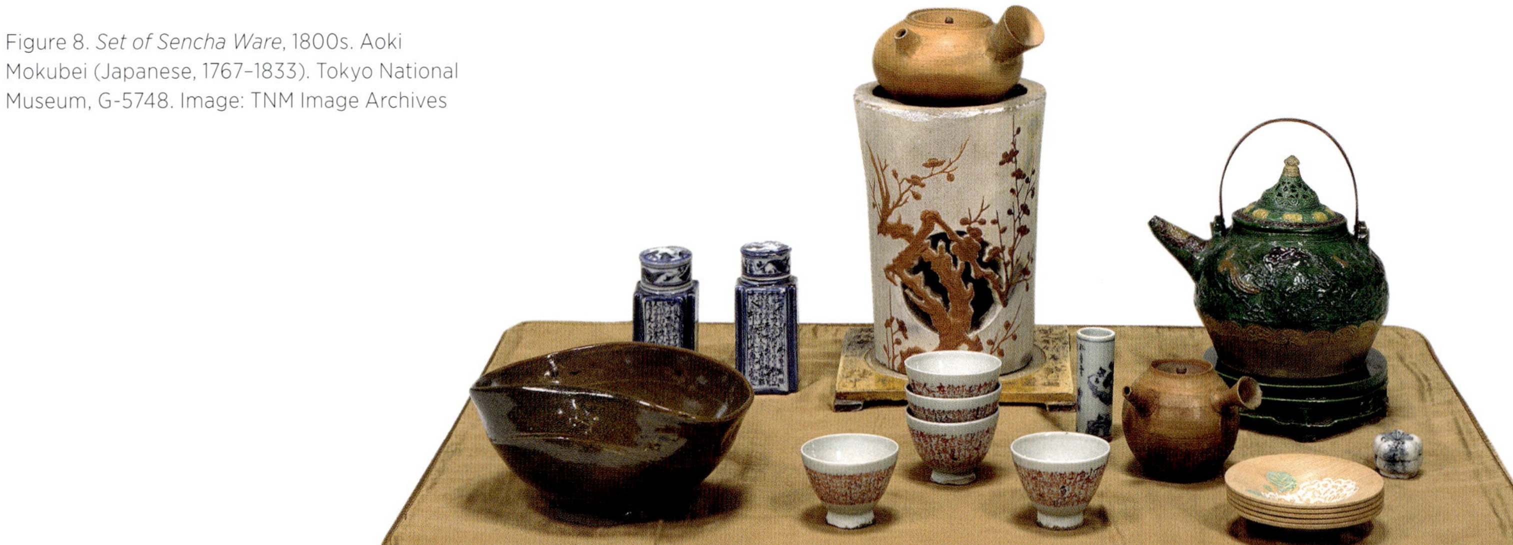

Figure 8. *Set of Sencha Ware*, 1800s. Aoki Mokubei (Japanese, 1767–1833). Tokyo National Museum, G-5748. Image: TNM Image Archives

the city of Uji. Until the mid-eighteenth century, the temple's chief priests were monks from China, and to Edo-period intellectuals who admired Chinese civilization, this temple was an important venue where they could come in contact with rare books, paintings, and writing materials brought from China. Two teapots thought to have been used by Yinyuan to prepare this form of tea are still stored at Manpukuji.

Although introduced to Japan in the mid-seventeenth century, *sencha* became widespread only after the mid-eighteenth century, when it became possible to grow *sencha* tea leaves domestically. In 1738, Nagatani Sōen (1681–1778), a tea cultivator in Uji, made further advancements in Japanese tea production with a new way to process tea leaves. Whereas harvested tea leaves were roasted in China, Sōen invented a steaming process, which produced a vibrant green liquid when the tea was steeped. Around the same time, the Ōbaku monk Baisaō (1675–1763), who had learned to prepare tea in the Chinese way (i.e., by steeping loose leaf tea) in Nagasaki, held simple gatherings around Kyoto where he served this novel form of tea. It began to catch on in Kyoto, Osaka, and ports in western Japan among intellectuals and wealthy townspeople, including the famous painters Ike Taiga (1723–1776) and Yosa Buson (1716–1784) (fig. 9).

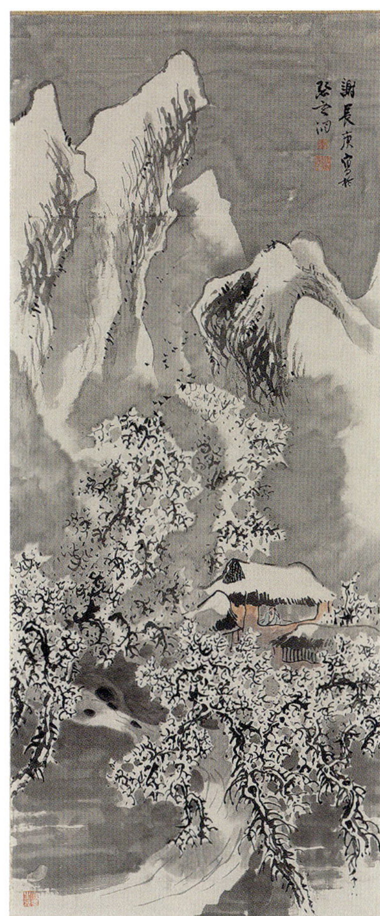

Figure 9. *Snow Landscape*, c. 1770s. Yosa Buson (Japanese, 1716–1784). Ink and color on paper; 174.6 x 67.3 cm. The Cleveland Museum of Art, Bequest of Mrs. A. Dean Perry, 1997.111

As with *sencha*, many aspects of Japanese culture arose out of a sense of admiration for China. Before oil painting was introduced from Europe in the nineteenth century, Japanese painting borrowed the tools and techniques of Chinese painting and evolved by adapting these. Both Buson and Taiga painted works known as *bunjinga*, "literati paintings," or as *nanga*, literally "Southern paintings," since their landscapes were inspired by the so-called Southern school of Chinese painting, produced not by professional artists but by literati such as bureaucrats and intellectuals who took up painting as a pastime. Initiated by bureaucrats harried by their duties and sometimes caught up in life-threatening political strife, these literati-style paintings portraying an ideal valley deep in the mountains offered world-weary individuals, at least when alone in their study, a means to be transported to that other world. In mid-Edo-period Japan, this style of painting became popular particularly in Osaka and Kyoto among merchants and lower-ranking samurai who had no avenue to demonstrate their abilities, even if they were talented. As far as *nanga*'s geographic concentration, the ability to obtain exemplary Chinese paintings, as well as books explaining this style of painting, was limited largely to two cities connected to China: Osaka, which as the nation's economic hub was linked by sea to Nagasaki, the sole port permitted trade with China; and Kyoto, which was home to Manpukuji and other Zen temples with ties to Chinese temples and monks. The material simplicity of *nanga* also contributed to its spread. Historically, Northern school professional painting required obtaining mineral powders of various colors and having the specialized knowledge needed to turn them into paint by blending with a gelatinous binder. By contrast, most Southern school paintings, which developed as an amateur pastime, employed only ink and colors that could be dissolved in water. The fact that this style of painting was possible as long as one had brushes and ink, even without knowledge of specialized painting techniques, boosted its popularity.

Alongside literati-style paintings inspired by Chinese models, the Chinese style of tea—*sencha*—also came to enjoy great popularity beginning in the nineteenth century. As described below, Seifū Yohei III initially aspired to become a nanga artist before he became a ceramist. Among his paintings is *Rain Clearing Over a Summer's Mountain*, which depicts a scene of humid summer haze, after the rain has stopped and the sun has come out [8]. Only the roof of a temple pagoda is discernible in the haze. Paintings such as this, when displayed at a *sencha* gathering, were meant to evoke in participants the feeling that they were in the setting depicted in the painting. Imagining that they were gathering with friends deep in the mountains of China, rather than in the metropolis of Kyoto, they would consider themselves literati and engage in refined conversation while savoring their *sencha* as Chinese tea.

Transportation routes also contributed to *sencha*'s growing prevalence. From Kyoto or Uji, Osaka could be reached by boat in half a day. As a strategic maritime transport hub, the city was connected with ports around Japan. The route linking Nagasaki, Kyoto, the temple Manpukuji, Uji tea, and Osaka allowed *sencha* to spread throughout the country.

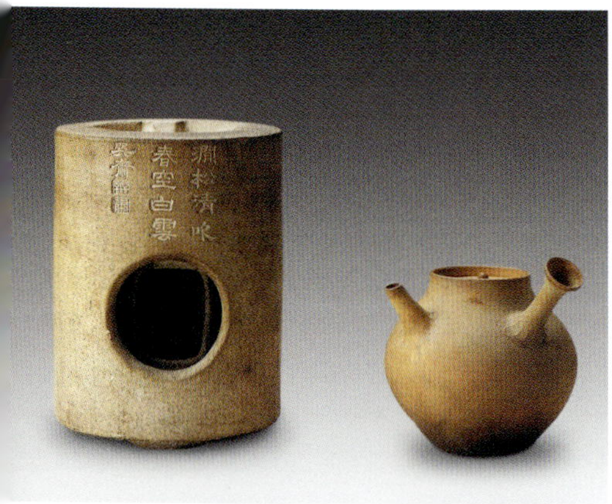

Sencha's popularity led to an immediate shortage of Chinese-made utensils used with this kind of tea. At the time, the implements regarded as necessary included not only teapots and teacups but also a tea kettle and brazier for boiling water and a trivet for the brazier. Many utensils for *sencha*, including those used by Baisaō, were Chinese ones imported to Japan, often via Nagasaki.[1] After this form of tea became fashionable, however, imports alone were not enough to meet the demand. Before long, utensils copied after ones made in China began to be produced in Japan. The fiction writer Ueda Akinari (1734–1809) observed in his book on *sencha*, *Trifling Stories of Pure Wind* (*Seifū sagen*; 1794): "If you happen to acquire a teapot that came from China a long time ago, you should have it copied by a famous Kyoto potter in case it gets broken."[2] Kiyomizu Rokubei I (1738–1799), the founder of the celebrated Kiyomizu family of ceramists, which has continued in Kyoto for eight generations, is known to have been esteemed for his skill in making teapots (fig. 10). Both Baisaō and Rokubei I were active around the end of the eighteenth century. It was early in the following century that Seifū Yohei I moved to Kyoto to become a potter, apprenticing himself to Nin'ami Dōhachi, also known as Takahashi Dōhachi II (1783–1855), renowned as a maker of *sencha* utensils.

Figure 10. *Pot and Furnace*, 1700s. Kiyomizu Rokubei I. Stoneware; pot: h. 12.3 cm; furnace: h. 18.8 cm, diam. 14.6 cm. Private collection

The Seifū Yohei Lineage

Since the founding of the Seifū Yohei lineage, the production of *sencha* utensils was a pillar of the family business. The name Seifū comes from the classic "Poem of the Seven Cups of Tea" (C. *Qiwan chage*, J. *Shichiwan chaka*) by the Tang-dynasty poet Lu Tong (?–835): "Bowl number seven I can barely get down: / I feel only pure wind (C. *qingfeng* 清風, J. *seifū*) blowing, swishing beneath my arms!"[3] The word *seifū* was also inscribed on the banner Baisaō set up when he made tea outdoors. The fact that the Seifū family's name symbolizes Japanese *sencha* culture also indicates that their main line of ceramics work consisted of making utensils for this type of tea.

Yohei I, the lineage founder, was born to the Yasuda family in the city of Kanazawa, which faces the Sea of Japan. His home province of Kaga (in present-day Ishikawa Prefecture) produced its own ceramics, known as Kutani ware, but for his training as a potter, Yohei I chose Kyoto, which produced the more technically advanced porcelain ware. He moved to Kyoto around the 1820s and became apprenticed to Nin'ami Dōhachi, a leading potter in the city. He later struck out on his own, and it is likely that his teacher gave him the name Seifū Yohei. His works include many exquisitely painted copies of Chinese porcelain (fig. 11), and he also produced stoneware with overglaze color enamels that emulated works in the style of Ogata Kenzan (1663–1743) at which his teacher excelled.

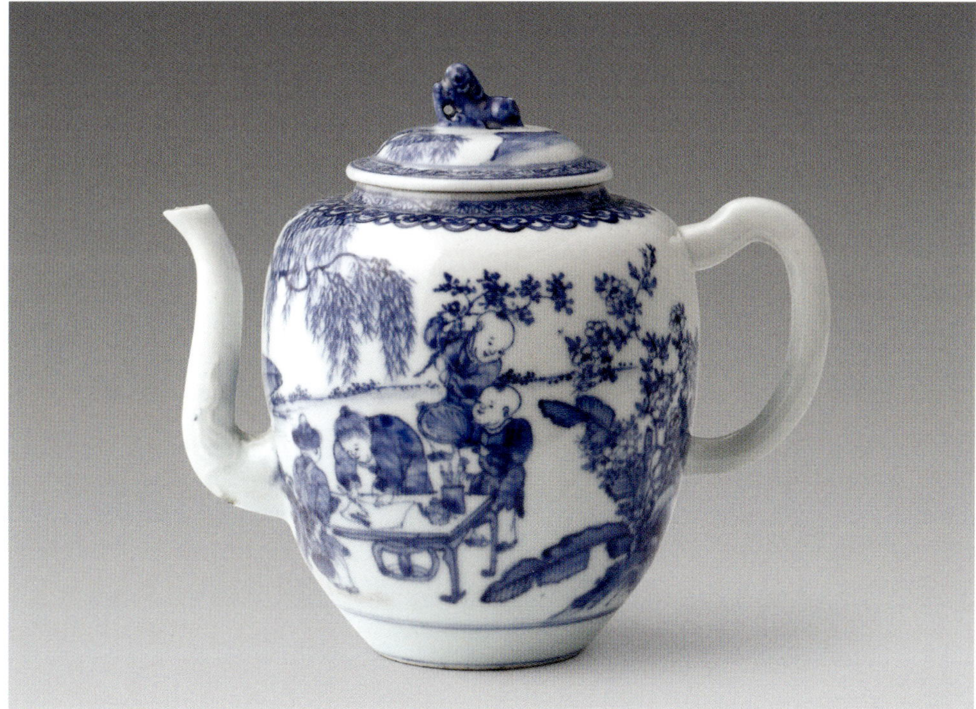

Figure 11. *Ewer with Blue-and-White Decoration*, 1800s. Seifū Yohei I. Porcelain; h. 17 cm. Private collection

When Dōhachi II died in 1855, Yohei I faced a crisis. He had a falling-out with Takahashi Dōhachi III (1811–1879), who claimed that Yohei was imitating the family style, and consequently lost their backing and access to their kiln. The number of climbing kilns in Kiyomizu Gojōzaka was restricted to avoid overproduction. As a result, potters without their own means of firing works had to borrow space from a kiln owner. Having parted ways with the powerful Takahashi family, Yohei must have faced the pressing problem of inability to fire his works. So he built a small kiln behind his house, one that fell outside the scope of the kiln-use permit system. Unfortunately, the effort was unsuccessful, and he failed to produce any porcelain wares there. Hence it is highly likely that Yohei produced virtually no works from around 1857 until his death in 1861.

Shrewd decisions by his successor, Seifū Yohei II 二代清風與平 (1845–1878), enabled ceramics production to resume. Yohei II wed Kiyomizu Miyo, daughter of Kiyomizu Rokubei III (1820–1883), who was an influential figure in Kiyomizu and Gojōzaka along with the Takahashi Dōhachi family.[4] Thanks to these marriage ties with Rokubei's family, he was able to mend relations with the Takahashi family and regain access to a kiln. Having avoided the threat of being forced to close down its operations, Yohei II built up the family business. He excelled at copying blue-and-white ware of the Ming dynasty (1368–1644), and he established a reputation for his skill in flower designs drawn with cobalt blue pigment imported from China, known as *tōgosu*. His success also seems to have stemmed from his move into the foreign market that opened under the new Meiji government. In response to demands from Western nations for a trading port near Kyoto and Osaka, Japan chose Kobe as one of its major ports. The city is known today for producing some of the best beef in the world, but at the time, it was a small fishing village with a population of just a few hundred. The opening of the port in 1868 transformed Kobe. For Kyoto potters, whose clientele had long consisted of wealthy Japanese, this finally opened up an avenue to foreign trade and allowed Kyoto ceramic ware to reach the West.

The Victoria and Albert Museum in England holds a pair of vases that Yohei II exhibited at the 1876 Centennial Exposition in Philadelphia, *White Porcelain Flower Vases with Molded Design of Plum Blossoms* (fig. 12). These relief flower decorations were modeled after Chinese Dehua (J. Tokka) porcelain. Yohei II also devised ingenious combinations of shape and design, producing *sui generis* works. *Flower Vase with Overglaze Color Design of Grasses and Flowers* held in the British Museum (fig. 13) has a flower design in overglaze color enamels, and the base is covered with decorative gilding known as *kinrande* ("gold brocade"), a technique adopted from Ming- and Qing-dynasty (1644–1911) ceramics. In this way, Yohei II gradually attracted attention in Kyoto ware circles: in Kiyomizu Gojōzaka, where imitations of Chinese porcelain prevailed, his method of

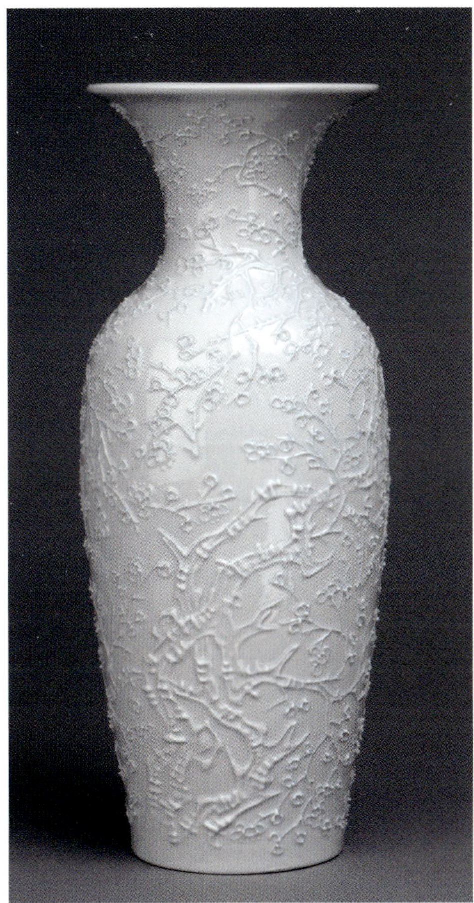

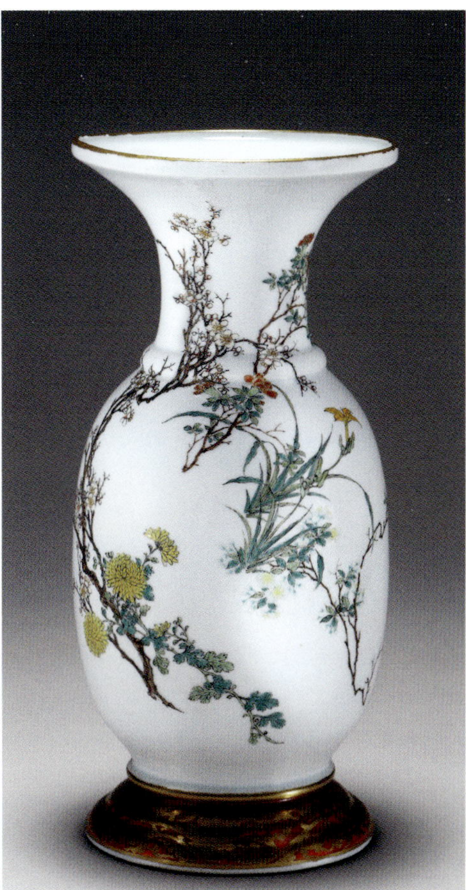

Figure 12. *White Porcelain Flower Vase with Molded Design of Plum Blossom* (one of pair), 1875. Seifū Yohei II. Porcelain with raised slip-trailed decoration; h. 42.1 cm. Victoria and Albert Museum, 370A-1877. Image: © Victoria and Albert Museum, London

Figure 13. *Flower Vase with Overglaze Color Design of Grasses and Flowers*, 1870–78. Seifū Yohei II. Color-enameled and gilded porcelain; h. 38.1 cm, diam. 17 cm. The British Museum, Donated by Sir Augustus Wollaston Franks, 1700. Image: © The Trustees of the British Museum

incorporating Chinese porcelain styles from different eras stood out as innovative. He eventually made his breakthrough with works that differed from the existing styles of the Kiyomizu and Takahashi families, carving out a position for himself in early Meiji Kyoto. In this new endeavor, he was supported by Okada Heikichi—the future Seifū Yohei III—who had been adopted into the Seifū family upon marrying Yohei II's younger sister.

Seifū Yohei III: From Birth to Aspiring *Nanga* Painter

Okada Heikichi was born in 1851 in the village of Ōshio in Harima Province (in present-day Hyōgo Prefecture). As the name Ōshio ("large salt") indicates, this region was supported by the salt industry, which harvested sea salt from the extensive sand dunes overlooking the Seto Inland Sea.[5] The Okada family ran a soy sauce brewing business, and Heikichi's father, Ryōhei, was a Confucian scholar, known for his skill in bird-and-flower paintings. Heikichi enjoyed reading and sketching and reputedly showed no interest in typical childhood pastimes such as walking on stilts, instead spending his time drawing on salt pans whenever he saw flowers or creatures such as insects and fish. He also enjoyed playing the game *go*, but after his father rebuked him for a major quarrel with a friend over a match, he never again engaged in competition. The people of Ōshio, an area known for its hot-blooded youths, reportedly called the quiet and serious Heikichi an extraordinary child. When his father questioned him about his future, Heikichi replied that he wanted to become a painter, so sometime around 1863, he was sent to study under Tanomura Chokunyū (1814–1907) in Osaka.

Chokunyū's teacher and father-in-law, Tanomura Chikuden (1777–1835), was an eminent *nanga* painter in the first half of the nineteenth century. As discussed above, *sencha* and *nanga* were popular in the latter half of the Edo period, particularly in Kyoto and Osaka. As *nanga* painters, both Chikuden and Chokunyū took part in intellectual circles focused on the appreciation of paintings and calligraphic works brought from China as well as those created in Japan in the Chinese style. And at venues where *nanga* were produced and admired, *sencha* was also served as something that accorded with literati tastes.

In 1862, the year before Heikichi began his training, Chokunyū became famous for hosting a major *sencha* gathering in Osaka. Held in commemoration of

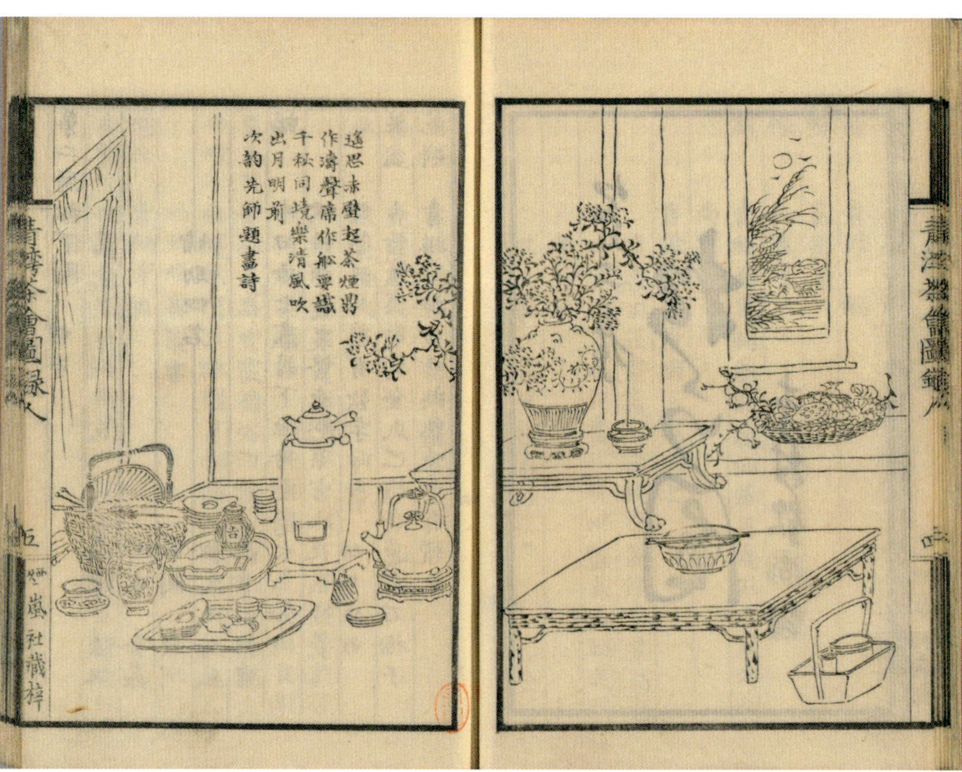

Figure 14. A scene from the Azure Bay Tea Gathering. Tanomura Chokunyū, *Seiwan chakai zuroku: Jin* (Naniwa: printed by the author, 1863), pp. 4–5. Image: National Diet Library Digital Collections

the one hundredth anniversary of Baisaō's death, the Azure Bay Tea Gathering (Seiwan chakai) (fig. 14) was attended by thousands of people. Under Chokunyū, then, Heikichi was no doubt not only able to learn *nanga* but also to come into contact with famous objects associated with *sencha*, from imported Chinese paintings and calligraphic works to renowned vases and writing implements such as ink, inkstones, brushes, brush holders, and brush rests. In this optimal environment for cultural cultivation, he doubtless acquired all the knowledge needed to become a potter.

Chokunyū subsequently moved to Kyoto and in 1880 became the first principal of the Kyoto Prefectural Painting School (the forerunner of today's Kyoto City University of Arts), founded to support the city's traditional arts and crafts. He retained his ties with Kyoto in his later years, becoming the chief priest of a minor temple on the grounds of Manpukuji, the focal point of *sencha* culture in Japan. As for Heikichi, even after turning to ceramics and eventually assuming the name Seifū Yohei III, he became a special member of the Japan Nanga Institute (Nihon Nanga'in), established in 1890 by Chokunyū, artist Tomioka Tessai (1837–1924), and others, and some of his *nanga* are extant (fig. 15).[6] The relationship between teacher and student continued until Chokunyū's death, and among Yohei III's ceramic works are quite a few that Chokunyū inscribed. Chokunyū had connections with supporters of *nanga* and *sencha* around Japan, and this teacher-student relationship undoubtedly contributed to Yohei's later success as a potter.

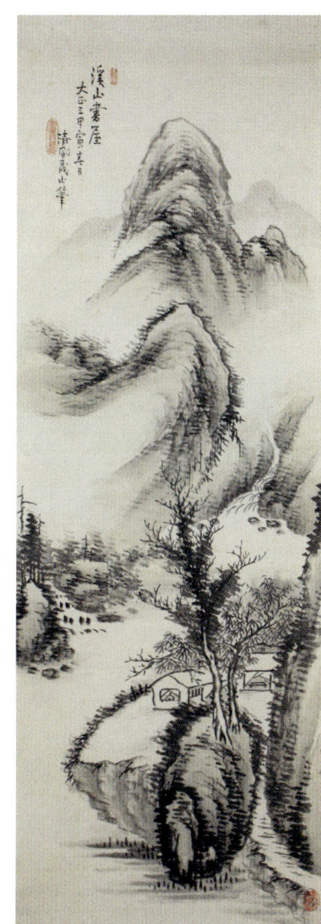

Figure 15. *Landscape*, 1914. Seifū Yohei III. Ink on paper; 124 x 41.3 cm. Private collection

From Training to Family Headship

Heikichi trained under Chokunyū for two years. In the winter of 1865, he succumbed to beriberi and was forced to return home to Ōshio to recuperate. By the spring, he had made a complete recovery, but his parents, fearing a relapse, refused his request to return to Osaka. Around that time, a ceramics dealer who regularly traveled between Kyoto and Ōshio visited the Okada home and told them that the Seifū Yohei family in Kyoto was looking to adopt a youth interested in painting and pottery. His parents agreed to this suggestion, and Heikichi was adopted into the Seifū family in the summer of 1866. His artistic development after moving to Kyoto was remarkable. He commenced training as a ceramic painter, but he realized that to truly master the ceramics business, he needed to study techniques across the whole production process. In between his work and household duties, therefore, he sought experience in all aspects of ceramics, from preparing the raw materials to firing the kiln.

Heikichi began his training at a time of political turbulence, when samurai concerned with the growing threat of foreign powers plotted a rebellion that would eventually lead to the Meiji Restoration. Kyoto was caught up in the unrest, partly because it was the site of the emperor's palace. In 1864, over 60 percent of the city burned down in a major fire sparked by street fighting between the shogunate troops and pro-imperial rebel forces. With the reinstatement of imperial rule in 1868 and the emperor's move to the capital, now named Tokyo, most of the nobles serving the court also took up residence there. Then with the abolition of feudal domains and the establishment of prefectures in 1871, samurai who had been stationed in Kyoto returned to their hometowns in various domains across Japan, abandoning their houses. Ever since Kyoto became the capital of Japan in 794, industries and crafts had served a wealthy clientele at the center of Japanese politics and culture. All of these changes, therefore, marked the beginning of tough times, not only for the ceramics industry but all Kyoto industries.

While the city was recovering from the devastating fire, Heikichi continued to devote himself to his training, and six years after he had commenced his studies, he mastered all aspects of ceramics manufacturing. In recognition of his efforts, the head of the Seifū family, Yohei II, gave Heikichi permission in 1872 to strike out on his own. By then, Heikichi was already married to the family head's younger sister Kuma. Yohei II, who had no sons, adopted as his heir Heikichi's eldest son, Baikei, while Heikichi founded a new lineage with his remaining family, taking the name Shinkai Seizan 新開清山.[7] He was active under this name for about eight years. Virtually nothing is known about his works during that time, but he seems to have produced mostly conventional blue-and-white ware and porcelain with overglaze color enamels.[8]

After Yohei II died in 1878, in accordance with the provisions of the deceased's will, Heikichi returned to the Seifū family as guardian of the still-young Baikei. For about a decade, under the name Seifū Seizan 清風靖山, he assisted the young head of the family; but around 1887, Baikei met a premature death. Seizan changed his name to Seifū Yohei III (art name Seizan 晟山) and was active under that name from then on. It is customary in the world of traditional Japanese industries to change one's name upon succeeding to family headship (by taking on the style name of one's predecessor), but Yohei III was unusual in changing names three times during his career.

Exemplary Imitation of Qing-Dynasty Porcelain

Throughout the 1880s, Seifū Yohei III steadily built a track record as a producer of exemplary Kyoto ware, becoming known as a leading ceramist in Meiji Japan. Behind this rise was his creation of works that took advantage of the popularity of porcelain at home and abroad.

In the first place, he continued producing the *sencha* utensils that had been part of his family's work ever since Yohei I and II. This is of significance given the robust domestic market for high-quality ceramics at that time. The *chanoyu* master Takahashi Yoshio (Sōan, 1861–1937) commented on the early Meiji market for *sencha* utensils:

> After the emperor's carriage went to Tokyo in 1868, all the government officials gathered there and took up residence, so they needed to decorate their houses from scratch. . . . Since many of these people had plain literati tastes, their interiors also naturally adopted this style. In this way, it was the literati style that first brought a ray of hope to the world immediately after the Meiji Restoration.[9]

Thus, despite the upheaval to Kyoto industries at the end of the shogunate, there remained constant demand into the Meiji period for objects of literati taste, including *nanga*, *sencha* utensils, and writing implements. And it was Kyoto that was known for artisans skilled in copying the archetypal Chinese ceramics used in *sencha*. Because these artisans focused on producing "imitations," however, Kyoto was looked down on by twentieth-century ceramics scholars who emphasized "originality" as a marker of modern artistic quality. One example is the following description from 1945 of early modern Kyoto ware by William Bowyer Honey, curator of the porcelain collection at the Victoria and Albert Museum:

> The porcelain of Kioto (Kiyomizu, etc.) was the work of a host of clever potters, mostly copyists, such as Eisen, Eiraku, Moku Bei and Makuzu Kōzan, who created no original style of any great importance; blue-and-white and red-and-green in Ming style were favourable decorations.[10]

Yohei III's early works, from the late 1870s and 1880s, were copies of Chinese porcelain and were thus no exception to the ceramics generally produced in his city. He began with the *sencha* utensils that had been the Seifū family's forte in previous generations. Simply copying famous objects made it difficult, however, to distinguish himself from other ceramists. Moreover, the fact that Yohei I had almost faced business closure for producing copies of works by the Takahashi Dōhachi family meant it was risky to turn his hand to designs that were the specialties of other families.

What Yohei III focused on instead was developing new glazes. In 1872, while still operating under the name Shinkai Seizan, he perfected a combination of a creamy white-tinged translucent glaze over an ivory clay body, resulting in an effect similar to Ding ware, which he called *taihakuji* ("great white porcelain") [28–30, 32, 35, 36], then in 1873 he developed *namakoyū* ("sea cucumber glaze") to replicate the streaking effect on Jun ware of the Northern Song dynasty (960–1127).

In 1882, he developed works he called *hisokuji* (C. *mise ci*; "mysterious color porcelain"), named after a type of green-glazed ceramic produced in present-day

Zhejiang Province, China, from the ninth to the eleventh century. He did so using *kinutayū*, or "mallet glaze," a blue-green glaze resembling that typically found in green-glazed wares of twelfth-century Longquan, also in Zhejiang [89–92].

At the same time, he worked on developing overglaze colors reminiscent of the five colors of Ming-dynasty *wucai* ware, as well as of enamels made in the Qing dynasty. Yohei commented on this *hyakka nishiki*, or "hundred-flower brocade," technique of overglaze color enamels [16, 22, 23, 42]:

> China has very good raw materials for porcelain manufacturing, but even in Japan, it is not impossible to find them if one takes the trouble to seek them out. I set my sights on chemistry, in the belief that it was essential to understand the methods of analytical chemistry. I studied various methods of analytical chemistry and gradually invented a range of glaze manufacturing methods, which I collectively called *hyakka nishiki*.[11]

The Meiji period brought technical advances in Japanese porcelain as the importation of minerals previously unavailable in Japan—not just artificial cobalt but also chromium, cadmium, and uranium, for example—enabled new color glazes. Nevertheless, Yohei sought, where possible, to produce works using materials found in Kyoto or elsewhere in the country. Whenever he could find time, he would head off into the mountains around Kyoto and collect minerals, seeking out materials that could be used as glazes. He would prepare them himself, and he steadily succeeded in developing new methods.[12] He chalked up many achievements, developing ten methods in the 1870s and eleven in the 1880s. His skill as a glaze maker was commented on by the American writer and photographer Eliza Scidmore (1856–1928) when she visited Yohei in the late 1880s. She recorded that the works using these techniques to imitate Chinese porcelain were of such quality that even connoisseurs in China misjudged them:

> Seifu is the king of potters and first ceramic artist of Kioto to-day. Connoisseurs are extravagant in praises of his genius, and his establishment in the Kiyomidzu quarter, near the top of Teapot Hill, is visited by every foreigner who goes to Kioto. Seifu is a grave and serious man, who has toiled long and late over the problems of his glazes, and has achieved wonderful results in celadon, imperial yellow, coral red, and aubergine purples in such brilliant covers to his carefully moulded forms. For years the produce of his kilns in crackle and monochrome glazes went directly to China, where they confounded Peking experts, but with the more recent acknowledgement of the skill of other Japanese potters in the same lines these triumphs in classic lines are now signed openly and proudly sold.[13]

Yohei's works using techniques hitherto unavailable in Japan began to win him awards in exhibitions at home and abroad. In 1890, he was the only potter to win first prize in the art category at the Third National Industrial Exhibition, Japan's largest exhibition and the venue where works to be exhibited at world expositions were selected. He immediately became known as a leading Japanese ceramist. The work for which he won the award was a bowl with a fish design. The exhibition report explained that Yohei received this award for his high level of technical skill, particularly the quality of the purple glaze and the work's resulting gentle and elegant grace.[14] Unfortunately, it is not known whether this work is extant, so its details are unclear.

A National Artist and a National Style

In 1893, three years after winning the award at the Third National Industrial Exhibition, Seifū Yohei III became the first ceramist to be designated an Imperial Household Artist, a position established by an 1890 policy to support the nation's artists and craftspeople. Appointees, who were provided with an annuity, were tasked with producing items needed by the imperial household to decorate the Meiji Palace and to present to state guests as gifts. After World War II (1939–1945), the Imperial Household Artist system was abolished, but it was the prototype for two subsequent forms of artistic recognition: membership in the Japan Art Academy and designation as an Important Intangible Cultural Property (better known as Living National Treasures).

Over a period of about fifty-five years, a total of seventy-nine people were appointed Imperial Household Artists, of which only five were from the field of ceramics. Because of this designation, Yohei III has been regarded as a leading Meiji-period ceramist. Three years after Yohei's appointment, Miyagawa Kōzan I (1842–1916) from Yokohama, who under the name Makuzu was as much admired as Yohei, also received the honor. The fact that Kōzan was nine years older than Yohei is indicative of the extent of the latter's reputation.

There are no extant records that shed light on why Yohei was appointed an Imperial Household Artist, but we do have a record of why he was awarded the Green Ribbon Medal, another government honor, in 1895. The reasons cited were his invention of countless glazes in an attempt to surpass Chinese porcelain, as well as the fact that instead of keeping his recipes secret, he made them widely available to other ceramists.[15] In keeping with this reputation, Yohei continued until his later years to develop and share many new techniques, focusing mainly on glazes.[16]

Yohei and Kōzan, beyond their appointments as Imperial Household Artists, shared two other characteristics. The first was that both trained in Chinese classical poetry and prose and in Chinese ceramics, pursuits that derived from their literati tastes.[17] Both were educated as literati, and both produced *nanga*. They also partook of *sencha* and produced works modeled on Chinese ceramics. This background is thought to have acted in their favor in Japan's industrial exhibitions, since as described in Takahashi Yoshio's memoirs,[18] many high-ranking government bureaucrats and intellectuals at that time were, like Yohei and Kōzan, people with literati tastes. It is well known, for example, that Japan's first prime minister, Itō Hirobumi (1841–1909), and the literary giant Natsume Sōseki (1867–1916) both loved *sencha*.

Another characteristic shared by Yohei and Kōzan was the nature of their technical developments. Both artists modeled their glazes not on the Ming-dynasty blue-and-white ceramics and overglaze color enamels in which Kyoto ware ceramists specialized but rather on Qing-dynasty ceramics of the Kangxi (r. 1661–1722), Yongzheng (r. 1722–1735), and Qianlong (r. 1735–1796) eras. In particular, the political disturbances in China in the latter half of the nineteenth century led to an overseas exodus of Qing-dynasty artistic masterpieces, including ceramics that only the emperor and his close relatives and high-level bureaucrats had been permitted to see. Japanese and Western ceramists were astonished at the level of technical expertise evident in such Chinese ceramics, and they focused their efforts on reproducing them. In response to this trend, which began simultaneously in Japan and the West in the 1890s, Yohei and Kōzan tackled the technical development of underglazes and high-firing glazes that produce new or vivid colors.

As noted above, Yohei was awarded the Green Ribbon Medal for having developed these new techniques and for sharing them with other ceramists. This disclosure is thought to be closely related to the new Patent Monopoly Ordinance, which came into effect in 1885. Prior to this, there had been no laws in Japan that protected intellectual property rights. As a consequence, techniques were kept secret and passed down only within families and artistic schools, as evidenced by the expressions "secret transmission" and "transmission [of artistic secrets] to one child [a designated successor]," commonly used to describe the privileged transfer of knowledge in traditional artistic lineages. In time, the Meiji government realized that this approach was not conducive to the technological development vital to modernize the new nation. With the introduction of the Patent Monopoly Ordinance, inventions were given legal protection. A technology, even if made publicly available, was protected for a certain period as the property of its developer, who was also recognized as such. Yohei's innovative spirit is clearly evident in the fact that ten years after this ordinance came into effect, he was awarded the Green Ribbon Medal and commended for his development of new techniques and for making them publicly known.[19]

Some of Yohei's technical inventions were on display at the Paris Exposition of 1900, where he exhibited four large vases—*Porcelain Flower Vase with Underglaze Blue, Flower Vase with Iron Oxide Brown-Spotted Green Glaze, Tenmoku* (C. Tianmu) *Flower Vase with Dragons in Clouds*, and *Kanpakuji Flower Vase with Carved and Incised Image*.[20] Another unique contribution was Yohei's translucent pink and yellow *kyokusai* ("morning-sun color"). The Sannomaru Shozōkan of the Imperial Collections holds the *Morning-Sun Color Flower Vase with Mountain Cherry Blossom* from 1905, which is regarded as a masterpiece (fig. 16). Although the precise details of the methods and materials used to make works with the glaze and clay body combination known as *kanpakuji* ("bright-jewel white porcelain") [54–56], which resulted in a pink-tinged translucent cream color effect, and *kyokusai*, which resulted in a pink-and-yellow-tinged translucent cream color effect, are not known, it is clear that they involved technically accomplished and highly delicate work. Presumably, kaolin clay was built up over the ivory clay body, and designs such as flowers were carved and molded in low relief. These areas were covered with paper to mask them, then gradations of pale, translucent colors were applied to the exposed areas, and finally, the entire surface was given a translucent ivory glaze and the piece was fired. On the Sannomaru Shozōkan vase, this technique was used for the mountain cherry blossom motif, long established in Japan as a symbol of the arrival of spring. There was no precedent for serene-looking ceramics that combined relief designs

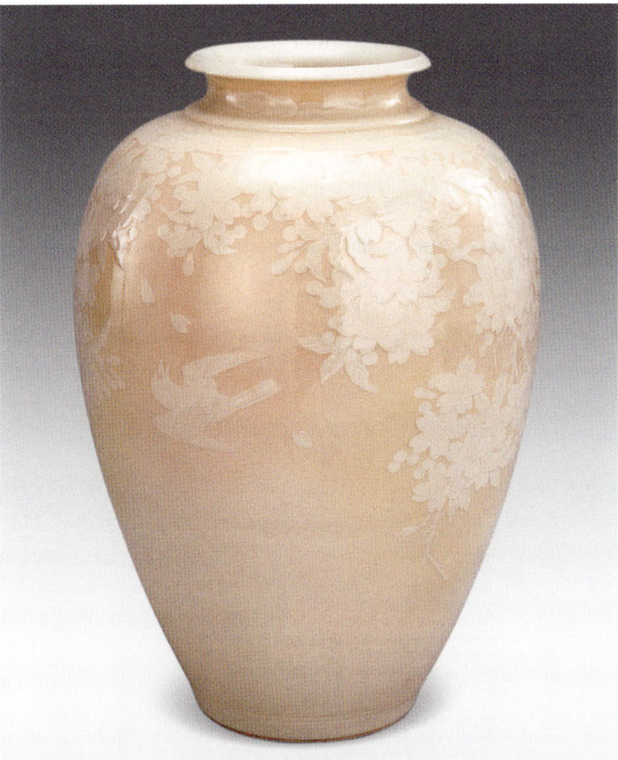

Figure 16. *Morning-Sun Color Flower Vase with Mountain Cherry Blossom*, c. 1905. Seifū Yohei III. The Museum of the Imperial Collections, Sannomaru Shozōkan

with pale colors, so this has been regarded as a quintessential Seifū Yohei III technique since being developed.

In this way, Yohei's works gradually moved away from his previous approach of using sophisticated techniques to emulate Chinese ceramics. It is likely that from around 1900, Imperial Household Artists were expected to create new Japanese-style works, given their position as eminent national artists.

Around the same time, changing cultural trends brought about other developments in ceramics design. *Chanoyu* began to undergo a revival, supported by enthusiasts such as up-and-coming businessmen. Moreover, in response to the Sino-Japanese War of 1894–1895 and nationalist sentiment, Yohei began also to produce *chanoyu* utensils, such as teabowls and water jars, rather than implements for *sencha*, with its intimate associations with China. In this way, the admiration for Chinese culture that had been shared by nineteenth-century Japanese gradually faded in the new century, and the production of Japan's own arts for the nation's benefit gradually got under way.

The Allure of Limited Available Works

Unlike most Meiji-period potters, Seifū Yohei III did not actively seek to export his works to the West. In an 1897 interview, he commented on this choice:

> [In the past,] I was frequently visited by a certain well-known merchant, who urged me to carry out export sales and to observe the market situation. Because he was so persistent, I went there once, even though I had little desire to do so. As I had long suspected, Japanese dealers are treated in a highly demeaning fashion by foreigners, and their commercial rights are violated. . . . So I resolved to abandon any idea of exports and decided that if someone likes my products, they can come to my store to buy them. I adopted an exclusive in-person-only principle and single-mindedly devoted all my efforts to improving my products.[21]

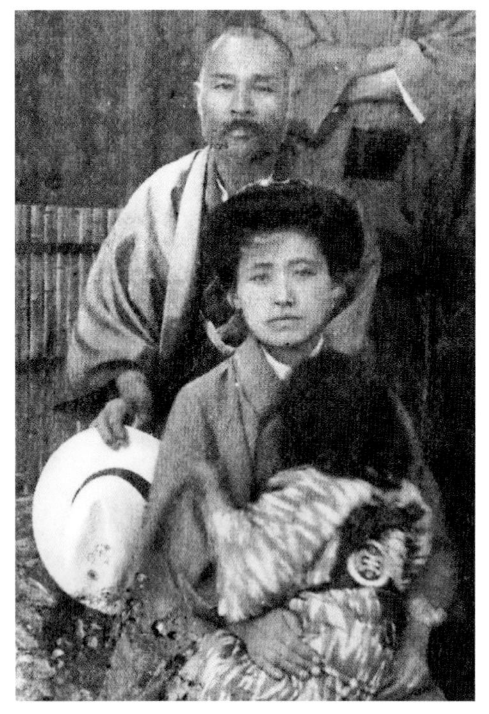

Figure 17. Photograph of Seifū Yohei III, his wife Kuma, and daughter Tama. Private collection

Although he does not specify the location of "there," Yohei probably visited the port of Kobe at the invitation of a foreign merchant. The outcome, however, was his decision not to become involved in overseas trade and instead to focus on selling only at his Kyoto store. Based on the account above, we can conclude that except for works exhibited at the international exposition and ones purchased in Japan in recent years, most Yohei works currently owned by Western art galleries and museums were purchased directly from his store.

Many foreign customers visited the workshop-cum-store in Gojōzaka, and Yohei's daughter Tama (dates unknown) helped out by interpreting for them. The novelist Okada Seizō (1913–1994), Yohei's grandson, commented about the role of his mother Seifū Tama (fig. 17) in the shop:

While helping with cleaning at her father Seifū Yohei III's workplace, Tama attended a Catholic-run English school. She mainly served American tourists, who often dropped by Gojōzaka, where rows of ceramics shops stood in those days. Sometimes the American ambassador would ride up in a one-man rickshaw.[22]

If one wanted to acquire a work by the esteemed Seifū Yohei III, one of only two Imperial Household Artists in the field of ceramics, there was no option but to make the trek to Gojōzaka and purchase it oneself.

Even for Japanese clientele, Yohei works were difficult to obtain because they were produced and sold in such small numbers. Seifū Yohei IV 四代清風與平 (1871–1951) commented on the Seifū family's production methods:

> If you fire an item such as a vase, only a tenth of ten finished pieces are of good quality—in other words, just one. Luckily, with this blue-and-white incense burner, we could get two good works out of every seven, and of course we smashed the other five to pieces. I would smash all the second-rate items and not put them up for sale at all.[23]

We might argue that because of this policy of producing small batches of quality products and selling them only in the Kyoto store, acquiring a work by Yohei III was an attraction for foreigners visiting Kyoto. Limited in number, unlike the many other ceramic works that were produced for export and on a large scale, these works had the mark of distinction.

Among these is *Taihakuji Flower Vase with Iris Design*, a large vase purchased in 1959 by the Museum of Fine Arts, Boston. Interestingly, the Los Angeles County Museum of Art holds what is thought to be the preliminary drawing for this work (fig. 18). The sketch was formerly owned by Charles Morse (1852–1911), a businessman who represented a construction company in Illinois. He was involved in building a pavilion for the world exposition in Chicago in 1893. That experience led him to visit Japan in 1897 and again in 1907, and he purchased many works directly from Yohei.

Also of great interest are the twenty-three small works donated by Margaret Watson Parker (1867–1936) to the University of Michigan Museum of Art because Parker purchased these when she visited Kyoto in 1907 with Charles Morse. They are valuable materials that allow us to learn about Yohei's later works and his notes of authentication on the boxes containing these works. Very few works by Yohei, apart from those submitted to expositions, have a certain production date. With the works in this collection, however, because he did not export his works overseas, we can infer that nearly all were purchased during Parker's 1907 visit. The seals and the works' titles on the boxes also reveal the

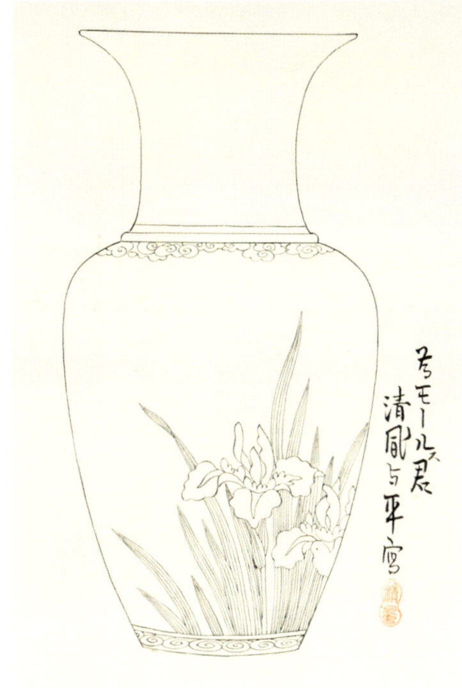

Figure 18. *Study of Vases* (one of two), late 1800s–early 1900s. Seifū Yohei III. Hanging scroll; ink on paper; 46.9 x 32 cm. Los Angeles County Museum of Art, Gift of Caroline and Jarred Morse (M.81.61.3). Digital image: © 2023 Museum Associates / LACMA. Licensed by Art Resource, NY

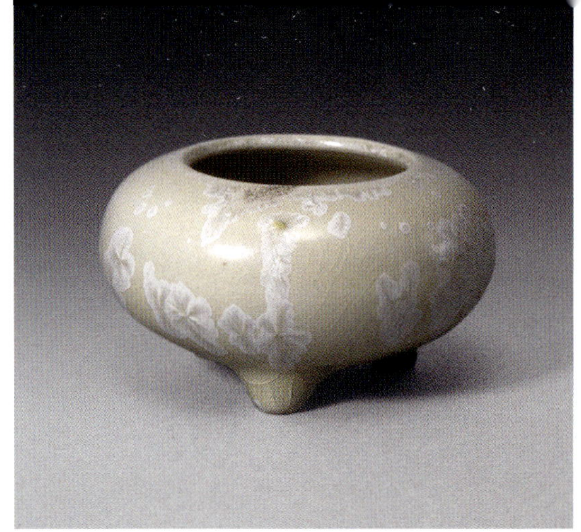

Figure 19. *Incense Burner*, c. 1880–1914. Seifū Yohei III. Porcelain with crackled glaze and white *kesshō* overglaze painting; 5.1 x 8.9 cm. University of Michigan Museum of Art, Bequest of Margaret Watson Parker, 1954/1.498

kind of calligraphic style and seals used at that time. These pieces also indicate the kinds of techniques in which Yohei, who continually sought new glazes throughout his career, was engaged. Among these pieces, the crystalline glaze incense burner (fig. 19) is an invaluable work with few counterparts. The first person in Japan to successfully produce a crystalline glaze was Nōtomi Kaijirō (1844–1918), likely in 1901. This work makes clear that six years later, in 1907, Yohei was putting this glaze to practical use and selling the resulting works.

Knowing the limited production and sale of works by Yohei III helps us understand the rarity of the works donated from the Heusinger Collection to the Cleveland Museum of Art. This is one of the foremost collections of Yohei's works, both in number and substance.

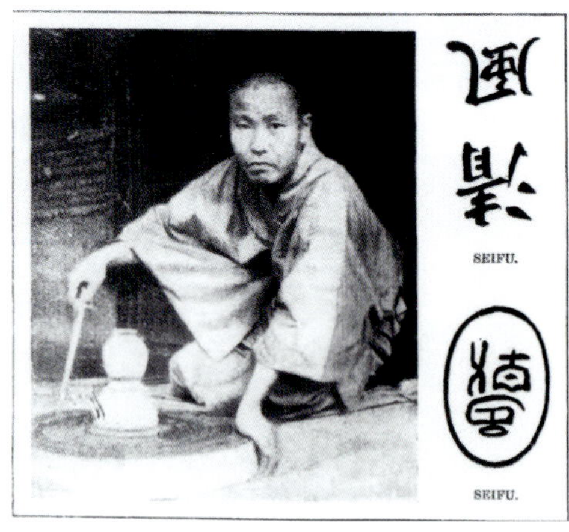

Figure 20. Photograph of Seifū Yohei III. Source: Eliza Ruhamah Scidmore, "The Porcelain-Artist of Japan," *Harper's Weekly* 42, no. 2144 (January 1898): 83–88

Seifū Yohei III's Death and Successors

The Heusinger Collection includes not only works by Seifū Yohei III but also pieces by the next two generations of family heads, Yohei IV and Yohei V. This section discusses Yohei III's activities late in his life as well as the family fortunes after his death.

Even in his later years, Yohei III maintained a vigorous work schedule and exacting attitude toward his work (fig. 20). His successor and second son Yohei IV described him:

> In later life he would get up at about ten o'clock and work all day, absorbed in designing until two in the morning. He didn't touch a drop of alcohol, and he had no other interests. Making things was apparently his sole pleasure, so he rarely went out. He taught us in detail about manufacturing, but things didn't [always] go as he liked, so he would often complain.[24]

Okada Seizō gave a similar description of his grandfather and his unyielding standards:

> When at work, Yohei wore an apron as wide as a skirt, with a cord to tuck up the sleeves of his kimono. His gray hair was trimmed short, and the white collar peeping out from his plain navy cotton kimono gave an immaculate impression right until his final years. Throughout the entire [production process], at each step until a piece was finished, Yohei was constantly on the lookout to ensure that not even a speck of dust could get in. What he was most afraid of was how easily dust was absorbed into moist clay. Yohei's eyesight, which remained sharp until he died, never missed even the tiniest piece of trash in the corners of the workshop. Whenever he found any, he would pick it up in his fingertips and cart it off to a distant trash can, then wash his hands and scrub his fingertips with a fresh cotton towel until they were red. Even the ground around the kiln, where pine firewood of a uniform size was piled up to the same height, was swept as clean as the wood-floored room with the potter's wheels. In the midst of all this, Yohei would run his brush in indigo blue or red over a piece of unglazed pottery, as if brushing a Japanese-style painting on a piece of silk.[25]

Yohei thus continued his keen pursuit of ceramics research and production in this way until late in life. He died from illness in July 1914 at age sixty-four.

The diverse range of porcelain manufacturing techniques that Yohei III had developed were inherited by Seifū Yohei IV, born in Gojōzaka on August 1, 1871, as Yohei III's second son. He learned the ceramics industry from his father and painting from Tanomura Shōsai, a son of Tanomura Chokunyū, his father's former teacher. He was active at home and abroad, and like his father, he won recognition, even winning a gold medal at the 1915 Panama-Pacific International Exposition in San Francisco.[26] The award-winning work involved low-relief designs, underglaze blue, and a yellow glaze—techniques at which Yohei III had excelled. At the same time that he employed such techniques learned from his father, Yohei IV also developed new ones, such as a dark olive-green glaze.

World War II brought a change to the family's fortunes. Right before the end of the Pacific War (1941–1945), Gojōzaka was widened to prevent the spread of fires caused by bombing. As a consequence, the Seifū family home and workshop, which were located on the southern side of the street, were demolished except for the climbing kiln and part of the workshop.[27] On top of that, in the postwar period, the switch to the new yen meant that the family's assets became worthless, like those of many other wealthy people. Yohei IV died in 1951 without recovering from these adversities.

Seifū Yohei V 五代清風與平 (1921–1991), who took over as family head after Seifū Yohei IV, was unable to continue producing works under the Seifū name because after the war the Seifū family lost its assets and sold the climbing kiln to raise money to make ends meet. He instead worked as a ceramics painter at a Kyoto ware factory. It was not until 1971, at the age of fifty, that he started producing his own works (see [77]). Renting a room in the workshop of Tsukinowa Yūsen (1908–1998), who was known as a bonsai pot artist, he carried out the entire ceramics process by himself, from turning on a pottery wheel to painting the fired pottery. He was fascinated by Yūsen's works, and in time he, too, became known as a bonsai pot artist. In 1974 he moved his workshop to the Kiyomizuyaki Pottery Complex in Yamashina, to the southeast of Kiyomizu Gojōzaka. He died from illness on December 5, 1991, at the age of seventy.[28] The name Seifū Yohei was carried on by Matsumoto Masaaki (1948–2001), the husband of Seifū Yohei V's daughter, but no further details are known.

The Fate of the Seifū Family and Its Climbing Kiln

Although the Seifū family workshop was destroyed in the war, part of the climbing kiln owned by Seifū Yohei III in his later years still stood in Kyoto until 2017 (fig. 21). It was constructed by Kiyomizu Shichibei (active 1840s–1860s). From the days of Yohei II, the Seifū family had been permitted by Shichibei's family to share this kiln for firing products. (The two families were related through Kiyomizu Rokubei III, father-in-law to Yohei II.) The kiln's ownership changed hands several times from 1882 onward, and Yohei III acquired it sometime around 1907. After the war, the Seifū family transferred the kiln to a new owner.[29] The fact that Yohei III did not own his own kiln until late in life, even

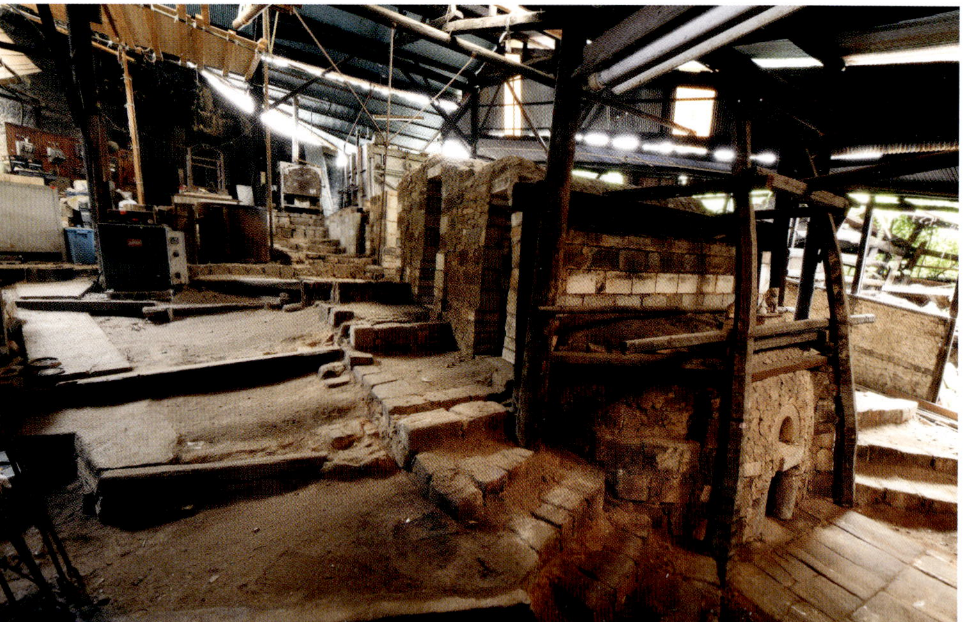

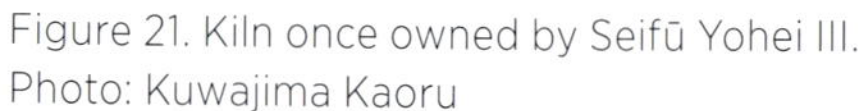

Figure 21. Kiln once owned by Seifū Yohei III. Photo: Kuwajima Kaoru

though he was an Imperial Household Artist, was nothing unusual in Gojōzaka, where rented kilns were common. Rather, his ability to own a kiln in the late Meiji period is inextricably linked to his appointment and can be regarded as proof that he had accumulated sufficient wealth to purchase a kiln.

In the Taishō period (1912–1926) there were an estimated thirty kilns in Kiyomizu Gojōzaka alone. After World War II, however, this number declined as the chopped pine used as fuel became more difficult to obtain and Gojōzaka became increasingly urbanized. These factors made it difficult to operate climbing kilns, which continuously emit black smoke. The 1971 Kyoto Prefecture pollution prevention ordinance imposed regulations on emissions from the chimneys of climbing kilns within the city bounds. In 1973 the Kyoto Ceramics Cooperative Association temporarily revived a communal kiln in which anti-smoke and anti-noise measures had been implemented, but because of a fire in 1980, thought to have started from this communal kiln, local residents started a movement to abolish climbing kilns. As a result, in the spring of 1982, their use within the Kyoto city limits was brought to an end.

The kiln previously owned by the Seifū family changed hands, and upgrades were made. Yet because this ordinance came into effect, the kiln was not fired up even once after the upgrade. Since it had previously been owned by Yohei III, a leading Meiji-period potter, there were moves to preserve it as an industrial heritage site. Ultimately, however, this climbing kiln and the workshop were demolished around 2017.

Conclusion

Seifū Yohei III lived at a time of tremendous change. Japanese society and culture, which had been almost entirely isolated from the world for two and a half centuries and was rooted in admiration of China, opened up to the world. Looking to the United States and Europe, Japan sought to bring about an industrial revolution through westernization. Yohei III experienced these tumultuous years in the old capital of Kyoto: the initial mayhem caused to the local economy by the restoration, followed by the westernization and modernization of the ceramics industry and subsequent participation in international expositions as Japan demonstrated its new developments to the West. Amid all of this, he maintained his focus on the cultural models of his early training, developing and promoting technological innovations modeled on Chinese ceramics. After being appointed as an Imperial Household Artist, Yohei moved away from Chinese designs. He aimed instead to create works that were more Japanese in style. He left a legacy not only through his works but also through his contributions to Kyoto's ceramics industry. His achievements formed the cornerstone of its development, which continues to this day.

Nevertheless, the history of Japanese ceramics has not looked kindly on the artist. Although he received national recognition as the first potter designated an Imperial Household Artist in the history of Japanese art and craft, the Meiji period was regarded as a time for modernizing and internationalizing the ceramics industry. Amid the growing popularity of *sencha* since the Edo period, Yohei's lack of interest in exporting his works meant that his attitude toward the creation of ceramics was poorly received until recent years. The twentieth century was a time when Japanese admiration for Chinese culture was on the wane and when *chanoyu* and teabowls, as symbols of Japan's own unique culture, became focal points of Japanese porcelain history.

Since around 2000, interest in Meiji-period arts and crafts has gradually risen. This improved image is evident in the fact that Yohei III's *Large Vase with Butterflies and Peonies* (see fig. 4), in the collection of the Tokyo National Museum, was designated an Important Cultural Property in 2017. Opportunities to see his works at exhibitions in Japan are on the rise. It is expected that Seifū Yohei works in Japanese collections will gain greater recognition in the future and attract further study. In that sense, too, James and Christine Heusinger's donation to the Cleveland Museum of Art of works by multiple generations of the Seifū Yohei studio, collected over many years, is indeed fortuitous and timely.

1. Osaka Museum of History, *Kimura Kenkadō.*

2. Ueda, *Seifū sagen*, 495.

3. Translation by Jonathan Chaves, in Addiss, *The World of Kameda Bōsai*, 120–21.

4. Kyoto Prefecture, *Tōjiki setsu*, 4.

5. Ōshio Kōminkan Kyōdoshi Henshū Iinkai, *Ōshio ni ikiru hitobito*; Shin'ei, *Toki no kaze.*

6. Watanabe, "Kyōyaki to sono meikō ni tsuite," 15–23.

7. Kyōto Bijutsu Kyōkai, "Teishitsu gigei'in Seifū Yohei shi rireki," 14.

8. Several works are mentioned in Seki, *Sandai Seifū Yohei.*

9. Takahashi, *Kinsei dōgu idōshi*, 29–30.

10. Honey, *The Ceramic Art of China*, 188. Okuda Eisen (1753–1811), Eiraku Hozen (1795–1854), and Aoki Mokubei were ceramists active in the Edo period; see Sinéad Vilbar's essay in this volume on their contributions. Miyagawa (Makuzu) Kōzan I (1842–1916) was a ceramist of the subsequent generation and a student of Mokubei's; his contributions are discussed in the next section of this essay.

11. Kuroda, "Seifū Yohei-shi," 31.

12. Kuroda, 30–31.

13. Scidmore, "The Porcelain-Artists of Japan," 86.

14. Dai Sankai Naikoku Kangyō Hakurankai Jimukyoku, "Meiji nijūsannen dai sankai naikoku kangyō hakurankai shinsa hōkoku," 155–56.

15. Kuroda, "Seifū Yohei-shi," 38–39.

16. On the techniques that Seifū III developed, see Maezaki, "Kindai tōji to tokkyo seido," 87–94.

17. On the relationship between Seifū Yohei III, Miyagawa Kōzan I, and literati tastes, see Maezaki, "Naturalism in Meiji-Period Ceramics," 33–41.

18. Takahashi, *Kinsei dōgu idōshi*, 29–30.

19. Maezaki, "Kindai tōji to tokkyo seido," 73–108.

20. For details of Yohei III's works exhibited at the Paris Exposition, see Okamoto, "Sandai Seifū Yohei ni tsuite," 47–54.

21. Kuroda, "Seifū Yohei-shi," 36.

22. Okada, *Jibun ningen*, 113–14. Since Okada Seizō was born a year before Yohei III's death, we can assume that he heard this account from his mother Tama.

23. Kuroda, *Ikka issairoku*, 183. No information is available regarding the incense burner mentioned by Yohei IV.

24. Kuroda, 184.

25. Okada, *Jibun ningen*, 113.

26. Watanabe, "Kyōyaki to sono meikō ni tsuite," 20.

27. Watanabe, 20.

28. Ōe, "Yūsen to Seifū Yohei no kōryū," 125–27.

29. Mashimizu, *Kokon kyōgama deichū kanwa*, 63.

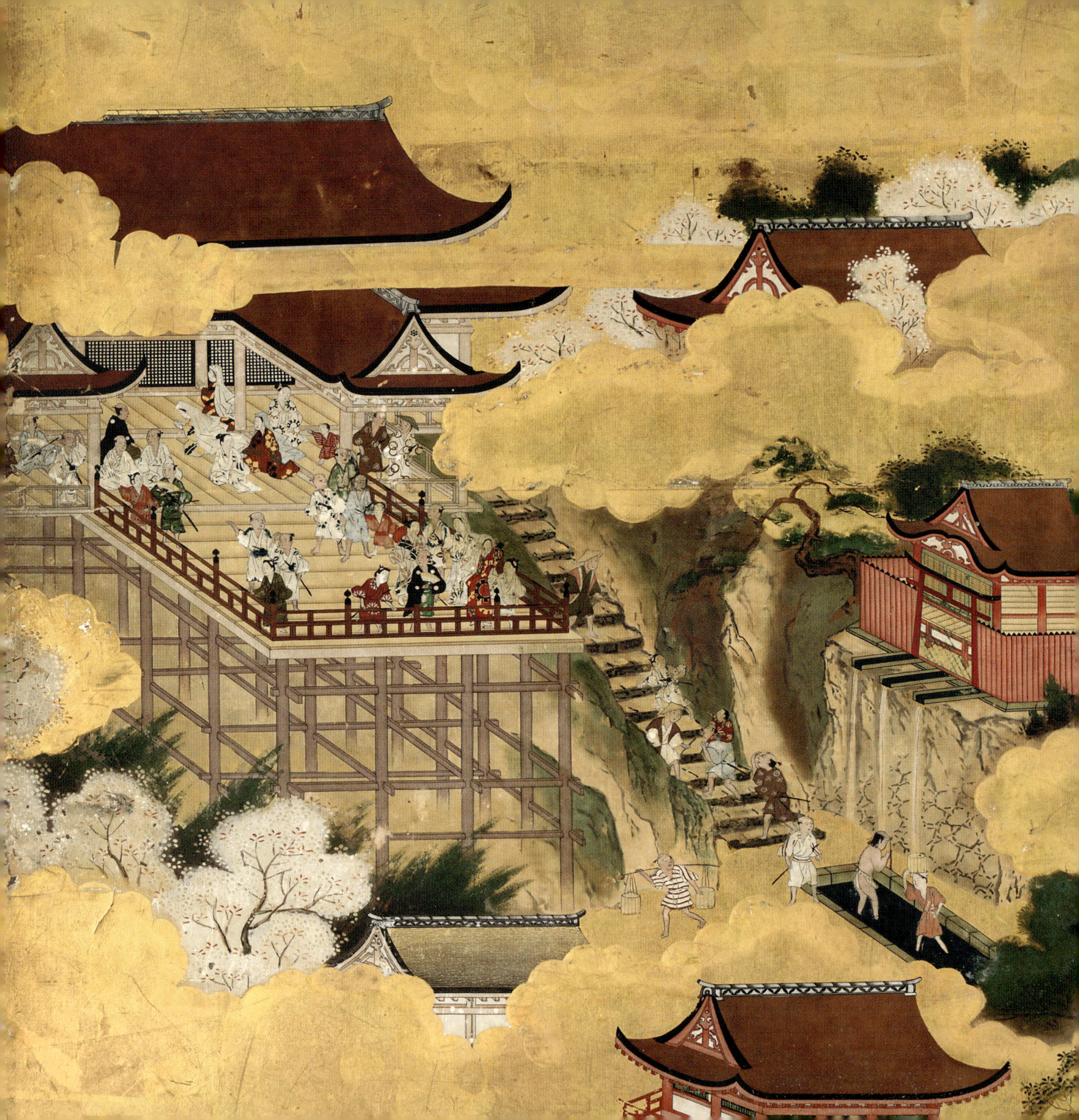

PORCELAIN IN KYOTO

SINÉAD VILBAR

Figure 22. *Views of Kyoto* (detail), 1600s. Six-panel folding screen; ink, color, gold, and gilding on paper; 110.3 x 307.2 cm. The Cleveland Museum of Art, Bequest of Mrs. A. Dean Perry 1997.119

Kyoto, situated in the Kansai region of western Honshu, the largest of Japan's main islands, was the country's capital from 794 until 1868. It was in this city that the generations of ceramists who produced under the name Seifū Yohei spent their careers. The studio's most famous member, Yohei III (1851–1914), came of age just as the capital moved to its present location in the Kantō region of eastern Honshu, giving a new identity to the metropolis of Edo, where the overthrown Tokugawa military regime had been headquartered. Yet even as Tokyo ("eastern capital") drew Kyoto elites into its orbit, for the Seifū Yohei studio, the slope of Kyoto's Gojōzaka, or Fifth Avenue, remained the center of the world.

Kyoto continues to hold tiny galaxies of culture within its vast creative universe. Now as during Yohei III's time, these galaxies can be slow to reveal themselves in the rush of daily life, but if one pauses long enough to apprehend their basic forms, their richness and depth will begin to reward even the slightest glance in the right direction. In the centuries since the city was established at the end of the eighth century with the aspirational name Heian-kyō, or "capital of peace and tranquility," it was home to grand imperial compounds with curated gardens and, later, to great shrines and temples, as well as warriors' residences. The everyday activities and maintenance of these complexes required ateliers specializing in all sorts of arts and crafts. Townspeople also contributed to culture, and the provinces provided a constant influx of new talent, including Yohei I and Yohei III.

Any ancient city has many layers, with the activities and identities of neighborhoods changing over time. Kiyomizu Gojōzaka, the former location of the Seifū studio and shop conjures not only contemporary photographs advertising Kyoto's famous vistas but also fourteenth-century illustrated handscrolls and seventeenth-century screen paintings showing the unmistakable platform of the temple Kiyomizudera presiding over the valley below (fig. 22). With such a robust history as a cradle for ideas and their material representations, any artist active in this neighborhood would experience both creative stimulation from peers and trepidation in the face of previous generations of talent.

As Shinya Maezaki observes in his essay in this volume, the Seifū studio and its focus on elegant porcelains emerged with the ability to fire porcelain in Kyoto combined with the trend of drinking *sencha*. To better understand these circumstances and how they are manifest in the studio's output, one must consider the overall history of porcelain production in Japan, as well as the kinds of objects involved in *sencha*. This essay therefore first presents a brief history of porcelain manufacture and appreciation in Japan as it relates to ceramic studios in Kyoto. It then discusses some basic features and purposes of Japanese *sencha* utensils. It concludes with a discussion of connoisseurship of Seifū studio works.

In Japan, climbing linked chamber kilns were introduced, most likely from Korea, to Kyushu, the southernmost of Japan's main islands, in the late sixteenth century. These kilns were initially used to fire stoneware. In the 1610s, the discovery of high-quality porcelain stone in the Arita area of northern Kyushu, combined with efficient climbing kilns that could fire at sufficiently high temperatures, made Japan's first porcelain production possible.[1] From that time until

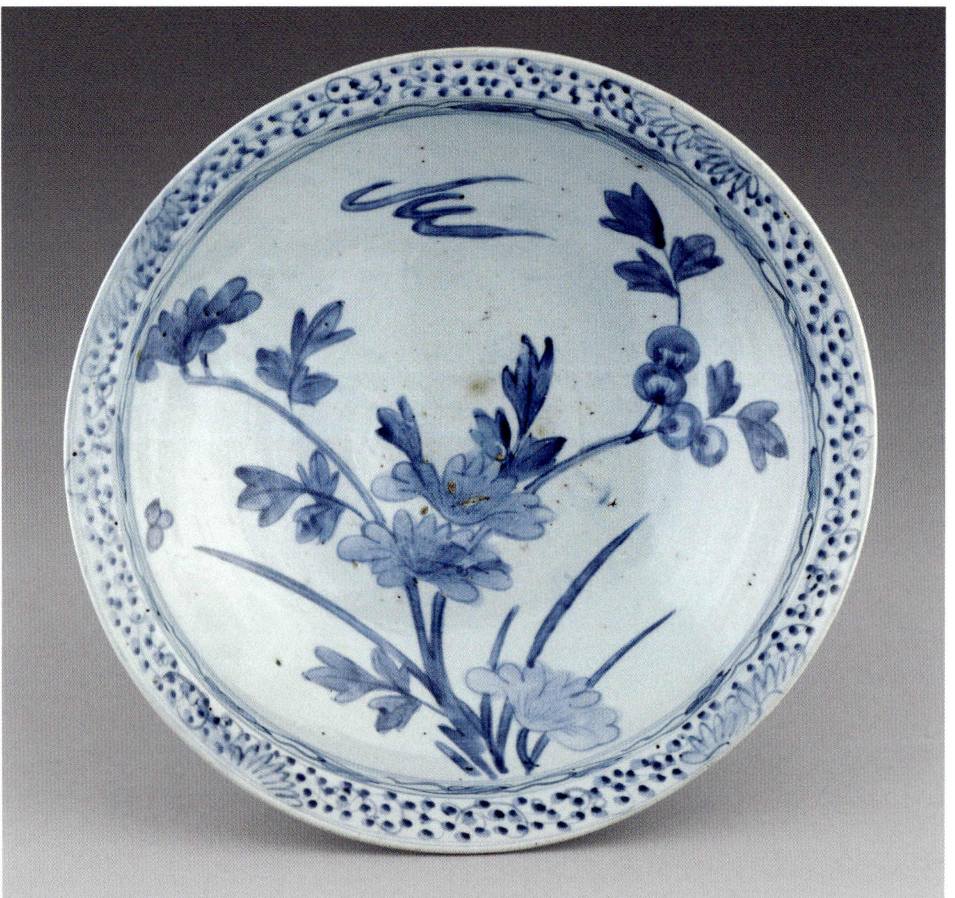

Figure 23. *Bowl with Flowers and Grasses*, 1620s. Porcelain with underglaze blue (Arita ware, early Imari type); h. 13.7 cm, mouth diam. 46.8 cm, base diam. 12.2 cm. Agency for Cultural Affairs, Government of Japan. Photo: Kodaira Tadao, courtesy of Kyushu National Museum

the early nineteenth century, porcelain production on the archipelago took place almost exclusively in Kyushu. There were kilns firing porcelain in some areas of Honshu in the mid-seventeenth century, but these operations appear to have been short-lived.[2] Two significant exceptions are sites in today's Aichi and Gifu Prefectures: both produced porcelain from the later eighteenth century.[3]

In terms of decoration, the Kyushu-based ceramists wished to replicate what they saw in Ming-dynasty porcelains from Jingdezhen, the Chinese city renowned for porcelain production. At first, Japanese kilns were able to make works only with designs in underglaze cobalt blue. Today, these pieces are often called early (*shoki*) Imari, after the port in northern Kyushu from which Japanese porcelains were first exported (fig. 23). Success with overglaze enamel decoration followed in the mid-seventeenth century (fig. 24). By the 1670s, what are now called classic Kakiemon-style porcelains, with their fine overglaze enamel designs in multiple colors, were favored by clients overseas and in Japan.[4]

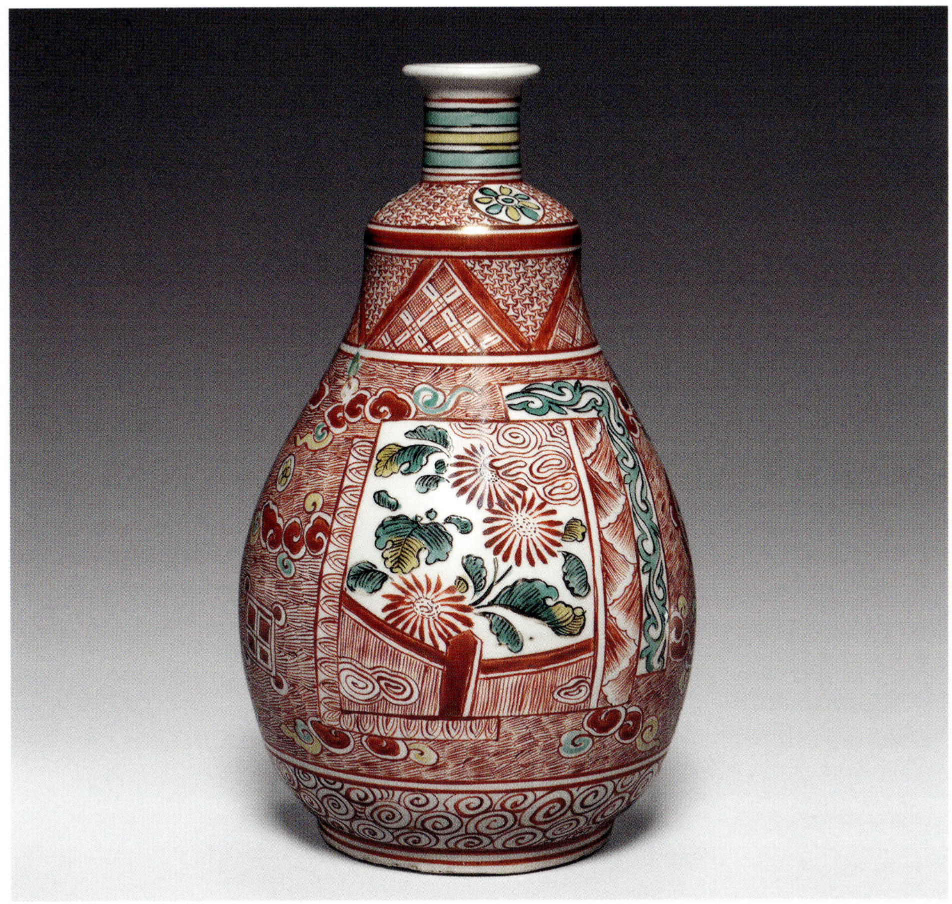

Figure 24. *Tea Whisk–Shaped Sake Bottle*, 1660s–early 1670s. Porcelain with overglaze enamel (Arita ware, early *iro-e* type); h. 25.4, diam. 14.7 cm. The Cleveland Museum of Art, Severance and Greta Millikin Purchase Fund 2014.391

Figure 25. *Dish with Ginkgo Leaves*, late 1600s–early 1700s. Porcelain with underglaze blue (Arita ware, Nabeshima type); diam. 20 cm. The Cleveland Museum of Art, Purchase from the J. H. Wade Fund 2017.61

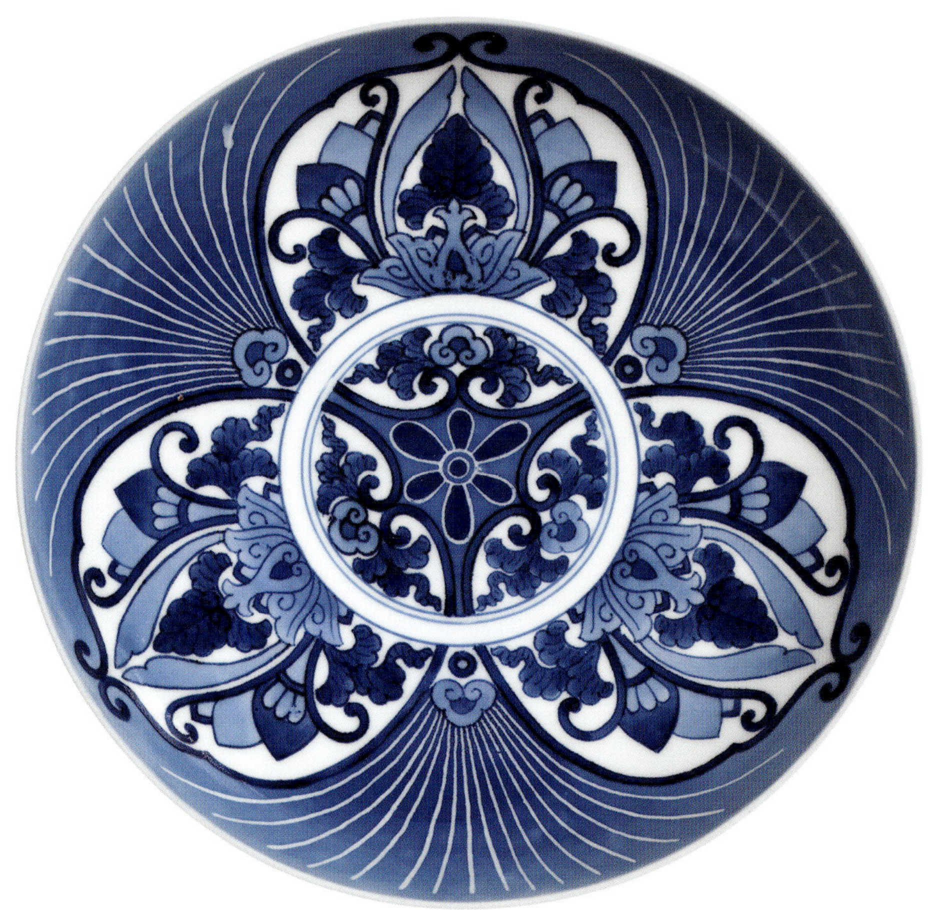

While Japanese porcelains increasingly supplied the domestic market, the desire to capture the international market was an important motivating factor in Japanese porcelain development during the seventeenth century. Chinese exports at the time were in disarray because of the collapse of the Ming dynasty and the trade restrictions set in place in the early Qing dynasty. Before China's political situation stabilized and its exports fully resumed in the eighteenth century, numerous porcelains were exported from Japan to Europe. What those outside Japan did not see were the extremely high-quality Kyushu porcelains called Nabeshima ware that began to be made in the late seventeenth century (fig. 25). Named after the regional ruling family that ordered their production, Nabeshima pieces were made as tribute wares for the shogunate in Edo and as gifts to other regional rulers. It was, however, not until the Meiji period that these works and their copies became known beyond Japan, as Edo-period Nabeshima designs started to be replicated and original works from prominent families found their way to auctions and art dealers.

While the rulers of Kyushu desired to retain control over the techniques and production methods that allowed their domains to profit from both the domestic and international markets, their porcelain studios' secrets eventually began to spread to other areas. A domain in what is now Ehime Prefecture on the island of Shikoku commenced limited porcelain production in the late eighteenth century with a ceramist recruited from Kyushu. In the first decade of the nineteenth century, Katō Tamikichi (1772–1824) brought porcelain techniques gained during his study in Kyushu to Seto, in what is now Aichi Prefecture, thereby significantly expanding local production. In Kyoto, the first to succeed in producing porcelain was Okuda Eisen (1753–1811), who did so experimentally and as a hobby.

In seventeenth- and eighteenth-century Kyoto, the most sought-after porcelains were still treasured works from the Song (960–1297) and Yuan (1271–1368) dynasties imported from China in the past. These were exemplified by the works in the Ashikaga shogunal collection. Also of interest were late Ming wares in underglaze blue and, less often, with overglaze color enamels, made to order or on speculation for the Japanese market. The earliest of those in underglaze blue are now called *kosometsuke*, or "old underglaze blue [works]" (fig. 26). Chinese *sencha* tea utensils, including stoneware kettles, teapots, and braziers, as well

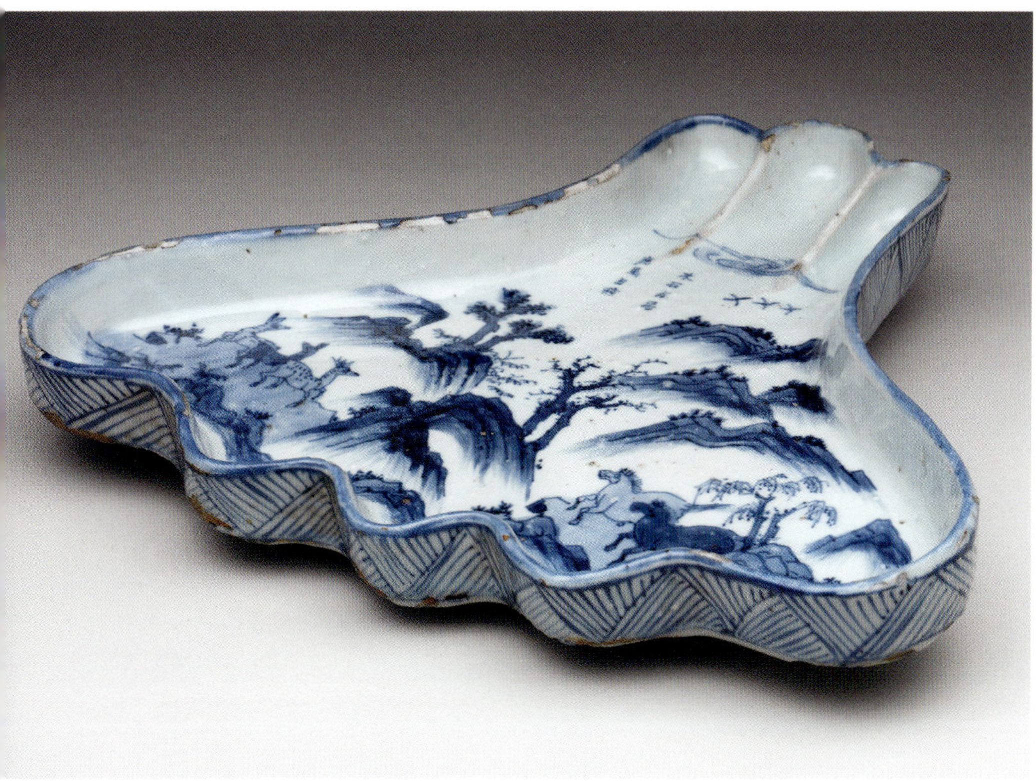

Figure 26. *Dish in Shape of Mount Fuji with Horses and Deer*, c. 1625. Porcelain with underglaze blue (Jingdezhen ware); h. 5.3 cm, w. 25.1 cm, l. 28.5 cm. The Metropolitan Museum of Art, Purchase, Barbara and William Karatz Gift, Gift of C. T. Loo and Company, by exchange and Rogers Fund, by exchange, 2010

Figure 27. *Tea Storage Jar*, mid- to late 1600s. Nonomura Ninsei. Stoneware with white glaze (Shigaraki style); h. 28.3 cm, diam. 28.7 cm. The Cleveland Museum of Art, Purchase from the J. H. Wade Fund 1978.6

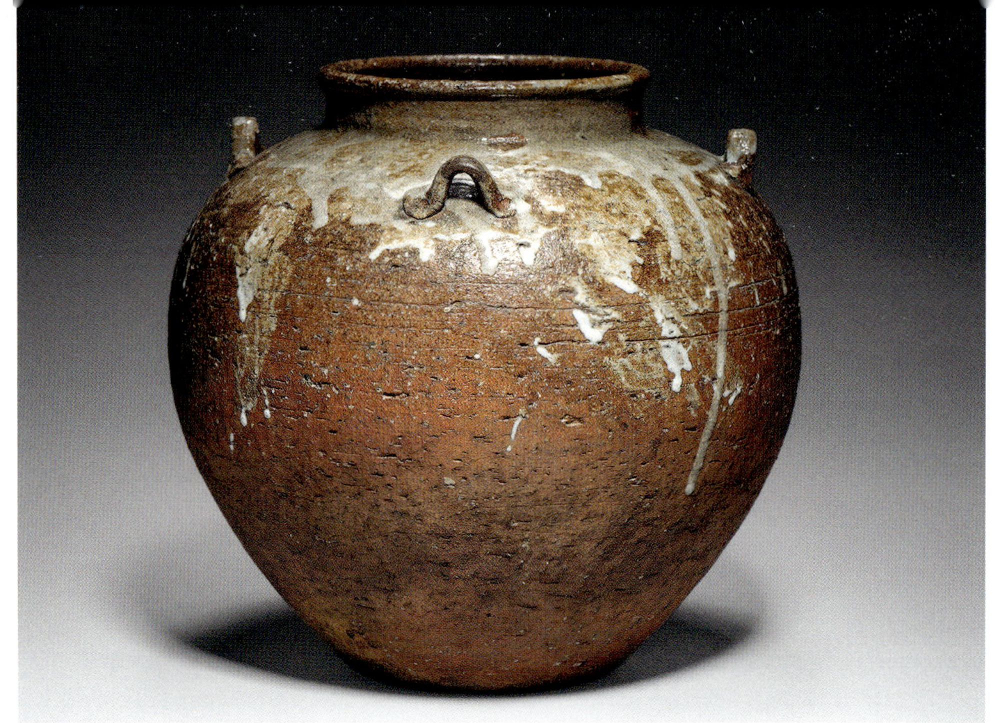

as porcelain serving cups, came to Kyoto through Nagasaki in the seventeenth century. However, it was not until the latter part of the eighteenth century that *sencha* spread beyond elite circles in Kyoto and Osaka. The seventeenth- and early eighteenth-century heroes of Kyoto ceramics were instead making ceramics for *chanoyu* and the associated kaiseki repast. Following in the footsteps of Chōjirō (?–1589?), recognized as the first potter of the Raku lineage, the famous

Figure 28. *Square Dish with Plovers over Waves*, c. 1709. Dish: Ogata Kenzan. Design: Ogata Kōrin. Stoneware with underglaze iron oxide; h. 2.7 cm, l. 22 cm, w. 22 cm. The Cleveland Museum of Art, Purchase from the J. H. Wade Fund 1966.365

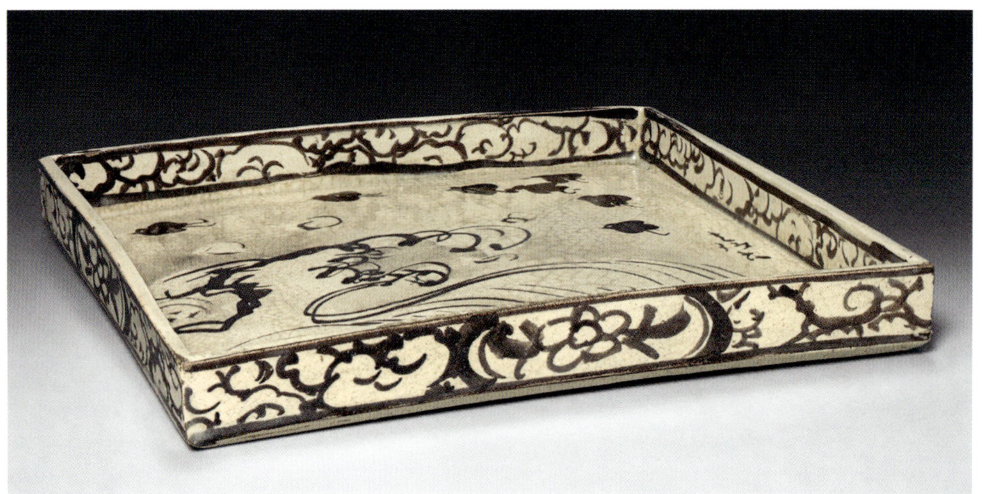

calligrapher Hon'ami Kōetsu (1558–1637) in his later years made earthenware teabowls at his artists' compound outside Kyoto.[5] Nonomura Ninsei (active 1640s–1690s), who is thought to have grown up near Kyoto in Tanba, in what is now Hyōgo Prefecture, made stoneware favored by *chanoyu* masters who desired a refined version of the imperfection lauded by other tea masters who prized rusticity (fig. 27). From 1709, the brothers Ogata Kenzan (1663–1743) and Ogata Kōrin (1658–1716) collaborated on stoneware for *chanoyu*, with Kenzan making the forms and Kōrin painting their designs (fig. 28). Kenzan also made colorful works on his own that were much admired and copied (fig. 29). It is Ninsei and Kenzan whose names are most strongly associated with the bold and colorful aspect of Kyoto ware.[6]

Three important figures in Kyoto ceramics of the later eighteenth to early nineteenth century, and thus in the history of the Seifū studio, were Kiyomizu Rokubei I (1738–1799; see fig. 10); Takahashi Dōhachi I (1740–1804), who hailed from Ise; and Okuda Eisen. Although Eisen—purportedly the grandson of immigrants who fled the Manchu invasion of Ming-dynasty China—is credited with being the first to successfully produce porcelain in Kyoto, as discussed earlier, Dōhachi is also said to have sometimes worked in porcelain, according to an 1802 publication titled *Quick Guide to Sencha* (*Sencha hayashi nan*).[7] Nin'ami Dōhachi (Takahashi Dōhachi II, 1783–1855) was one of Eisen's students (fig. 30), as was Aoki Mokubei (1767–1833) (see fig. 8). Mokubei was known for his exquisite *sencha* utensils, as well as his involvement with the Kaga domain's Kutani kilns. It was, of course, Nin'ami Dōhachi to whom Yohei I was apprenticed following his move to Kyoto from Kanazawa. While Yohei I failed to get on with Takahashi Dōhachi III after Nin'ami's death, a misstep that ended his career and

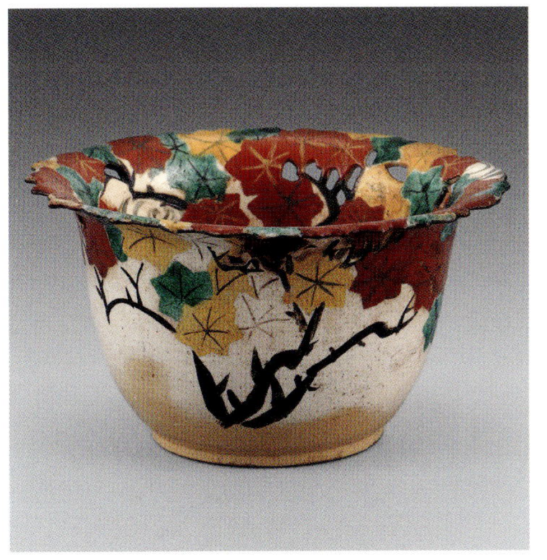

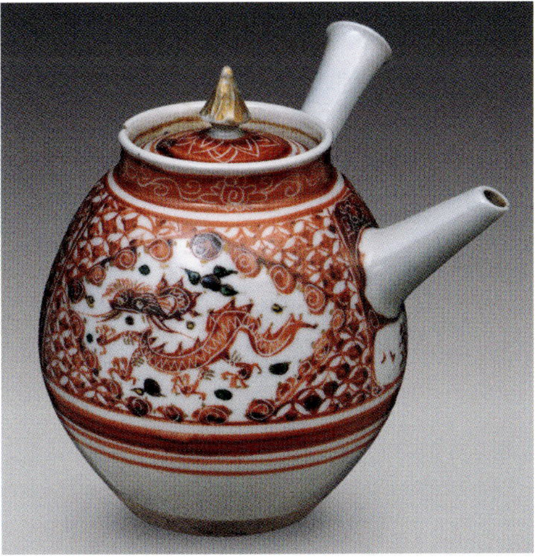

Figure 29. *Bowl with "Tatsutagawa" Autumn Foliage and Stream Design in Openwork*, c. 1712–31. Ogata Kenzan. Stoneware with overglaze enamel; h. 11.5 cm, mouth diam. 20.2 cm, base diam. 9.8 cm. Okada Museum of Art. Important Cultural Property

Figure 30. *Teapot with Dragon*, 1825. Nin'ami Dōhachi, also known as Takahashi Dōhachi II. Porcelain with overglaze enamel; h. 11.7 cm, diam. 10.5 cm, w. with handle 11.0 cm. The Museum of Fine Arts Boston, Morse Collection, Museum purchase with funds donated by contribution, 92.6168a–b. Photo: © 2023 Museum of Fine Arts, Boston

could have extinguished the Seifū Yohei lineage before it properly began, it was Yohei II and his relationship with Kiyomizu Shichibei (active 1840s–1860s), the eldest son of Kiyomizu Rokubei II (1790–1860), who also worked in porcelain, that created a path forward for the Seifū Yohei studio in the tight-knit Kyoto community of ceramicists (fig. 31).

The trajectory of Yohei III was similar to that of his contemporary Miura Chikusen I (1854–1915), a student of Dōhachi III. Chikusen was born into a family of tatami mat makers in Kyoto. Like Yohei III, Chikusen maintained a strong practice in creating *sencha* utensils even as the tides turned toward lionizing *chanoyu* as a uniquely Japanese taste for tea as part of a nationalizing fervor in the late nineteenth century and early twentieth century (fig. 32). In addition, he was likewise a student of Tanomura Chokunyū. Yet unlike Yohei III, who studied with Chokunyū for a brief but meaningful period before being redirected to an

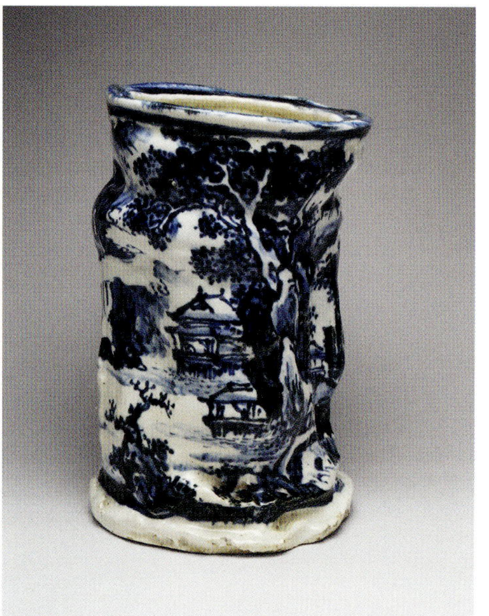

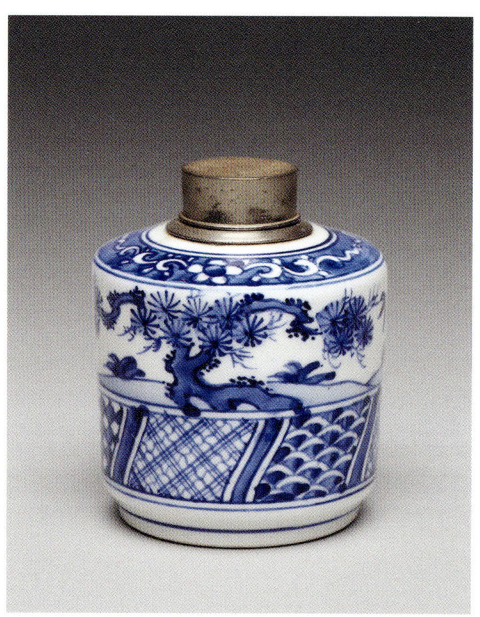

Figure 31. *Vase with Landscape*, c. 1900. Kiyomizu Shichibei. Porcelain with underglaze blue; h. 29 cm, diam. 18 cm. National Museums Scotland, Presented by David and Anne Hyatt King through the Art Fund, V.2015.10.273. Image © National Museums Scotland

Figure 32. *Tea Container*, 1880–1915. Miura Chikusen I. Porcelain with underglaze blue, silver lid; h. 11.4 cm, diam. 7.6 cm. Portland Art Museum, Gift of Margaret G. Forsythe, 2015.97.1

apprenticeship with Yohei II, Chikusen I did not start his training with the *nanga* painter until he was already active as a ceramist. Both Chikusen and Yohei III exhibited in international expositions in Chicago and Paris, yet Chikusen was not selected as an Imperial Household Artist. He did, however, found a successful lineage. The most recent head of the studio, Miura Chikusen V (1934–2021), was both a ceramist and a respected scholar of ceramics history.

In a discussion of porcelain in Kyoto, the work of Eiraku Hozen (1795–1854), although taking a step backward in the present chronology, cannot be overlooked. After being adopted into the Nishimura Zengorō lineage of brazier

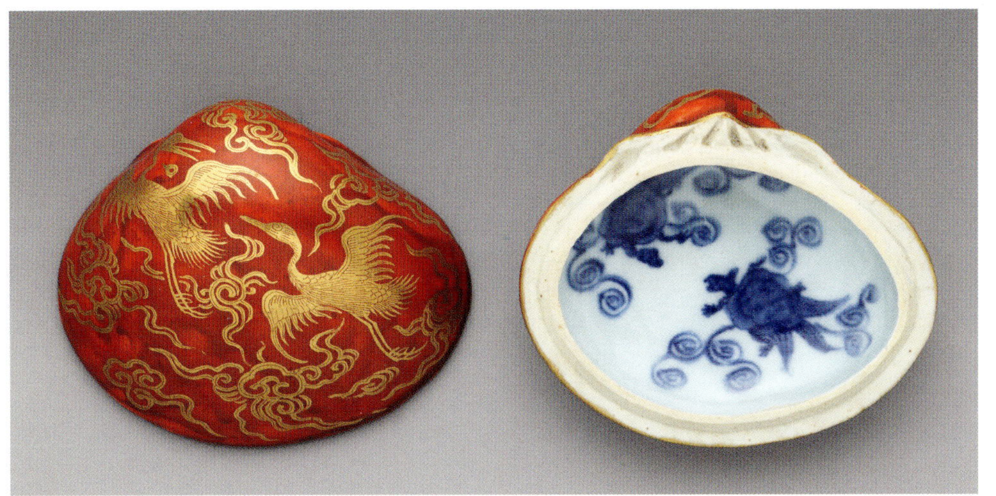

Figure 33. *Incense Container (Kōgō) in the Shape of a Clamshell, with Cranes and Tortoise Motifs*, early to mid-1800s. Eiraku Hozen. Porcelain with underglaze blue and overglaze red and gold; h. 6 cm. The Metropolitan Museum of Art, Gift of Mrs. V. Everit Macy, 1923, 23.225.252a–b

makers, he became one of the specially designated artists who produced tea utensils for the branches of the Sen family of *chanoyu* fame. Hozen worked in porcelain, creating works in underglaze blue and overglaze color and gold (fig. 33). He also produced stoneware with a variety of surface decorations based on Chinese porcelain prototypes, not just in Kyoto but in other provinces as well, at the request of regional rulers. Hozen excelled at pieces copied after *gosu aka-e*, or ceramics with multicolored overglaze enamels made in the Zhangzhou area of southern China in the sixteenth and seventeenth centuries (fig. 34). Hozen is perhaps best known, however, for his stoneware copies after Chinese *fahua* pieces (fig. 35). Pronounced *hōka* in Japanese, the technique involves relatively high-relief surface molding so that glaze collects in the recessed areas. The prototypes

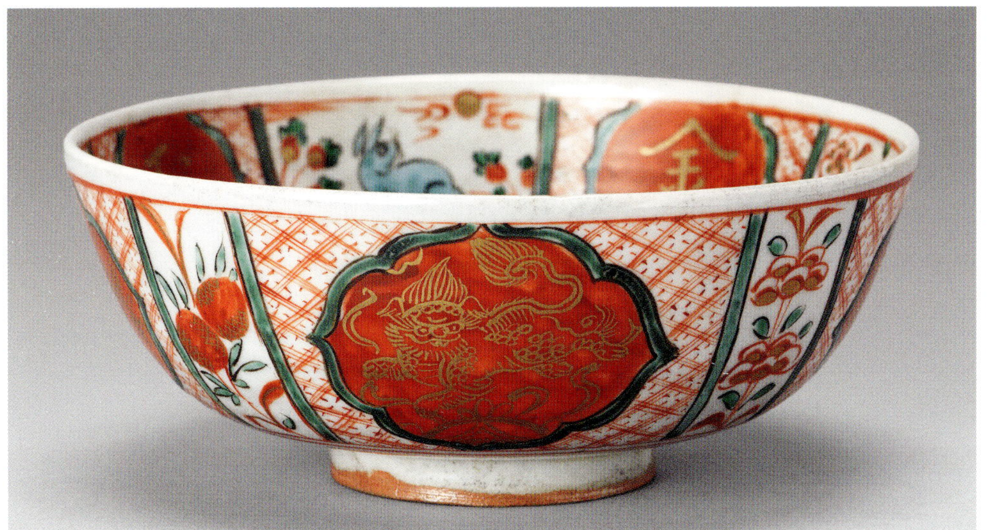

Figure 34. *Bowl*, early to mid-1800s. Eiraku Hozen. Stoneware with underglaze blue and overglaze color enamel and gold; h. 7.4 cm, mouth diam. 17.6 cm, foot diam. 6.8 cm. Kyoto National Museum

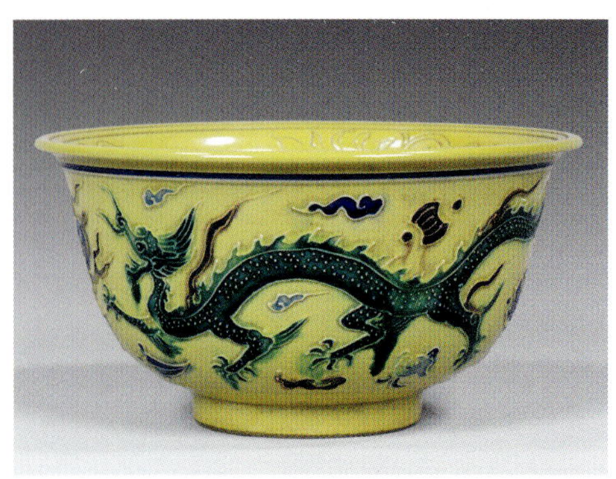

Figure 35. *Bowl with Dragon*, early 1800s. Eiraku Hozen. Stoneware with three-color glaze; h. 9.2 cm, mouth diam. 17.3 cm, foot diam. 7.1 cm. Tokyo National Museum, G-212. Image: TNM Image Archives

for these works were called *kōchi* ware, after the Japanese name for the people of Vietnam. While in fact Chinese, these works came to Japan from Southeast Asian ports and were thus associated with the region. As Patricia Graham has outlined in her immersive exploration of Japan's *sencha* culture, *chanoyu* aesthetics and practice had a significant impact on the reception of *sencha*. Indeed, the copies after Ming-dynasty Chinese export wares that featured prominently in Kyoto porcelain and stoneware production for both *chanoyu* and *sencha* would have seemed odd in the context of drinking tea in China.[8]

The collapse of the Tokugawa shogunate in 1868 greatly impacted the operation of the Seifū studio. Meiji authorities led Japan's transition from an isolationist country often guided by its unique vision of China's cultural legacy to a nation that wished to participate fully in international affairs and to distinguish itself, for both posterity and profit, on the world stage. Yohei II had a keen interest in the international market as an opening that would create room for him beyond the complicated world of Kyoto ceramics, with its kilns so tightly controlled by so few. The favorable assessment of a coffee set he showed in an 1872 exhibit of Kyoto-made products organized by the prefectural government led to his involvement in national and international exhibitions as a designer and as an artist.[9] Notably, Yohei II's works were selected to represent Japanese ceramics of his era in an exhibit on the history of Japanese ceramics presented by the government of Japan at the Philadelphia Exposition of 1876.[10] Yohei III was also active in the studio in the 1870s, so he would have been familiar with Yohei II's successes in working with the government and winning acclaim in Japan and internationally. Nonetheless, he chose instead to focus on developing glazes and, ultimately, to obtain a kiln in Kyoto, even while his own elevation to the level of Imperial Household Artist may have afforded him other options.

In the years between Okuda Eisen's first experiments with Ming-style porcelains in the 1780s and Yohei III's explorations of Qing-dynasty forms and glazes in the 1900s, *sencha* culture in Japan had changed substantially. It became far removed from the pictures of intimate meetings of cherished friends in remote locations or occasional festive convenings of recluses in nature. It had also moved beyond salon-like gatherings of artists and philosophers, or even the commercialized versions of such events. Massive public gatherings engineered in Osaka and northern Kyushu by Chokunyū in the 1870s were like a grand finale. By the early twentieth century, schools such as Kagetsuan in Osaka were enrolling students in courses where one could learn how to arrange utensils and to follow the proper sequence of steps when preparing *sencha*.[11]

A basic utensil set for *sencha* may include a tea container, a tea scoop, a charcoal brazier, a kettle, a teapot and teacups, and a hot water cooler, or *yuzamashi*. Additional items, such as saucers, wiping cloths, rinsing bowls, and incense burners, among others, may also be part of a set. In addition to ceramics, there will be objects in other media, such as bamboo, lacquer, wood, metal, and so forth. Both Yohei III and Yohei IV concentrated on making *sencha* utensils, in addition to their exhibition pieces; and they also made *chanoyu* pieces for select clients. Evidence of the latter can be seen in the documents associated with one water container, or *mizusashi*, in the Heusinger Collection (see [53]). The *mizusashi*, in fact, provides a useful point of entry for understanding the borrowing of terms, utensils, and forms between different realms of tea and gastronomic appreciation. In *chanoyu*, *mizusashi* are quite large containers that contain fresh water, which is transported to the vessel using a *suichū* (alternately pronounced *mizutsugi*), or water pitcher. As a rule, they are not moved around during use. In *sencha* practice, fresh water is kept instead in a *suichū*, which is moved about during use and can also serve a variety of other functions, from cleaning and cooling to filling other utensils. Historically, in China, sake pourers may have been appropriated for use as *suichū*, just as found objects, often foreign ones, were repurposed in *chanoyu*.

For those unfamiliar with *sencha*, it may be difficult to distinguish utensils that appear similar. For example, sake pourers called *chōshi* may easily be mistaken for teapots for serving tea. One way to know how the people making or using utensils understood them is to refer to their wooden storage boxes. Boxes made to go with a piece, usually from the time of production, are called *tomobako*. They customarily have inscriptions that provide key information about the piece, including its function. For example, one colorful work by Yohei III is a porcelain lidded vessel with a spout and two handles made of metal (see [16]). A quick look at the lid of its box explains that it is a *chōshi*. Meanwhile, a porcelain teapot with a fine underglaze blue design of bamboo by Yohei IV is described on its box as a *myōhei*, a term for teapot (see [60]).

A typical *sencha* set made by Yohei III contains a teapot, a hot water cooler, and a set of five teacups, all made of porcelain (see [27]). The teapot is most often a side-handled type called a *kyūsu*.[12] The hot water cooler may look rather like a pitcher or a creamer, with a handle and spout (see [28]), or it may look like a bowl that has been pressed in on both sides (see, for example, [19]). Regulating the temperature of the water used to steep the tea leaves, as well as the temperature of the vessels used to serve the beverage, is a crucial aspect of enjoying the tea and taking care of the utensils. Not only can water that is too hot ruin the tea's flavor, putting hot water into a cold teapot or cups can also damage the glaze on porcelain, causing it to crack.

Another important element in *sencha* is the brazier, or *ryōro*, upon which the kettle sits (see [31]). Incense burners, or *kōro* (see [33–36]), and incense containers, or *kōgō*, while certainly not exclusive to *sencha*, are also key objects in *sencha* practice. Along with the artwork selected for the occasion, such as hanging scrolls painted with landscapes of remote mountain valleys and riverfront cottages (see [8]), they are considered an integral part of the sensory experience. The comparatively large bowls used to serve sweets to guests are called *kashibachi* (see, for example, [11]). They generally have a stand-alone design that is meant to be juxtaposed or harmonized with other assembled utensils as the host desires.

Tea sets produced by the Seifū studio sometimes come together in a single box or cabinet with multiple compartments, each element wrapped in a cloth and placed in its own compartment. The components of a set may alternatively be packaged separately, with the teapot in one box, the hot water cooler in another, and the cups together in a third box. When boxed together, the set is typically identified as such on the box lid, without reference to the individual pieces. However, when boxed separately, the individual box inscriptions refer only to the objects contained in that particular box, so it may not be apparent that the works belong to a set. In general, the Seifū studio followed the standard practice in Japan for identifying the artist and object in box inscriptions. When a wooden storage box opens at the top, the outside of the lid (which is secured with a box cord) is inscribed on the right with the style and decoration of the vessels contained; another line of text to the left identifies the type of object, as well as the number included if it is a set of like objects, such as dishes or cups. One of several studio seals is often pressed to the left of the inscriptions. On the inside of the box lid are the artist's signature and a second seal. Further, a studio seal was impressed on each wrapping cloth. For storage boxes that open on the side by pulling up a sliding panel, the inscriptions on the panel's exterior and interior correspond with those on the inside and outside of a lid.

As an Imperial Household Artist, Yohei III had a seal with that title and applied it as well, making a total of three seals, one on the outside of the lid and two on the inside of the lid. However, there are instances in which he simply writes his government title in ink. With some frequency, it is not Yohei III's signature found on a box lid interior. Instead, there is an inscription by Yohei IV authenticating his father's work, next to which he generally applied his father's Imperial Household Artist seal. When placing a seal next to the identification of the artwork, father and son used a variety of different seals. Many read "Seifū," but they also include two used almost exclusively by Yohei III, a square one reading "Seifū Yohei" and one shaped like a lily pad with a phrase that may be glossed as "Golden Voice, Swaying Gem." Of course, only Yohei III used his style name, "Seizan" 晟山; Yohei IV used 成山, a homophone written with a similar but different first character. Yohei IV sometimes sealed himself "Seifū of the Thatched Hut" next to his signature. Like Yohei I and II, Yohei III often signed himself "Yohei," something Yohei IV never did.

Whatever the object, tea-related or otherwise, all of these identifying features on the box are in addition to the studio seal impressed into the base of the object or the signatory inscription painted on or incised into the base. In some cases, a seal or signature appears in an alternate location, for example, under the handle or just above the foot of an object (fig. 36). In still other cases, an object has no mark at all if the social position of the object's intended recipient called for it, as in the case of the imperial family. For a piece intended for international exhibition, not only the studio but also the artist's nation is likely to be identified, following a convention established in China in which dynasties or reign names were inscribed on the bases of porcelains.

In the visual appreciation of the porcelains of Yohei III and Yohei IV, the quality of light is a critical factor. Different lighting conditions bring out different aspects of the design and, importantly, highlight the translucency of glazes and at times the porcelain itself. The clay and glaze colors, along with

Figure 36. Box lid interior signature and seal of Seifū Yohei II and two different base marks, both reading "Seifū" appearing just above the feet of two sake cups. (See also [4].)

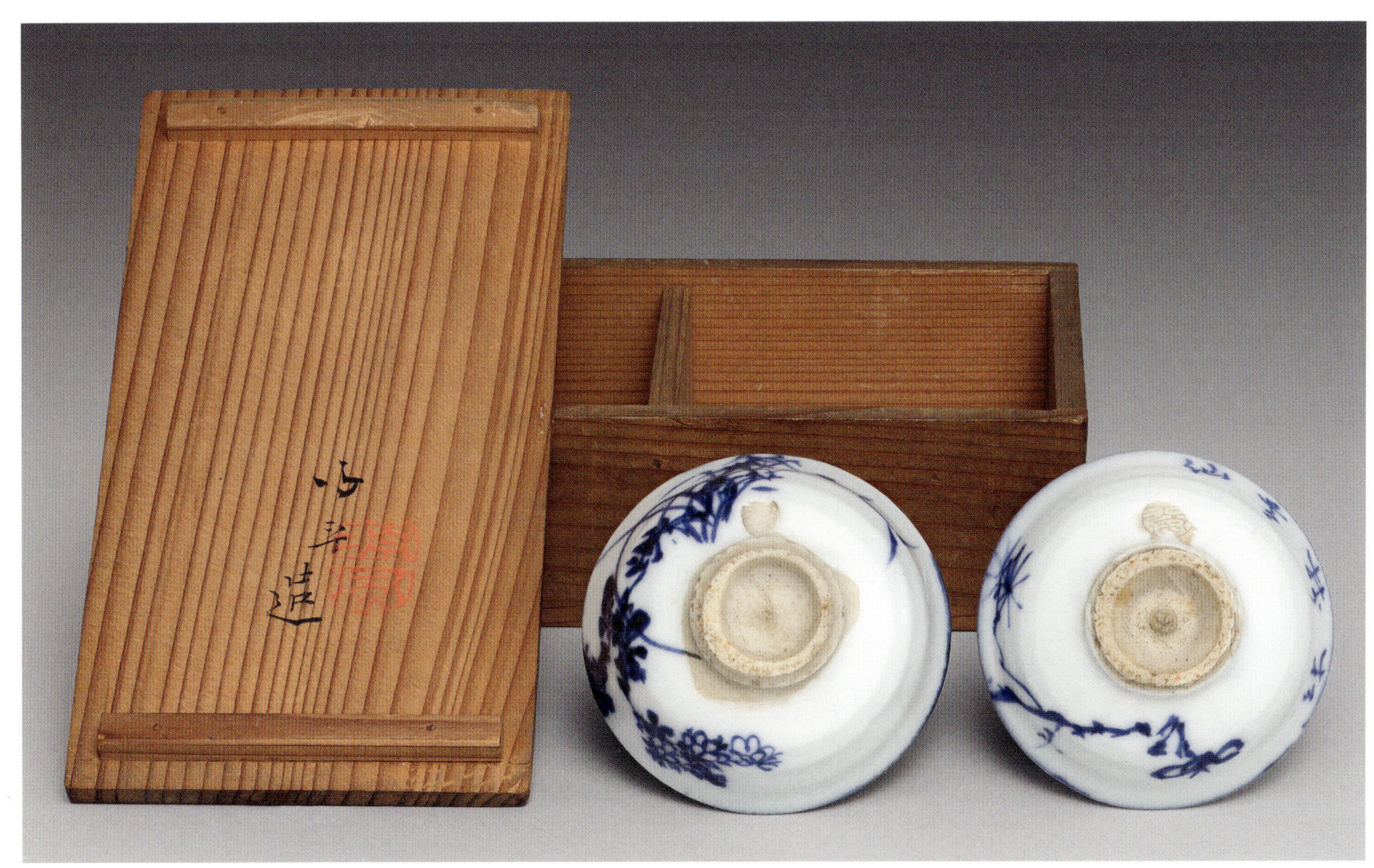

the combinations of techniques used, are sometimes bold, more often so in the work of Yohei IV (see, for example, [87]). Yet they are frequently remarkably subtle, so sustained looking and handling play a large role in how the pieces are experienced, as do the modeled clay elements and the way designs complement the shapes of the objects (see, for example, [54]). As Gisela Jahn so effectively describes one work (fig. 37), "Yohei III here conceives the vase as a volume that exists in a symbiotic relationship with the decoration: the motif is both fitted to the shape and takes command of it."[13]

Works made by the Seifū studio began with the clay of the earth, and many were intended to hold such marvels as cut flowers, alcohol, or tea. The level of care with which they were made shows respect for what they are meant to contain and the human connections they facilitate. A pair of seemingly humble sake pourers

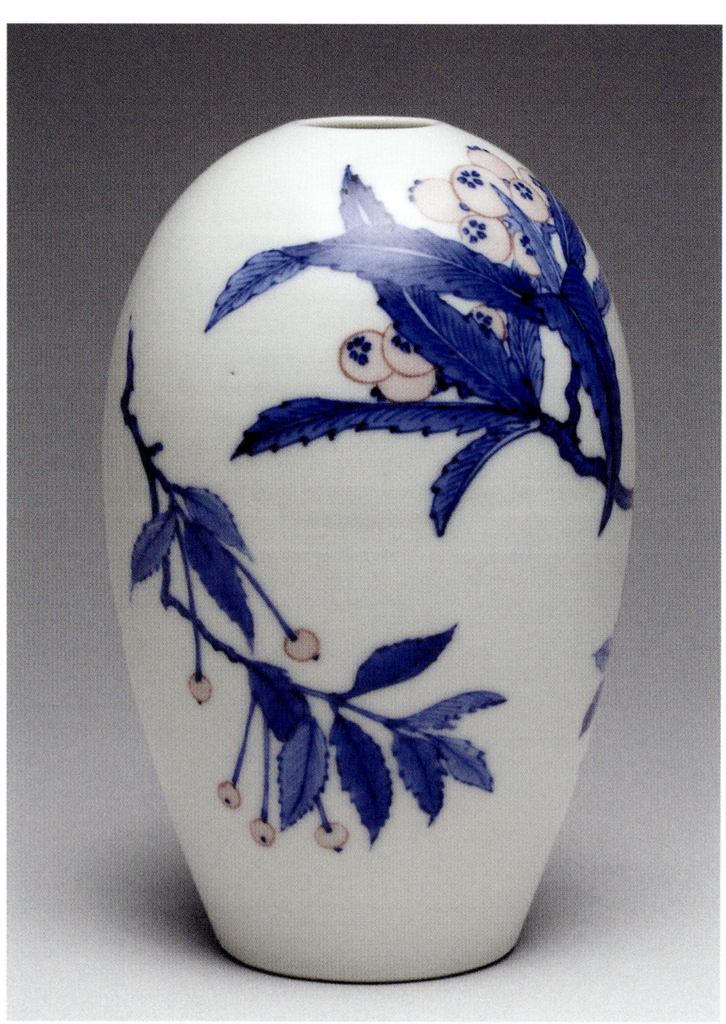

Figure 37. *Vase with Fruiting Plants*, 1890s. Seifū Yohei III. Porcelain with underglaze blue and overglaze enamel; h. 15 cm, diam. 9 cm. National Museums Scotland, Presented by David and Anne Hyatt King through the Art Fund, V.2015.10.307. Image © National Museums Scotland

may celebrate longevity and delight in a literary tradition that embraces multiple forms of poetic expression (see [17]). A set of teacups, each with its own short story, may create a bridge to a whole world for those gathered to use them (see [58]). A bowl may be a copy of another produced in a Chinese kiln and itself destined for international distribution (see [41]). A water container may also serve as a site for cultural reckoning, as when the life cycle of a flower prized in East Asia as a symbol of wealth is displayed across a Japanese *chanoyu* vessel whose glaze is associated with the seats of power in China and Korea (see [53]). As with the city in which they were made, each additional moment observing these objects may yield something missed on the first pass. Since most of the works in this group retain their boxes, the names of the glazes are identified and the combinations of seals, preserved. With this kind of archival information, as well as occasional clues as to specific owners and redistribution routes, the Heusinger Collection has the potential to yield an enhanced understanding of the Seifū studio as a whole and to serve as a window onto how Kyoto ceramists identified their own wares in relationship to the sweep of ceramics history in East Asia.

1. For a nuanced discussion of how porcelain came to be produced in Kyushu and the variety of factors that impact how the narrative is presented by different entities, see Nicole Coolidge Rousmaniere's synthesis of current scholarship in her *Vessels of Influence: China and the Birth of Porcelain in Medieval and Early Modern Japan*, 42–44, 120–38, 148–50.

2. These included kilns in Hiroshima and Ishikawa Prefectures. Rousmaniere, *Vessels of Influence*, 66.

3. Rousmaniere, 66.

4. Rousmaniere, 59.

5. On Hon'ami Kōetsu and the practice among tea enthusiasts of making earthenware teabowls that were then glazed and fired by professional ceramists, see Pitelka, *Handmade Culture*, 53–58.

6. The Cleveland Museum of Art's example of Ninsei's work is unusual in that it emulates Shigaraki ware, so it is less colorful. More colorful tea leaf storage jars by Ninsei are in the collections of the Idemitsu Museum and Tokyo National Museum, to cite two examples.

7. See Graham, *Tea of the Sages*, 94.

8. Graham's sophisticated and enjoyable narrative of Japan's nineteenth-century literati culture and *sencha* (or *bunjincha*, or "literati tea") weaves in a thoughtful discussion of Japanese taste for Chinese ceramics. Graham, *Tea of the Sages*, 41, 123–29.

9. See Maezaki, "Qing-Style Porcelain," 41.

10. Maezaki, 41–44.

11. See Graham, *Tea of the Sages*, 175–86.

12. The term *kyūsu* encompasses a number of types of teapots used in *sencha* but is generally used to mean the side-handled type. Pots of bisque-fired stoneware, called *bōfura*, can be set directly on the heating source. Pots left unglazed on the bottom, so that it is safe to place them in direct contact with the heating source, are called *kibishō*. Pots that cannot be set on the heating source are called *chatsugi*, and often have a handle at the back.

13. Jahn, *Meiji Ceramics*, 256.

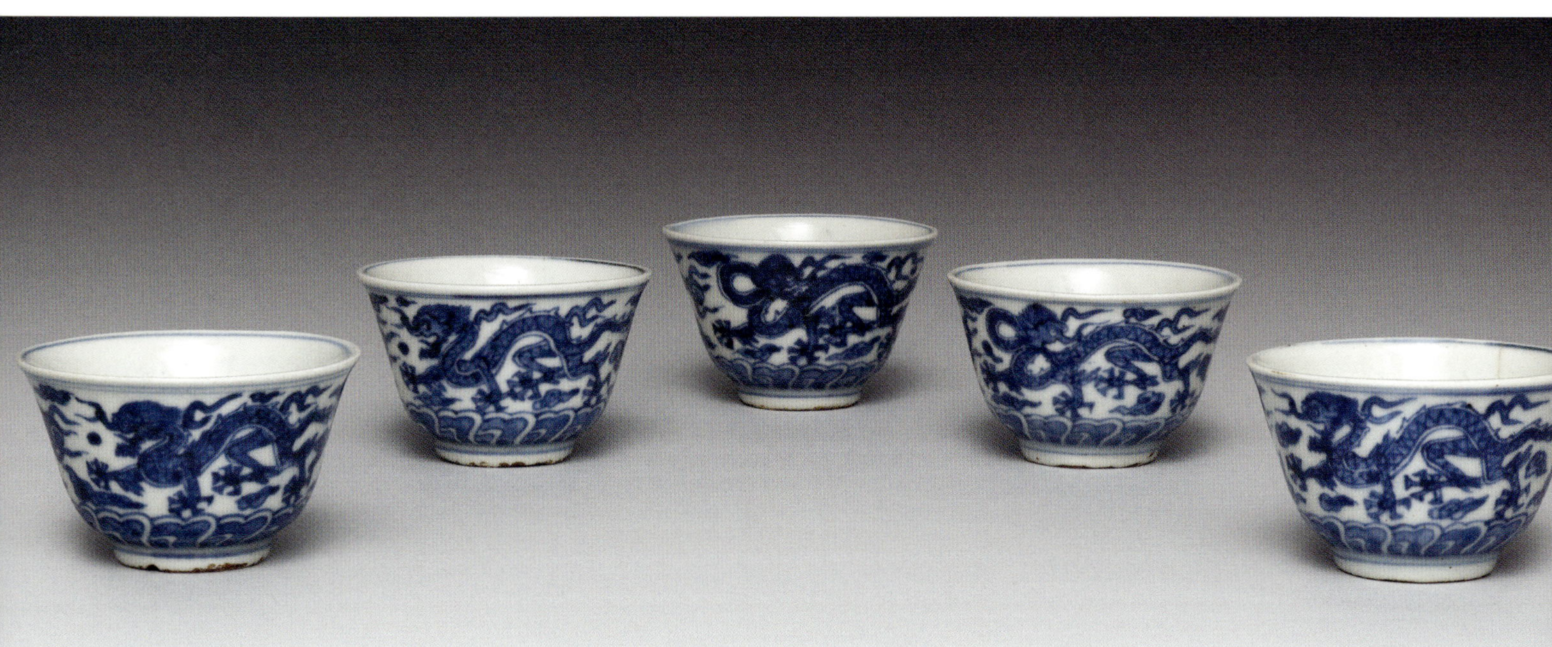

1 **TEACUPS WITH DRAGONS, 1840s–57**
Set of five teacups; porcelain with underglaze blue
Each: h. 4.5 cm, diam. 7 cm
2022.144

Yohei I painted each of the five cups in this set with a pair of five-clawed dragons, Chinese symbols of imperial power. The design is adapted from underglaze cobalt blue paintings seen on Ming-dynasty porcelain produced in Jingdezhen for the imperial court. One dragon's head faces forward while its eyes dart to see what is behind it; the other turns its whole head back to peek over its shoulder. With their mouths open and tongues extended, the slender, supernatural creatures race through a sky with tendrils of wafting cloud. A flaming jewel appears just ahead of the curve in the spectacularly long neck of the backward-facing dragon. Dragons in pursuit of flaming jewels are a common decorative motif derived from Buddhist texts, in which a jewel emerging from the head of the Dragon King is

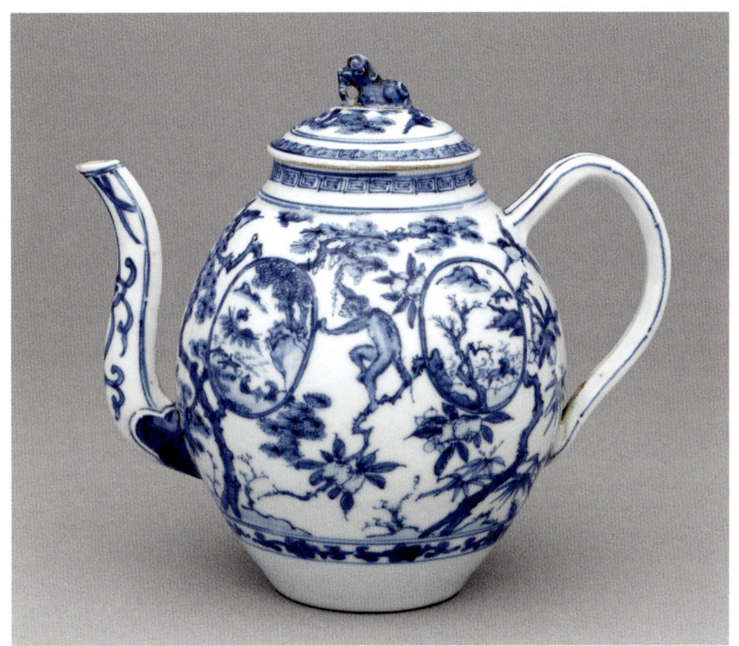
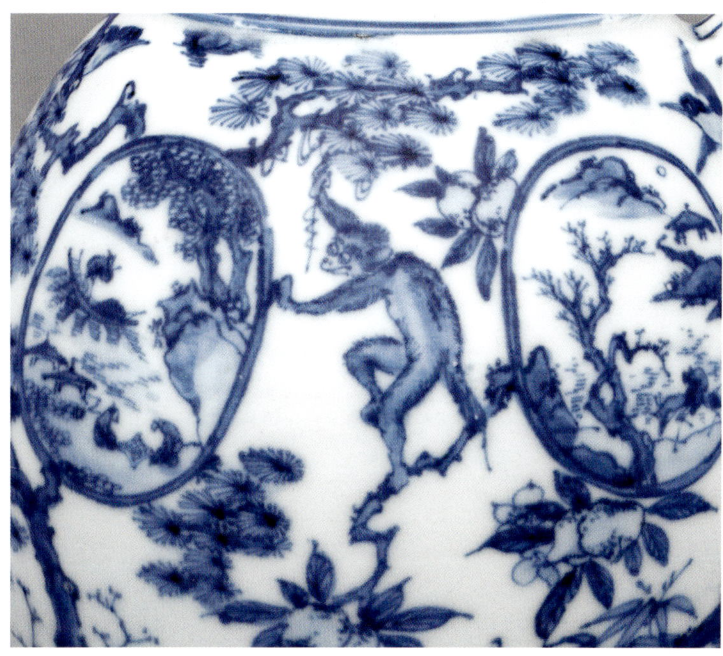

Figure 38. *Ewer with Auspicious Motifs*, 1840s–57. Seifū Yohei I. Porcelain with underglaze blue; h. 20.5 cm, diam. 11.3 cm. Hermann Ferré Collection. Photo: © Bruce M. White, 2022

said to be capable of fulfilling all wishes. Above the foot of each cup are repeating foliate motifs encircling the space beneath the dragons like a wide-open flower. The teacups would have been used for drinking *sencha*. They are all signed in blue on the base, and the lid of their storage box carries an attestation of their authenticity, recorded by Yohei IV in 1918.

A wide variety of Yohei I's reinterpretations of Chinese imagery in underglaze blue is on display in a lidded ewer in a private collection (fig. 38). On one side, a monkey or gibbon climbs a fruiting peach tree as birds fly above in a landscape filled out with bamboo and pine. As the other side (not pictured) features a deer and plum, the intent is to portray the land of the immortals. Embedded in the scene are two ovals framing individual vignettes of a figure traveling by donkey in moonlight (right) and a pair playing the board game *weiqi* (J. *go*) as someone guides a boat through the current in the distance (left), respectively. A small figure of an elephant serves as the handle for the lid.

2 BOX WITH BUTTERFLY, 1855–57

Porcelain with underglaze blue
H. 10 cm, l. 11 cm, w. 11 cm
2022.149

This sturdy box, with comparatively thick walls and resulting heft, is sparsely decorated with a single butterfly motif in dark underglaze blue cobalt in one corner of the lid and with repeating floral patterns along the lid and base. Single broken lines of underglaze blue define the edge of the box lid's top where it curves to meet the sides and again where it meets the base of the box. Another blue band runs around the upper rim of the base where it meets the lip, left unglazed for a better grip of the lid when the box is closed. Yohei I's signature on the center of the recessed base is set within a wide blue square. The porcelain box is meant to call to mind a famous story attributed to Zhuang Zhou (c. 369–286 BCE), also known as Master Zhuang, or Zhuangzi, pronounced Sōji in Japanese. The second chapter of *Zhuangzi*, his eponymous collection of anecdotes, records the story as follows:

> Once, Zhuang Zhou dreamt he was a butterfly, a butterfly flitting and fluttering about, happy with himself and doing as he pleased. He didn't know that he was Zhuang Zhou. Suddenly, he woke up and there he was, solid and unmistakable Zhuang Zhou. But he didn't know if he was Zhuang Zhou who had dreamt he was a butterfly, or a butterfly dreaming that he was Zhuang Zhou. Between Zhuang Zhou and the butterfly there must be some distinction! This is called the Transformation of Things.[1]

The lidded box resembles *kosometsuke*, the porcelains in underglaze blue made to order or on speculation for the Japanese market during the early to mid-seventeenth century in Jingdezhen, China. These works were often made from designs submitted by Japanese clients, many of whom were masters of *chanoyu*, who sought the wares for their tea practice. The relative roughness of the clay and the distortions in the fired object were intentional, as they created the rustic effect desired by Japanese tea communities. It is possible that the model for this box was a smaller lidded box meant for storing incense.[2]

1. Zhuang Zhou, *Chuang Tzu*, 45.

2. An 1855 publication pit famous incense burners against each other in the manner of a sumo wrestling tournament, and one of the "contestants" was an incense burner described as having a "Zhuangzi butterfly motif." See Nomura Museum and Aichi Prefectural Ceramics Archives, *Katamono kōgō banzuke no sekai*, cat. no. 69 (53, 140) and cat. no. 150 (91).

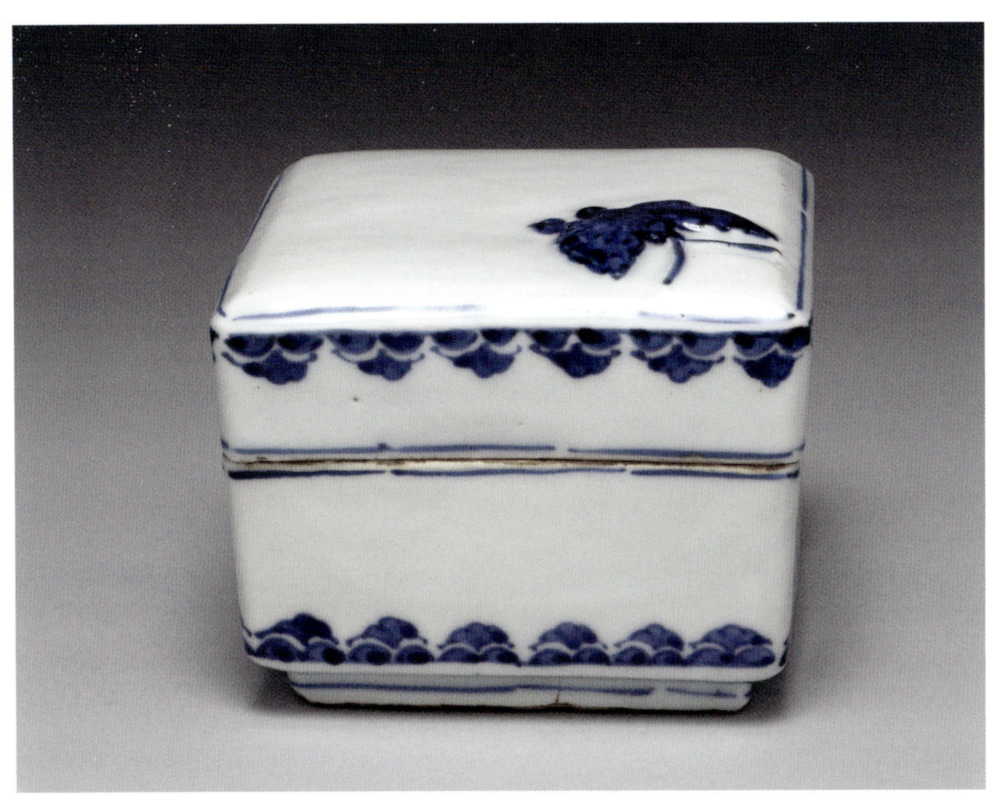

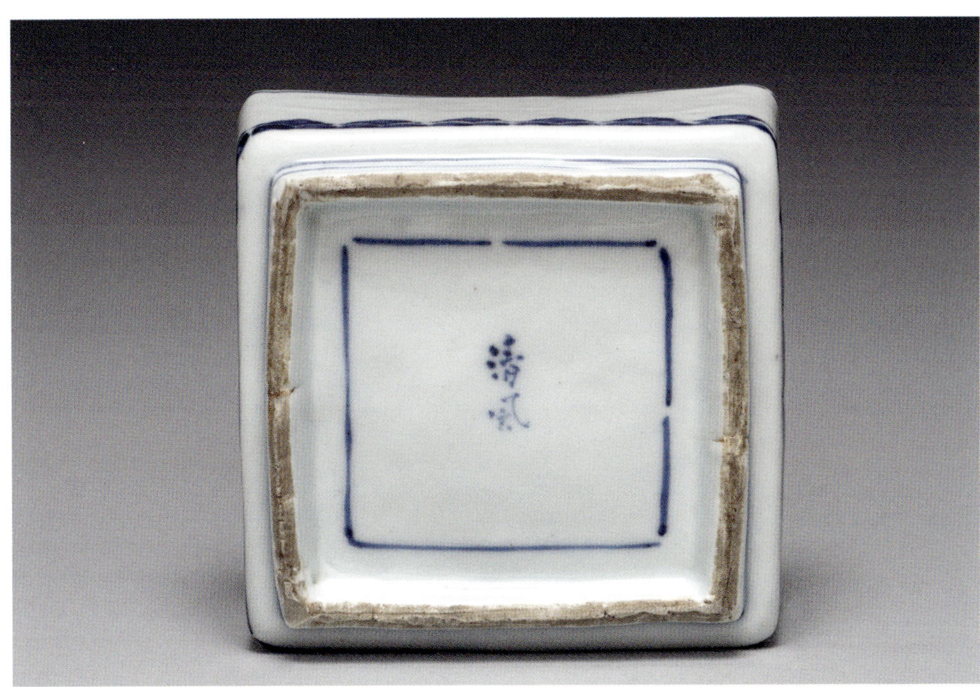

3 NESTING DISHES WITH SCATTERED PINE NEEDLES AND MAPLE LEAVES, 1861–78

Pair of dishes; stoneware with underglaze blue, iron oxide, slip, crackled glaze, and overglaze color enamel
Inner dish: h. 6.7 cm, l. 14.4 cm, d. 11.5 cm; outer dish: h. 7.5 cm, l. 15.3 cm, d. 12.7 cm
2022.147

This pair of nesting dishes is decorated with blue and brown iron oxide pine needles and brown pine cones under the glaze and overglaze red maple leaves. The thick, knobby application of the iron oxide gives the pine cones a low relief. The combination of the blue and brown for the needles imparts a sense of depth to the design, with the blue needles apparently at a greater distance. The maple leaves are translucent with opaque red vein structures. Where he intended to place the maple leaves, Yohei I first applied a white color, which can be seen around the leaf edges under the glaze. This layering on top of the white brightens the color of the translucent red. Brown iron oxide edges the entire rim of both deep dishes. There is a shiny, transparent, crackled glaze over the designs with

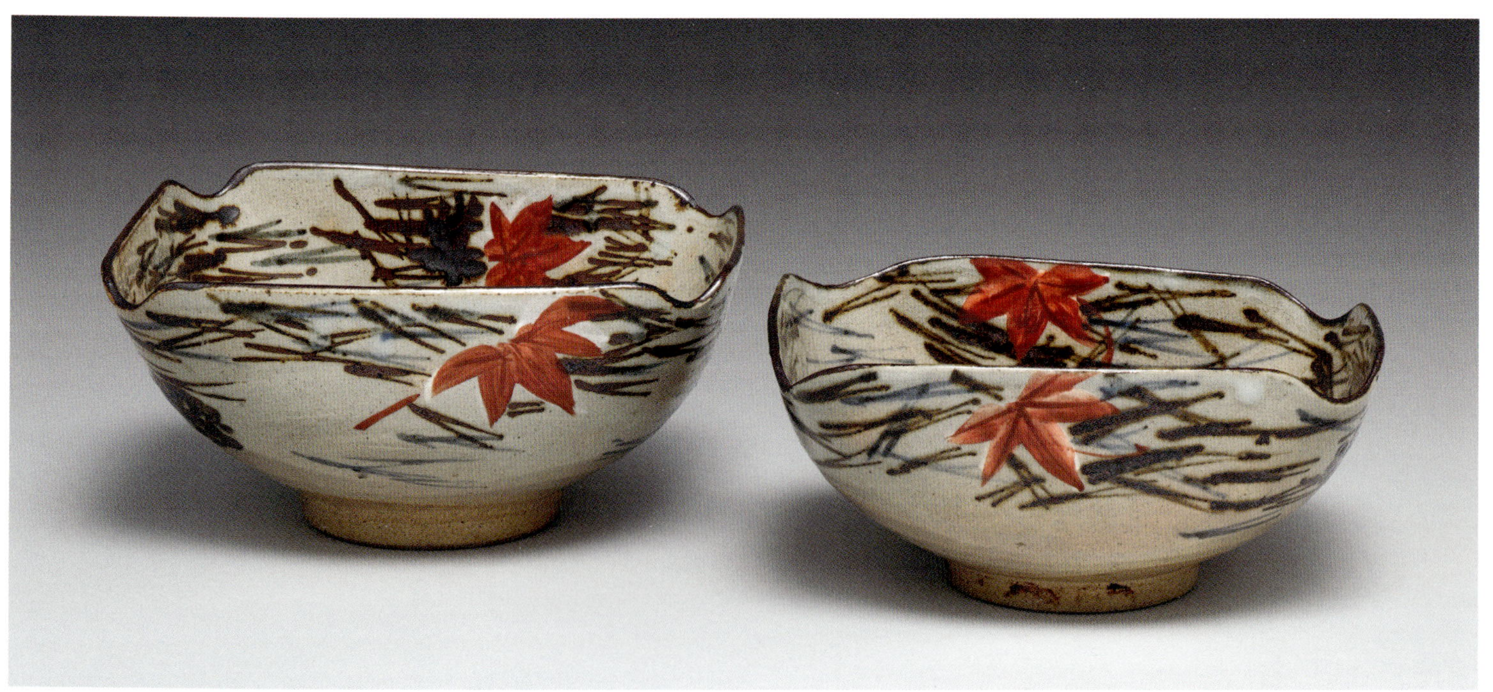

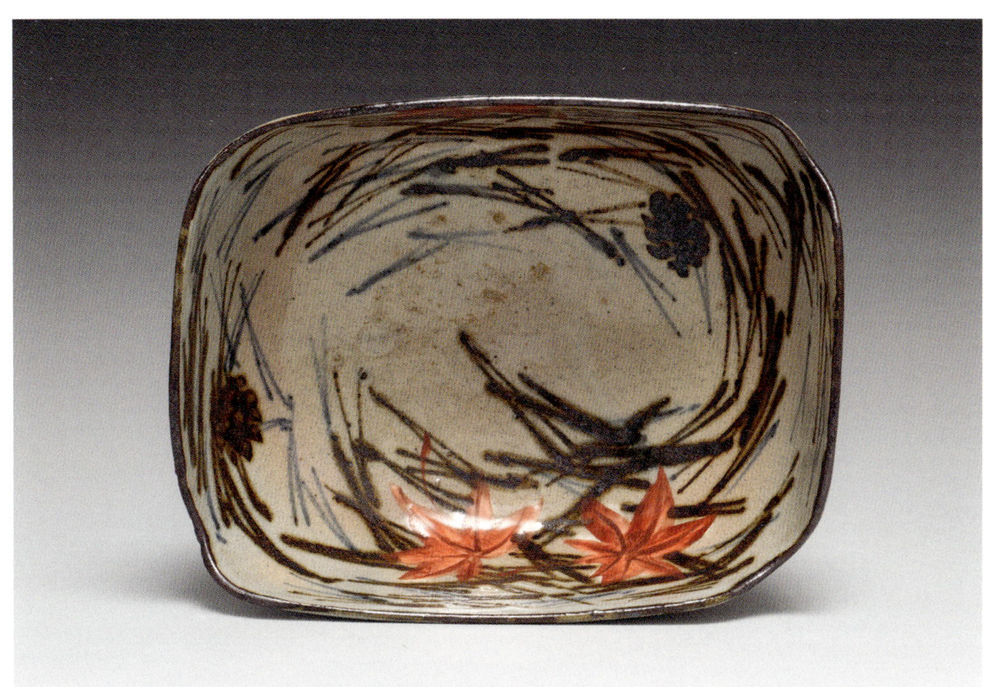

milky and peach effects coming through the soft, warm grayish slip. The dark dots in the clay body remain visible through the slip and glaze. In places, the glaze has entirely shrunk away from the body, leaving unglazed spots in the basin of the smaller dish. The lower part and foot of each dish is left unglazed but for a small area in the footring. However, only the smaller dish is stamped with one of Yohei I's seals. The dishes are rounded on the sides, but they open up into four straight lengths at their lips with a dipping curve at each corner, creating a shape like an open flower. These two dishes bear some resemblance to bowls by Yohei I with wintry scenes of pine and red ivy in snow, one of which is in the Morse Collection at the Museum of Fine Arts, Boston. Comparatively, the painting on these Yohei I dishes is somewhat looser in execution.

4 SAKE CUPS WITH AUSPICIOUS FLORA, 1861–78

Pair of sake cups; porcelain with underglaze blue
Each: h. 3 cm, diam. 7 cm
2022.145

In this pair of sake cups, one has an exterior painted under the glaze with images of bamboo, orchid, and chrysanthemum and an interior with both chrysanthemum and a bough of plum, or prunus. The mate has a plum branch and a hint of pine on the outside, along with four characters just under the rim reading "pine, plum, and immortal plant" (*shōbaishisen* 松梅芝仙). "Immortal plant" is a synonym for the *reishi* (C. *lingzhi*), or numinous mushroom, which is said to be capable of conferring immortality upon those who consume it. On the inside of this cup is a pine bough.

While bamboo and pine appear on different cups in the pair, plum is seen in both, bringing the pair into closer dialogue and perhaps alluding to the Three Friends of Winter. This Chinese grouping of pine, bamboo, and plum as auspicious symbols spread to many cultures in East and Southeast Asia and in Japan is known by the names of the three plants, *shōchikubai*. The pine is evergreen; the bamboo, which also remains verdant year-round, has hollow stalks that bend,

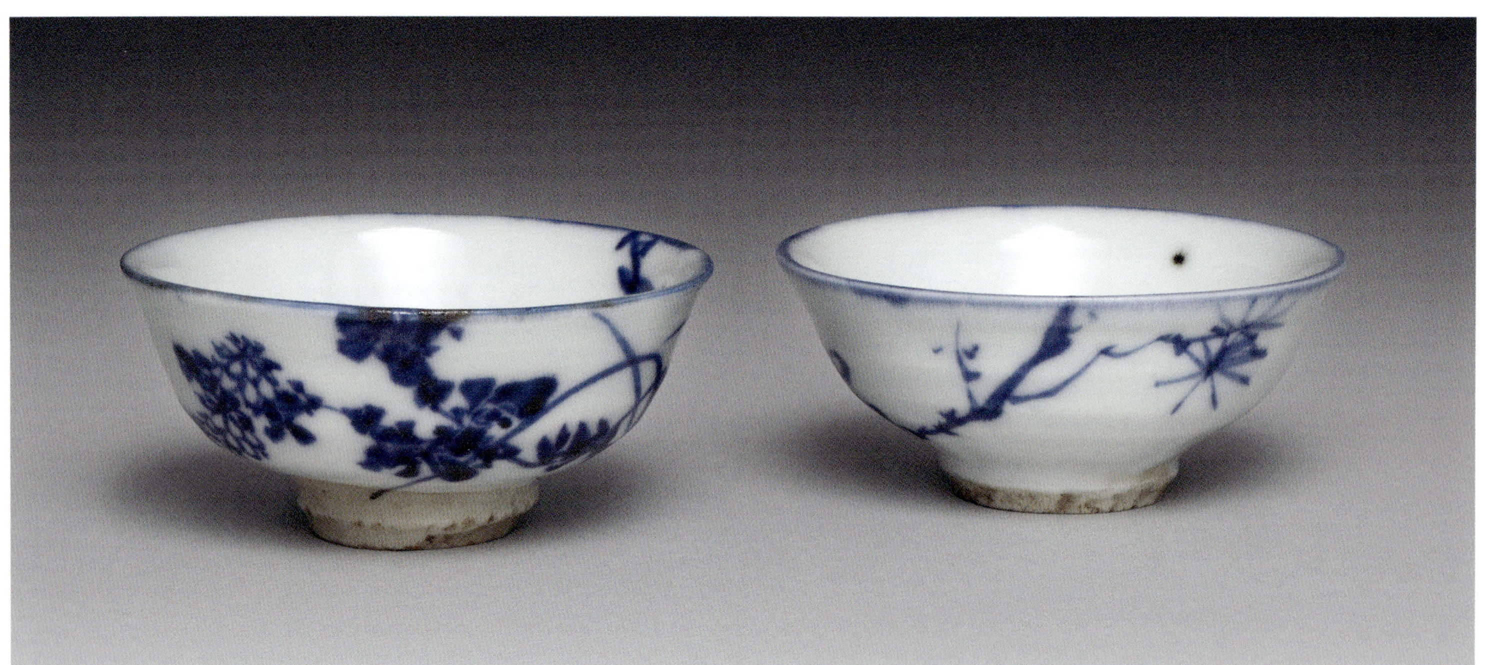

not break, in strong wind; and the plum is among the first to flower in the New Year, when it remains cold. Together, these plants symbolize many of the virtues attributed to the cultured scholar: steadfastness, fortitude, determination, perseverance, resilience, humility, and flexibility.

Another symbolic grouping of plants called the Four Nobles often features orchid, bamboo, chrysanthemum, and plum, all of which appear on one of the cups. In this arrangement, chrysanthemum is associated with autumn, while the brave plum is connected to winter, just before the onset of spring. The autumn chrysanthemum blooms undaunted toward the end of the season, as cold winter approaches. The dignified, fragrant orchid symbolizes spring in this group, and bamboo, summer. Aspiring ink painters often depict these four plants to hone their brush technique.

The pair of sake cups covers both of the themes, along with a calligraphic nod to the extraordinary mushroom. These modest cups are important for the connoisseurship of the art of Yohei II because their original box is intact with a signature and seal on the interior of the lid. Another seal accompanies the identifying inscription on the lid's exterior. In addition, each of the two cups has a different seal impressed into its side just above the foot. Like Kiyomizu Shichibei, with whom he shared kiln space, Yohei II produced many works painted in blue under the glaze, works often described as *sometsuke* or *seika*, as is written on the box for these sake cups. *Sometsuke*, the Japanese term, literally means to apply dye, while *seika*, a Japanization of the Chinese term, translates to "blue flower." It was owing to his marriage to Kiyomizu Miyo, a daughter of the influential ceramist Kiyomizu Rokubei III, that Yohei II was permitted to fire his works at the kiln of Rokubei's older brother, Shichibei.[1] The uncle-in-law was a heavy drinker, a habit that prevented him from taking over his father's kiln, but made him a close companion of Yohei II, who was similarly inclined. According to a biography authored by Yohei III, Yohei II trained in his youth with the Kyoto-based painter Maeda Handen (Chōdō) (1817–1878), who had training in both the Maruyama school and literati painting modes.[2] Yohei's designs on these cups fall firmly into the latter category of painting in both execution and symbolism.

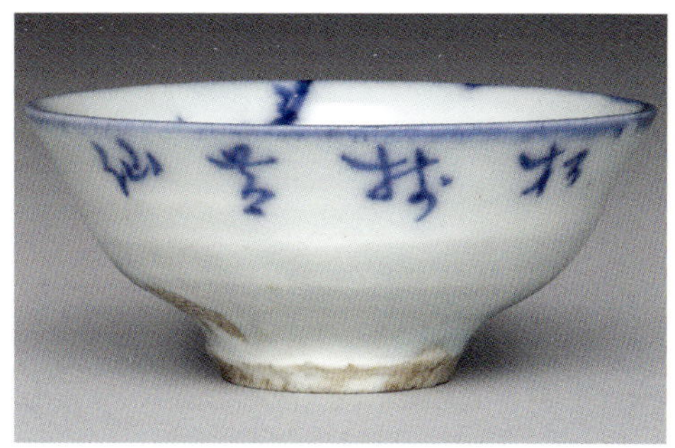

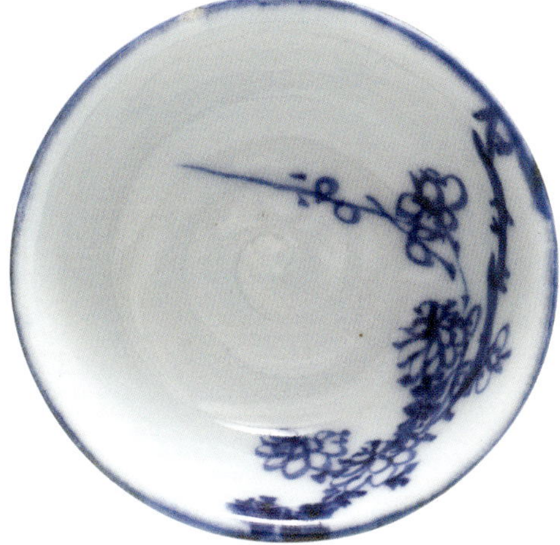

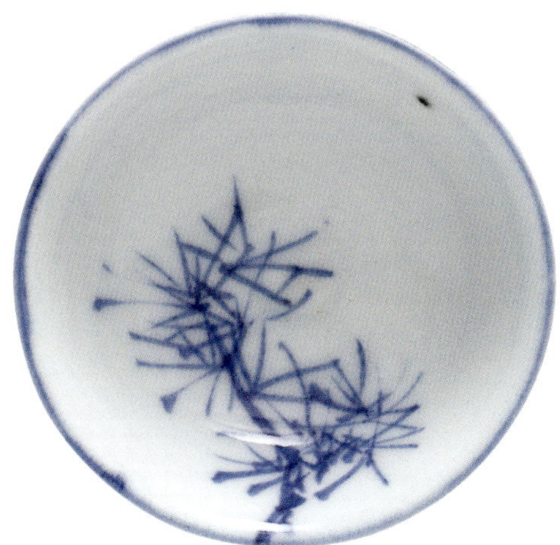

1. See Maezaki, "Qing-Style Porcelain," 39–40.
2. Maezaki, 38.

5 COVERED BOWL WITH SEVEN TREASURES, 1861–78

Stoneware with overglaze color enamel and gold
H. 20 cm, diam. 29.5 cm
2022.146

The box lid for this large covered bowl by Yohei II identifies it as in the style of Ninsei, a reference to Nonomura Ninsei. Overglaze enamels in red, green, and white sit within lattices of jewel-shaped gold forms scattered across the lid and base in a design known as the seven treasures. At the center of the lid is a knob in the shape of a peach with a stem and leaves. The leaf veins are detailed in gold. A prominent feature of the piece is the appearance of warm pink dots known as *gohon*. Here creamy at their center and with a gradation to almost red at the edges, they appear during firing due to high iron content in the clay. Pieces with this effect were made in emulation of certain ash-glazed ceramics imported from Korea. The originals were made to order for the Japanese market at a kiln in Busan. The kiln was established within the Japanese diplomatic compound in that port city by the lord of Tsushima in 1639 and continued production until 1717.[1] In the seventeenth century, teabowls from Korea in a variety of styles were extremely popular among practitioners of Japanese-style tea, and they were soon copied by ceramists active on the archipelago, including in Kyoto.

1. See Watanabe, "From Korea to Japan and Back Again," 93–94. See also Hur, "Korean Tea Bowls (Kōrai chawan) and Japanese Wabicha," 6–9.

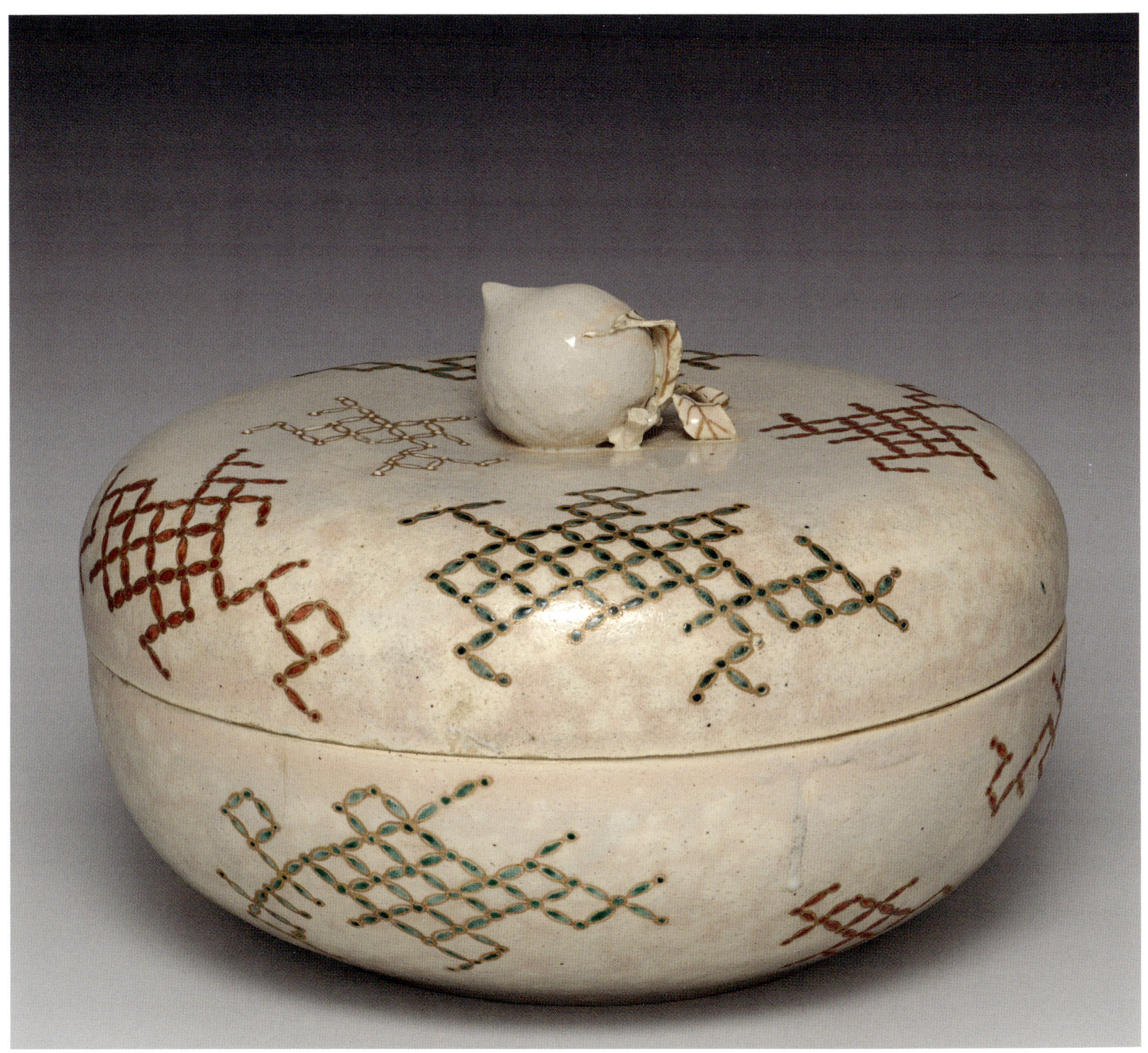

6 SWEETS DISH WITH LANDSCAPE, 1874

Porcelain with underglaze blue
H. 5 cm, diam. 16 cm
2022.148

Dated works by members of the Seifū studio are comparatively rare outside of pieces known to have been on public exhibition. This porcelain sweets dish with an underglaze blue landscape painting by Yohei II has on one side an inscription dating it to 1874, just a few years before his death. The full inscription reads, "The year Meiji 6 [1874], fifth month, for Mr. Nakayoshi" 明治六年五月為仲吉君属. The recipient's name also appears on the interior of the box lid. This low-profile dish has a complex landscape with a river or lakefront residential compound set among pine and willow trees and approached by a plank bridge over the water. A single figure sits within one of the buildings, gazing out toward the bridge as if anticipating a visitor. On the inside of the dish, a background of mountain peaks is painted at the top, while the foreground, at the bottom, shows a stand of pine and a single willow, following the curve of the dish up to the rim. The blank space in between suggests the vastness of nature, dwarfing humanity. The thinly potted dish is of a sensitive, accomplished design created with a literati spirit.

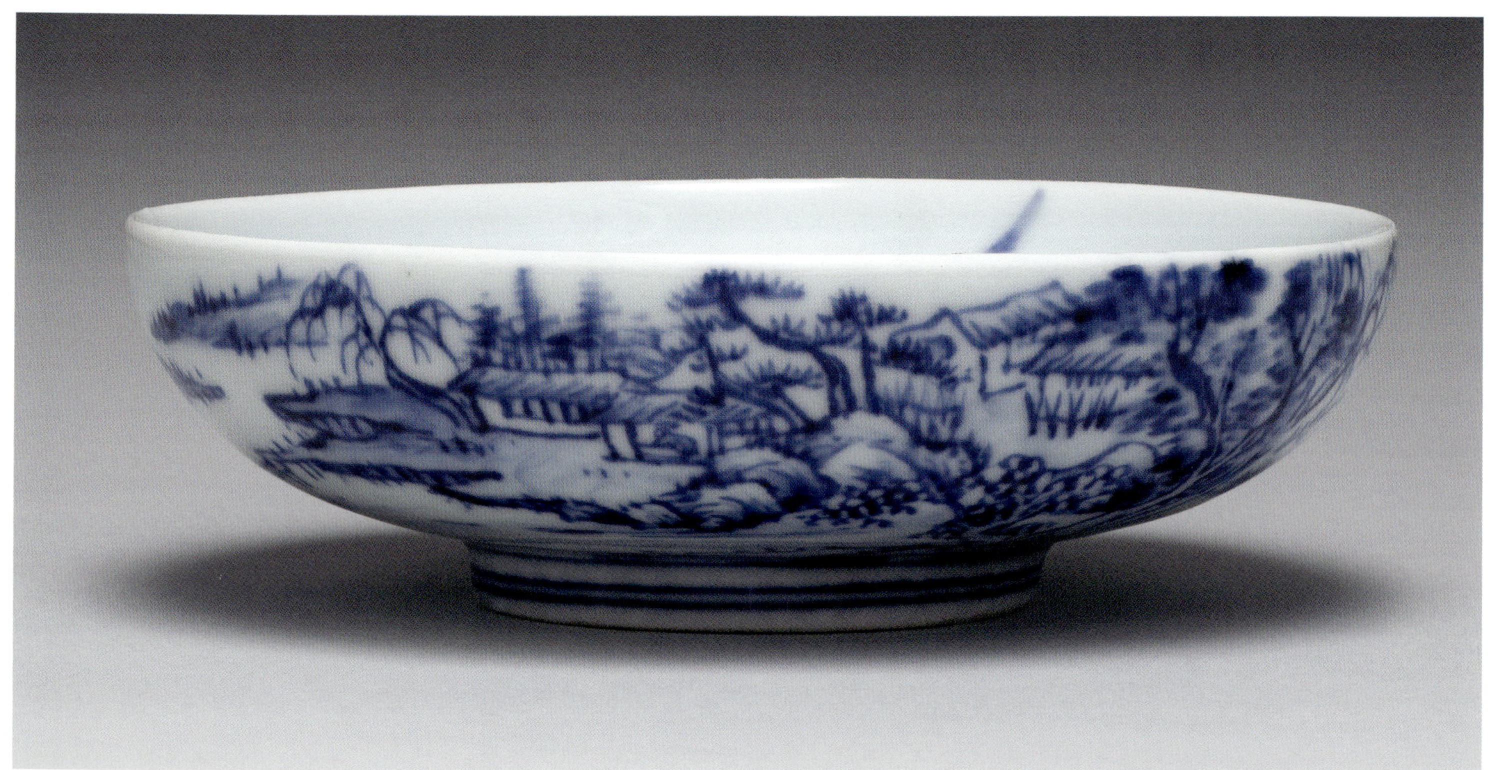

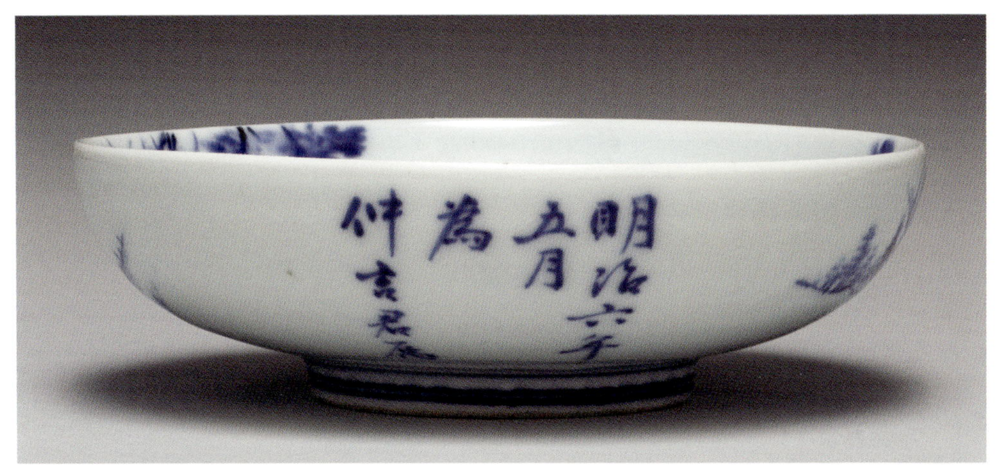
明治六年
五月
為
仲吉君

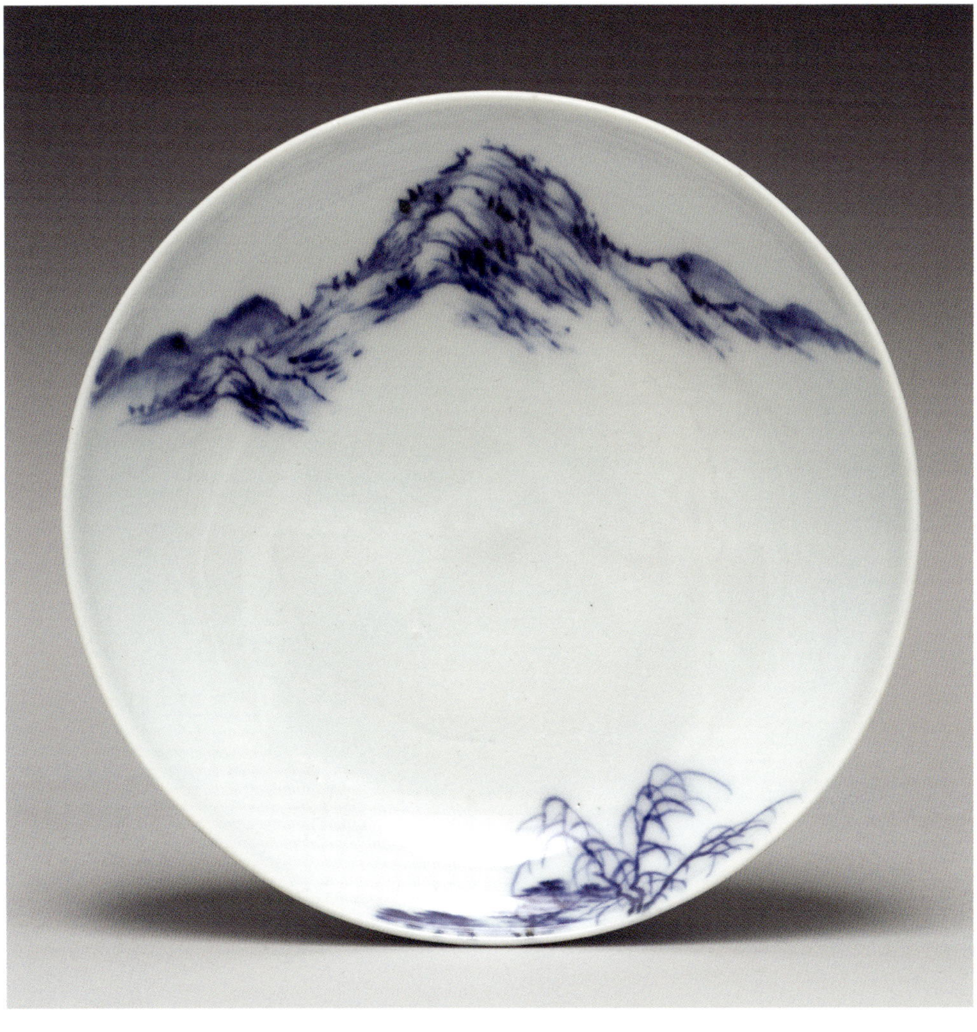

7 DINING SET, 1875–78

Nine of ten settings; porcelain with molded designs and cream glaze
Each: small dish: h. 2.9 cm, diam. 11.5 cm; each medium dish: h. 3.2 cm, diam. 16.4 cm; each drinking cup: h. 6.7 cm, diam. 9.3 cm; each covered bowl: h. 7.5 cm, diam. 11.5 cm
2022.150

Each item in this set has a delicate low-relief design of flowering plum branches over scattered, intersecting lines meant to resemble the cracked-ice surface of a frozen body of water and is signed on the base in gold pigment. While Yohei II produced many fine works in underglaze blue, like those produced by Kiyomizu Shichibei, he also made works in quite different styles later in his career, from the early 1870s. In 1873, he was appointed purveyor to the Industrial Center of Kyoto Prefecture, a designation associated with Kyoto's efforts to reach an international market through the port of Kobe; and from 1875 until his death, he was involved in national-level projects to present Japanese ceramics across the world.[1] It was during this period that Yohei III was apprenticed to Yohei II, and it has been suggested that this set may in fact be an early example of Yohei III's work, which he signed with his teacher's name.[2]

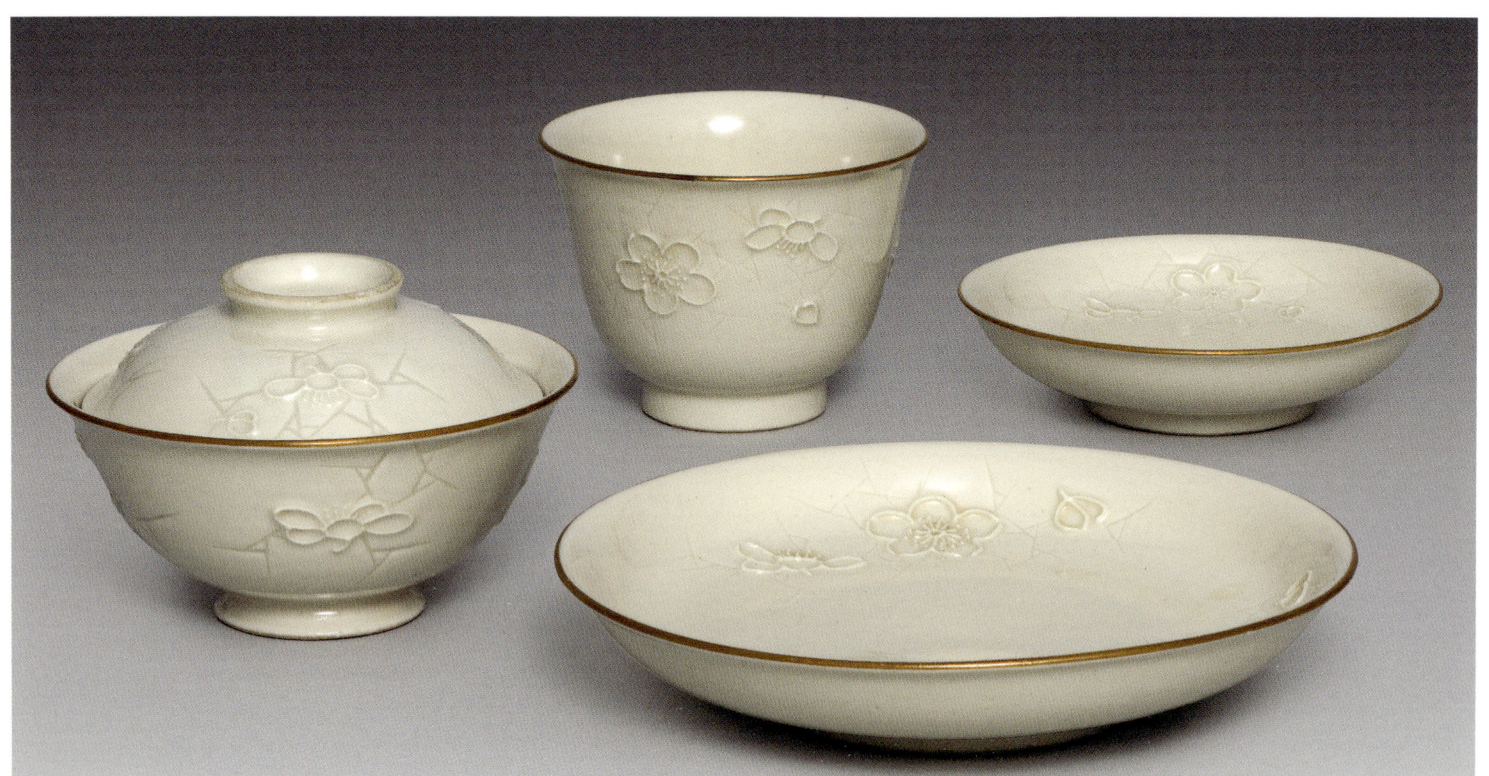

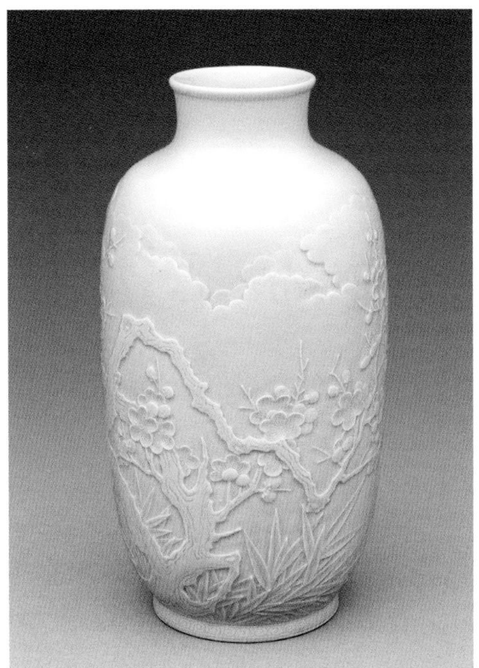

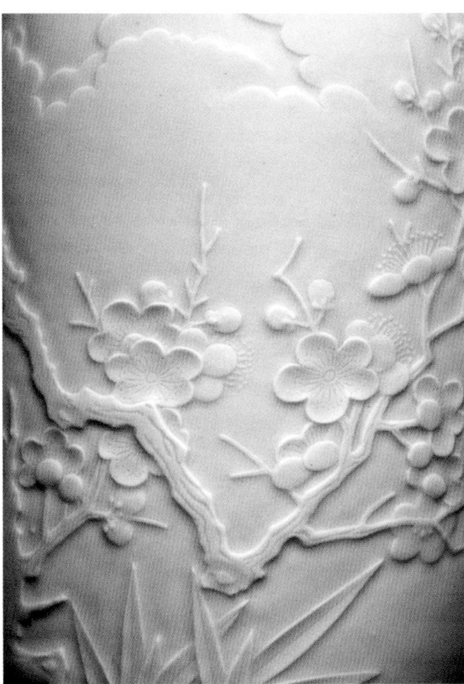

Figure 39a, b. *Vase with Plum,* 1893–1914. Seifū Yohei III. Glazed porcelain with molded designs; h. 25 cm, diam. 12.3 cm. Hermann Ferré Collection. Photo: © Bruce M. White, 2022

Decorated with flowers resembling Japanese textile motifs, the set calls to mind the design of Yohei II's 1875 pair of vases with plum blossoms in the Victoria and Albert Museum (see fig. 12). Here, the elaborate trees created for a formal public exhibition setting have been translated into the approachable blossoms of the genteel domestic environment. While the designs are consistent across the pieces, each raised flower petal and pistil and each incised line in the ice was done by hand, so the cups, bowls, and dishes are similar yet unique. The dining wares have a creamy white coloration that the four boxes containing them identify as Korean in style. The bottoms of two boxes once identified the set's owner, but the information has been deliberately obscured with black ink. However, inscriptions still visible appear to indicate two occasions, once at the end of July 1886, and once again in June 1916, when parts of the set were requested from Hokura in Niigata Prefecture. The location corresponds to a neighborhood in the present-day city of Jōetsu. The surname Tsuji 辻 also appears on a paper tag affixed to one of the box cloths. Future research may possibly reveal more about their provenance. A vase by Yohei III in a private collection combines the formal grandeur of the Yohei II vases in the Victoria and Albert Museum with the gentler design of this dining set, placing flowering plum trees against soft, scalloped-edge clouds resembling those in golden screens (figs. 39a, b).

1. See Maezaki, "Qing-Style Porcelain," 41–42.
2. Maezaki, 52.

ARTIST TO THE IMPERIAL HOUSE

PAINTING

SEIFŪ YOHEI III

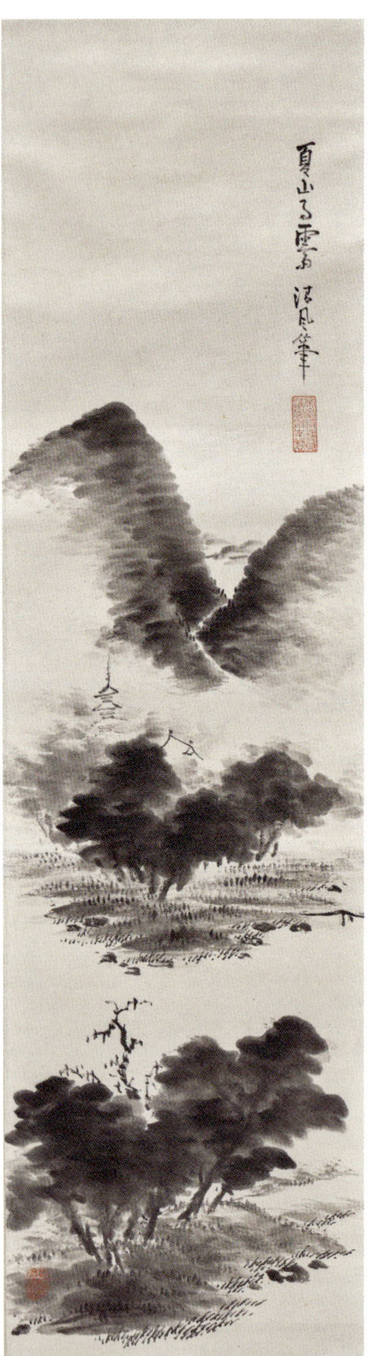

8 **RAIN CLEARING OVER A SUMMER'S MOUNTAIN, 1893–1914**
Hanging scroll; ink on paper
Painting: h. 122.1 x 32.8 cm; mounted: h. 183.5 x 44.8 cm
2022.151

9 **ROLLER ENDS FOR HANGING SCROLL, 1893–1914**
Pair of hanging scroll roller ends; porcelain with green glaze
Each: l. 3 cm, diam. 3 cm
2022.152

Before entering into his apprenticeship with Yohei II, Yohei III trained as a painter in Osaka. He continued to paint throughout his career as a ceramist. Yohei IV authenticated this painting as having been done by his father in a box lid inscription dated to the summer of 1919. The signed inscription by Yohei III in the painting's upper right gives the title *Rain Clearing Over a Summer's Mountain* and is accompanied by his Imperial Household Artist seal. His signature seal is found in the lower left on the grassy riverbank. The composition follows a basic literati painting convention: it is divided into a foreground, middle ground, and background, with trees in the front, a temple in the middle, and mountains at the back. The brushwork, too, with its ovals of ink wash and dry-brushed dots and lines, has the casual feel of a painting made for one's own amusement or dashed off for a friend. As part of his ceramic practice, Yohei III also made roller ends to be placed at either end of the wooden dowel around which the lower part of a hanging scroll mounting is wrapped. These served both as weights for the painting and as knobs for handling it when rolling and unrolling. The pair here is made of porcelain with a green glaze.

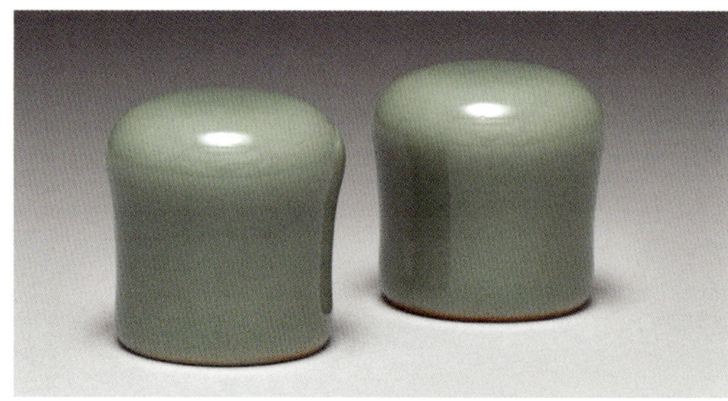

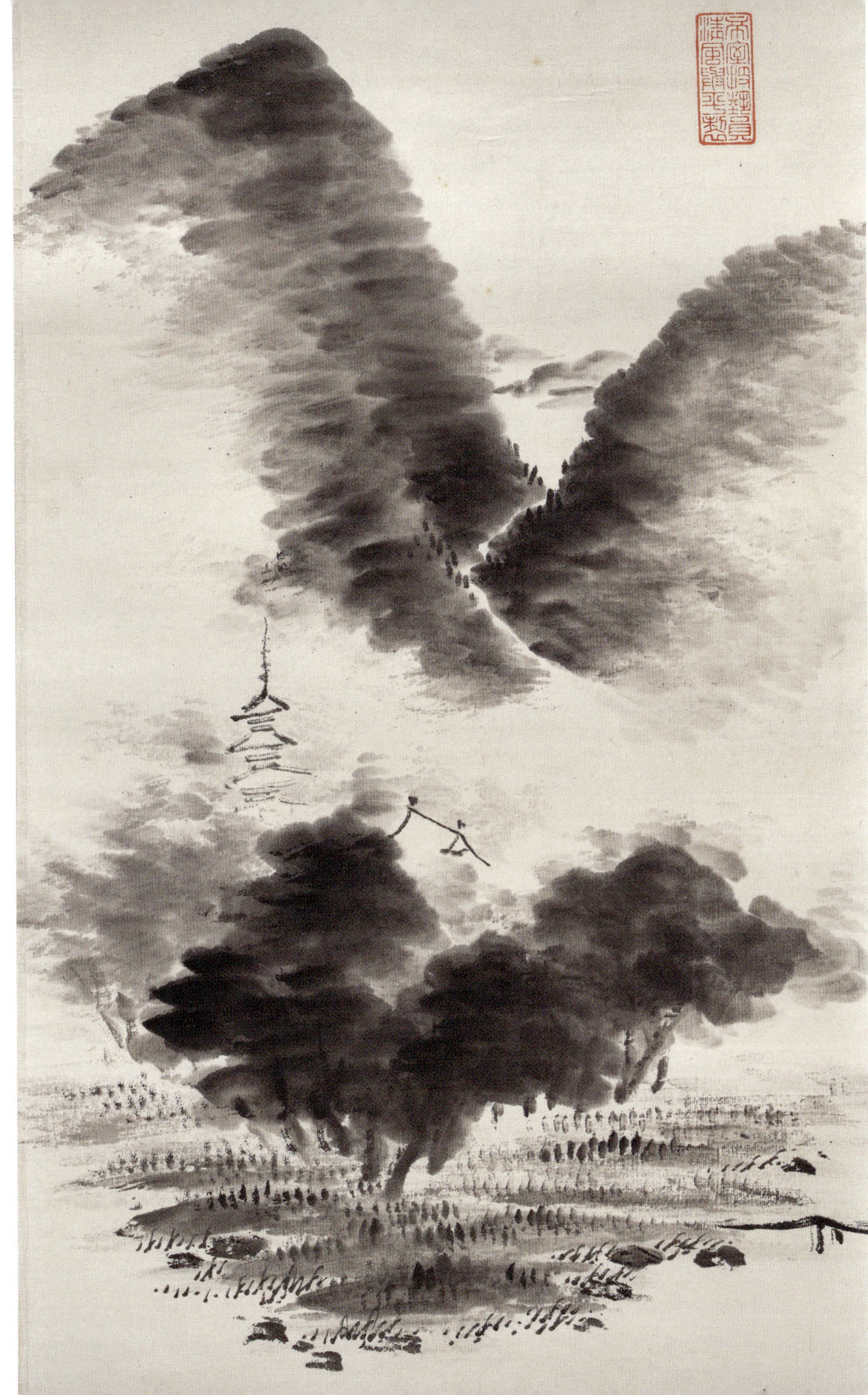

Detail of [8]

10 BOWL WITH CHINESE LANDSCAPE, 1893–1914

Porcelain with underglaze blue and iron oxide
H. 8 cm, diam. 21 cm
2022.153

This bowl has a landscape with figures in blue and iron oxide. The scene is set along a river with mountains in the distance, likely in the Jiangnan region of southern China, famous for compositions of the Eight Views of the Xiao and Xiang Rivers and of West Lake in Hangzhou. There are two people in the foreground: one person fishes along the riverbank across from a rustic hermit's lodge sited on stilts over the water's edge; on the other side of the bowl, a person with a tall staff gazes at the full moon, accompanied by his servant. Between them, a flock of geese makes its way across the sky; this visual trope and the many bare tree branches suggest the season may be autumn. The foot has a double band in blue, while another blue band encircles the bowl just beneath the rim, which is covered in red iron oxide. The inside of the footring is also circled in blue around the impressed mark.

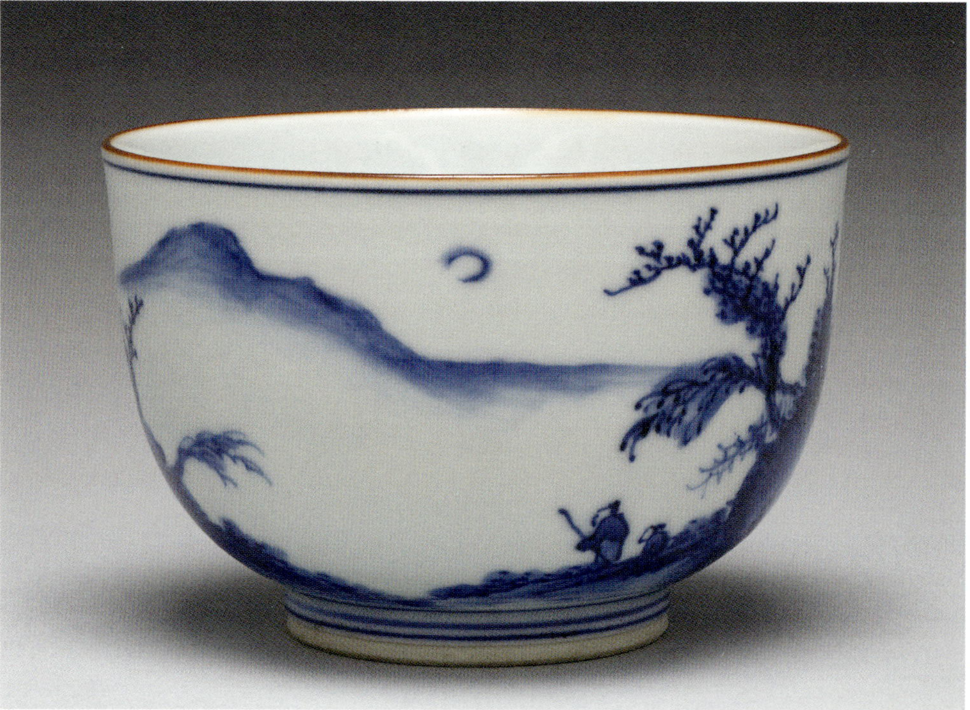

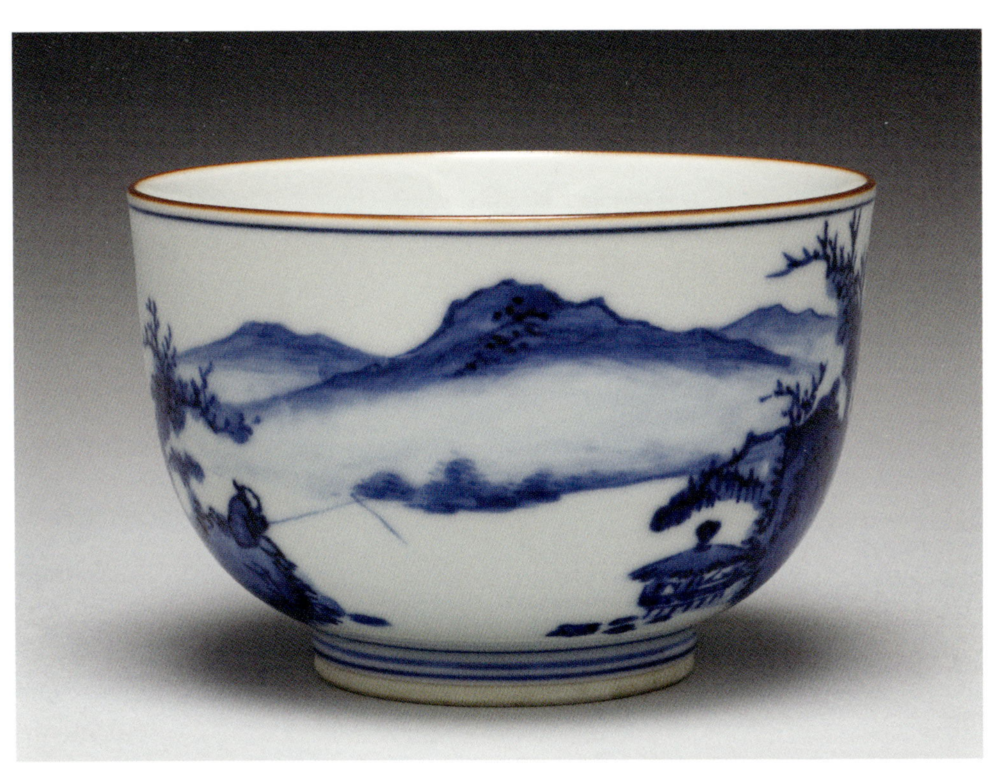

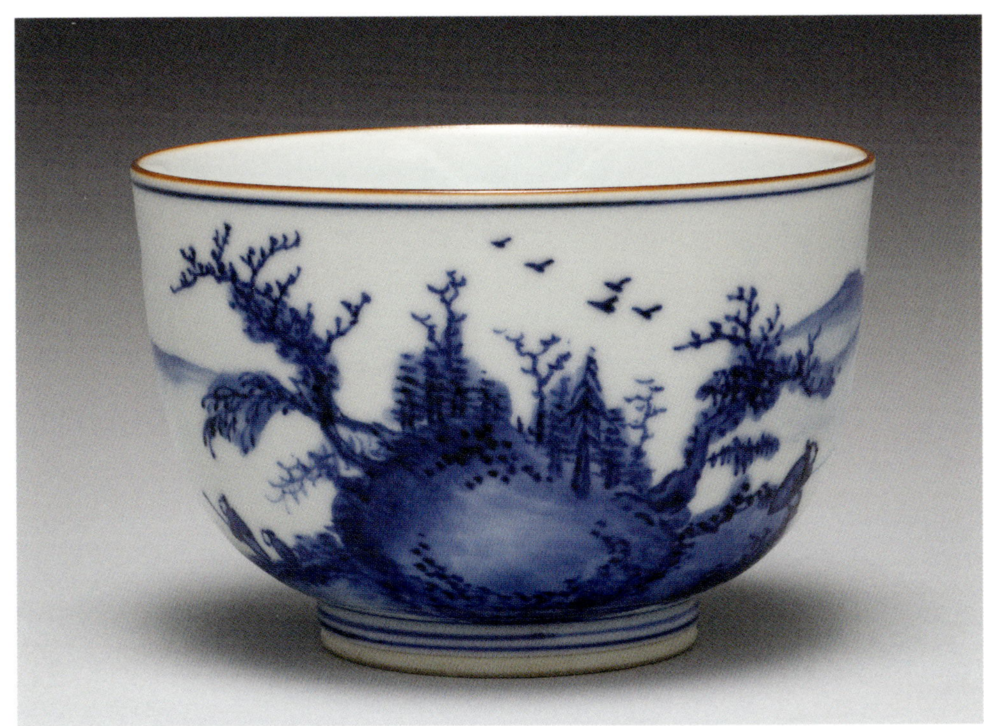

11 SWEETS BOWL WITH EGRETS AND WILLOW IN SNOW, 1912–14

Porcelain with underglaze blue and iron oxide
H. 10 cm, diam. 19.5 cm
2022.154

For this sweets bowl, Yohei III designed a dramatic surround of egrets in a willow tree under heavy snow. The entire design is painted in cobalt blue under the transparent glaze. If one turns the bowl clockwise, two egrets come into view, one after the other. As they ascend, both struggle against the wind amid snow-laden weeping willow branches. They are followed by a stretch of willow branches that evoke the bitter cold. The sky is painted with blue washes all around the designs. The imagery culminates in a group of three egrets huddled together in the crotch of the tree. Of course, it is also possible to read the scene in the other direction, in which case the sheltering egrets look toward one of the flying egrets, who looks back at them, and it is the egret with wings outspread, looking directly down, who concludes the scene. Two thin bands of blue set off the design just under the bowl's rim, and a band of brown iron oxide runs along the rim. Another two bands of blue run around the middle of the foot. The inside of the bowl's box lid has an attestation by Yohei IV that it is the work of Yohei III.

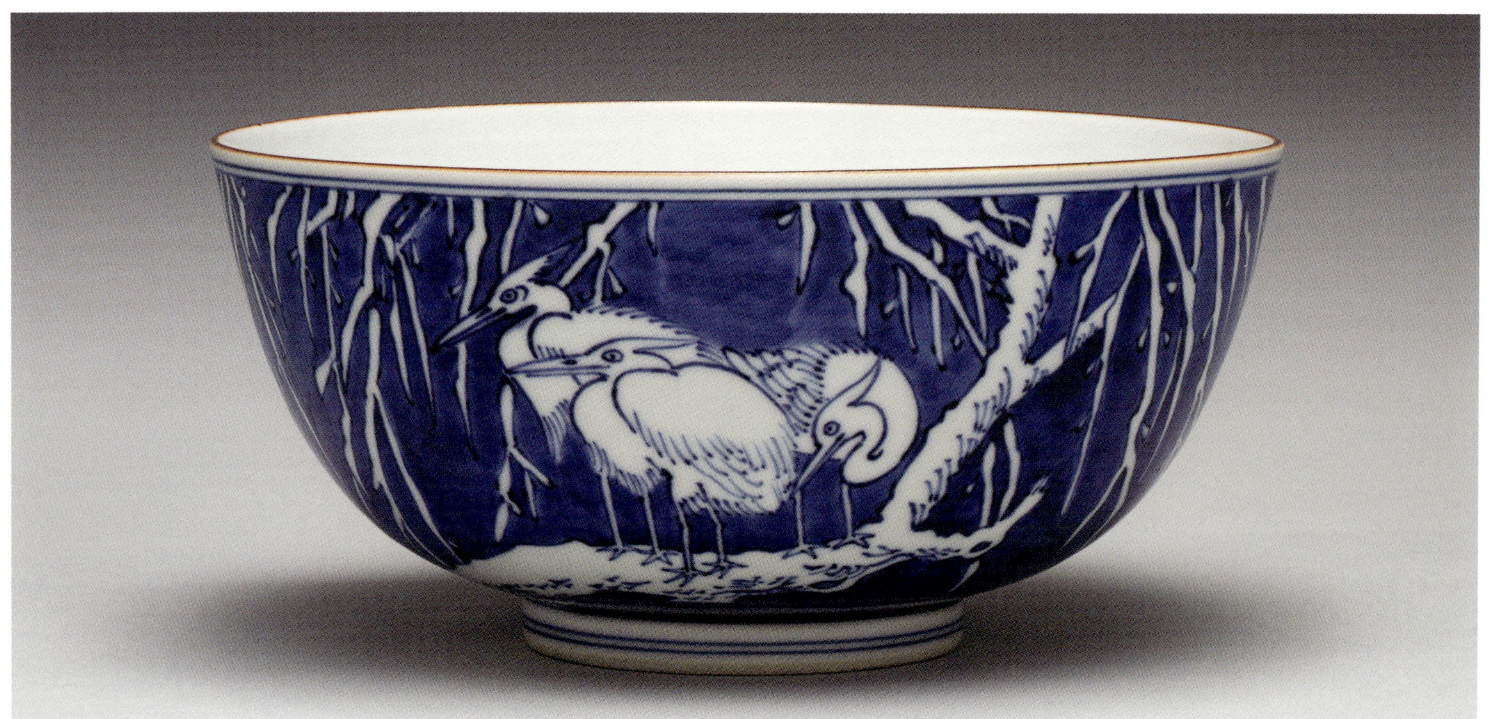

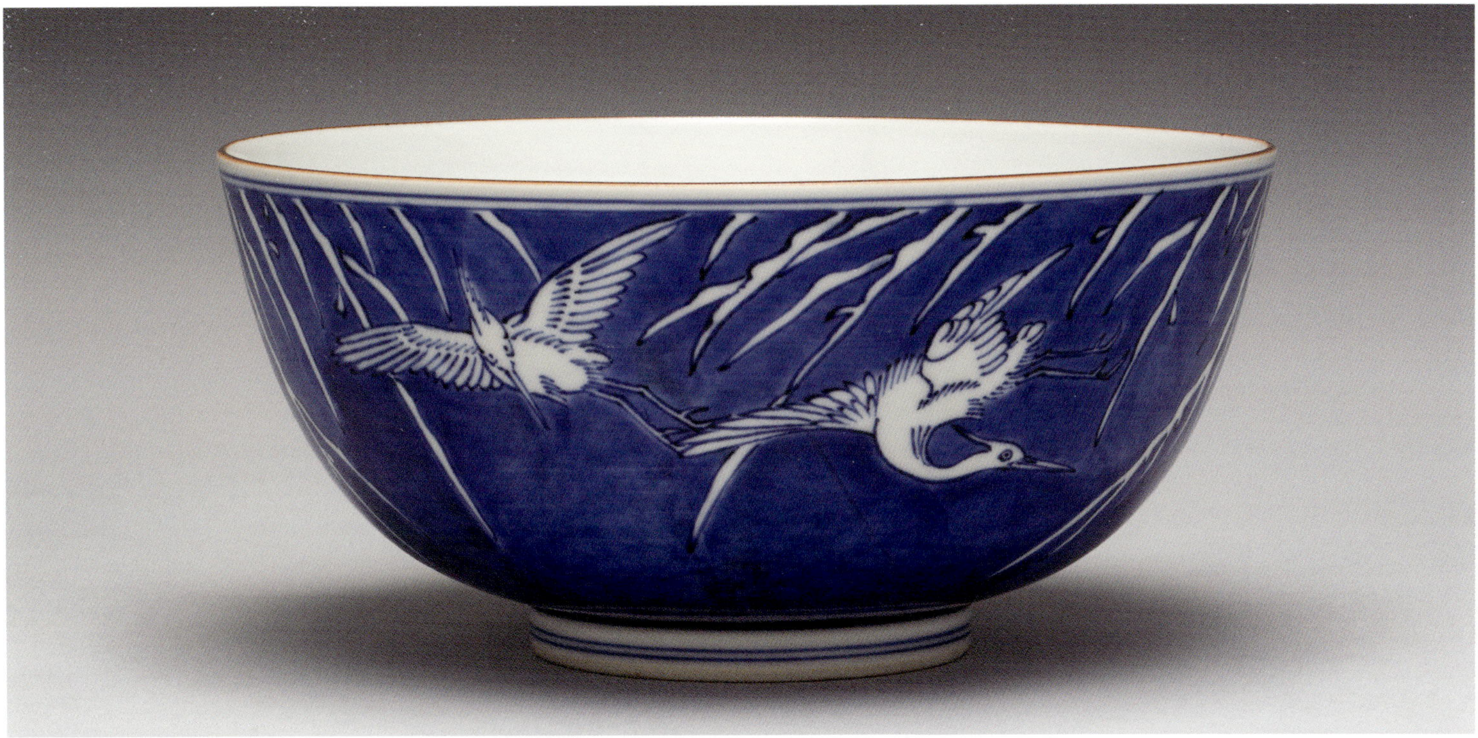

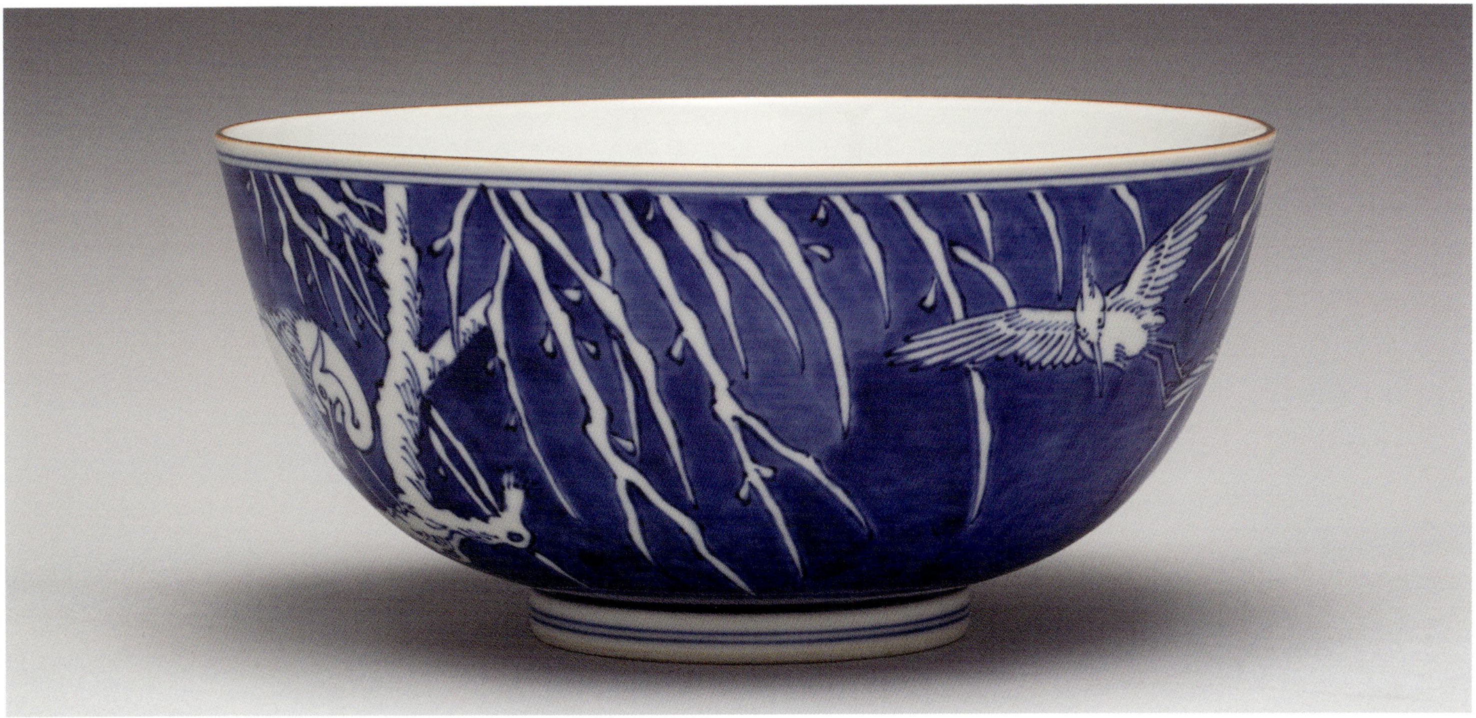

12 **HIGH-FOOTED BOWL WITH LOTUS POND, 1887–92**
Porcelain with underglaze color and molded designs
H. 10 cm, diam. 23 cm
2022.155

13 **DINING BOWL WITH CLEMATIS, 1893–97**
Porcelain with underglaze color and molded and incised designs
H. 6.9 cm, diam. 19 cm
2022.156

The two bowls here, one with a high foot and the other with a wide, low profile, are both especially well-executed examples of Yohei III's work in underglaze blue combined with other underglaze colors. The high-footed bowl is of a *takatsuki* shape, often used for offering bowls set before altars. Its flared foot has two raised bands, and the lip of the basin is everted. The exterior is painted delicately with an underglaze design of large lotuses, with the leaves, stems, and open flower in blue line and wash. He creates dewdrops by leaving domes of clay unpainted on the surface of one of the leaves so that one feels them when touching the bowl.

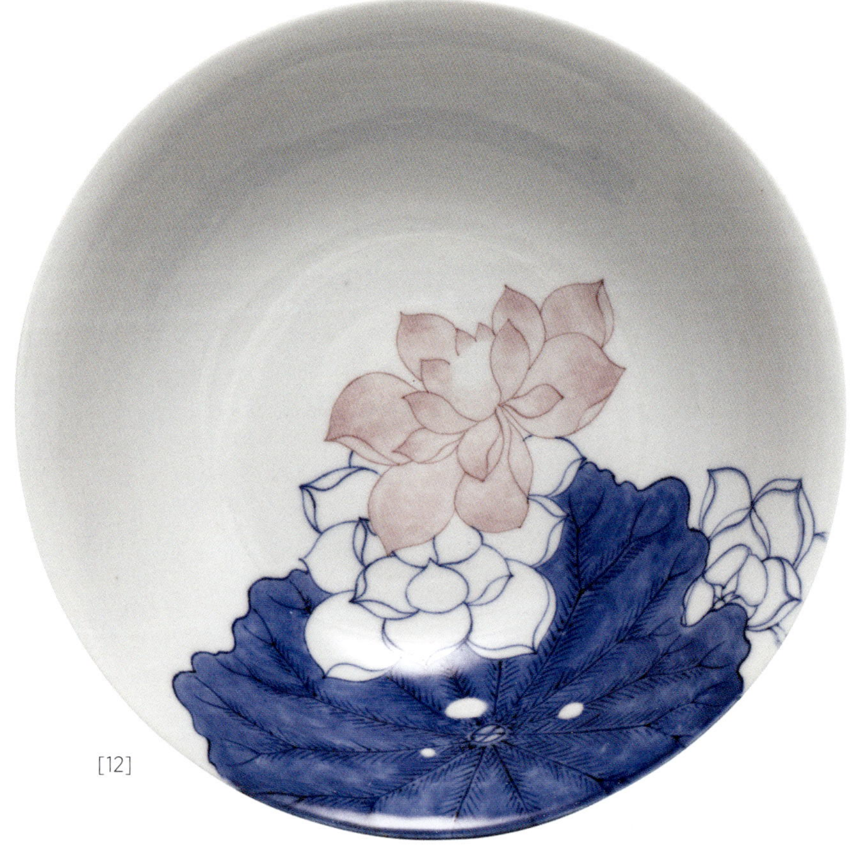
[12]

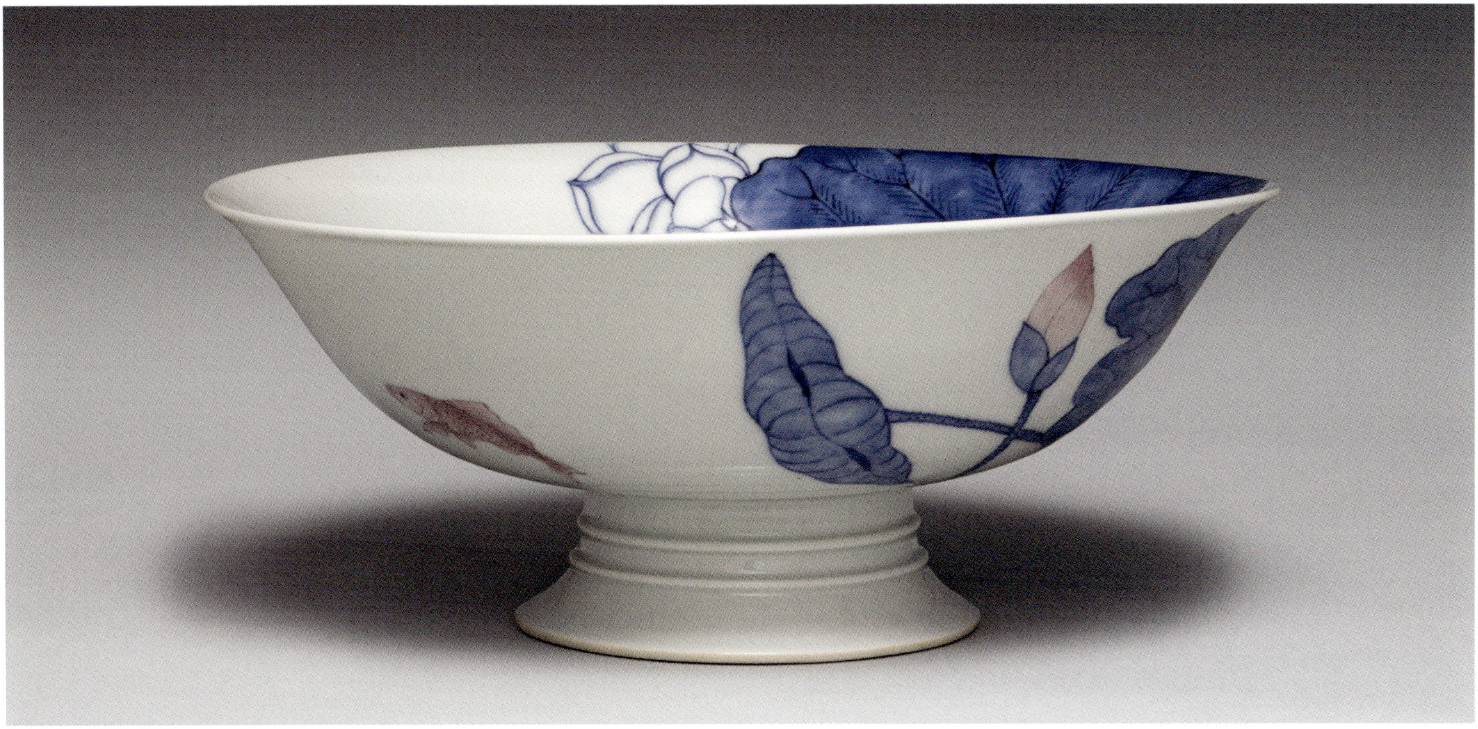

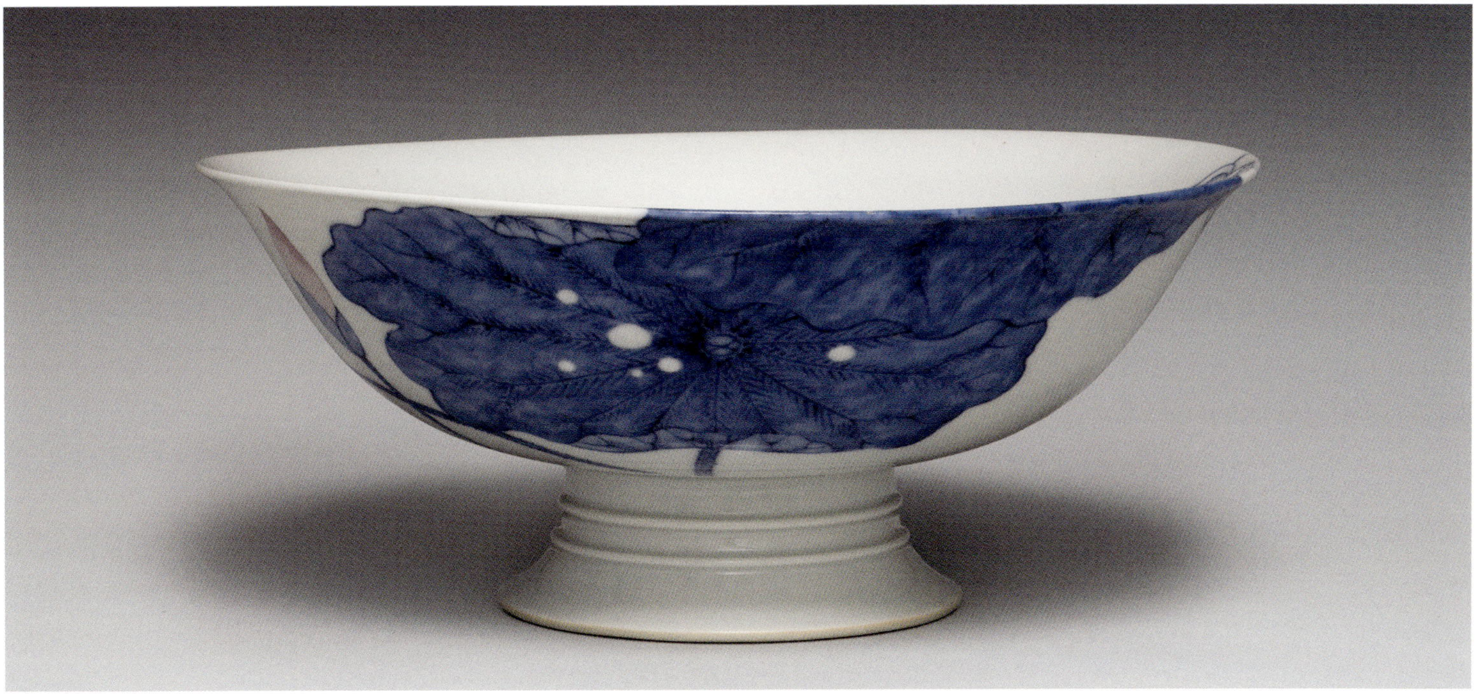

[12]

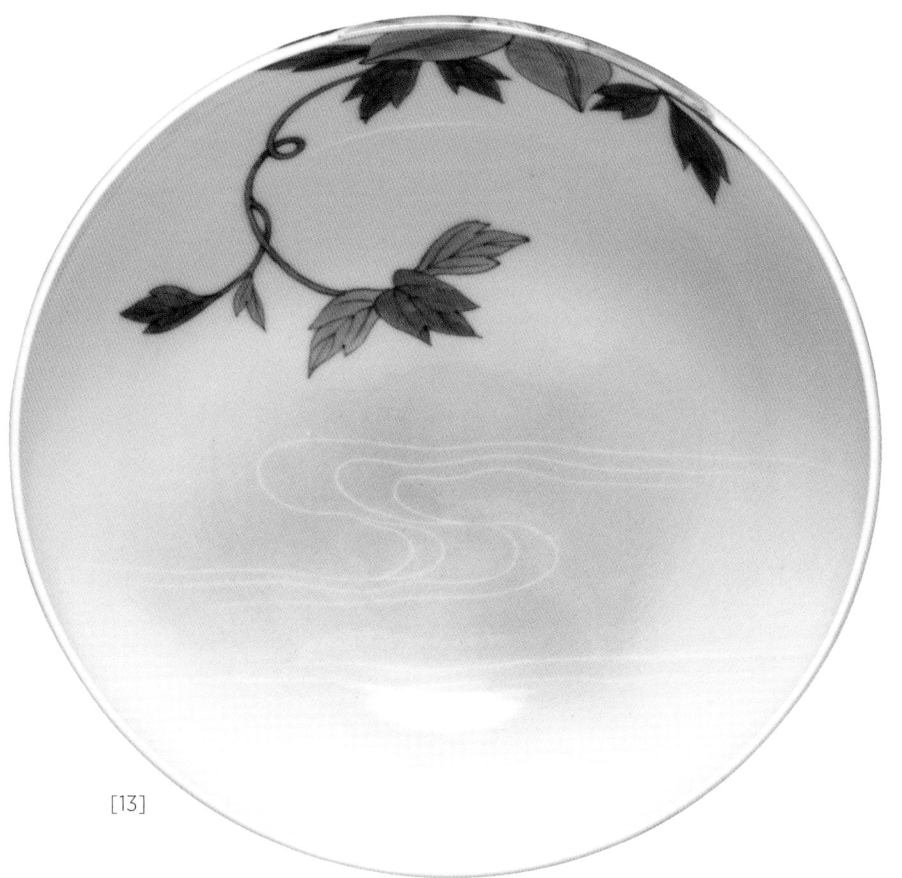

[13]

A lotus bud and two swimming fish are painted under the glaze in red with washes to achieve pink, while the outlines are in red. A foliate motif with tendrils and little round fruits in blue floats along between the fish. The basin, down to where it joins the foot, has been covered with a bluish white color. The interior of the bowl has a single large lotus leaf with raised dewdrops and three lotus flowers in full bloom, two white and one pink. The center of the pink one has been left unpainted.

The low-profile dining bowl has paintings of flowering clematis vines under the glaze in blue and red. Water is depicted with blue in the bottom of the bowl. The lines of white used to show motion on the water's surface were created using either a reserve technique, where blue was omitted, or a masking technique, where parts of the surface were covered before applying the blue. A pair of butterflies flutters across one side. The foot is decorated with a pattern of spirals in blue, and the lip curves in slightly. The overall effect is one of seeing the flowering vine hanging down, hovering just above the surface of a pond, whose slight disturbances hint at unseen fish swimming below.

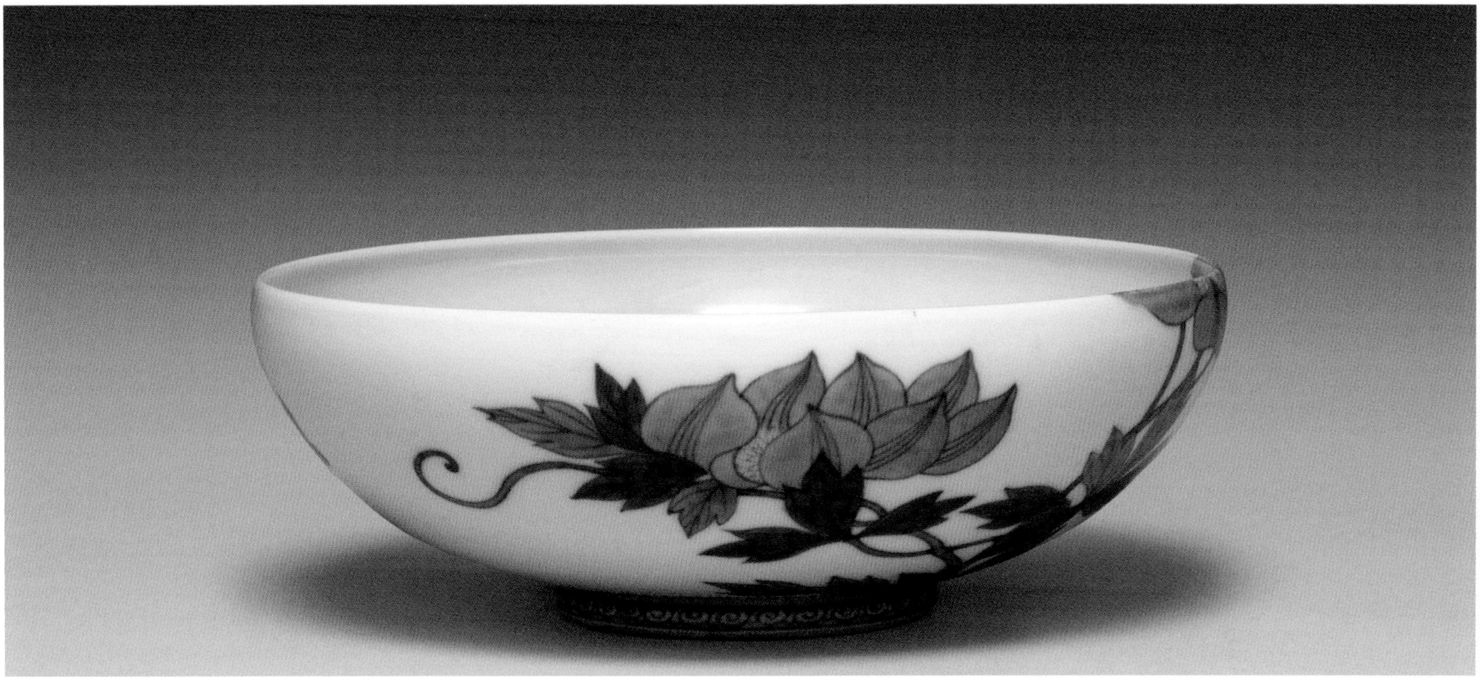

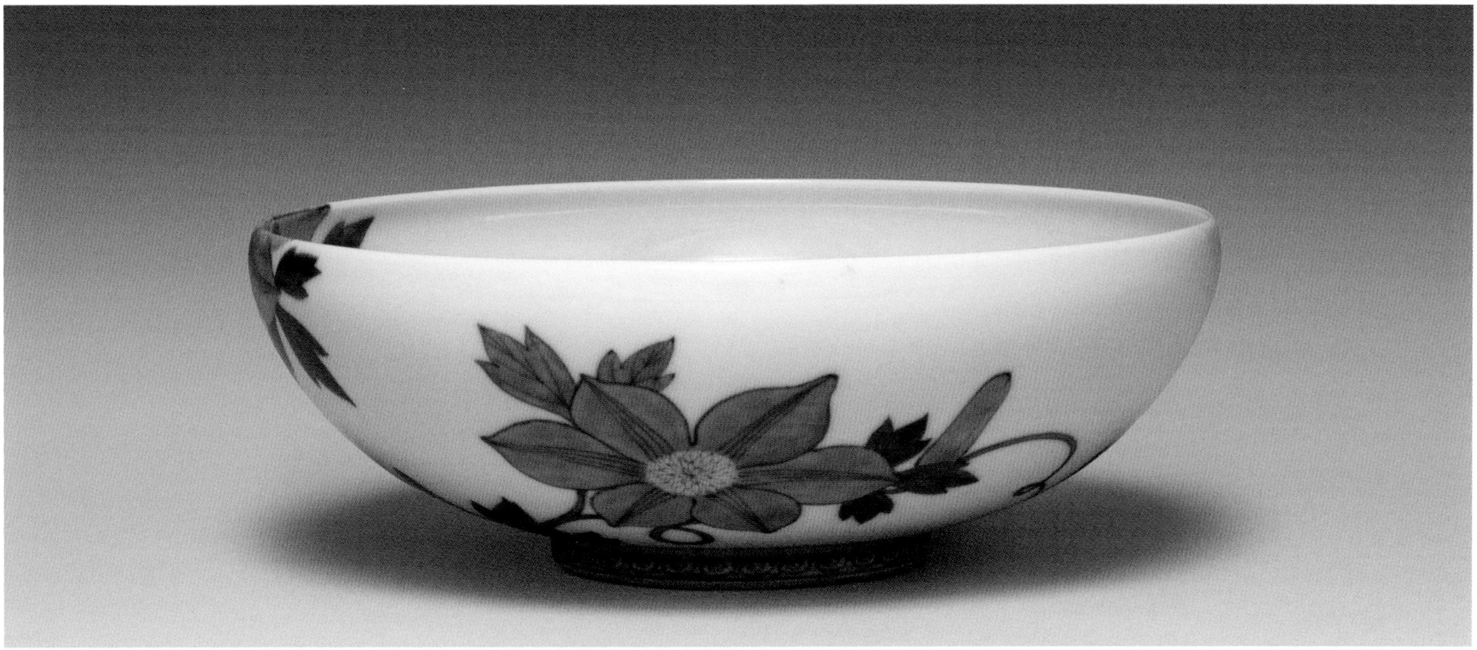

[13]

14 SAKE POURER, C. 1887

Glazed porcelain
H. with handle 23 cm, w. with spout 24 cm
2022.157

15 SAKE POURER WITH CHRYSANTHEMUM, ORCHID, AND PLUM, C. 1887

Porcelain with underglaze blue
H. with handle 23 cm, w. with spout 24 cm
2022.158

Each of these two sake pourers has a wide basin with a low foot; a generous spout open across the top half; a flat, round lid with a small knob recessed flush to the top of the container; and a tall, arched handle that meets the container where the top joins the basin at a sharp angle. While one vessel is glazed but otherwise undecorated, the other has a painting in underglaze blue of the Four Nobles: chrysanthemum, orchid, plum, and bamboo. Unlike the creamy white color of some Yohei III works, the white of these sake pourers has the bluish cast typical of porcelains produced in Kyoto. Both pourers are signed in underglaze blue on their bases.

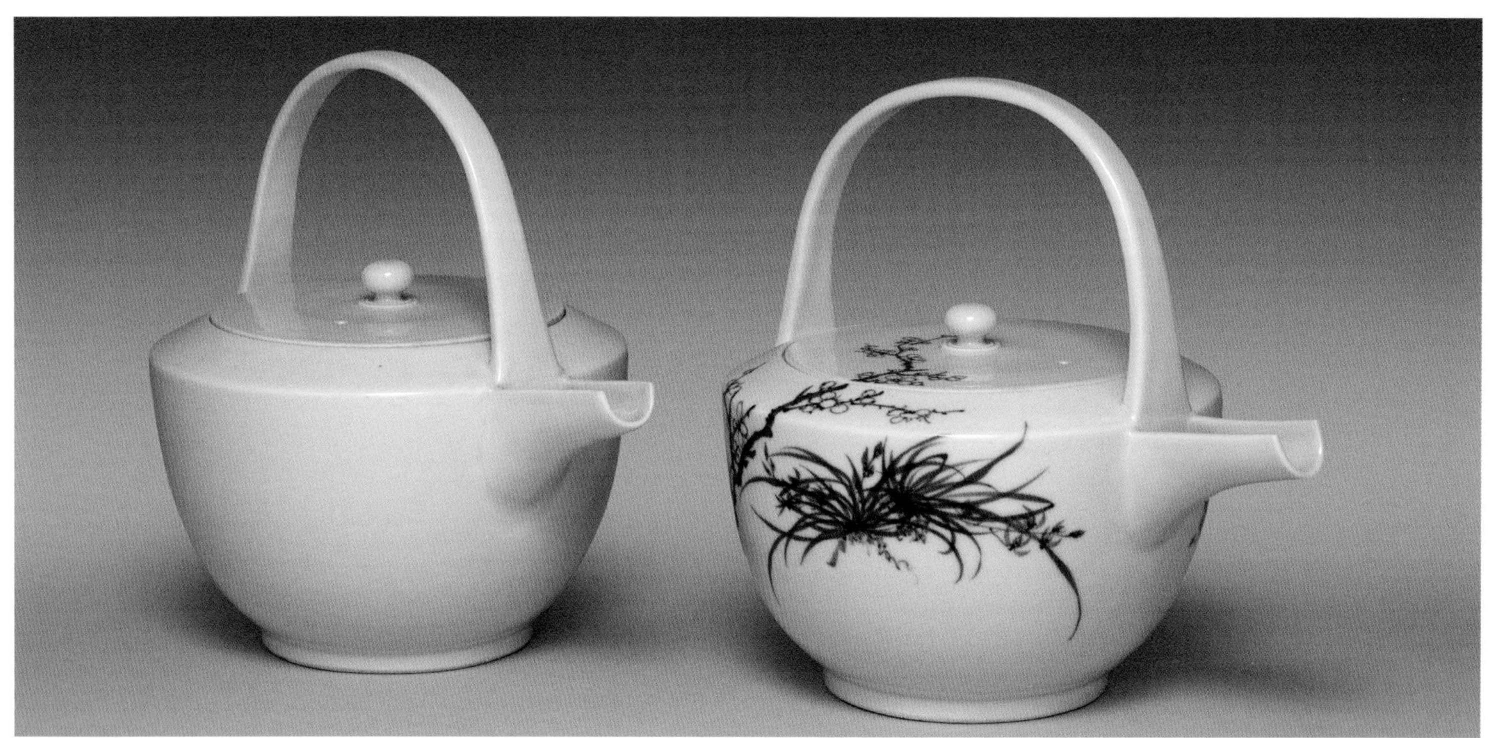

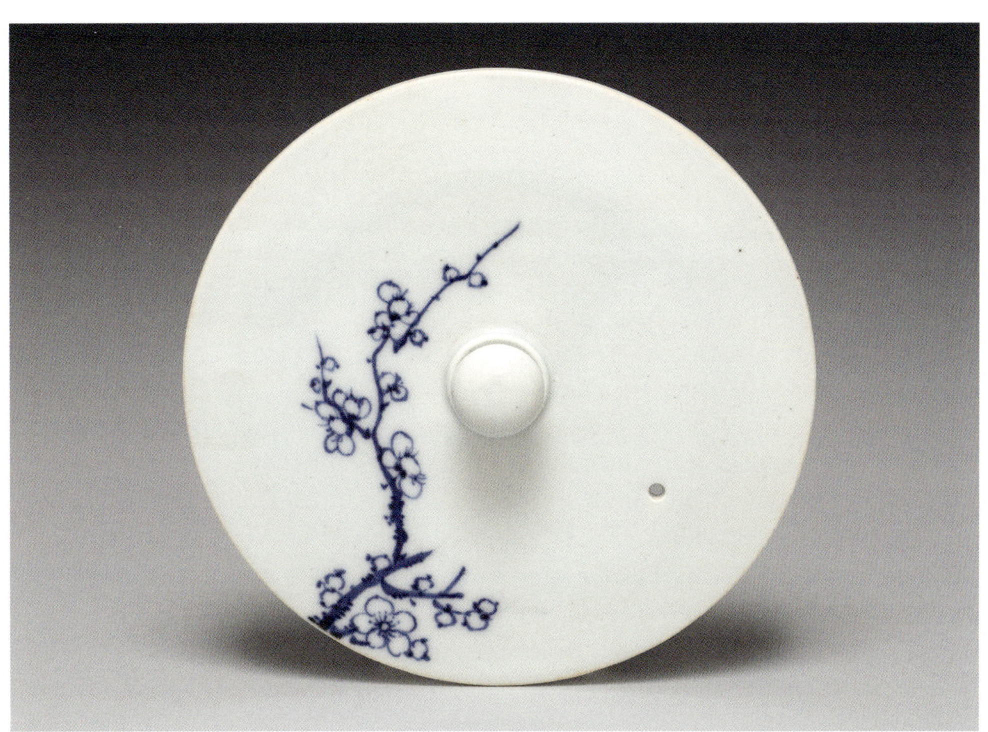

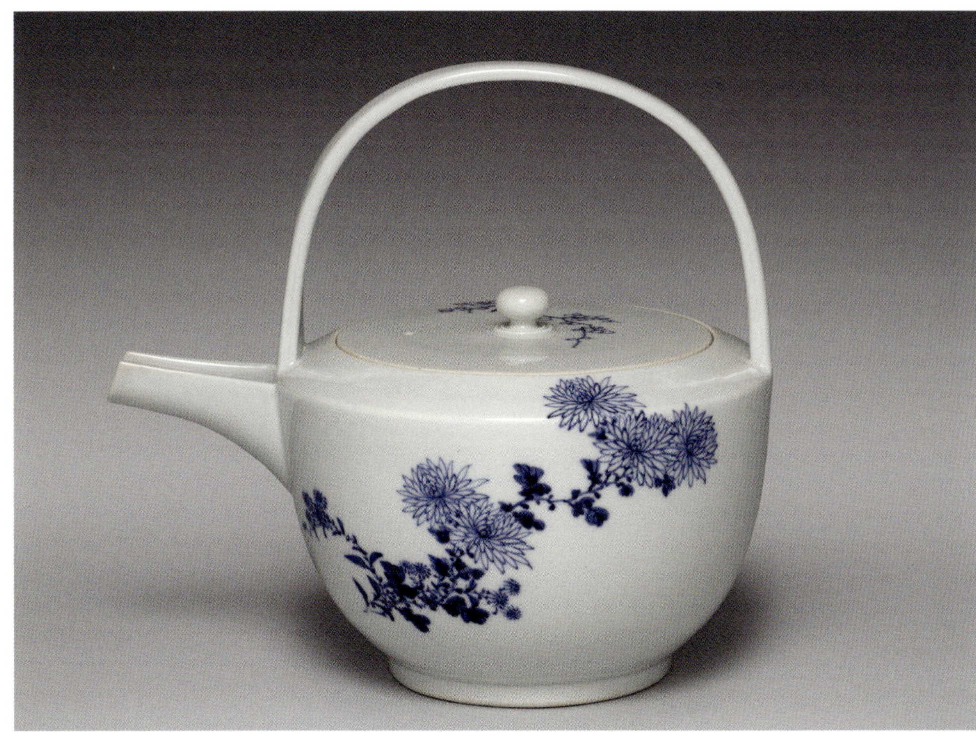

[15]

16 SAKE POURER WITH FLOWERS, 1893–1914

Porcelain with molded designs, overglaze color enamel, and metal handles
H. with handle 14.4 cm, w. with spout 13.1 cm
2022.161

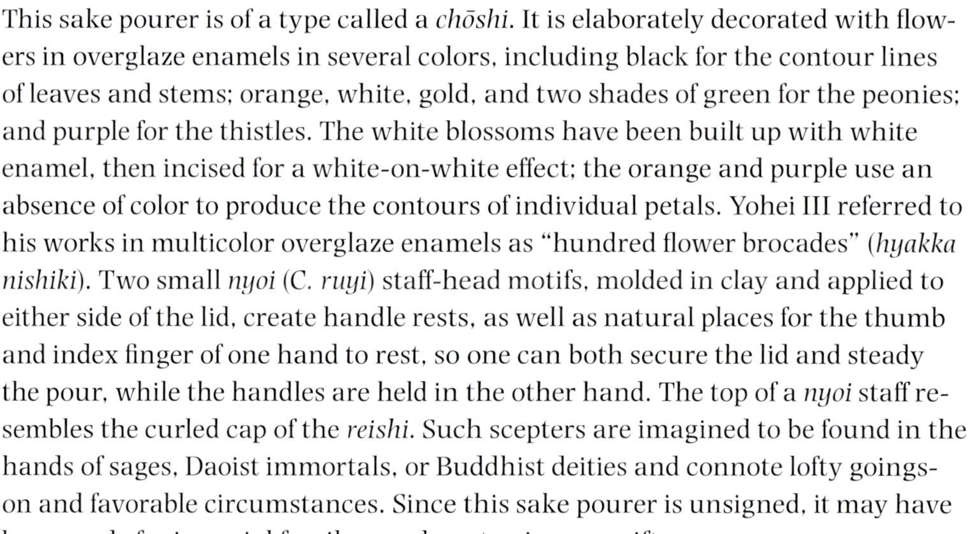

This sake pourer is of a type called a *chōshi*. It is elaborately decorated with flowers in overglaze enamels in several colors, including black for the contour lines of leaves and stems; orange, white, gold, and two shades of green for the peonies; and purple for the thistles. The white blossoms have been built up with white enamel, then incised for a white-on-white effect; the orange and purple use an absence of color to produce the contours of individual petals. Yohei III referred to his works in multicolor overglaze enamels as "hundred flower brocades" (*hyakka nishiki*). Two small *nyoi* (C. *ruyi*) staff-head motifs, molded in clay and applied to either side of the lid, create handle rests, as well as natural places for the thumb and index finger of one hand to rest, so one can both secure the lid and steady the pour, while the handles are held in the other hand. The top of a *nyoi* staff resembles the curled cap of the *reishi*. Such scepters are imagined to be found in the hands of sages, Daoist immortals, or Buddhist deities and connote lofty goings-on and favorable circumstances. Since this sake pourer is unsigned, it may have been made for imperial family members to give as a gift.

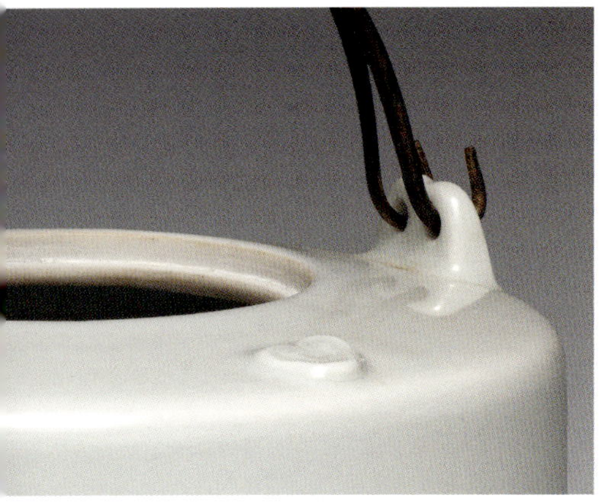

Detail of [16]

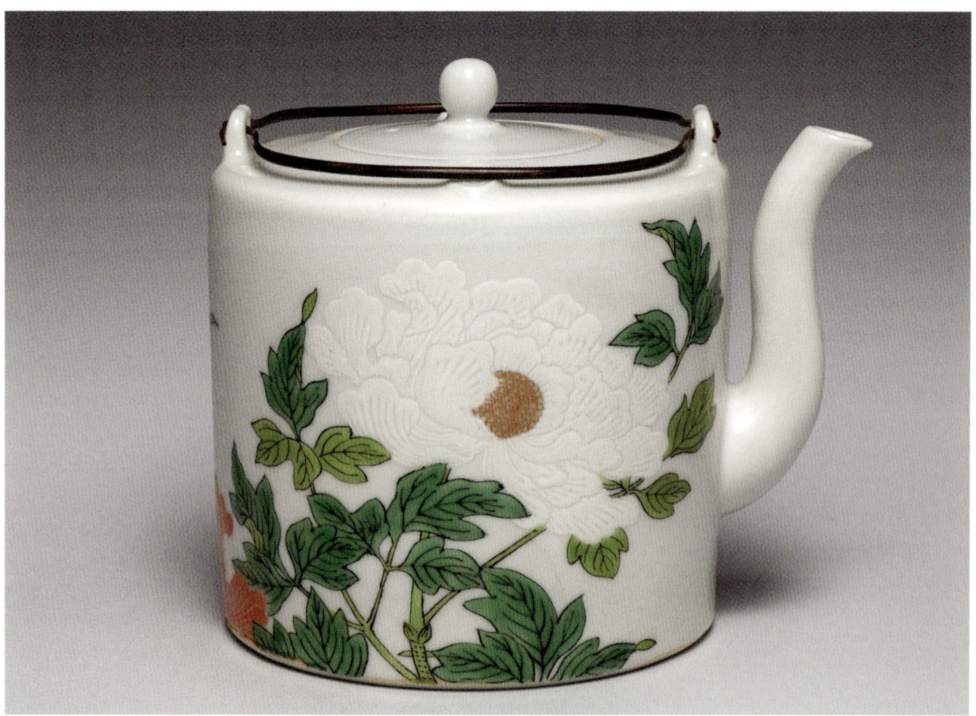

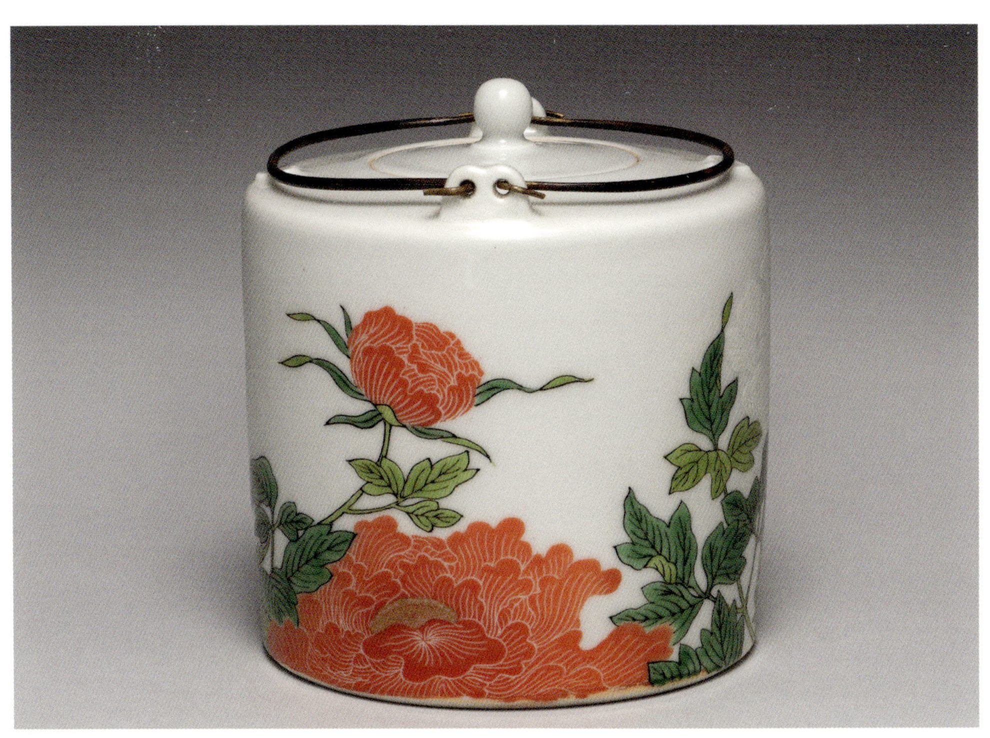

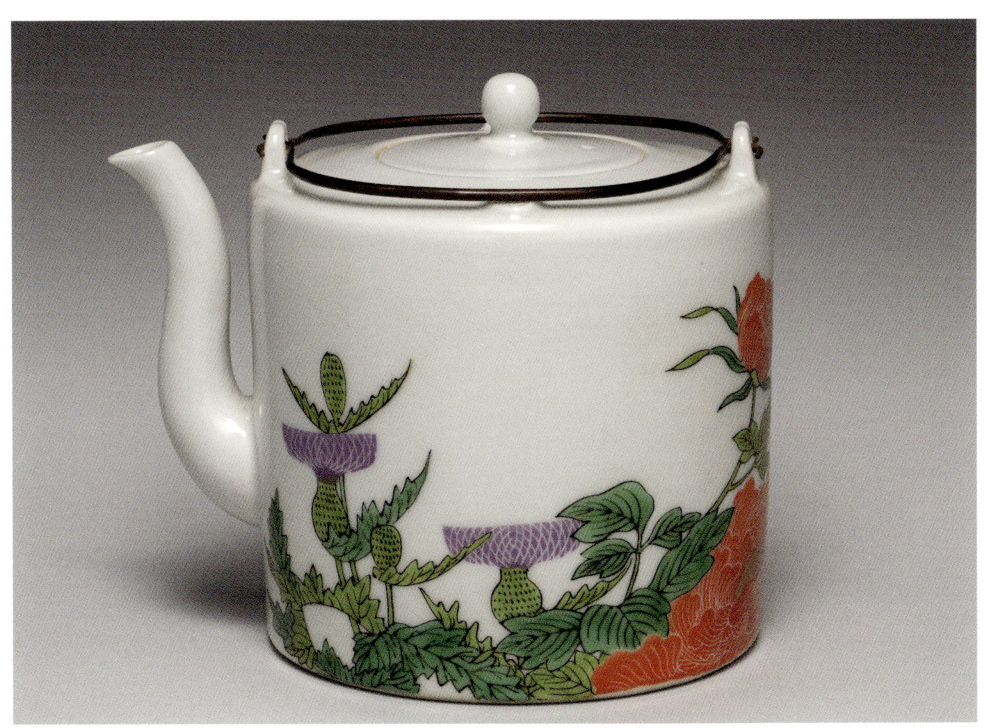

17 SAKE POURERS WITH TURTLES AND CRANE, 1893–1914

Pair of sake pourers; stoneware with crackled glaze and overglaze red
Crane pourer: h. 13.9 cm, diam. 7.1 cm; turtle pourer: h. 13.7 cm, diam. 7.1 cm
2022.159

One flask of this pair has stencil-like paintings of three turtles—a young one with its parents—while the other has a crane with a leg raised. Cranes and turtles are well-recognized symbols of longevity in East Asia, with the turtle said to live for ten thousand years and the crane for one thousand. Each flask also has a poem on the back, one in Chinese and the other in Japanese. The latter, which appears on the turtle flask, reads *kame iwaku kamiyo wa, ore no wakaki toki* 亀いわく神世ハ、おれ乃若き時. The seventeen-syllable poem begins with "turtle" and ends with "when I was young." It can be translated as, "the turtle said the world of the gods

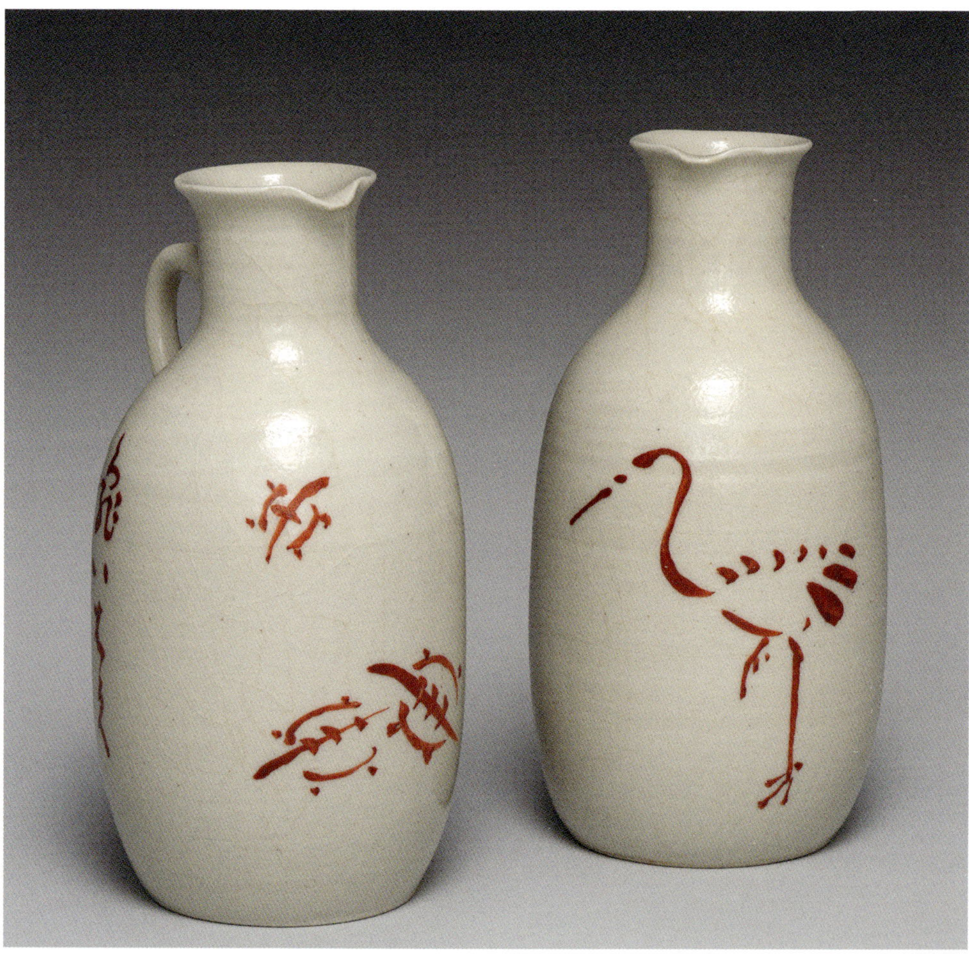

began when I was young." The poem on the crane flask is two nonconsecutive five-character lines from a poem called "Crane Feelings" by the famous Tang-dynasty poet Bai Juyi (772–846). One character in one of the lines has been altered. This creative poetic sampling results in a verse reading *zheng shi qun ji qian, tong you zhe tong zhi* 爭食羣雞前、同遊者同志. It could perhaps be translated, "before the flock of chickens competing for food, those traveling together have the same ambitions."[1]

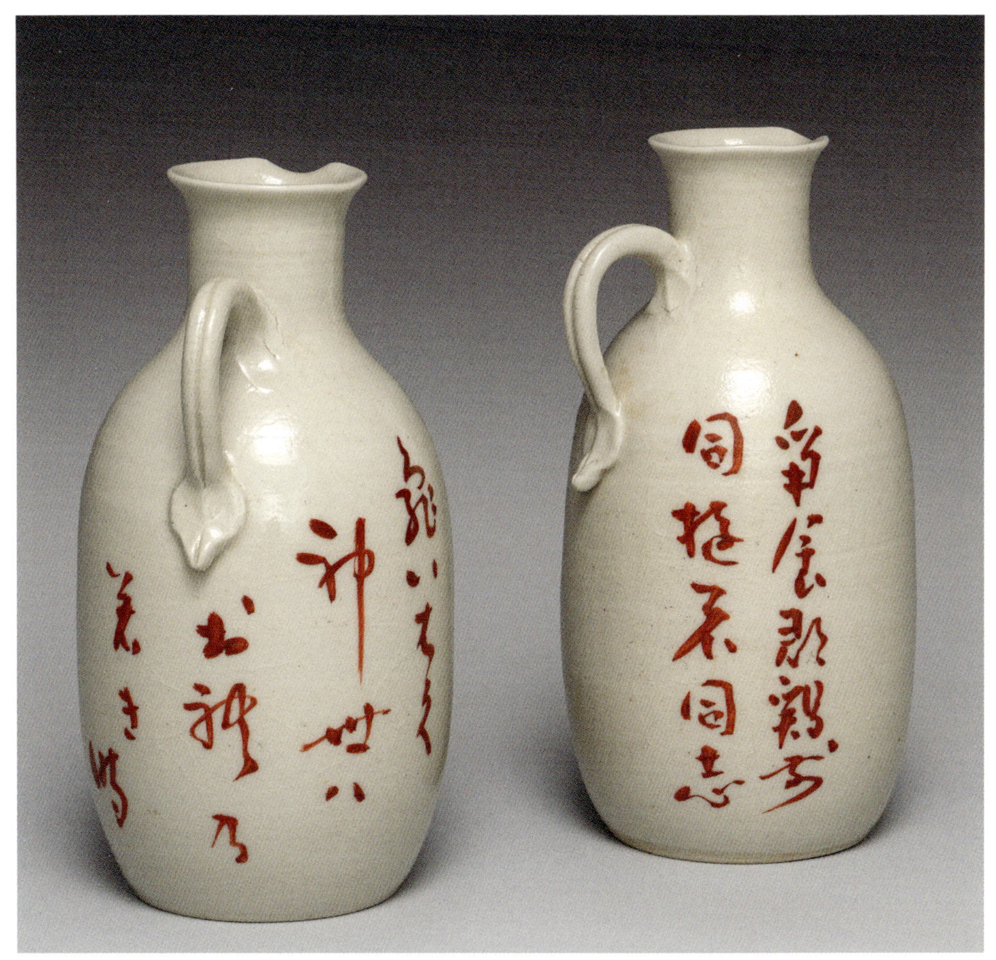

1. Professor Murata Takashi of Kyoto Women's University assisted with transcribing the poems.

18 TEAPOT WITH PINES, 1893–1914

Porcelain with underglaze blue
H. with lid 8 cm, w. with handle 10.5 cm, diam. 8 cm
2022.162

19 WATER COOLER WITH PINES, 1893–1914

Porcelain with underglaze blue and applied forms
H. 5 cm, l. 11 cm, d. 7.5 cm
2022.163

20 BOWL WITH PINES, 1893–1914

Porcelain with underglaze blue
H. 9 cm, diam. 18.7 cm
2022.164

Side-handled teapots known as *kyūsu* and hot water coolers, or *yuzamashi*, are essential components of *sencha* tea sets. The teapot is, of course, meant for steeping and serving the tea. *Yuzamashi* are used to cool boiled water to the ideal temperature for the type of tea to be brewed. The kidney-like shape of this one permits it to be cradled in one hand, following curvature of the palm, with the

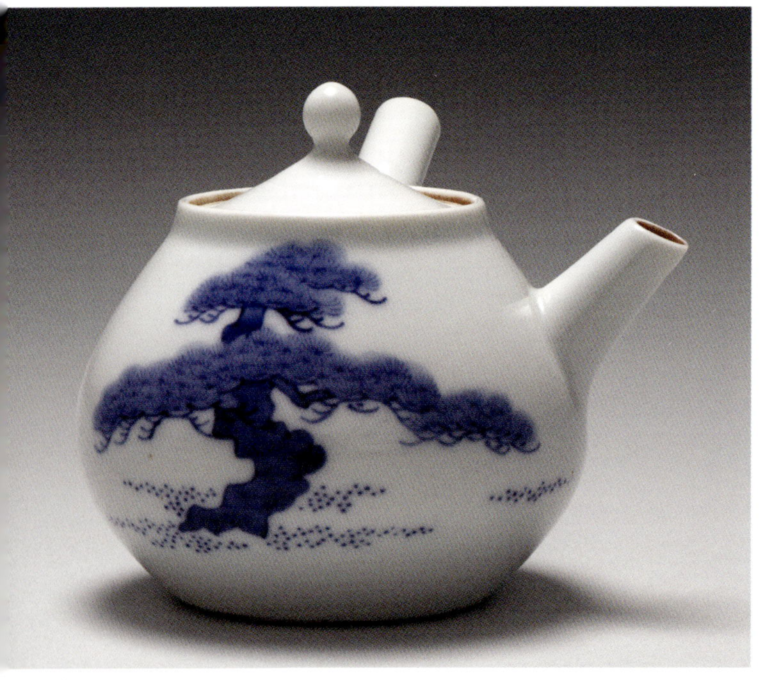

[18]

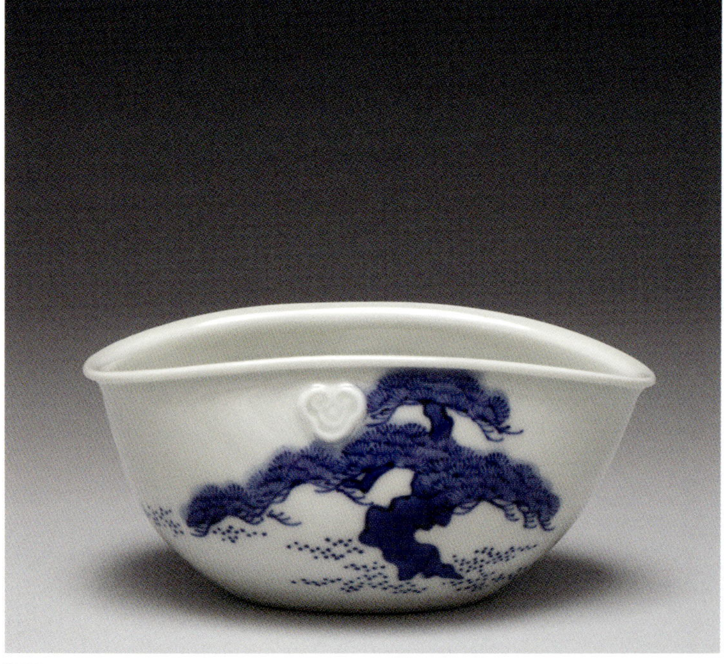

[19]

tips of the thumb and index finger each pressed against a *nyoi* staff-head-shaped applied form, perfectly placed to ensure a stable hold. Someone pinching the cooler in this way would have enough protection from the heat to maintain a steady grip but also sufficient contact along the base of thumb to assess the water temperature. On each of the cooler's two longer sides, a pine tree in grass or sand is painted under the glaze in cobalt blue. Evergreen, pines have associations with eternal youth and longevity. The tree on one side has two main roots and two large branches, while that on the other has a single, thick, curved line from root to tip with racks of needles spreading across the width of the sky. A blue oval is traced along the footring, and the center of the base contains an ovoid "Seifū" seal. The teapot also has a pine in underglaze blue on each side. The tip of one of these pines reaches onto the tiny lid, and as with the trees on the cooler, the trunks are curvy ribbons with little definition. Considering the execution of their designs, one might imagine the pot and cooler to have been part of the same set. In contrast, the bowl has slightly more detailed surface designs, painted in blue under the glaze: three pines, with two, three, and four racks of boughs, respectively, have more angular rather than curved trunks, with clearly articulated bark. The box for the bowl carries an attestation by Yohei IV that it is the work of his predecessor, while that of the teapot has a Yamamoto Shōseidō seal (see also [21]).

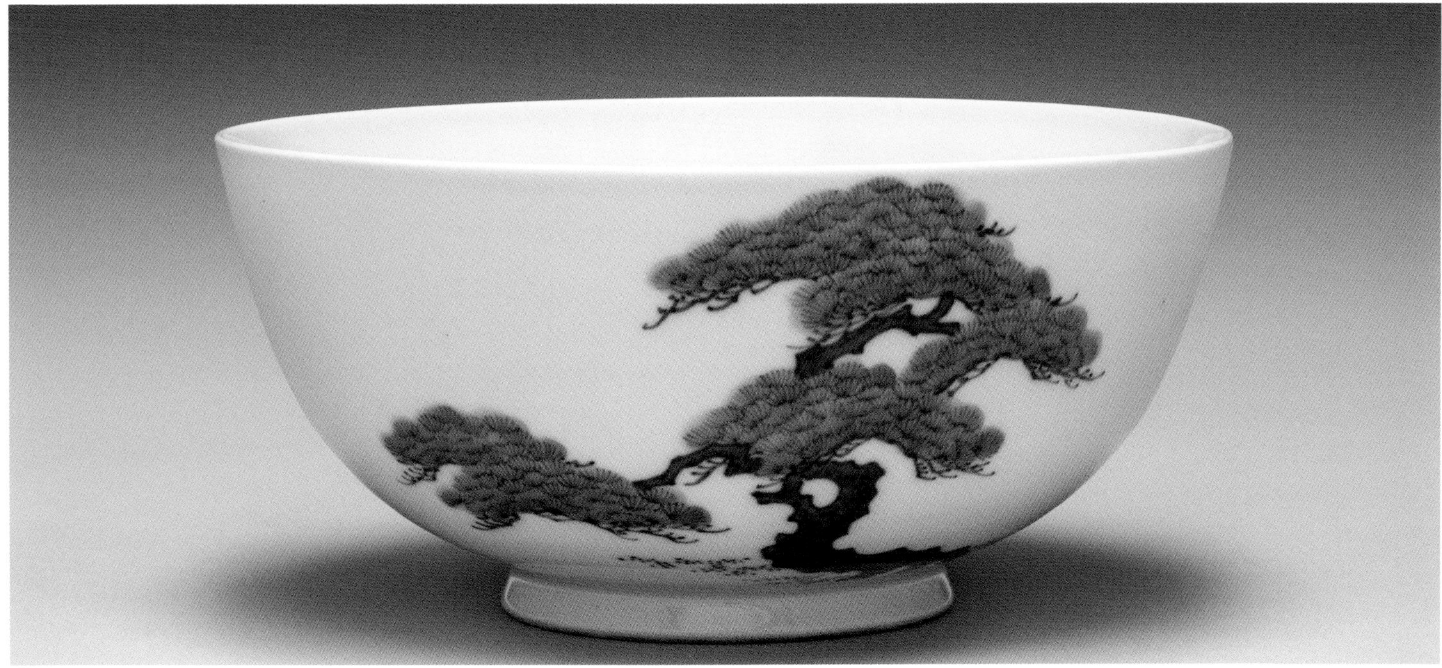

[20]

21 TEAPOT WITH CHERRY AT NIGHT IN GION, 1893–1914

Porcelain with underglaze blue and brown
H. with lid 9 cm, w. with handle 11 cm, diam. 8.5 cm
2022.165

22 TEAPOT WITH CHRYSANTHEMUMS, 1912–14

Porcelain with overglaze color enamel and gold
H. 8 cm, w. with handle 11 cm, diam. 8.5 cm
2022.166

23 TEAPOT WITH CHRYSANTHEMUM MOTIFS, 1912–14

Porcelain with overglaze color enamel and gold
H. 9.5 cm, w. with handle 12 cm, diam. 9 cm
2022.167

24 TEAPOT WITH BEGONIAS, 1897–1914

Porcelain with underglaze blue and overglaze color enamel
H. with lid 7.5 cm, w. with handle 10.5 cm, diam. 9 cm
2022.168

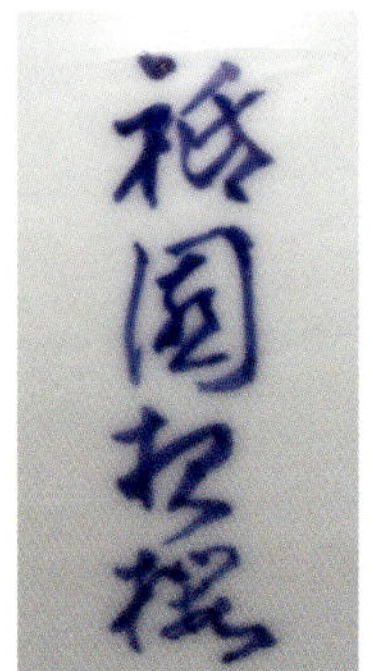

Details of [21]

These side-handled *sencha* teapots show differing shapes and a wide array of the decorative techniques Yohei III employed in his tea wares. The teapot with the cherry tree has a nearly spherical shape, and its recessed lid has an ovoid knob. It has both blue and a purplish brown under the glaze for the blossoms and embers on one side, and the vertical calligraphy identifies the tree as a cherry tree at night in the Gion area of Kyoto. To the right of the tree, smoke billows from a small lantern fire in a basket suspended on a post. In terms of collecting history, a paper inserted into the box of *Teapot with Cherry at Night in Gion* is of interest. It is a flyer for Yamamoto Shōseidō, a shop (no longer extant) that sold fine Kyoto ceramics in Osaka. Notably, some other works in the Heusinger Collection have seals from this shop placed over the side and lid of their boxes (see [18]).

Another teapot with recessed lid has a bold, realistic design of pale yellow and white chrysanthemums rendered in overglaze color enamels and dotted gold centers. Black contour lines define the yellow and white flowers and their green stems and leaves. Small pink and purple chrysanthemums are rendered as simple motifs, their shapes defined in contrast to the white ground of the pot. A teapot with the lid flush against the body, forming an oblong orb, is decorated with a sprinkling of similar chrysanthemum motifs in red, green, and purple overglaze color enamels with centers of pale red dotted with gold.

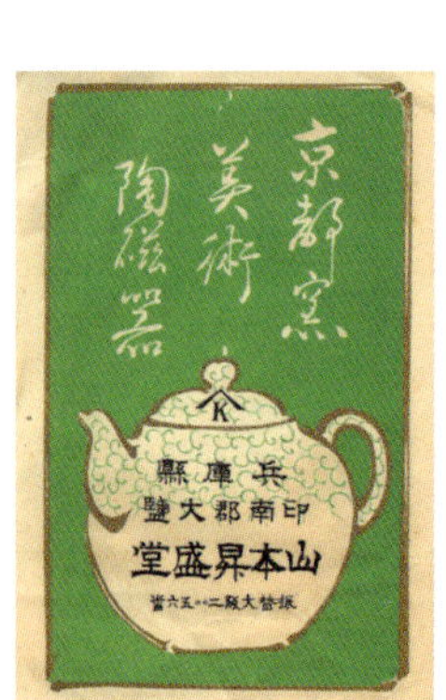

Flyer for Yamamoto Shōseidō that was inside the box [21]

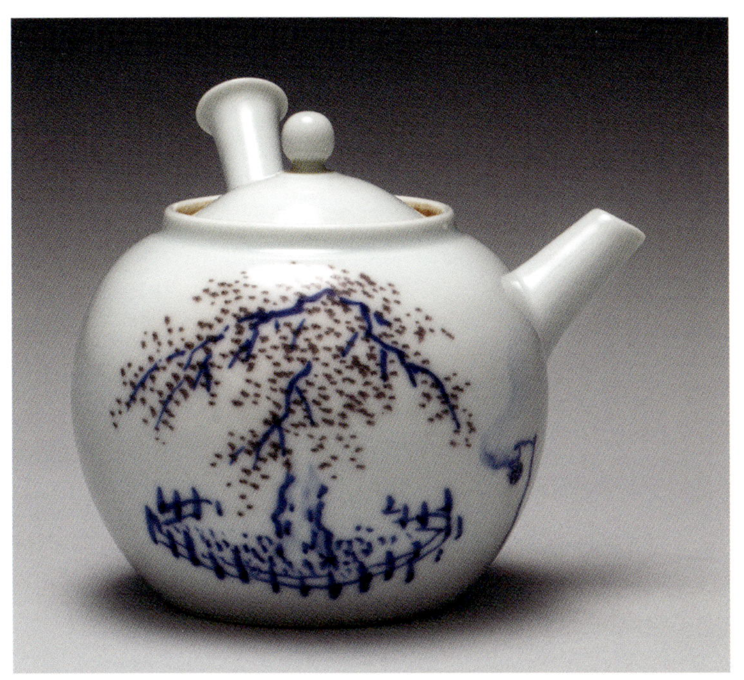

[21]

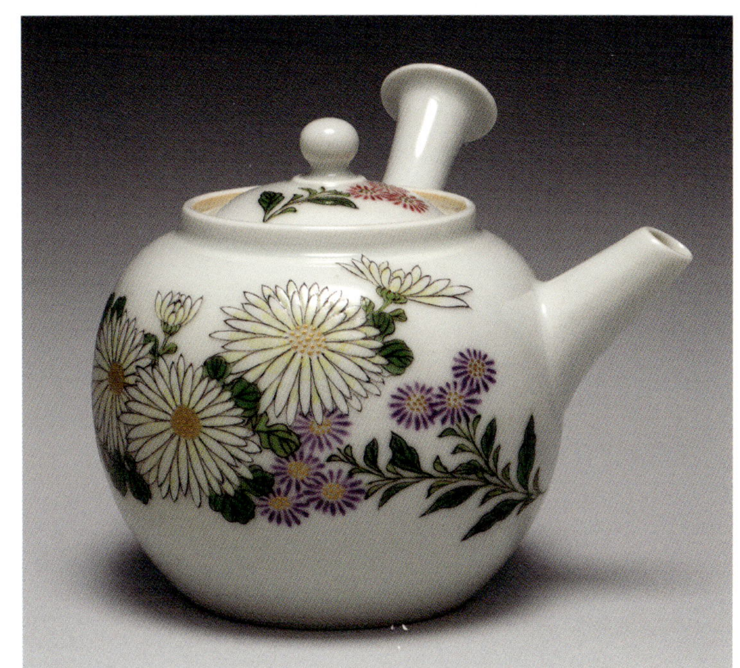

[22]

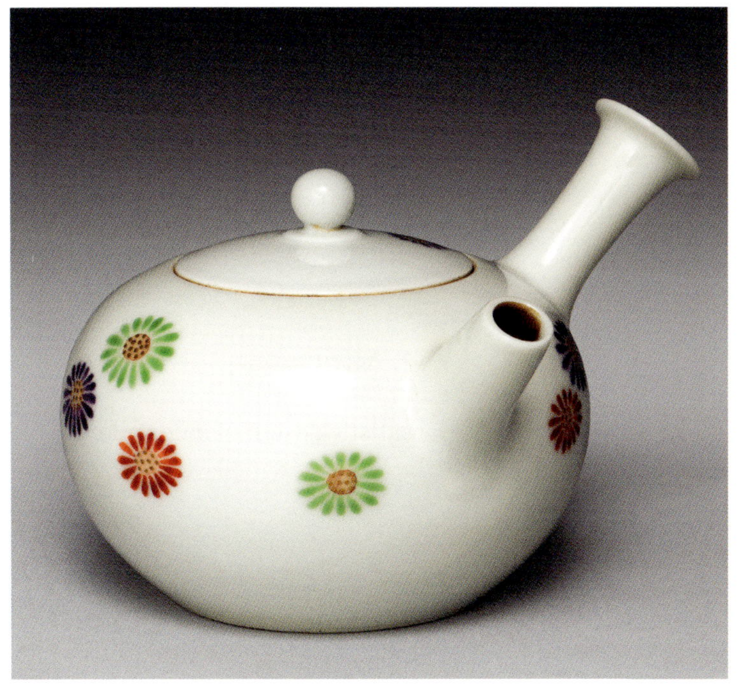

[23]

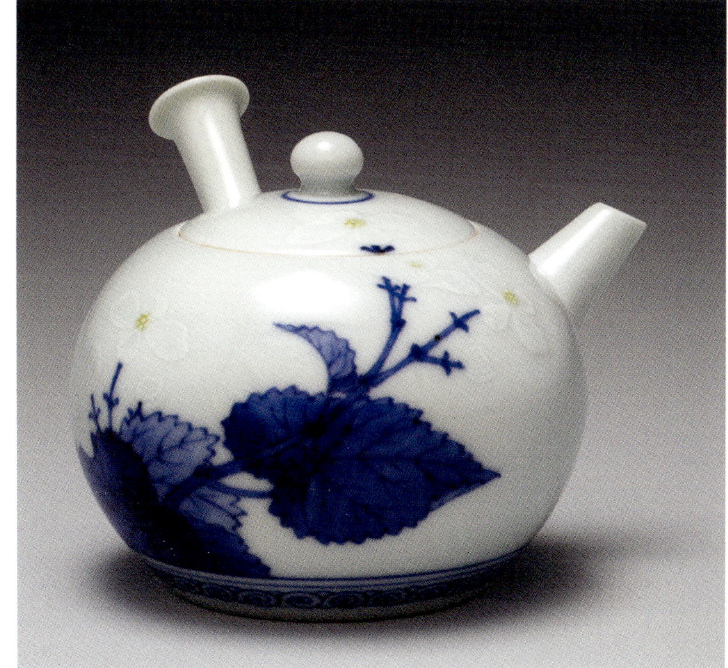

[24]

Of similar shape to the preceding pot, the teapot with the most complex surface treatment has a design of begonias in modulated underglaze blue for the leaves and stems as well as thick overglaze white with incised lines to define the petals, plus small areas of underglaze yellow at their low-relief centers. A band of underglaze blue gives further definition to the lid's handle, and the area just above the base has a double band of blue above a row of snail-shell curls. Unlike the other pots, which have marks on their bases, this one has "Seifū" incised into one of its sides in relatively large characters. It is the side that would face the host if the teapot were held by the handle with the right hand, which would be the expectation.

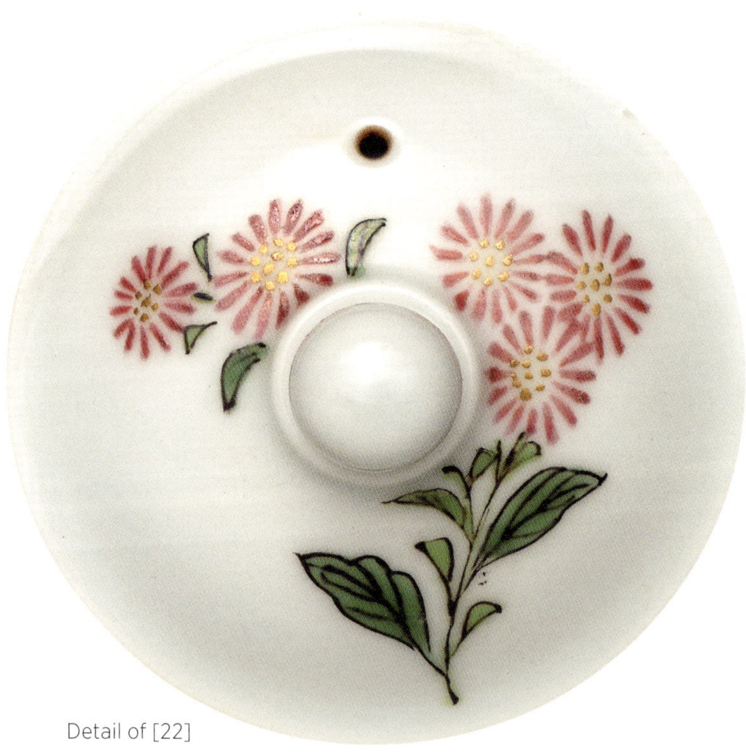

Detail of [22]

25 TEACUPS WITH A HUNDRED SAGES, 1893–1914

Set of five teacups; porcelain with underglaze blue
Each: h. 6.5 cm, diam. 9 cm
2022.169

Each of these five teacups has a painting of identical design in underglaze blue, but as the tiny figures are drawn entirely by hand, each cup has its own personality. The theme of the *sencha* cups is an assembly of sages or immortals, literally "a hundred venerable [people]" (*hyakurō*). The myriad figures crowd the scene in groups. The god of longevity, with his tall forehead, sits with his cranes, having flown in from Mt. Penglai on the Isle of the Immortals. Seven long-bearded sages sit around a stone table, chatting and drinking; one is seated on an enormous gourd. Of course, there is a stack of books on the table, and elsewhere, scrolls are being written upon or read—in one case held very close by a sage who is wearing glasses. The design was enormously popular in ceramics made for those engaged in literati culture.

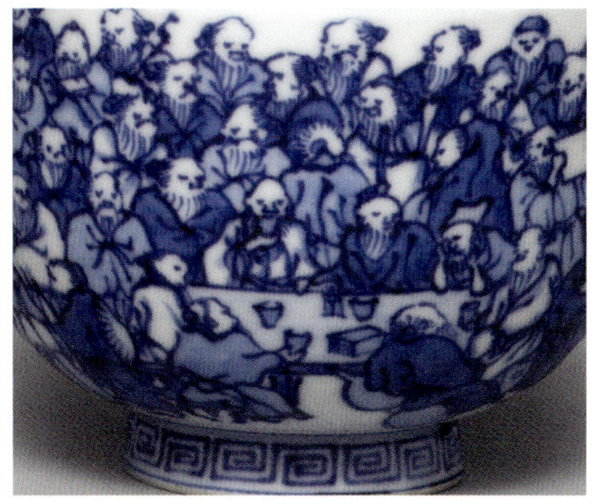

Detail of [25]

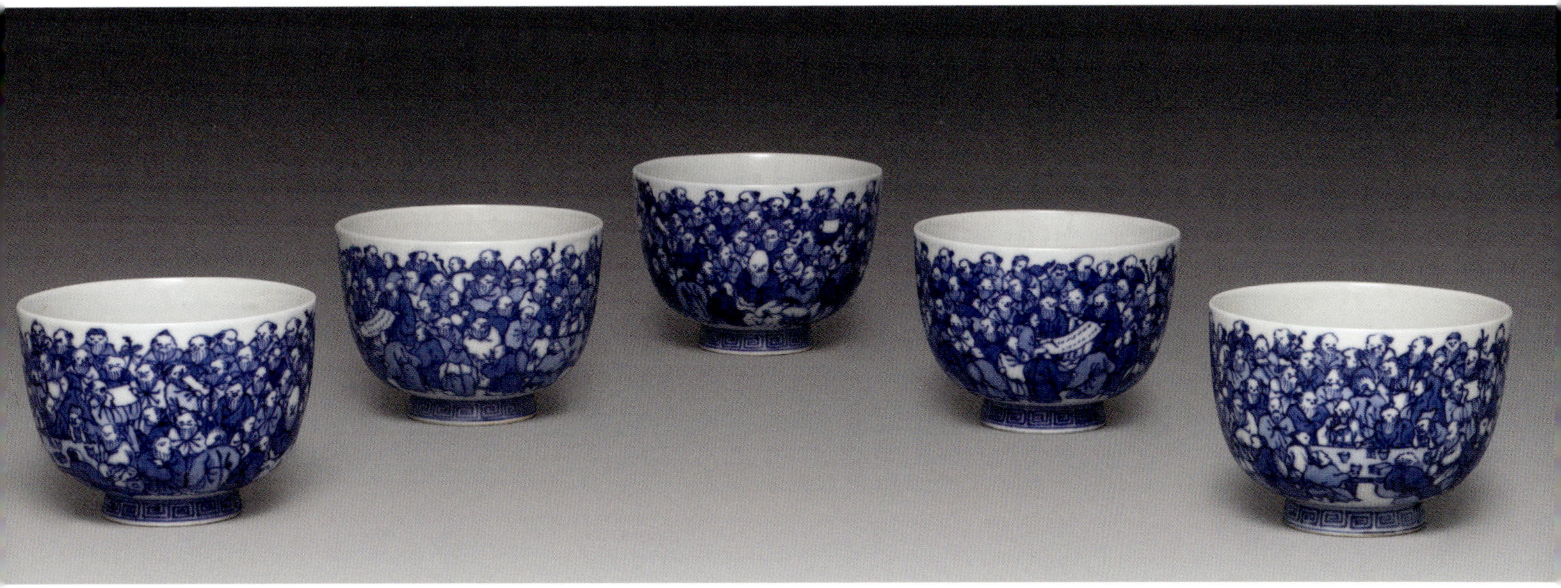

26 TEA SET WITH ORCHIDS, 1893–1914

Teapot with set of five teacups; porcelain with underglaze blue
Teapot: h. with lid 6.7 cm, w. with handle 10.7 cm; each cup: h. 5 cm, diam. 7.7 cm
2022.170

Although the teapot here is stored in a separate box from the five cups, these six pieces may once have been part of a tea set that included other tools such as a water cooler. The teacups have orchid flowers on both sides in underglaze blue, as well as a blue band inside the footring. The teapot has the same design and a blue band painted around the bottom of the lid's knob. The cups' long wood storage box is stamped on the exterior, over the lid and base, with a small red seal reading "Satō." The same seal appears on five small squares of yellow textile, one placed in the bottom of each compartment in the teacup storage box. These are additional to the customary yellow cloths stamped with a "Seifū" seal. Interestingly, four of the Seifū cloths are stamped with an ovoid seal, while the remaining cloth, which is a slightly lighter color, has an unusual seal that is not quite gourd-shaped and with the *fū* of Seifū in a stylized, unrecognizable form. The teapot has its own box with a Satō seal and is wrapped with an orange textile stamped with the same unusual Seifū seal.

A set with a very similar surface design is in the Brooklyn Museum. The Brooklyn set has a water cooler and a small pitcher, in addition to the teapot and cups, and all are in a single storage box. This box records the tea tools as made with *kanpakuji*, or "bright-jewel white porcelain," counted among Yohei III's most important inventions, and carved images. In fact, both sets have a white surface much closer in coloration to the cool white of porcelain clay used in Kyoto at the time, and the designs are simply painted. The Brooklyn set was thus likely mismatched at some point with a box intended for another tea set. Nonetheless, the box may have helped prevent the set's original components from being dispersed, and the set itself provides insight into how the other tools from the present set may have looked.

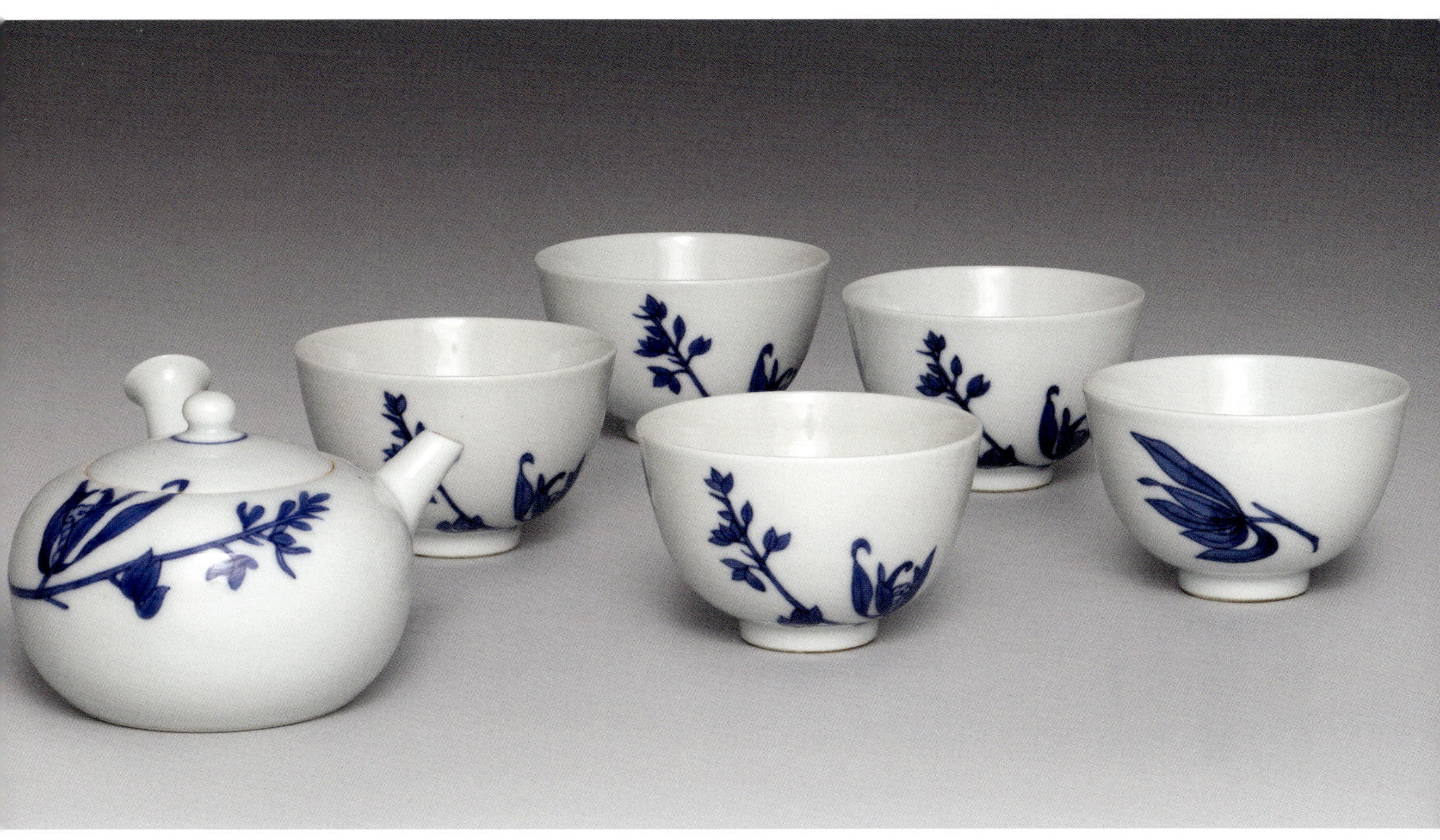

27 TEA SET WITH CHINESE LANDSCAPES, 1893–1914

Tea set with teapot, water cooler, and five cups; porcelain with underglaze blue
Teapot: h. with lid 9.2 cm, w. with handle 11.2 cm; hot water cooler: h. 5.4 cm, l. 11.9 cm, d. 7.4 cm; each cup: h. 5 cm, diam. 8.2 cm
2022.171

The theme of this *sencha* tea set is the Chinese scholar-recluse in an idyllic landscape. The teapot depicts two friends playing a board game on a promontory beyond a two-storied residence, while another figure comes across the entry bridge bearing bags of provisions, hung from the ends of a pole balanced across his shoulders. The kidney-shaped water cooler has a scene of a man gazing at a full moon in a dramatic mountain-scape stretching before a large compound in the woods. Another man, hunched over and carrying a heavy parcel tied to a pole over his shoulder, struggles to make his way up a hill to the site. The cooler also has a pair of applied *nyoi* staff-head forms for resting the tips of one's thumb and index finger, like those on the water cooler with pine trees (see [19]). Each of the five teacups has a landscape with an architectural structure and some human activity. One cup shows a man with a staff walking away from a residence toward a boat, loaded with what might be a musical instrument wrapped for travel. A second cup shows a man rowing a little skiff, which disturbs the otherwise still water. Behind him in the distance is an open-air pavilion. He is making his way toward a pair of figures playing a board game, much like the scene on the teapot. Down the hill from them is a residence; beyond this, a flock of geese approaches through the sky. A third cup shows a man in a traveling robe leaning upon his staff as he crosses a bridge to reach a two-story building with a pitched roof, possibly a temple, set between trees. Past this structure, another man sits fishing in a boat. A fourth cup shows a humbly dressed man with a broad-brimmed hat lugging a package tied to the end of a rod slung over his shoulder. In front of him is a two-story building flanked by deciduous trees and a man resting against the side of a sturdy stone bridge as he looks at a residence, or perhaps a set of roofed gates, further up the path. The last cup has a man walking toward a group of three pavilions announced with a banner hanging from a tall post; beyond this are two large deciduous trees sheltering a stand of small conifers. Across the water from this site is another man sitting on the bank fishing with a large woven basket for his catch beside him.

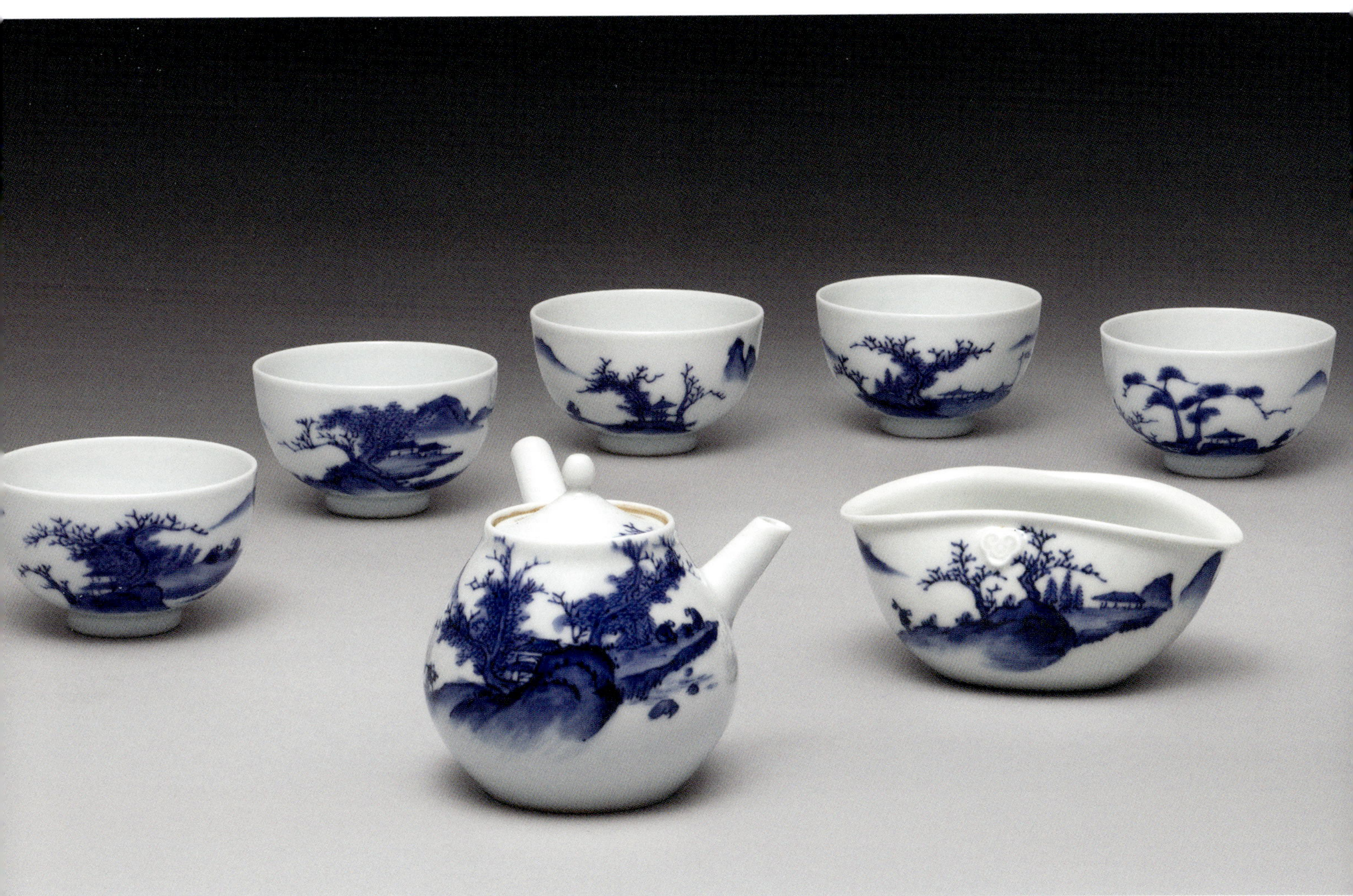

28 WATER COOLER WITH CHINESE GARDENS, 1893–97

Porcelain with molded and carved designs and cream glaze
H. 5 cm, l. 15 cm, w. 6 cm
2022.172

This water cooler has a handle with a dragon head. The body's two sides have garden scenes seen through windows. Designs of flowers and butterflies are incised in the spaces at both ends. Unlike most pieces by the Seifū Yohei studio, this one bears a seal beneath the handle rather than on the base. The glaze and technique are identified on the box as *taihakuji*, or "great white porcelain," an important early invention Yohei III devised in 1872 that involved the combination of a distinctive translucent, creamy glaze over an ivory-colored clay body. The garden on the right-hand side of the vessel, seen through a round window, has a decorative rock with grasses beneath a cloudy sky; and on a tiled verandah, there is a teapot, as well as a fan and two scrolls inserted into a double-handled urn or kettle atop a brazier. The garden on the left-hand side has two enormous flowers below what may be either a cloud or a rippling pond; a garden rock—or perhaps a carved wood sculpture—with a circular perforation sits on what appears to be a verandah. While the details may be open to interpretation, the setting is a rather glamorous Chinese residence or palace with a superbly tended garden in spring or summer.

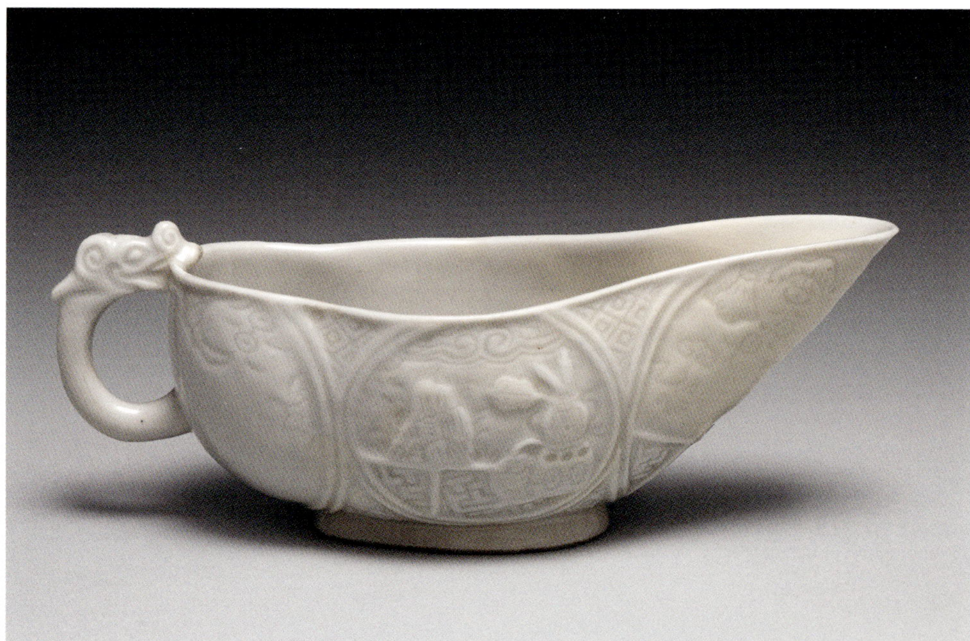

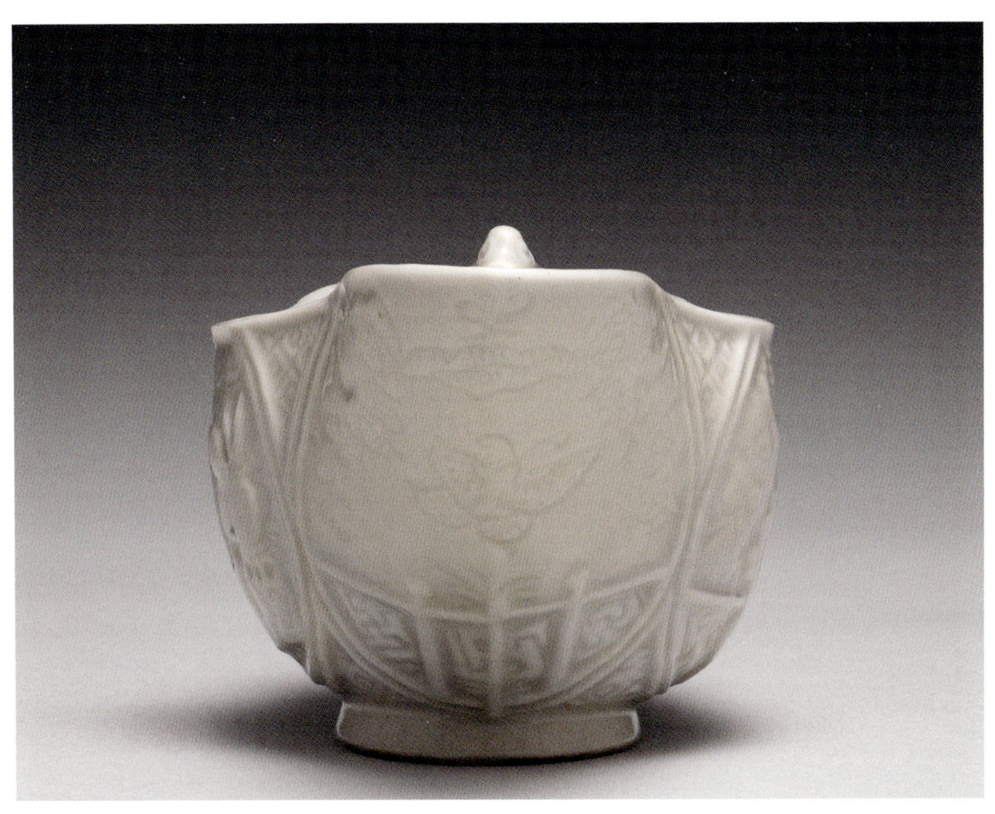

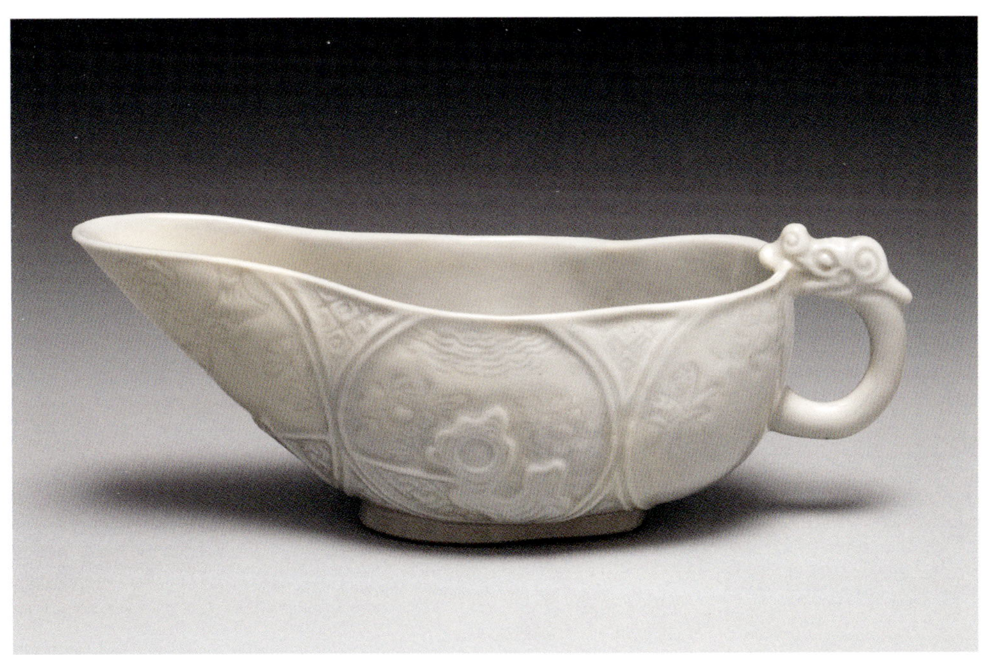

29 TEACUPS WITH FLORAL BAND MOTIF, 1893–1914

Set of five teacups; porcelain with incised design and cream glaze
Each: h. 4.5 cm, diam. 8.5 cm
2022.173

The five *sencha* teacups in this set are decorated with incised flowers and dots between a double band at the top and a single band at the bottom. They are in Yohei III's creamy *taihakuji* body and glaze. In their motifs, they are quite similar to an incense burner by Yohei III (see [36]), but the flowers are even more simple in design, with no open circle at the center. A label affixed to the side of the box refers to them as "*sencha* cups in emulation of Korean white [ware]." The reference to Korean ware indicates that even though Yohei was more directly inspired by Qing-dynasty wares from the Dehua kilns in Fujian Province in developing his porcelain clay and glaze for works such as these, the general understanding of the continental models still placed them, at least in terms of color, among pieces broadly associated in Japan with Korean white wares.[1] The delicate cups are thinly potted, so they have a highly desirable translucency.

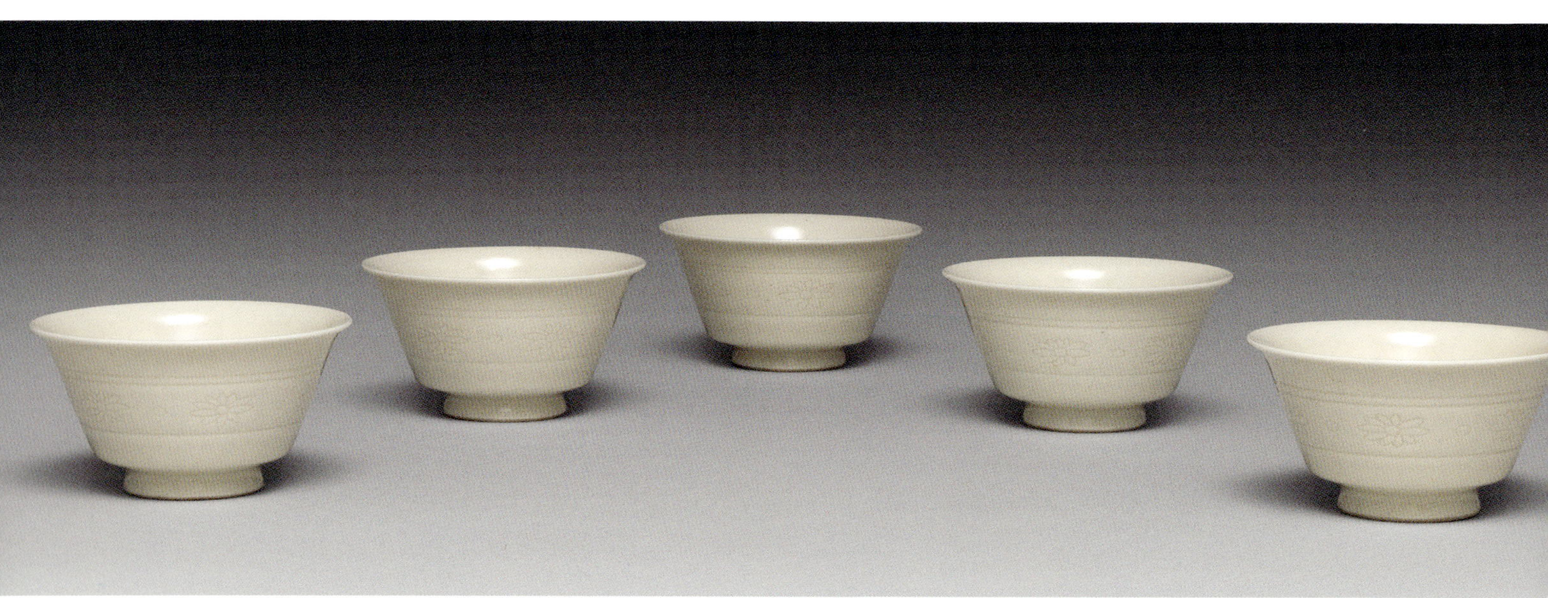

1. On Yohei III's emulation of Dehua ware, see Maezaki, "Qing-Style Porcelain," 150.

30 HAND-HELD TEAPOT, 1893–1914

Porcelain with molded and carved design and cream glaze
H. with lid 6 cm, w. with spout 9.5 cm, diam. 8.2 cm
2022.174

This teapot is of a variety used by advanced *sencha* practitioners. Called a *hōhin*, the pot is designed to be held directly by the fingers, with the body touching the upper part of the palm. This shape allows the host to manipulate the pot with a single hand and demonstrate dexterity. Direct contact between the ceramic body and the hand allows the host to closely gauge the temperature of the water within. There are differing grades of *sencha*, and for the finest one, *gyokuro*, the water temperature must be carefully regulated to achieve the proper flavor. This vessel is therefore efficacious for preparing this high-quality tea. The *hōhin* is also extremely portable, so it is well suited for impromptu gatherings. This pot's restrained design includes on the lid's handle a yin-yang motif, symbolizing the ideal balance between the forces of the universe. According to its box, it is an example of *taihakuji*.

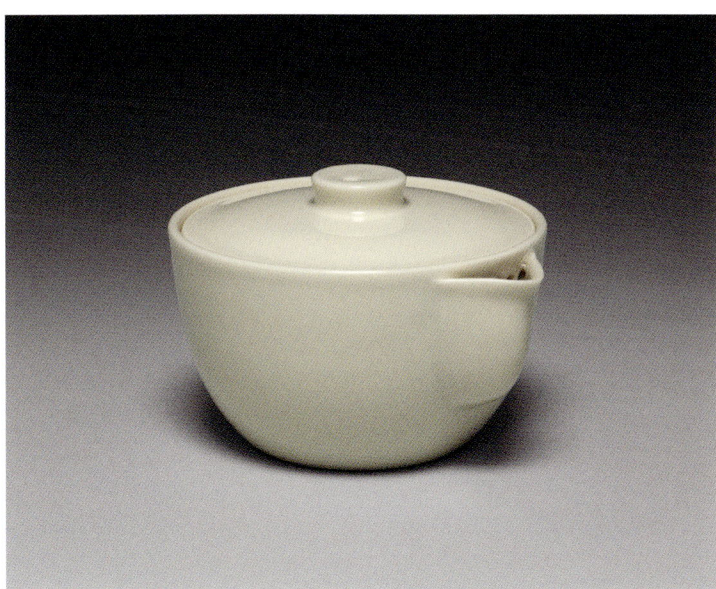

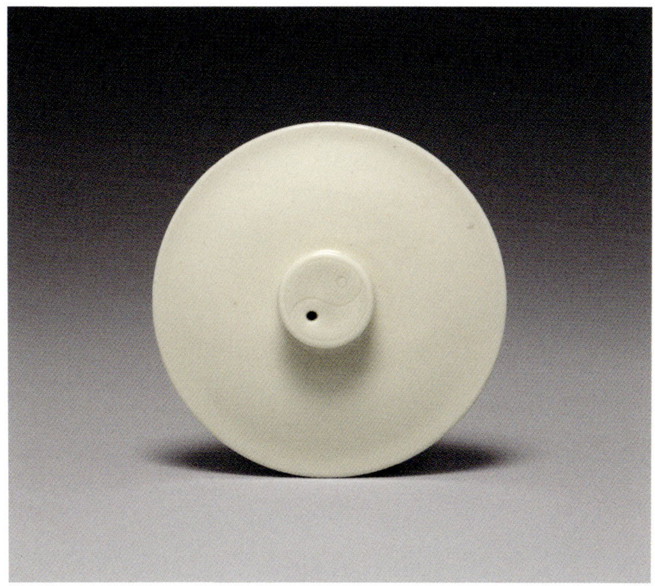

Detail of [31]. Daikokuten, standing upon two bales of rice.

31 BRAZIER WITH COINS MOTIF, 1893–1914

Stoneware with underglaze iron oxide designs and crackled glaze
H. 16.5 cm, diam. 15.5 cm
2022.175

Tall pottery braziers called *ryōro* are often used to heat the water for the tea served at *sencha* gatherings. This one sits on three sturdy legs, one of which bears the artist's seal on its face. A horizontal rectilinear opening above this leg allows air to circulate into the lower part of the brazier. The top part is outfitted with three prongs onto which the kettle can be lowered; below them is a basin, perforated with circular holes, that holds the charcoal fuel. The brazier is decorated under the crackled transparent glaze with a design of old coins in iron oxide. One coin is painted with the Japanese god of wealth, Daikokuten, standing upon two bales of rice. The motif is cleverly chosen, for most older coins are round with a central hole, often square, which echoes the cylindrical form of the brazier with its rectilinear "wind gate," or *fūmon*.

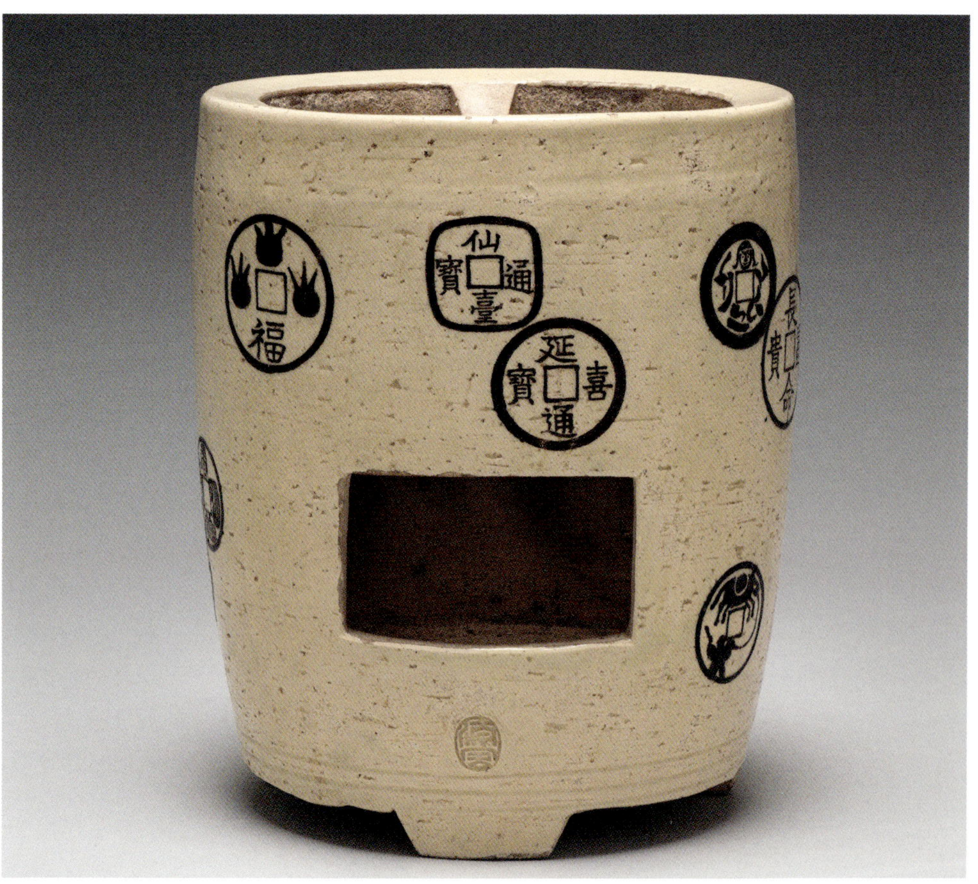

32 TEAPOT WITH *NYOI* STAFF-HEAD MOTIFS, 1893–1914

Porcelain with overlay decoration, cream glaze, and metal handles
H. 9.5 cm, w. with spout 13.5 cm, diam. 11.5 cm
2022.176

The simple, round form of this teapot is embellished with only a pair of *nyoi* staff-head motifs, one on each side. Two arched iron handles, parallel to each other, are hooked through holes in raised tabs at the front and back of the shoulders of the pot. The round lid is depressed so that an iron ring handle fastened with an iron clamp passing through the lid can lie flat inside the recessed area. The base of the pot has a "Seifū" seal. The box, however, is not original to the piece and has an inscription dated to 1960. The person who wrote it clearly admired Yohei III and his efforts to produce works that resembled Chinese ceramics. The inscription describes Yohei's journey to perfecting these copies but misidentified the Chinese kiln whose wares were the basis for this particular work.

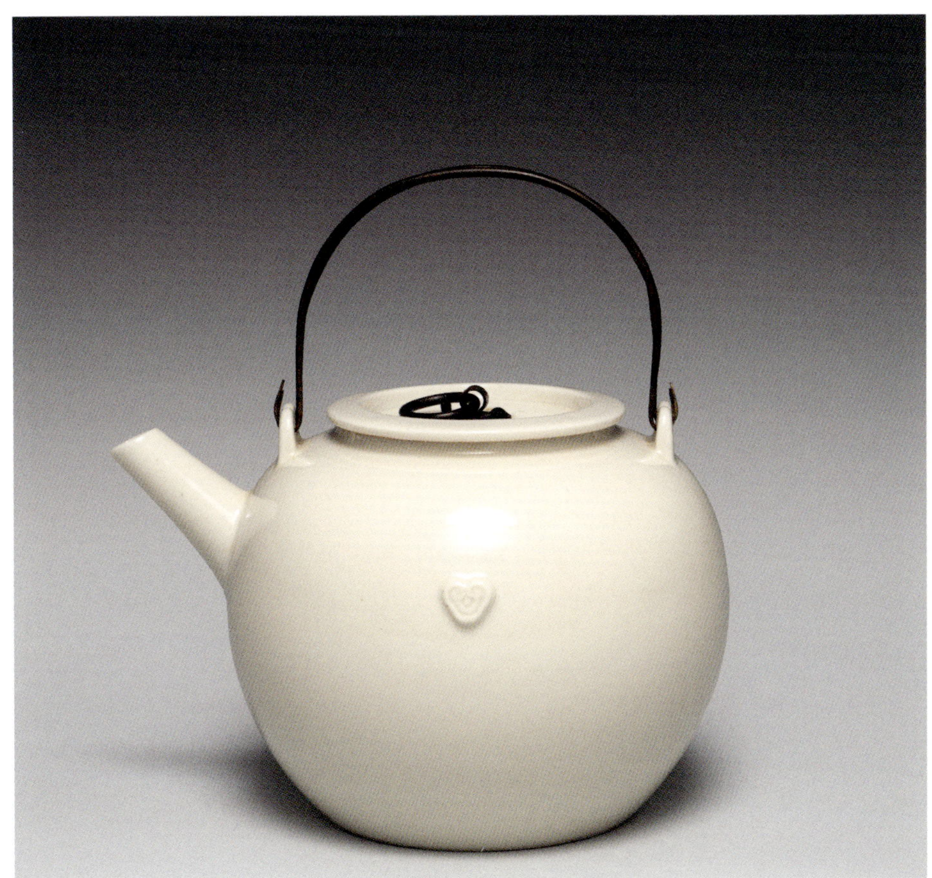

33 **INCENSE BURNER, 1895–1914**
Porcelain with molded design, tea leaf–colored glaze, and geometric openwork silver lid
H. with lid 14 cm, diam. 14.4 cm
2022.177

34 **INCENSE BURNER, 1893–97**
Porcelain with molded design, crimson glaze, and floral openwork silver lid
H. with lid 10.8 cm, diam. 11.4 cm
2022.178

35 **INCENSE BURNER, 1893–1914**
Porcelain with molded design, cream glaze, and floral openwork silver lid
H. with lid 11.4 cm, diam. 11 cm
2022.179

36 **INCENSE BURNER WITH FLOWERS AND DOTS, 1893–1914**
Porcelain with molded and incised design, cream glaze, and geometric openwork silver lid
H. with lid 8.5 cm, diam. 8.5 cm
2022.180

Yohei III made incense burners in a wide variety of designs and styles. Their silver lids were produced outside the studio by metalwork specialists. Each of these four burners is a tripod, but of two different basic shapes: two are globular and two, cylindrical. They vary further in the form of their legs, molded decorations, and glazes.

Two of the incense burners have distinctive colored glazes and linear molded decorations that run around the base of the collar and down the legs. The one with a variety of flowers on its lid has a glaze described as "crimson glaze" (*kōyū*); it is also dappled with dark spots of varied opacity and tiny pores throughout, which gives the container a rich, textured effect. The burner with a geometric-patterned silver lid has a glaze identified on its box lid as "tea leaf [color–glazed] porcelain" (*chayōji*).

The two cylindrical incense burners feature *taihakuji* body and glaze. The one with the floral-patterned silver lid has rounded, cabriole legs, resembling tiny table legs, attached to the exterior and the faintest decorative band around the bottom. The other, with a lid meant to look like a single flower, has tapering legs with a combined curvilinear and geometric design; the bands encircling the middle have simple, incised flower motifs alternating with single dots.

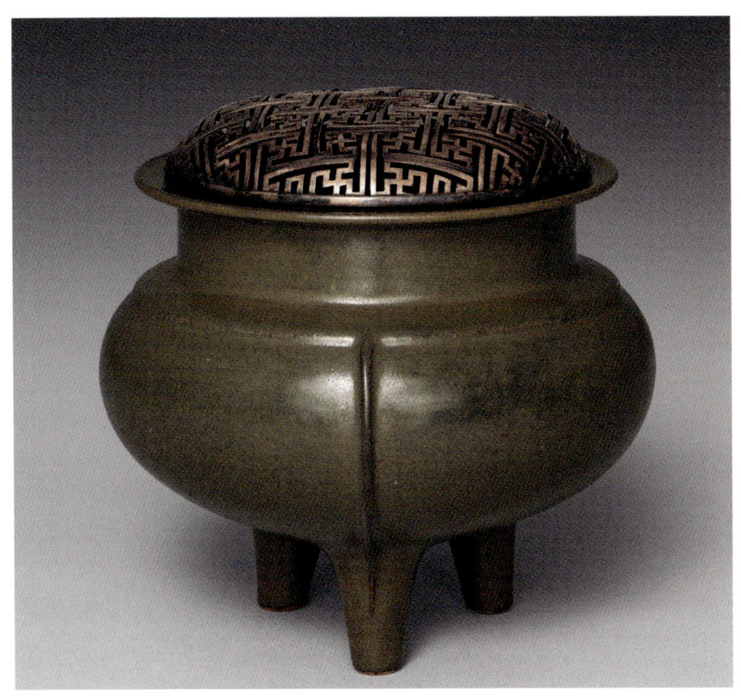

[33]

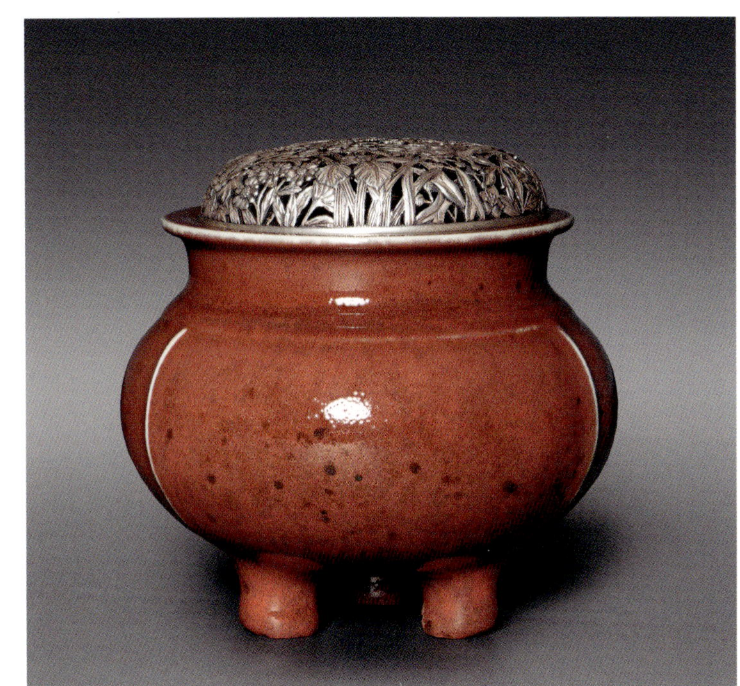

[34]

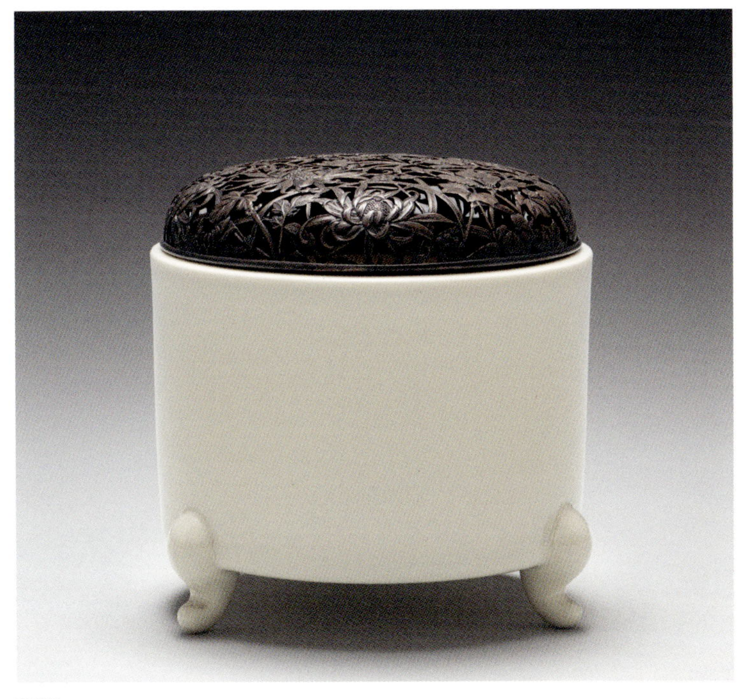

[35]

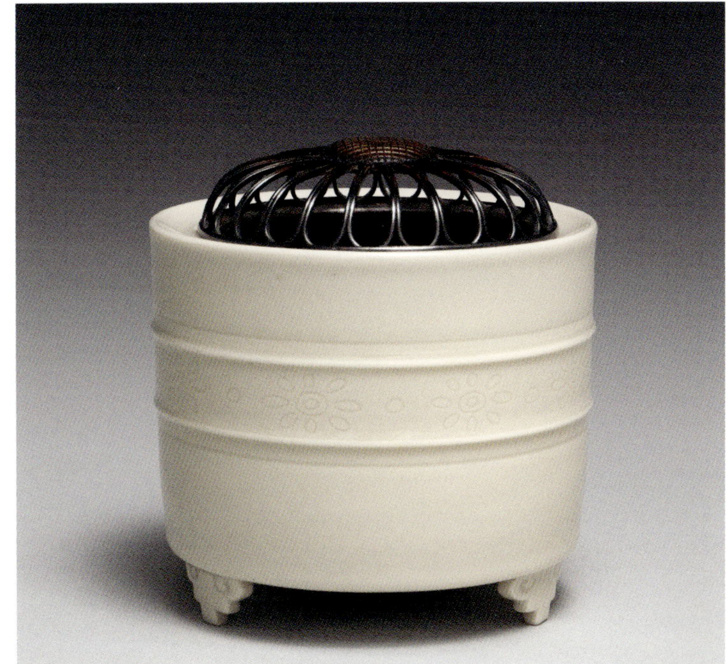

[36]

37 LIT CHARCOAL AND ASH CONTAINERS, 1893–1914

Set of two pairs of containers; porcelain with molded design and cream glaze
Each: h. 10 cm, diam. 12 cm
2022.181

The box lid for these six-lobed lit charcoal and ash containers, or *hiire*, identifies them as *kōhakuji*, another of Yohei III's translucent cream colors over ivory clay bodies. One might translate the name as "lustrous pearl[–glazed ivory] porcelain." A *hiire* was filled with ash with burnt coals at the center so that embers and tobacco ash could be discarded safely during a gathering. Each of the lobes on the containers has a round protrusion set below the rim. The stud-like pattern is called *ruiza*. The term is also used to describe the pattern that rings the shoulder of some flower vases or metal kettles used in *chanoyu*.

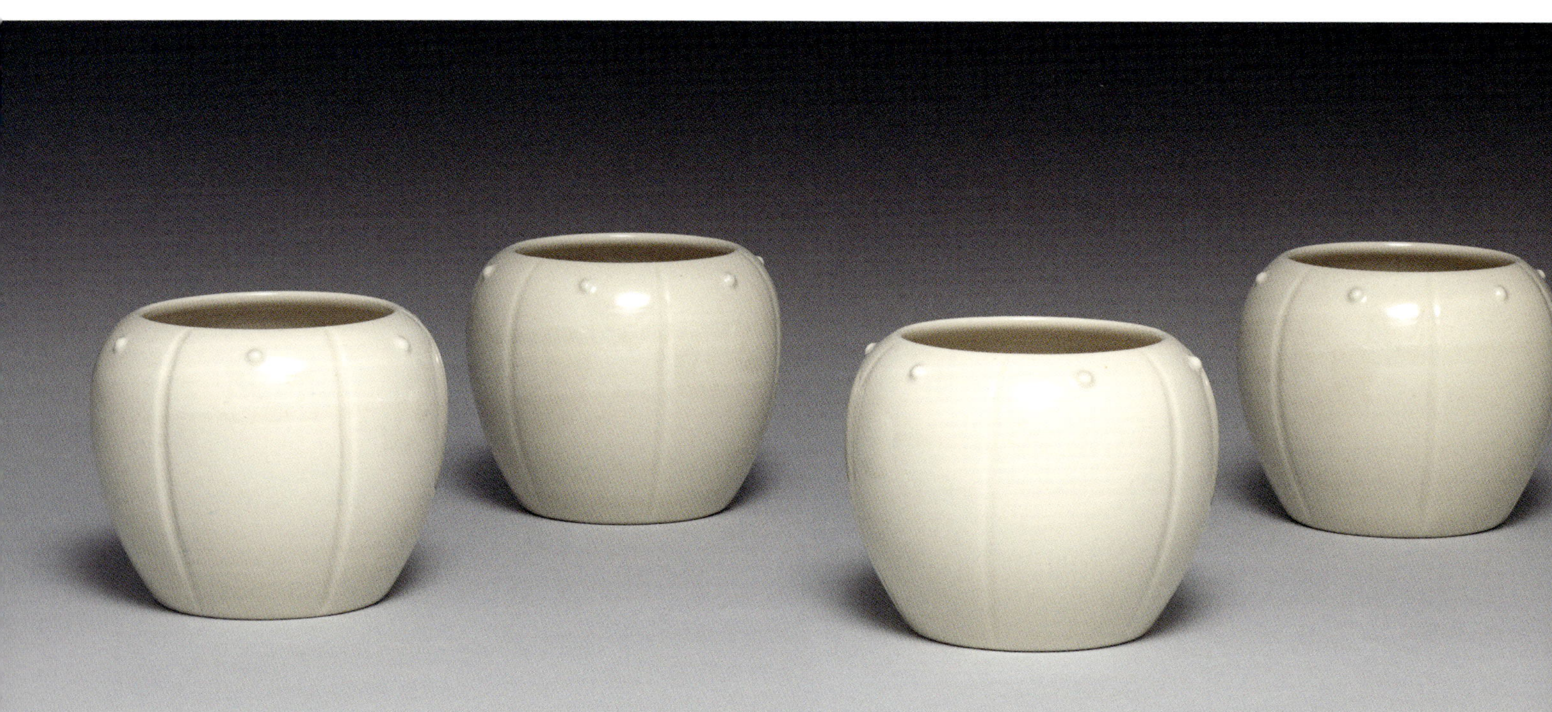

38 PINE-SHAPED DISH, 1893–1914

Stoneware with underglaze iron oxide and crackled glaze
H. 6 cm, l. 16.5 cm, w. 15.9 cm
2022.182

The clever design on this stoneware Awata-style dish makes use of the interior and exterior surfaces to present a close-up view of pine needles on the branch painted in underglaze iron oxide. The branch is shown on the outside of one side of the dish, while the needles fan out across the inside. The entire dish, when seen from above, reveals a shape resembling the mushroom cap–like motif appearing in textile designs and in classical Japanese paintings called Yamato-e to represent pine trees. Awata ware, named for the area of Kyoto where it was historically produced, is considered a subset of Kyoto ware. It is characterized by a very light brown body with a transparent crackled glaze.

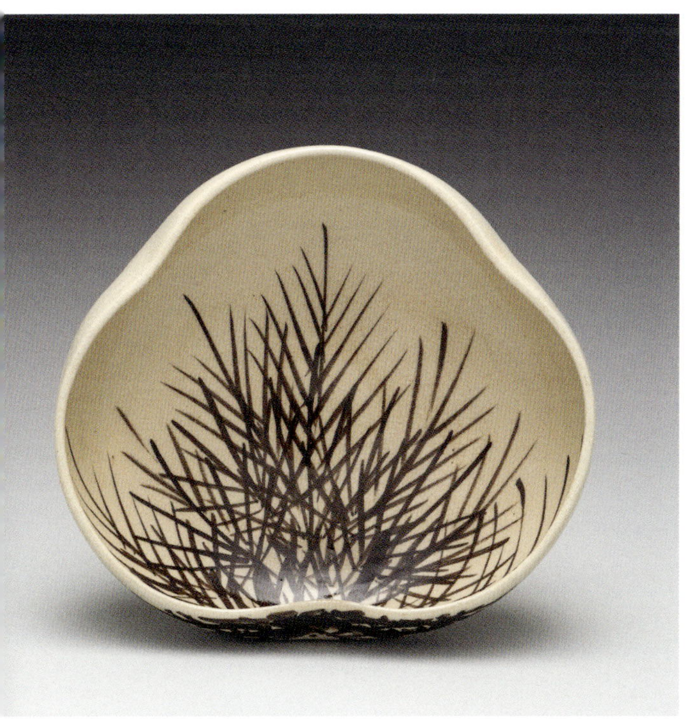

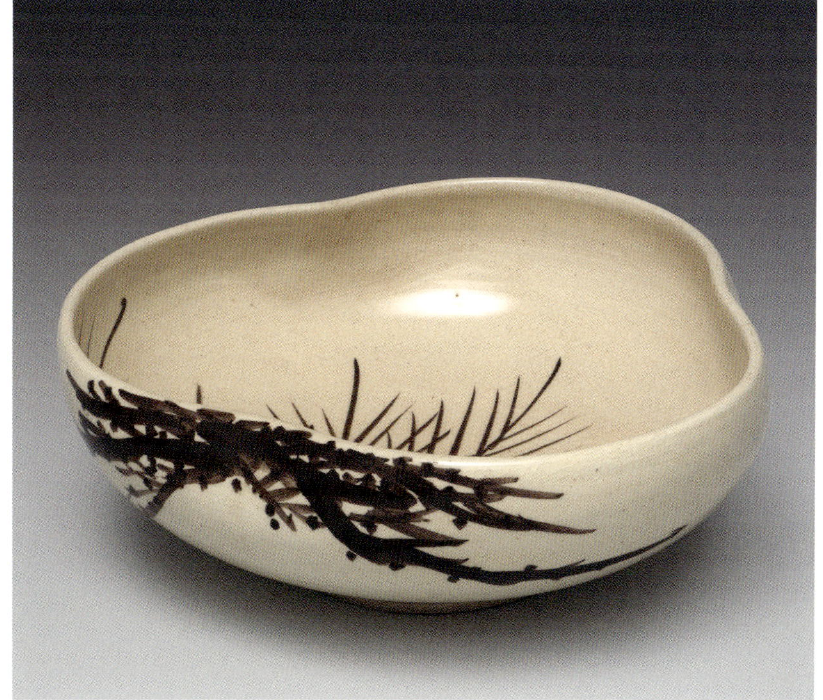

39 BOAT-SHAPED BOWL WITH PLOVERS, 1893–97

Stoneware with overglaze color enamel and crackled glaze
H. 5 cm, l. 17 cm, w. 8.5 cm
2022.183

Overglaze color enamels create an ocean-scape made complete by the bowl's boat shape. The bowl's form inserts a human presence into the scene, much in the way *rusu mōyō* is used in paintings to suggest people just out of view. *Rusu mōyō* is a pictorial device by which the presence of someone physically absent from an image is conveyed through the depiction of clothing or other items. The inside of the bowl has a scene of plovers flying through the sky over a profusion of seaweed in sand below. In addition to the black, gray, and green of the overglaze elements, warm pink banding and mottling in the clay come through the glaze and are remarkably effective at suggesting the seashore. On the outside of the bowl, on each side, birds fly about grasses in search of a meal.

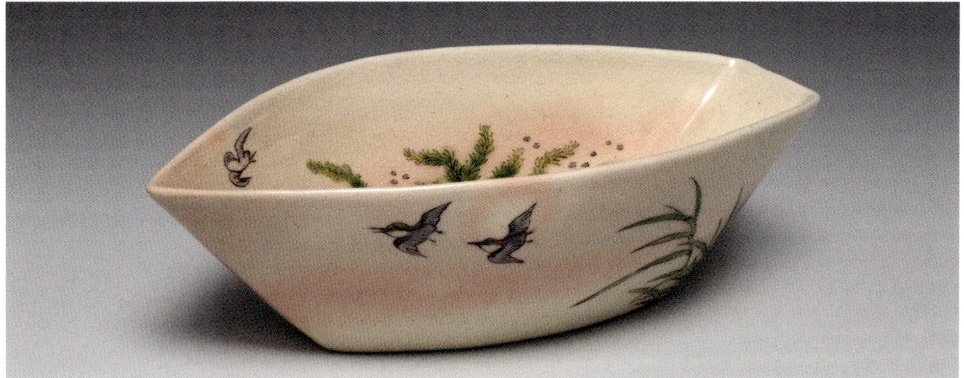

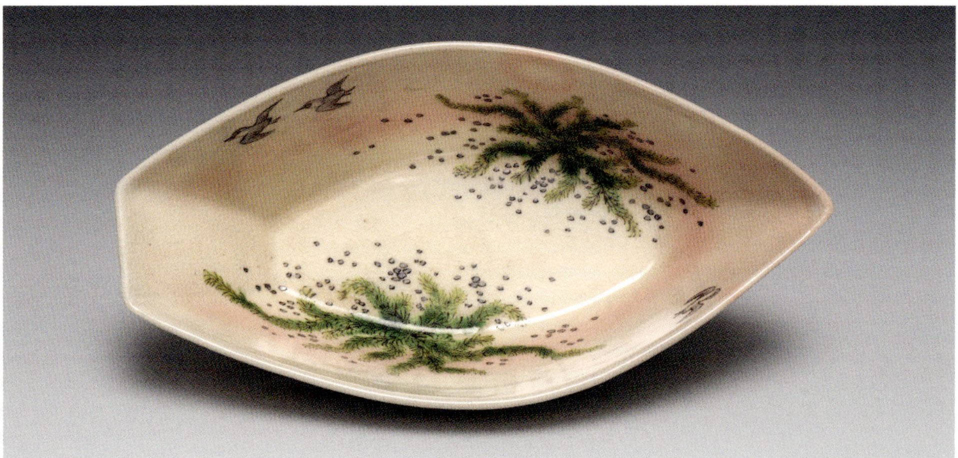

40 TEABOWL WITH PINKS, 1893–1914

Stoneware with overglaze color enamel, gold, and crackled glaze
H. 7.5 cm, diam. 11 cm
2022.184

This teabowl, for use in *chanoyu*, is a good example of Yohei III's mastery of the techniques involved in producing Kyoto ware. The painting of the pinks, with their blue centers, bright red petals, and green leaves, is carefully controlled with crisp gold borders throughout. There is crackling in the transparent glaze and obvious, thick dripping of the milky glaze over the outside of the mouth of the bowl. The pink spots would have appeared in the clay during firing, and the bottom of the inside of the bowl is entirely pink. A triangular wedge has been cut away from the foot, and a gently impressed band rings the bowl beneath the rim. The vessel comes with a bespoke brocade pouch with a silk fastening cord, as is customary for Japanese teabowls.

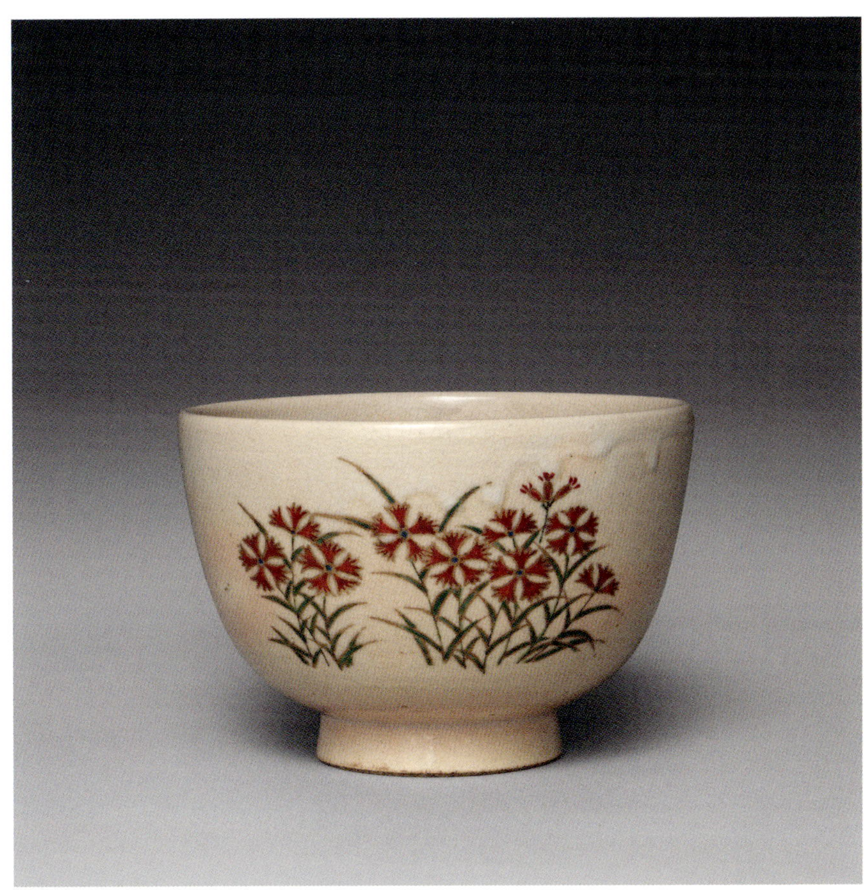

41 NESTING BOWLS WITH DAOIST IMMORTALS, 1893–1914

Set of three bowls; porcelain with underglaze blue
Inner bowl: h. 8.5 cm, diam. 20.2 cm; middle bowl: h. 9.6 cm, diam. 22.3 cm; outer bowl: h. 9.9 cm, diam. 23.9 cm
2022.185

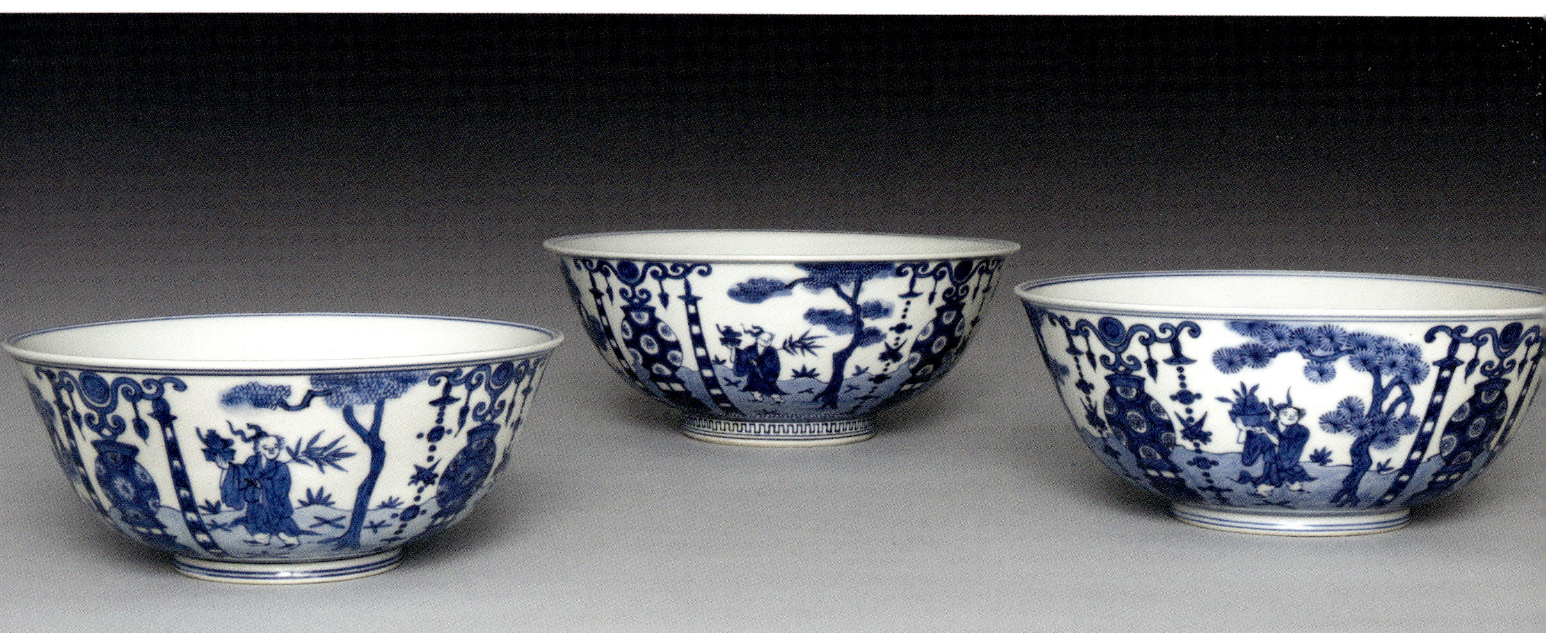

Yohei III was capable of ink painting–like compositions in underglaze blue, as well as more decorative ones like that on this set of three nesting bowls. Bowls with very similar designs in five colors were produced in the reign of the Wanli emperor (r. 1572–1620) during the Ming dynasty, and Yohei must have had direct access to one of these or to a close copy.[1]

A scene of Daoist immortals is presented on the bowls. On each one, the ground plane is defined with a blue wash. Four lanterns are evenly spaced around the bowl. Two are flanked with linked-piece metalwork banners of the seven treasures. The alternate altars are adorned with textile banners. In between them are four immortals, each standing beneath a tree with small plants surrounding his feet. Two of the immortals hold fruit on a tray. Another carries an elixir-filled ewer and a willow branch. The fourth holds a swastika (*manji*), here an auspicious symbol, and a flower. In the bottom of each bowl is a scene of two robed immortals who appear to stand on a precipice in a mountainous landscape high in the clouds, with celestial orbs over their heads. Curiously, the inscription inside each footring reads "Made by Seifū of Great Japan," in emulation

1. For a similar example, see Bonhams, "Fine Chinese Art."

of the dynasty and reign inscriptions that appear on Chinese ceramics; but one can also see through the translucent glaze another inscription, "Seifū Yohei," written in large characters within a double band of blue on the largest bowl.

A large bowl by Yohei III in a private collection features a related theme, one of the Seven Gods of Good Fortune, a distinctively Japanese configuration of supernatural figures of disparate origins, some South Asian, some Chinese, and others local (fig. 40a). It is embellished with images of the seven treasures in a translucent orange band near the base (fig. 40c), while the trees are emblazoned with gold. The interior features fish motifs in orange, gold, and green (fig. 40b). The detailed design and color scheme in combination with the strong composition on the bowl invite sustained enjoyment of the scene.

Detail of [41]

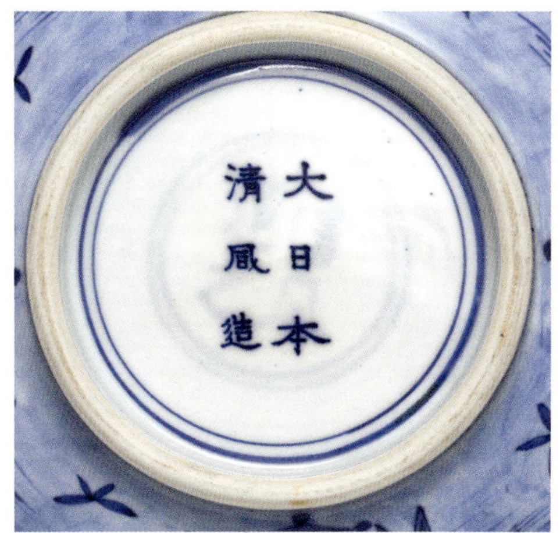

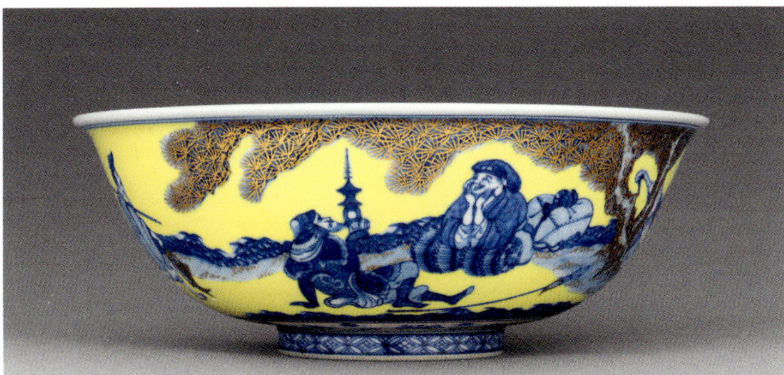

Figure 40a

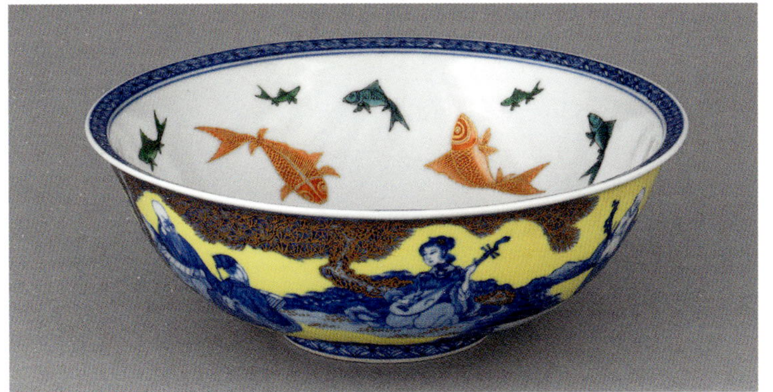

Figure 40b

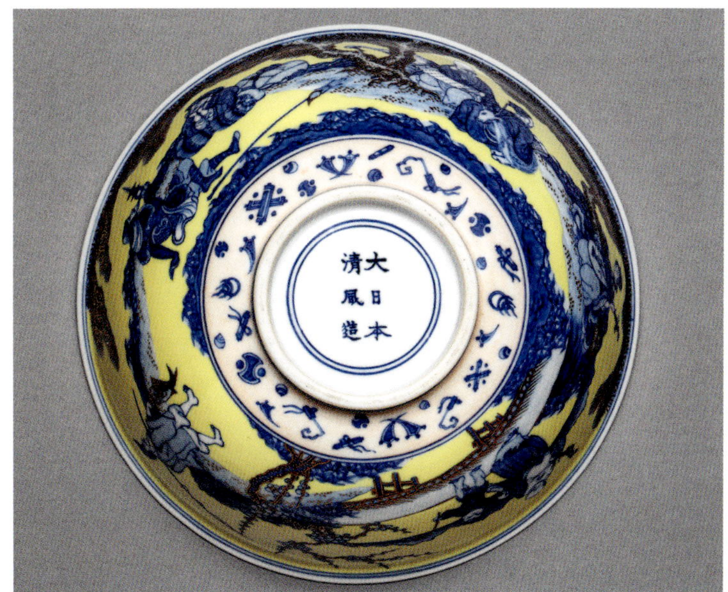

Figure 40c

Figure 40a–c. *Bowl with the Seven Gods of Good Fortune*, 1893–1914. Seifū Yohei III. Porcelain with underglaze and overglaze colors and gold; h. 6.5 cm, diam. 19.3 cm. Hermann Ferré Collection. Photos: © Bruce M. White, 2022

42 TEABOWLS WITH PEONY AND PLUM, 1893–1914

Set of five teabowls; porcelain with underglaze color, overglaze color enamel, and gold

Each: h. 5 cm, diam. 8 cm

2022.186

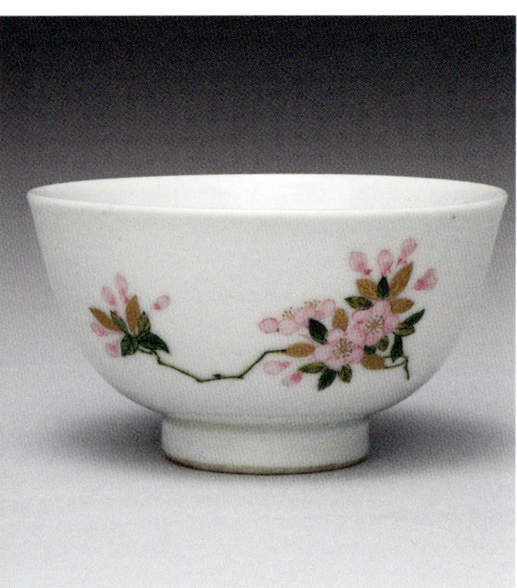

Other side of [42]

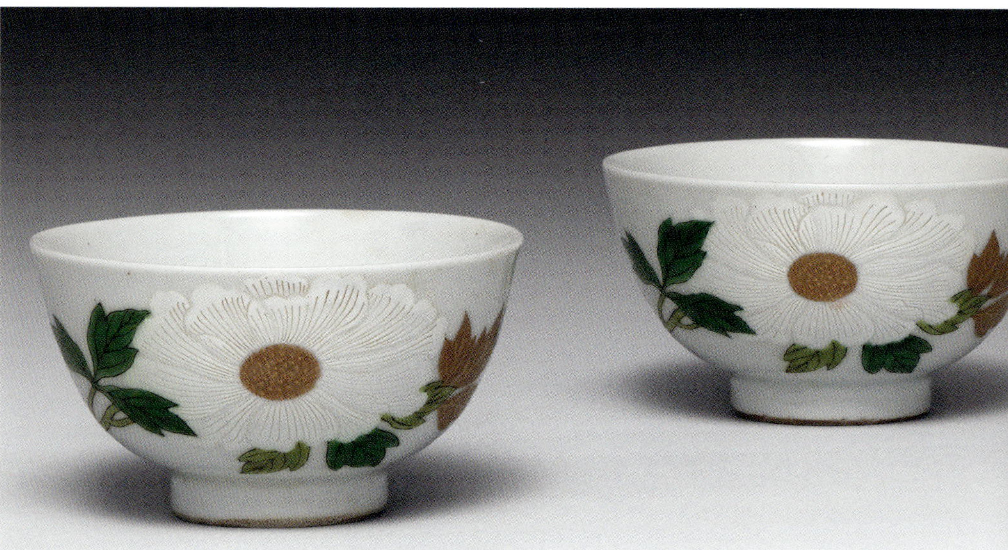

Overglaze color enamels are generally called *iro-e* (literally "color picture") in the terminology customarily used for Edo-period porcelain decoration. This set of teabowls is a fine example of Yohei III's skilled use of the technique, which is identified on this set's box lid with the alternate phrasing "porcelain with color painting" (*jisaiga*). Distinct from the way overglaze colors were used in Kakiemon ware from Arita, his designs and applications show a consciousness of Qing-dynasty porcelain decoration. Here, he combines Chinese models with a sensibility taken from Kyoto ware precedents, including painting with powdered gold (*kinrande*).[1] The colors used in the bowls are as follows: blue, black, gold, white, light green, green, and pink. The blue appears only inside the footring, as a double band of underglaze color. The black iron, used for stems and leaf veins, is painted over the glaze. The gold, also painted over the glaze, is used for leaves and the centers of flowers, for solid, glossy lines defining detail, or as a semimatte ground. The white of the peony flower is built up to a low relief over the glaze. Yohei has incised lines of varying widths into the pigment, carving away to the bowl's surface, to differentiate individual petals and their rippled shapes. The light and dark greens, as well as the pink, are painted over the glaze. Of note

1. *Kinrande* can also refer to the application of gold leaf, a more challenging technique.

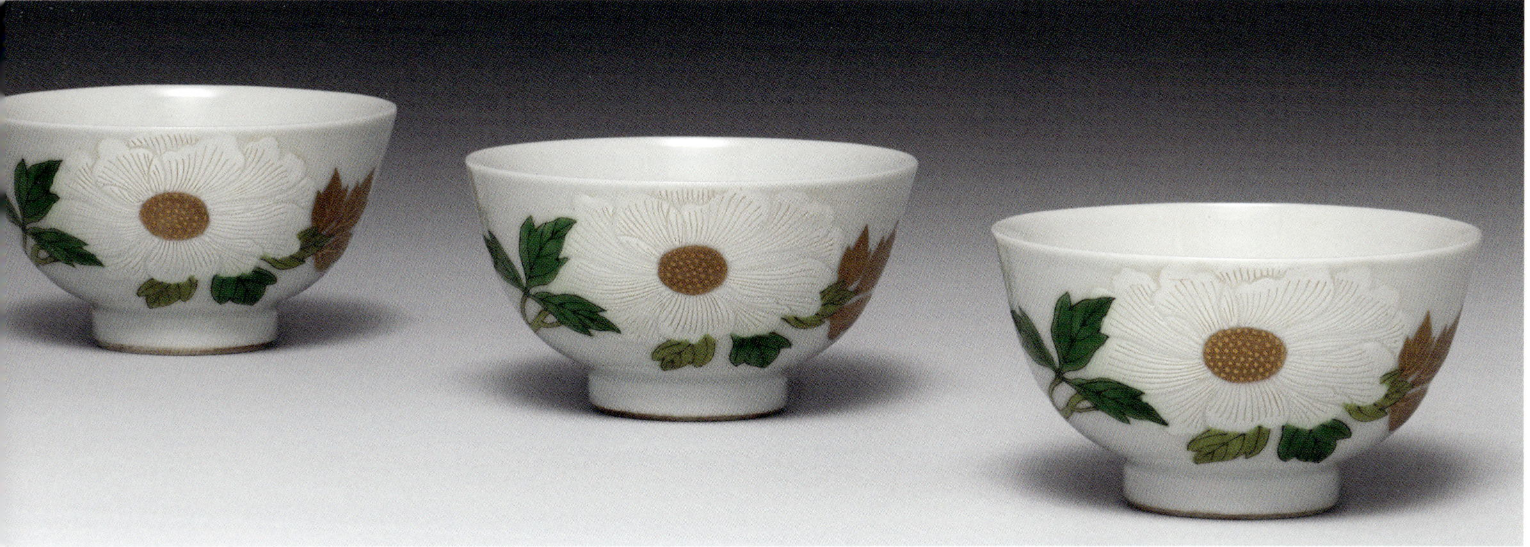

is how Yohei has first used thinly applied lines of light green to draw the plum branch before applying the opaque iron black. For the plum buds and flowers, he has used a diluted pink with an opaque pink for outline, both over the glaze. In his later works, Yohei used pink both over and under the glaze in a manner similar to underglaze blue, and it can be challenging in some cases to discern which technique he has used.

A lidded container in a private collection has a similar design but is augmented with the inclusion of white and purple magnolia blossoms (fig. 41). In contemplating the original decorative program of a set, of which these teabowls may have been a part, it is worth considering that perhaps not all objects included the full range of motifs. In such cases, the composition of the individual object may be best understood within the context of the extended ensemble. Here, the delicate pink plum on one side of the bowl seems slightly unbalanced with the bold white peony on the other, but when seen with other objects with the magnolia and its additional colors and shapes, it is possible to imagine a set with a complex, balanced design across multiple pieces.

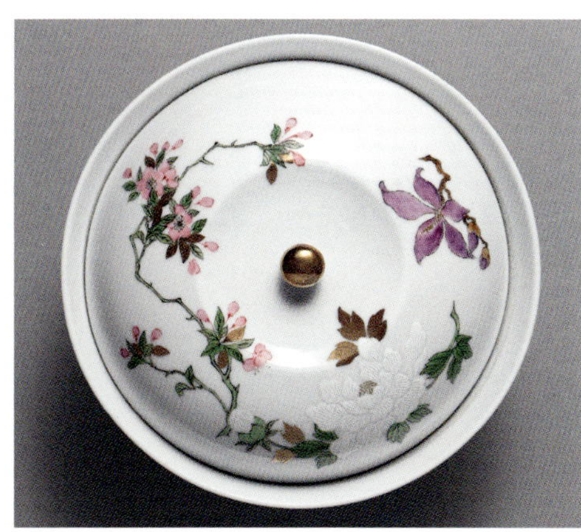

Figure 41. *Lidded Bowl with Peony, Plum, and Magnolia*, 1893–1914. Seifū Yohei III. Porcelain with overglaze color enamel, gold, and incised designs; h. 8.3 cm, diam. 13.5 cm. Hermann Ferré Collection. Photo: © Bruce M. White, 2022

43 **SAUCERS, 1893–1914**
Set of ten saucers; porcelain with green glaze
Each: h. 2.5 cm, diam. 8 cm
2022.187

44 **SAUCERS WITH MATCHING SHELLS, 1893–1914**
Set of five saucers; porcelain with molded designs and green crackled glaze
Each: h. 3 cm, w. 12 cm, d. 8.5 cm
2022.188

45 **SAUCERS WITH MATCHING SHELLS, 1893–1914**
Pair of saucers; porcelain with molded designs and green crackled glaze
Each: h. 3 cm, w. 12 cm
2022.189

46 **DISHES WITH IVY, 1893–1914**
Set of five dishes; porcelain with molded designs and green glaze
Each: h. 3.5 cm, diam. 11 cm
2022.190

Yohei III's main output for his sophisticated clientele was in the form of tea sets and dining sets. The dishes here show a range of his designs in green glazes. He often produced in pairs, sets of five, or sets of ten. For the set of ten small dishes in a simple, round form that emphasizes the glaze above all [43], the box lid designates the piece as *seiji*, or green-glazed porcelain, using a general term for the extensive palette of green glazes often called celadon in English. The box lid

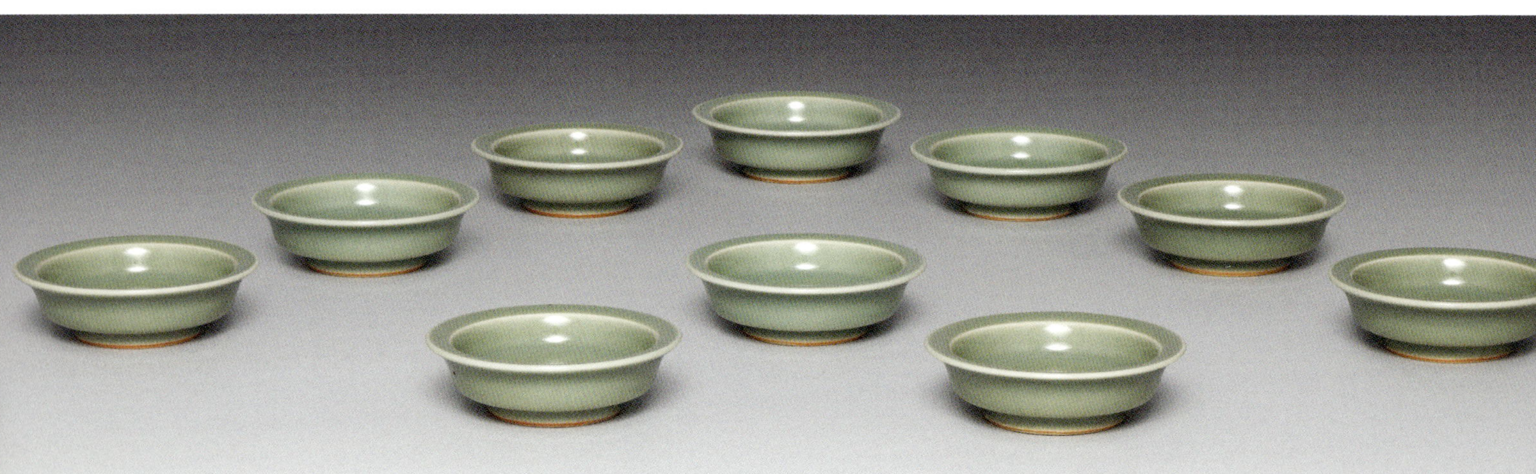

[43]

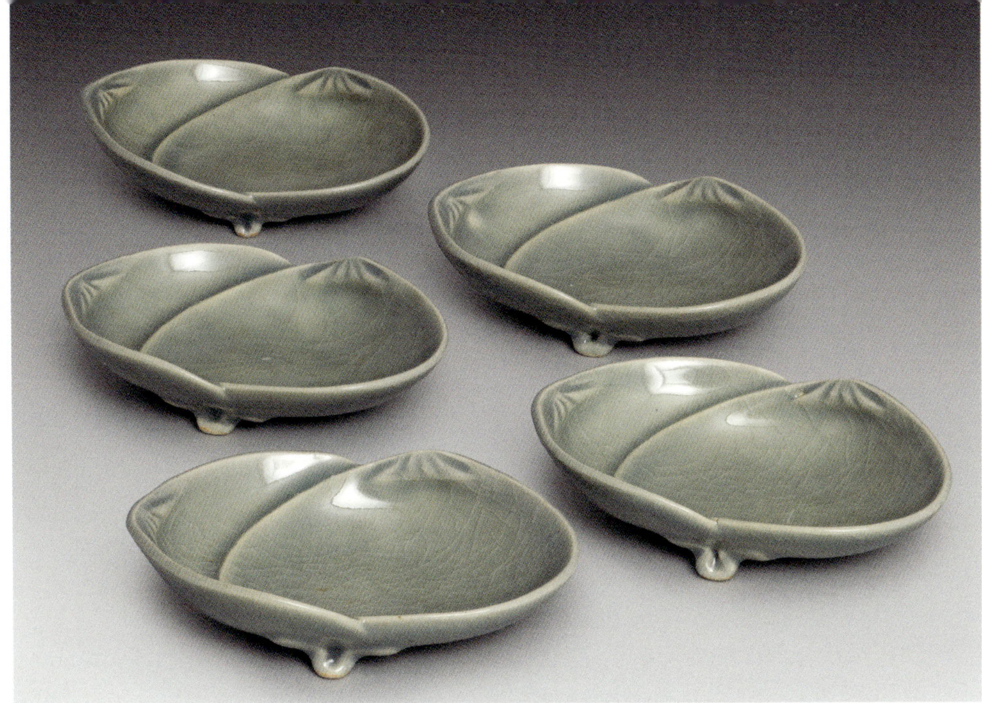

[44]

further identifies the dishes themselves as *tōchō*, literally "bean-sized saucers," a size that makes them suitable for dipping sauces. The set of five dishes with a more complex form is described as having a "water-colored glaze" (*mizuiroyū*) [44]. These are shaped like clam half shells, a reference to a game in which shell halves painted with narrative scenes or a variety of motifs must be matched back together by the players. The dishes have molded details to articulate the

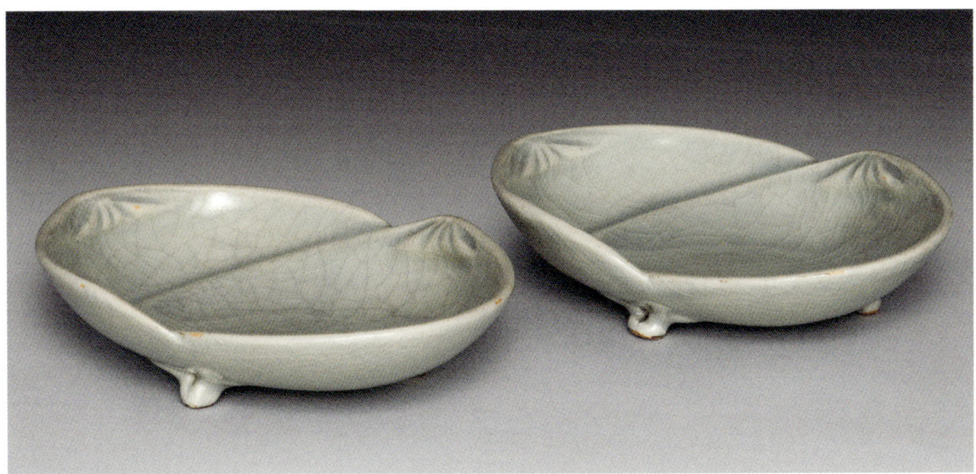

[45]

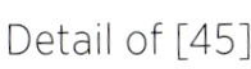

Detail of [45]

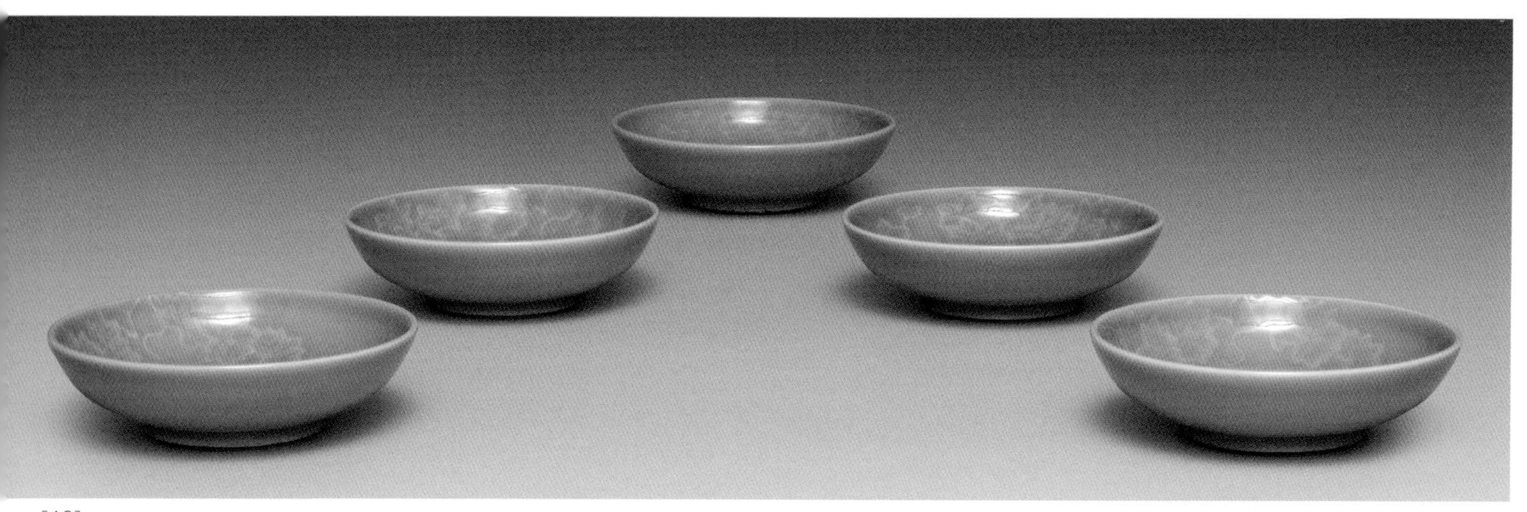

[46]

shell forms, and the crackling across each shell adds another dimension to the surface. Each dish is set on three small feet, formed by a pinched piece of clay and attached to an unglazed area on the underside of the dish. Curiously, while four of the dishes are stamped with the artist's mark, one has instead a signature carved into the base. Unlike the set of ten dishes, which are stored in stacks of five in a two-compartment box, each of the paired-shell dishes has its own compartment in a long, flat box. Yohei III also made shell dishes in pairs, like the one here [45], which has a box lid interior attestation by Yohei IV that the dishes were made by Yohei III with a cracked-ice (*hyōretsu*) pattern in the glaze, omitting reference to any glaze coloration. Like the set of bean-shaped saucers, both sets of shell dishes are also of the saucer type. The set of five dishes with a green glaze and designs of ivy vines in very low relief has unfortunately lost its box [46]. These dishes are slightly larger than the other dishes here and so may have been not saucers but rather small plates for meals.

47 MAPLE LEAF–SHAPED SAUCERS, 1893–1914

Set of five saucers; porcelain with molded design and blue glaze
Each: h. 2.5 cm, diam. 9 cm
2022.191

Like the five shell saucers in the previous entry, these maple leaf–shaped saucers have a long, horizontal box with a separate compartment for each piece. Now a set of five, these dishes were originally a set of ten, stored in two boxes of five each. From their housings, which accommodate differing numbers of objects, one can hypothesize that while some items created by the Seifū studio were intended to be acquired in larger sets, and thus were perhaps made to order, others, like the shells and the leaves, may have been items to be purchased off the shelf in set quantities that allowed clients flexibility in scale. The box for these five saucers describes them as "heavenly blue[–glazed] porcelain" (*tenseiji*). The veins of the leaves are slightly raised in the clay so that the glaze pools around them and they stand out as white where the glaze thins. There are longer lines at the points of the leaves and shorter ones following the wall of each indentation so that the design has both a horizontal and a subtle vertical dimension. Each saucer has a round foot.

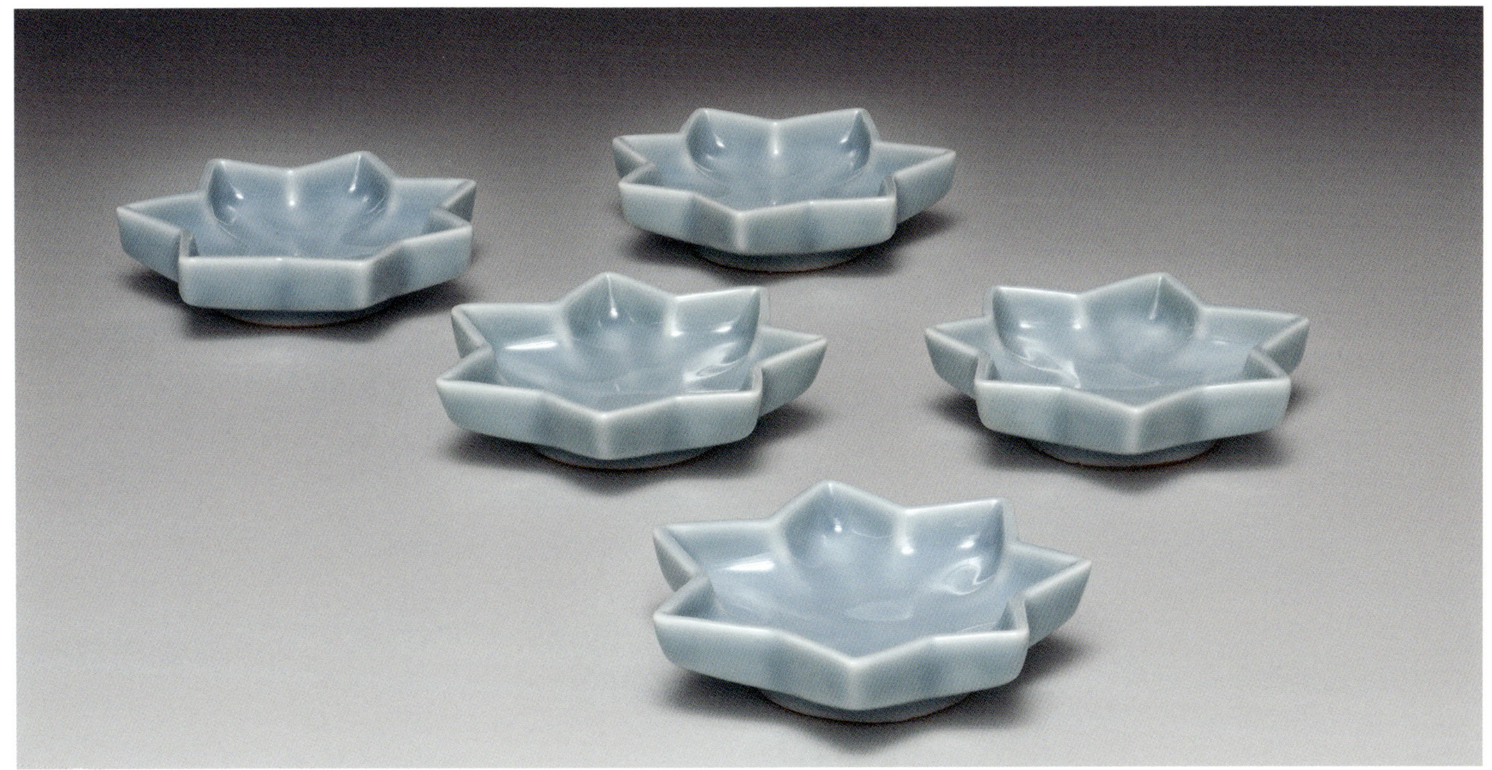

48 FLOWER VASE WITH FLORAL SCROLL, 1893–1914

Porcelain with underglaze color and green glaze
H. 24.5, diam. 12 cm
2022.192

The upper part of this vase is painted in underglaze blue with a floral scroll of leaves accentuated with a single chrysanthemum motif on each face and bound at top and bottom with single blue lines. The center of each chrysanthemum has a crescent-shaped design at the top filled with a very pale yellow wash under the transparent glaze. The box lid for the vase is short on detail; the inscription notes only that it is a flower vase with underglaze blue. It is possible that the box is a mismatch because the inscription does not mention the vase's more distinctive feature: the deep green glaze on its lower half, which is seen much less frequently among Yohei III's works. This glaze may be an example of a dark green porcelain glaze called *rōkanji*, which the artist invented in 1892. Maezaki conjectures that it may be present on a piece in the Museum of Fine Arts, Boston.[1] The piece in Boston is a bowl entirely in green and may be made of stoneware. It has a base mark Yohei III often uses on his stoneware objects. The name of the glaze comes from Chinese, in which it is pronounced *langgan*. It may literally mean "tinkling sound of jade" and could refer to malachite, among other proposed identifications.

A vase of the same shape in a private collection has an all-over pattern of the floral design in underglaze blue (fig. 42). The crescent shape is dark, matching the blue of the petals, while the remainder of the flowers' center is accented with a bright blue hue.

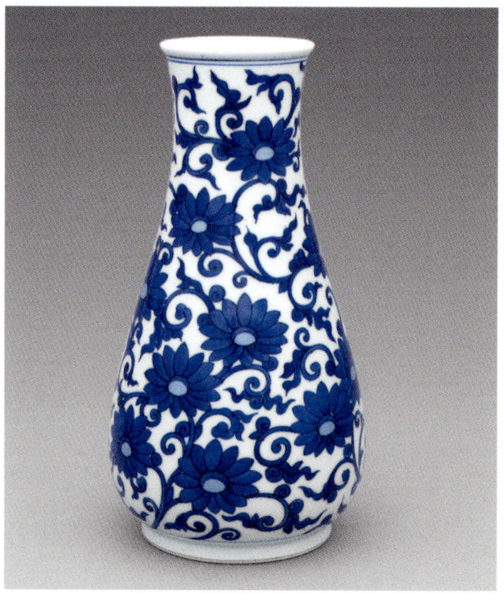

Figure 42. *Flower Vase with Floral Scroll*, 1893–1914. Seifū Yohei III. Porcelain with underglaze color; h. 25.5 cm, diam. 12 cm. Hermann Ferré Collection. Photo: © Bruce M. White, 2022

1. Maezaki, "Qing-Style Porcelain," 64.

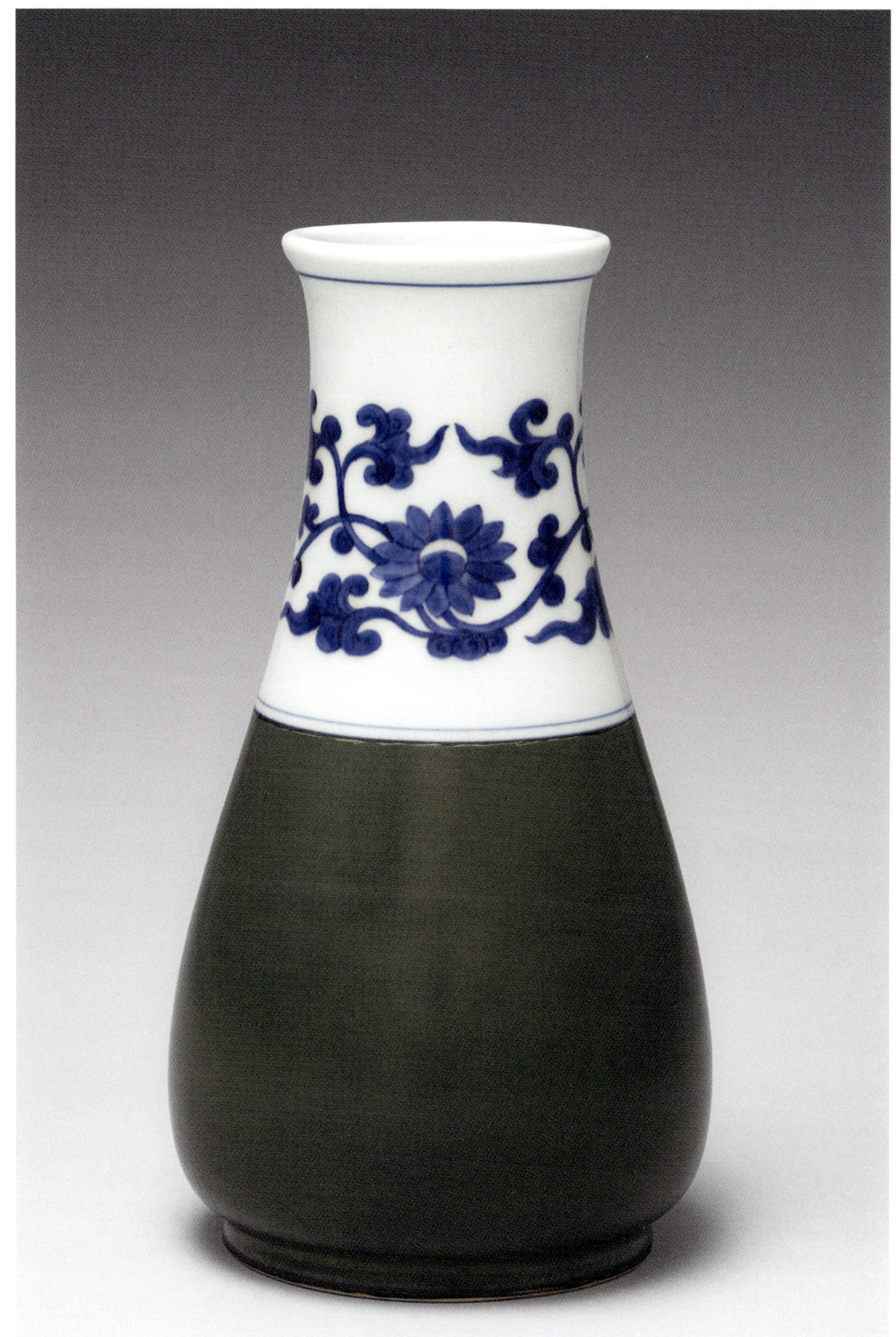

49 INCENSE BURNER, 1893–1914

Porcelain with coral red and crackled glaze
h. 5.3 cm, diam. 9.1 cm
2022.193

The tiniest of containers, this ovoid tripod is an incense burner. It likely once had an openwork metal lid. It is remarkable for its coral red color and crackled glaze. In contrast to the exterior, the interior has been left white under a transparent glaze. The "coral red glaze" is one Yohei III developed in 1887 and called *sangōyu*. Sensational among colors known at that time, Yohei III won first prize for his work glazed with it at the annual exhibition of the Japan Art Association (Bijutsu Kyōkai) in 1888.[1]

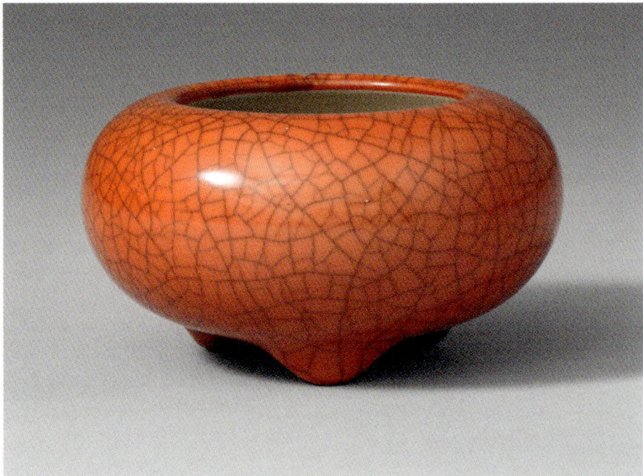

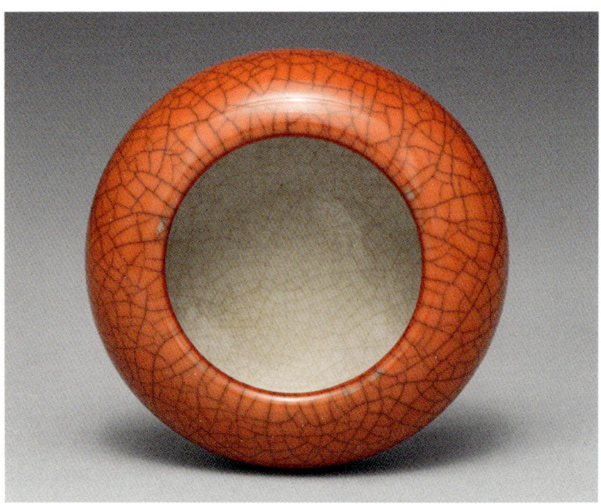

1. Maezaki, "Qing-Style Porcelain," 59.

50 SNOWFLAKE SIDE DISHES, 1893–1914

Set of six dishes; porcelain with lobed rims with underglaze iron oxide and pink glaze
Each: h. 5 cm, diam. 13.5 cm
2022.194

According to the box lid, this set of six side dishes, or *mukōzuke*, are "snow-flower style" (*sekkashiki*), having mouths shaped like snowflakes. Their mouths, which have six lobes and scalloped edges, are traced with brown iron oxide at the rim. The outside of each bowl is glazed with a very bright pink over the basin and foot, and the inside is left white. From directly above, one sees a snowflake-like shape, and from the side, they seem to float above a rosy ground. Their box has an inscription on the side noting that they were for a person with the family name Nakamoto.

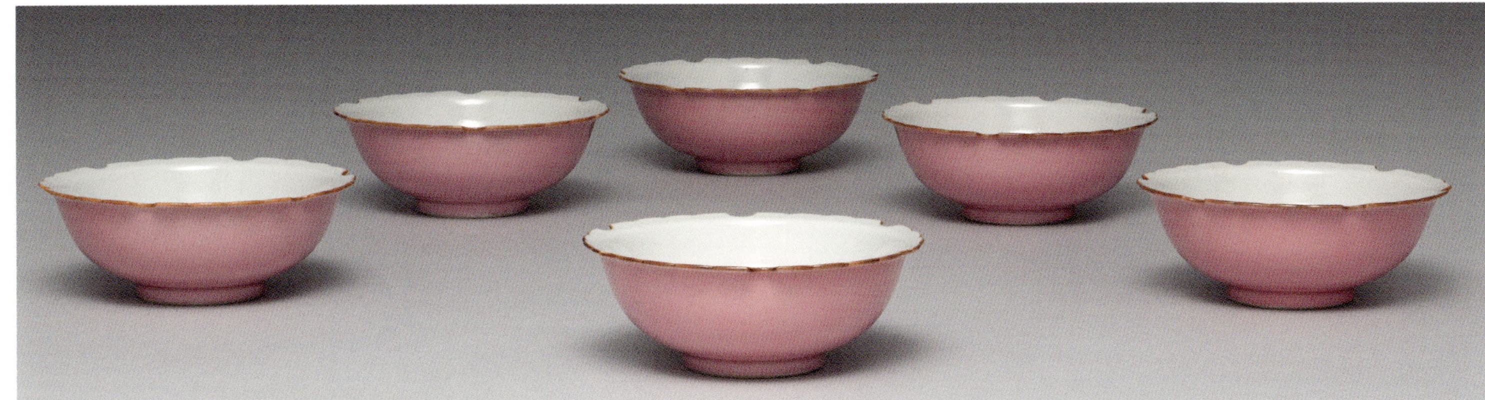

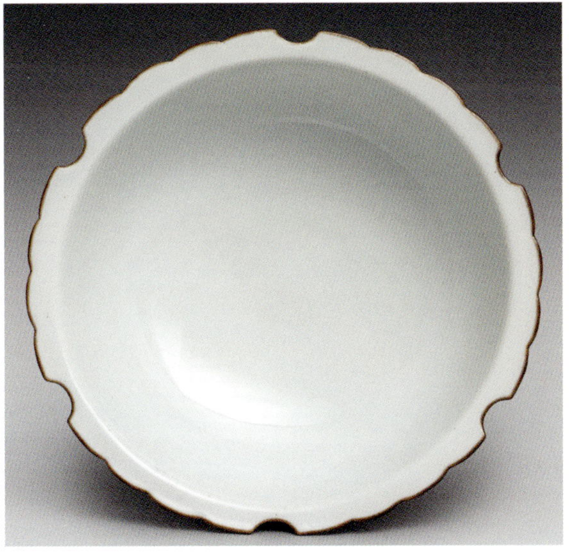

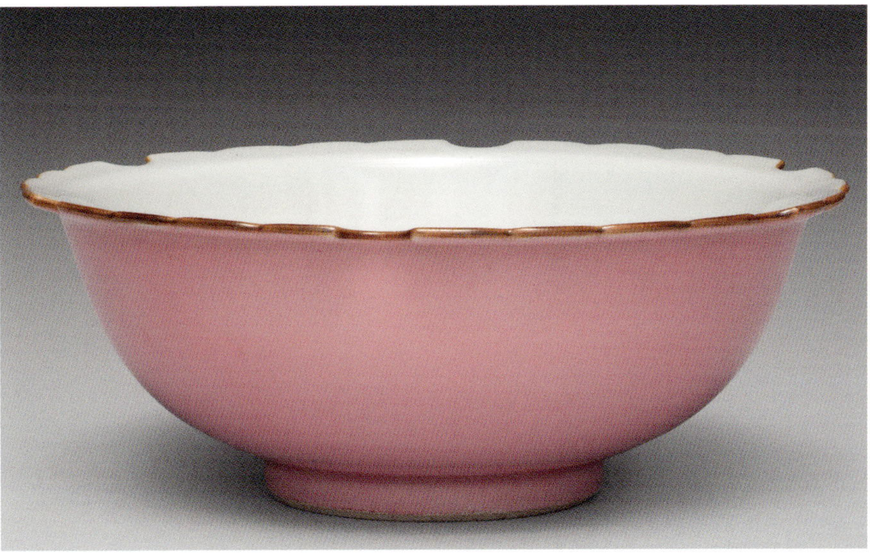

51 SWEETS BOWL, 1893–1914

Porcelain with yellow glaze
H. 4.5 cm, diam. 21 cm
2022.195

The simply elegant shape of this sweets bowl allows one to fully appreciate its yellow glaze. Like Yohei III's other monochrome, undecorated pieces, this one emulates Chinese prototypes. The box lid identifies the work's coloration with an unusual name, *hongama kōtekiji*. *Hongama* means "high-fired," and the inventive phrasing *kōteki* may mean something akin to "lustrous yellow." Although not represented in the Heusinger Collection, one striking series of works by Yohei III features insects in flora done in a limited palette of black, green, and white against a strong yellow background. One example of this decorative scheme in a private collection is an ovoid vase with a dragonfly hovering above white flowers on one side (fig. 43) and a grasshopper and butterfly on the other (not pictured).

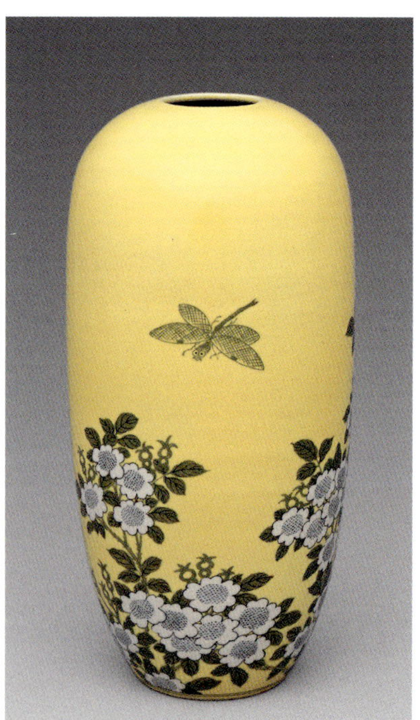

Figure 43. *Vase with Flowers and Insects*, 1893–1914. Seifū Yohei III. Stoneware with yellow glaze and overglaze color enamel; h. 30.5 cm, diam. 12 cm. Hermann Ferré Collection. Photo: © Bruce M. White, 2022

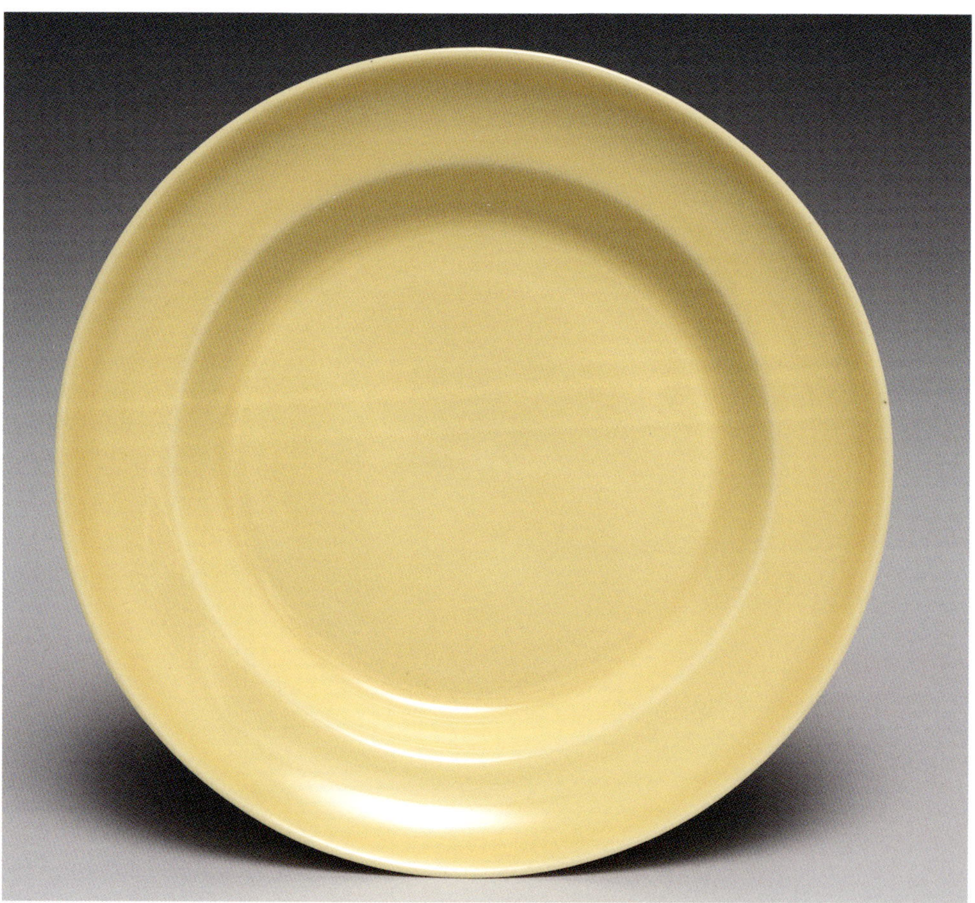

52 LONG-NECKED VASE, 1893–97

Stoneware with crackled glaze
H. 30 cm, diam. 15.5 cm
2022.196

The glazing of this long, narrow-necked and bulbous-based vase has a network of shallow cracks, created when the glaze fractured as it cooled from firing. It is called a cracked-ice pattern or glaze, since the effect resembles the surface of a frozen lake. The cracks here are of a consistently high density throughout the vessel. This pattern is observed also in the transparent glaze of some Kyoto ware, in some of Yohei III's green glazes, and in some of his vessels emulating Chinese forms. The interior of the box lid has an attestation to its authenticity by Yohei IV, and the footring is inscribed Seifū of Great Japan (Dai Nihon Seifū) in iron black.

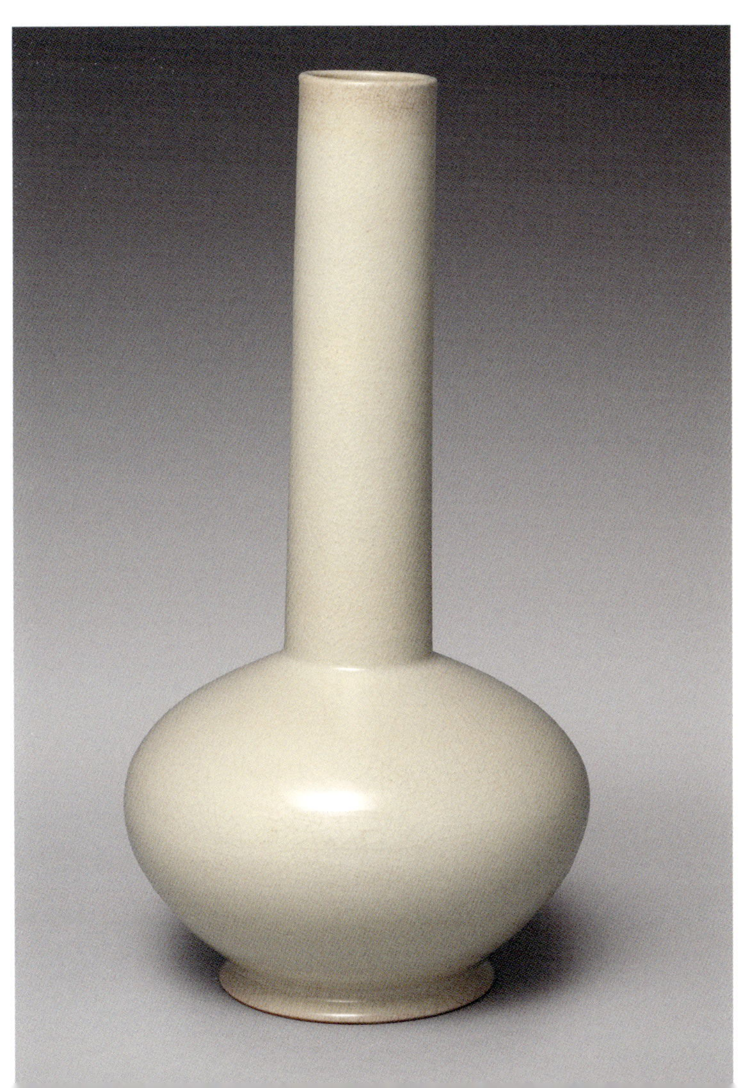

53 WATER CONTAINER WITH PEONIES, 1900–14

Porcelain with molded and carved design and green glaze and lacquered wood lid
H. with lid 17.8 cm, diam. 16 cm
2022.197

This ceramic is an especially accomplished example of Yohei III's combination of an all-over translucent colored glaze with molded and carved designs. It features the peony as its primary motif. The water container, or *mizusashi*, has a green glaze, and its design takes into consideration the rounded shape and the seated position of the host and guests. It begins low on the body with a flower just beginning to open and continues with another flower a bit higher up, with its petals fully extended and beginning to open outward. It finishes with a flower in full bloom, petals and leaves unfurled and spread outward from the center, now occupying almost the entire surface. The water container once belonged to the Hosokawa family, whose go-between corresponded with Yohei IV about the piece. Yohei IV thanked them for their payment and requested that despite his father's death in the previous year, they continue to favor the studio with their orders. The letter and its envelope, as well as an auction tag, remain with the object.

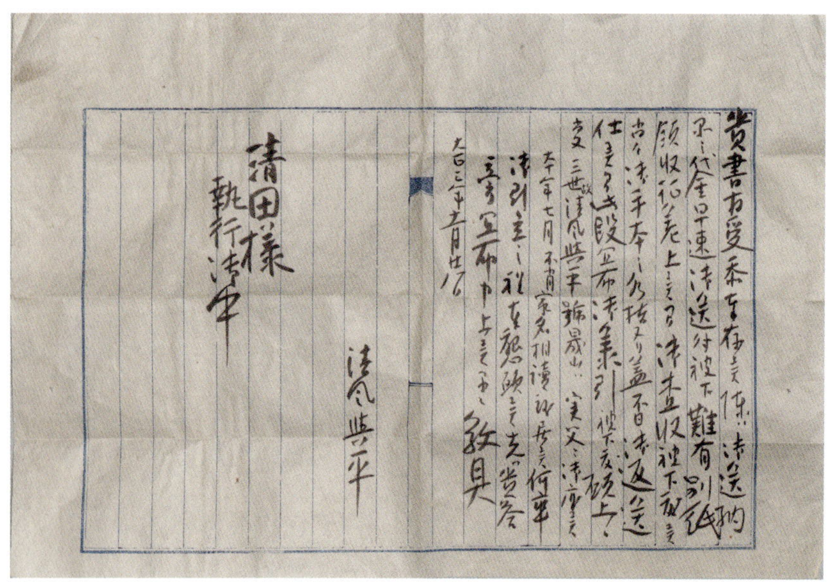

清風与平

清田様
執行御中

[53] Letter

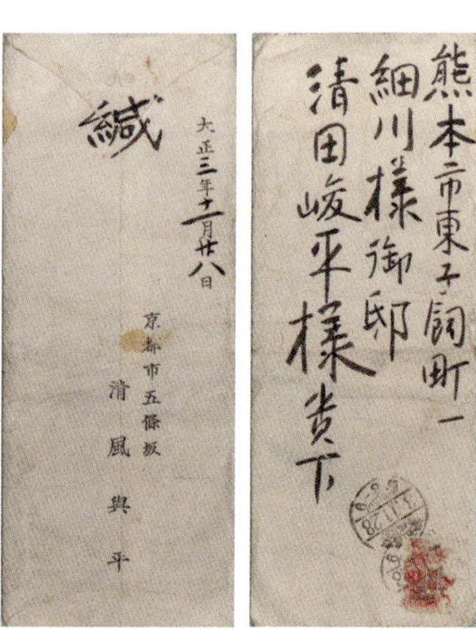

緘
大正三年十一月廿八日
京都市五條坂
清風與平

熊本市東子飼町一
細川様御邸
清田峻平様貴下

[53] Envelope (front and back)

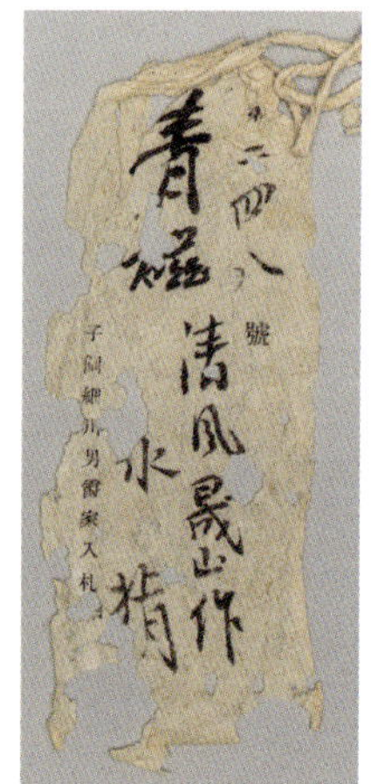

[53] Auction tag

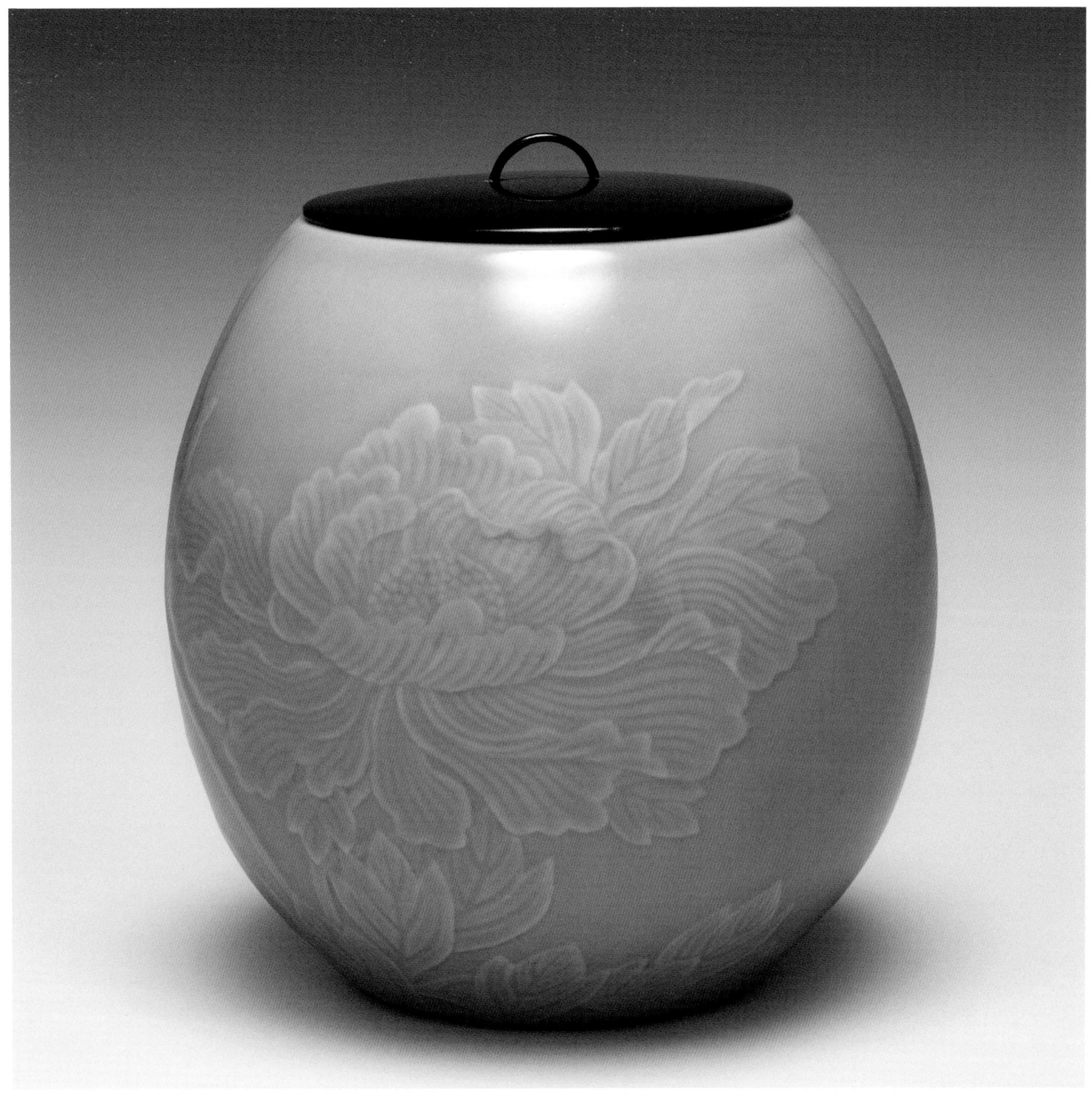

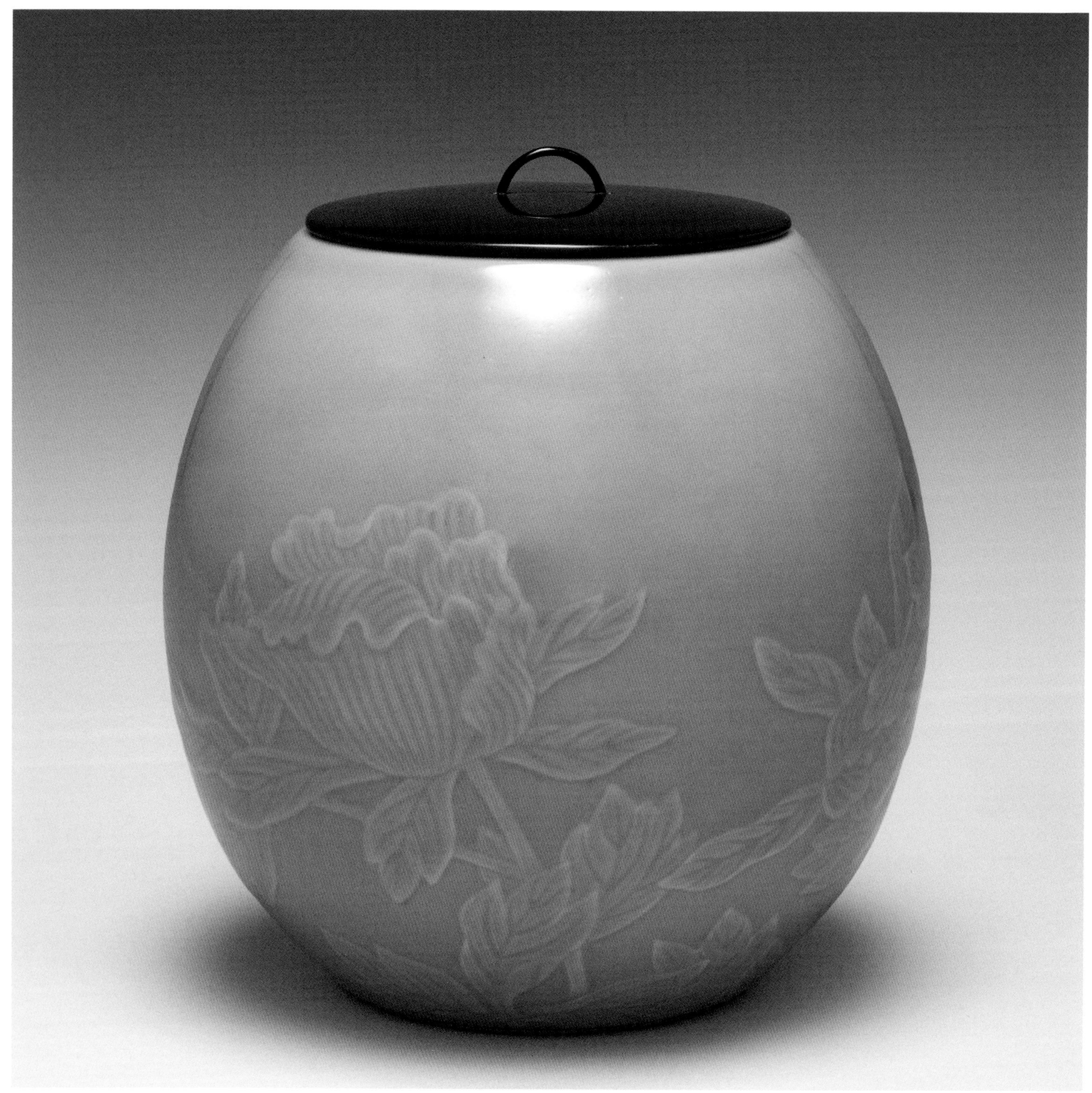

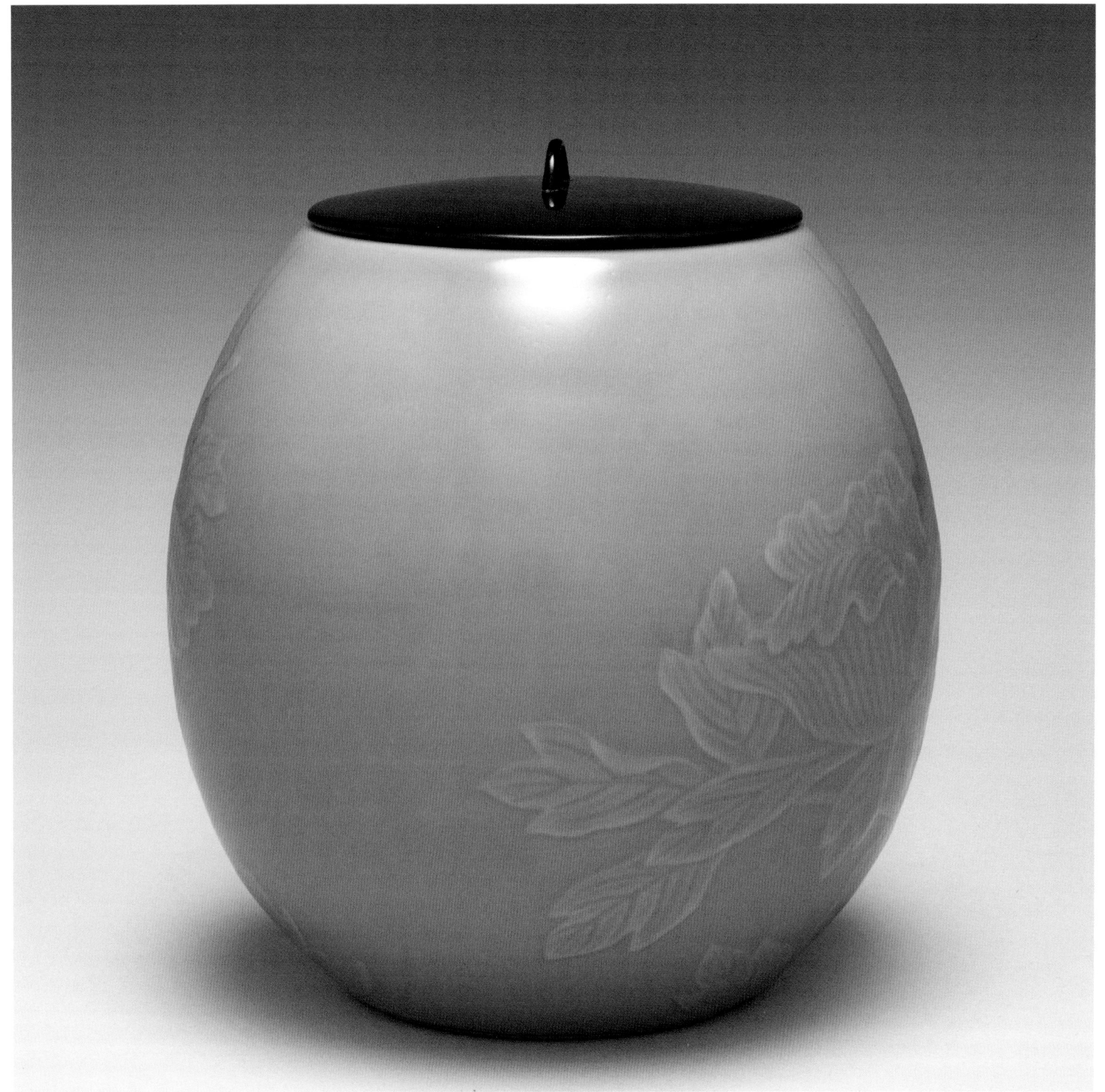

54 VASE WITH PEONIES, 1900–14

Porcelain with molded and carved design and pink-infused cream glaze
H. 17.8 cm, diam. 12.1 cm
2022.198

This flower vase has a creamy white glaze infused with pink. Sadly, the box has been lost, so we cannot know how it was described by the studio. However, through comparison with other works, it is possible to surmise that the work can be categorized as *kanpakuji* with in-glaze pink. A single huge blossom shoots up into the widest part of the vessel, near the top, so it will be visible from a distance. If this design is displayed in a space with a decorative alcove located some distance away from the entrance, even at a remove, it can announce the taste of its owner and immediately please a guest. On the other side of the vase, two butterflies, their wings overlapping, flit through the sky.

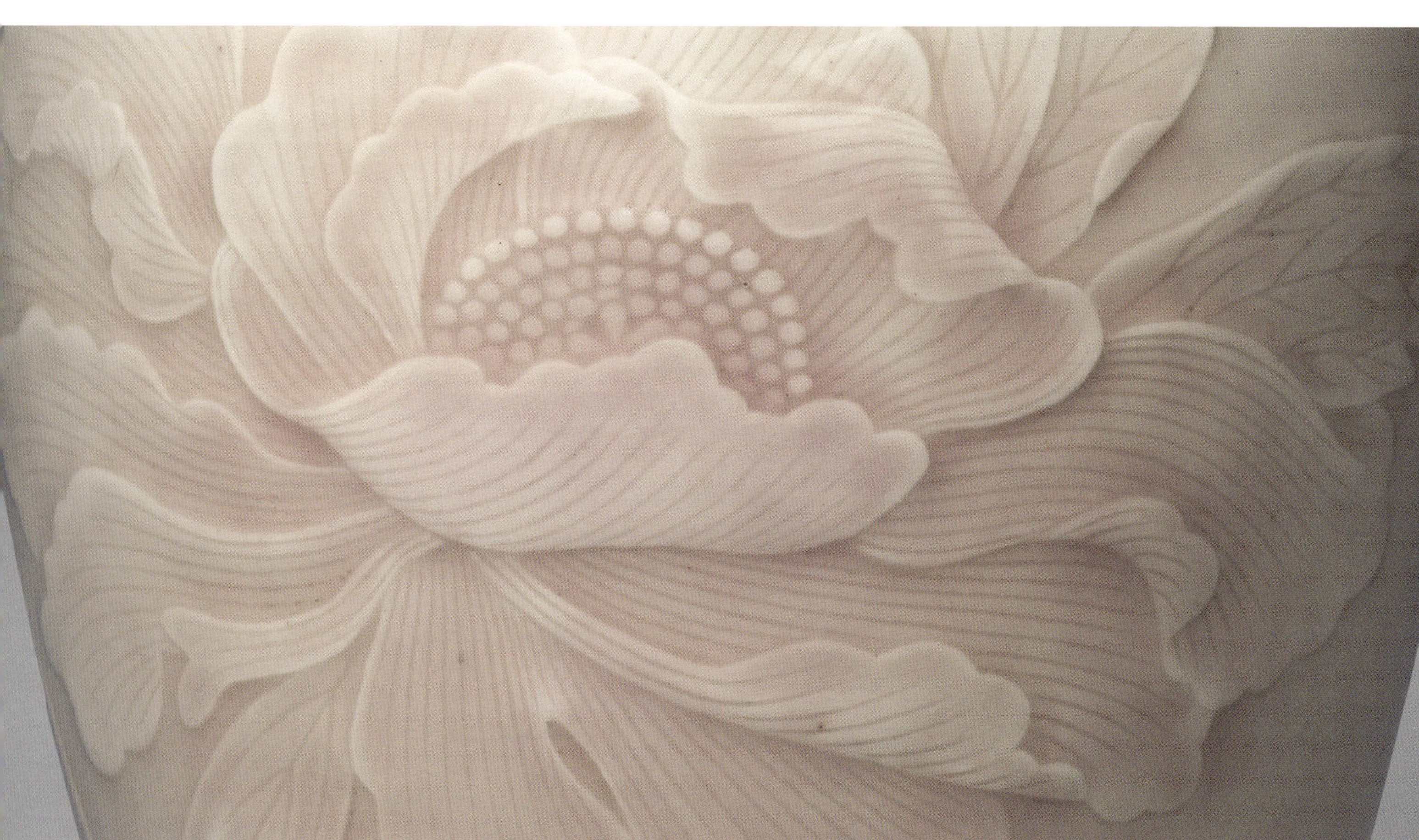

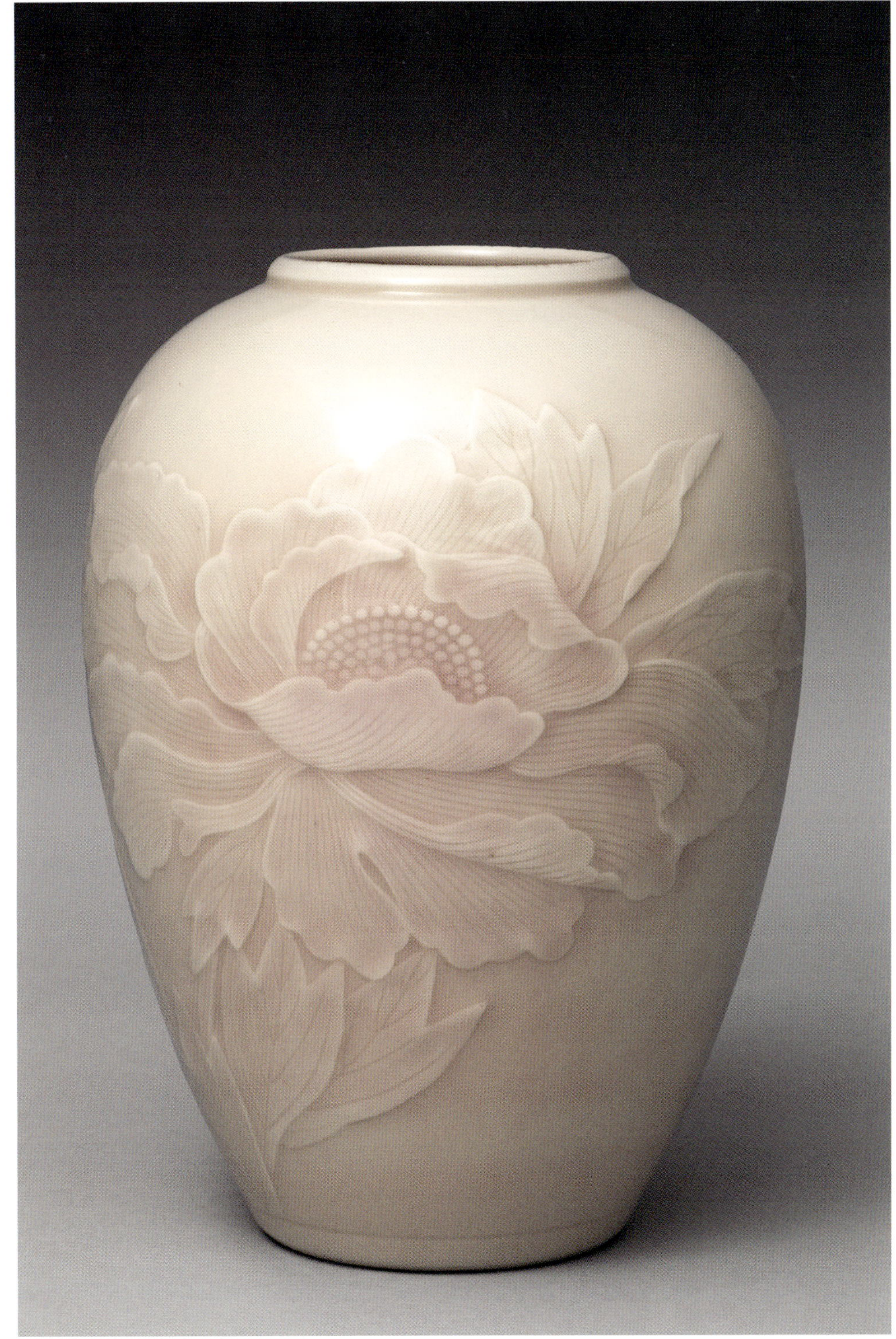

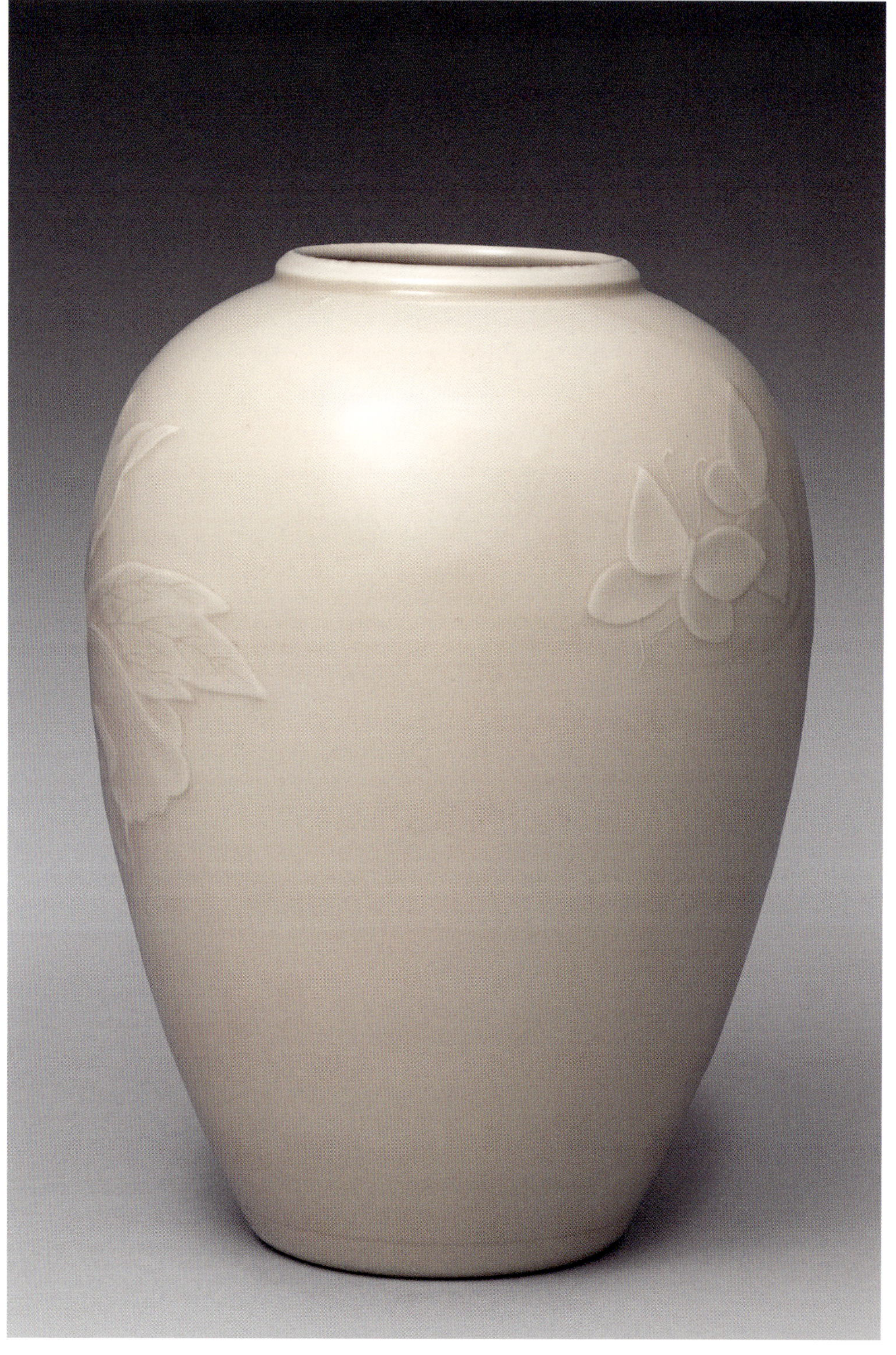

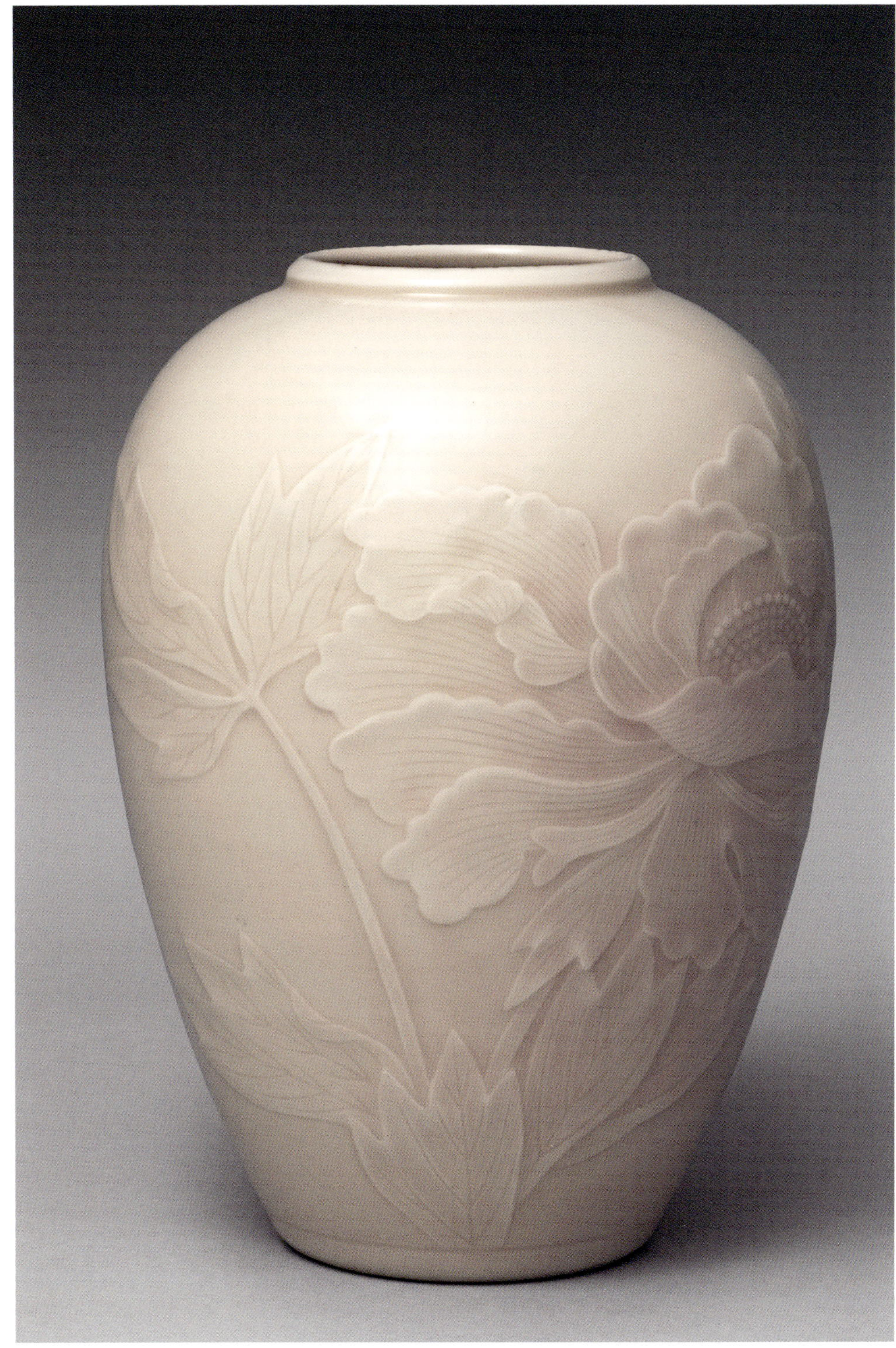

55 FLOWER VASE WITH PHOENIX IN PAULOWNIA, 1897–1914

Porcelain with molded and carved design and underglaze color
H. 20.6 cm, diam. 15.9 cm
2022.199

The phoenix's commanding presence on this vase was created by adding clay to the surface of the white clay body and then intricately molding and carving it. Then cobalt blue was used to paint the paulownia tree upon which the phoenix perches. Yohei III used a masking technique, covering the phoenix with paper before adding pink color to the area surrounding it. Firing with an all-over transparent glaze created a glossy surface, with the phoenix standing out boldly from the background. The mythical bird's long tail sweeps majestically around the vessel so that one must move around it to see the eyespots in its plumes. A symbol of imperial power in both China and Japan, the phoenix is said to alight only in the paulownia tree. Upon close inspection of its face, one can see that the phoenix's eye is in yellow under the glaze. The scene is set off at the bottom with a double band of underglaze blue above an incised ring of cloud.

Once Yohei III had created his creamy translucent *taihakuji* glaze, he began applying it over the entire surface of an ivory clay body with motifs in low relief to achieve a creamy white-on-white design.[1] He then began using the combination of gradated pink around raised motifs on a typical white porcelain clay body like the one for this vase. He masked his low-relief designs with paper before sprinkling diluted iron oxide glaze onto the surrounding areas through a net with a brush. These unpigmented elements stand out as starkly white against the gentle pink blush color that surrounds them.[2] Still later, he added pink to the translucent creamy glaze he used in *kanpakuji* works and used it over motifs in relief on an ivory clay body for an overall pink-tinged cream effect (see [54]).

1. On the evolution of Yohei III's glazing techniques with respect to gradation, see Seki, *Kyoto Ceramist Seifū Yohei III*, 100.

2. On this combination of techniques, see Maezaki, "Qing-Style Porcelain," 63.

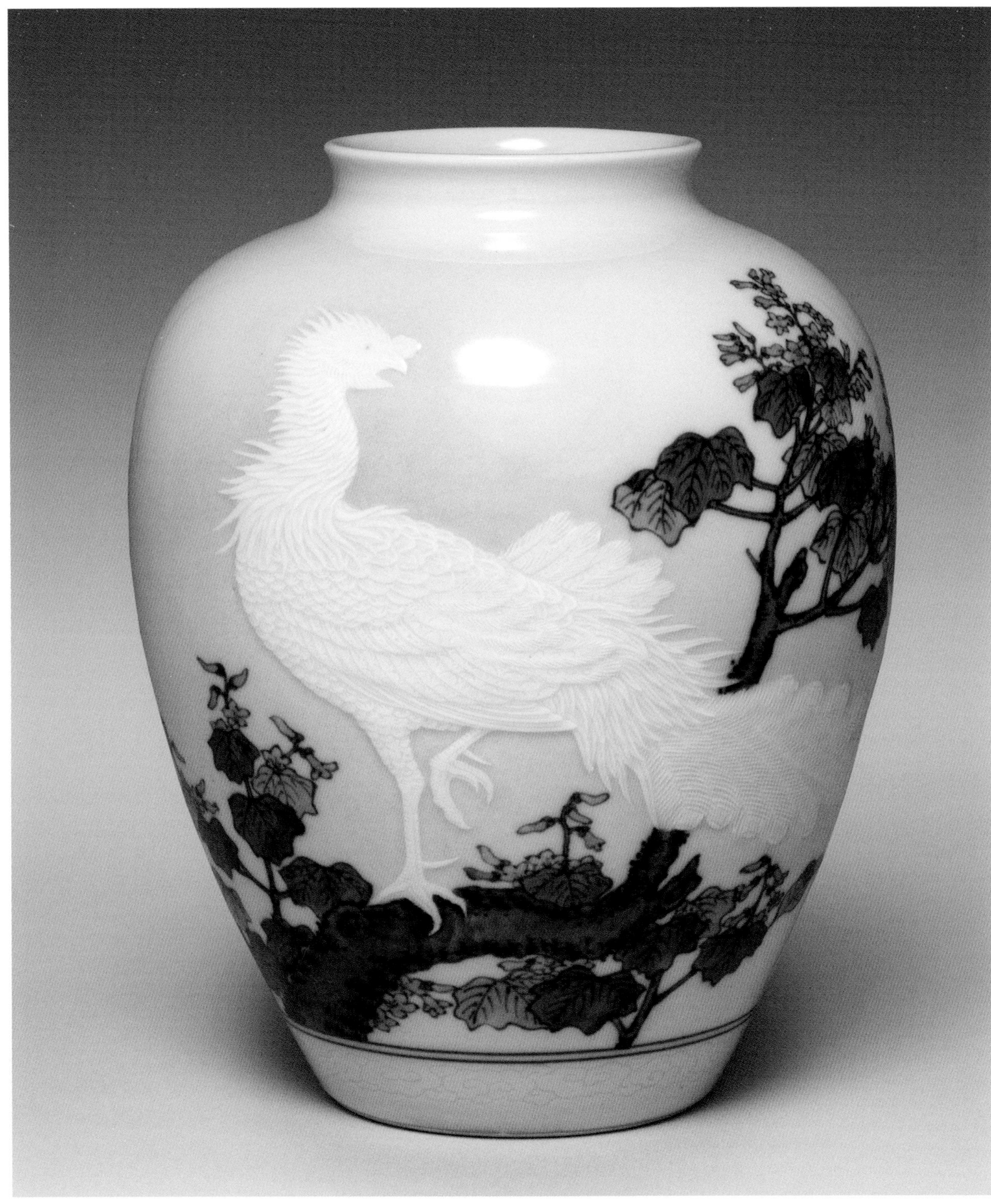

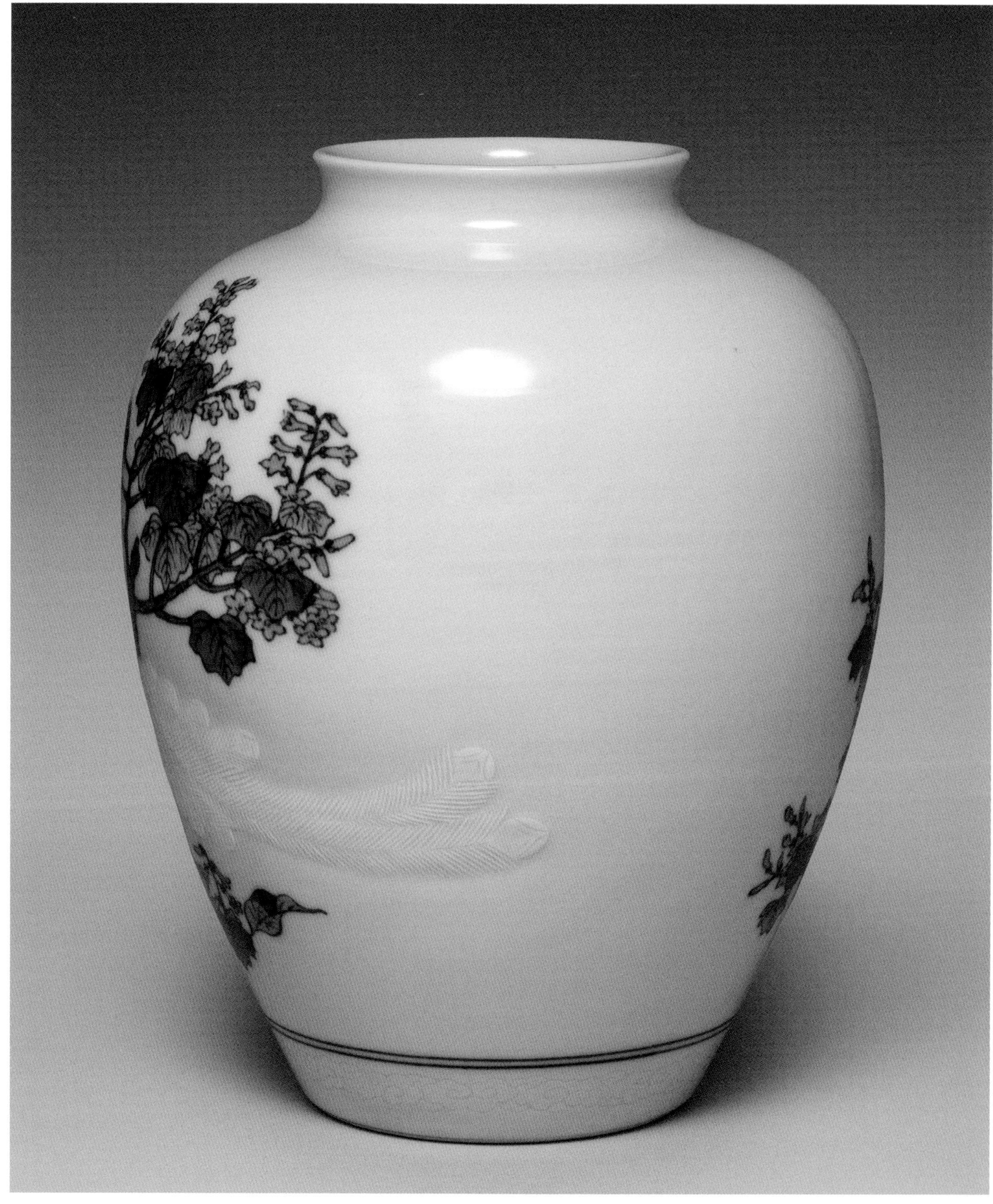

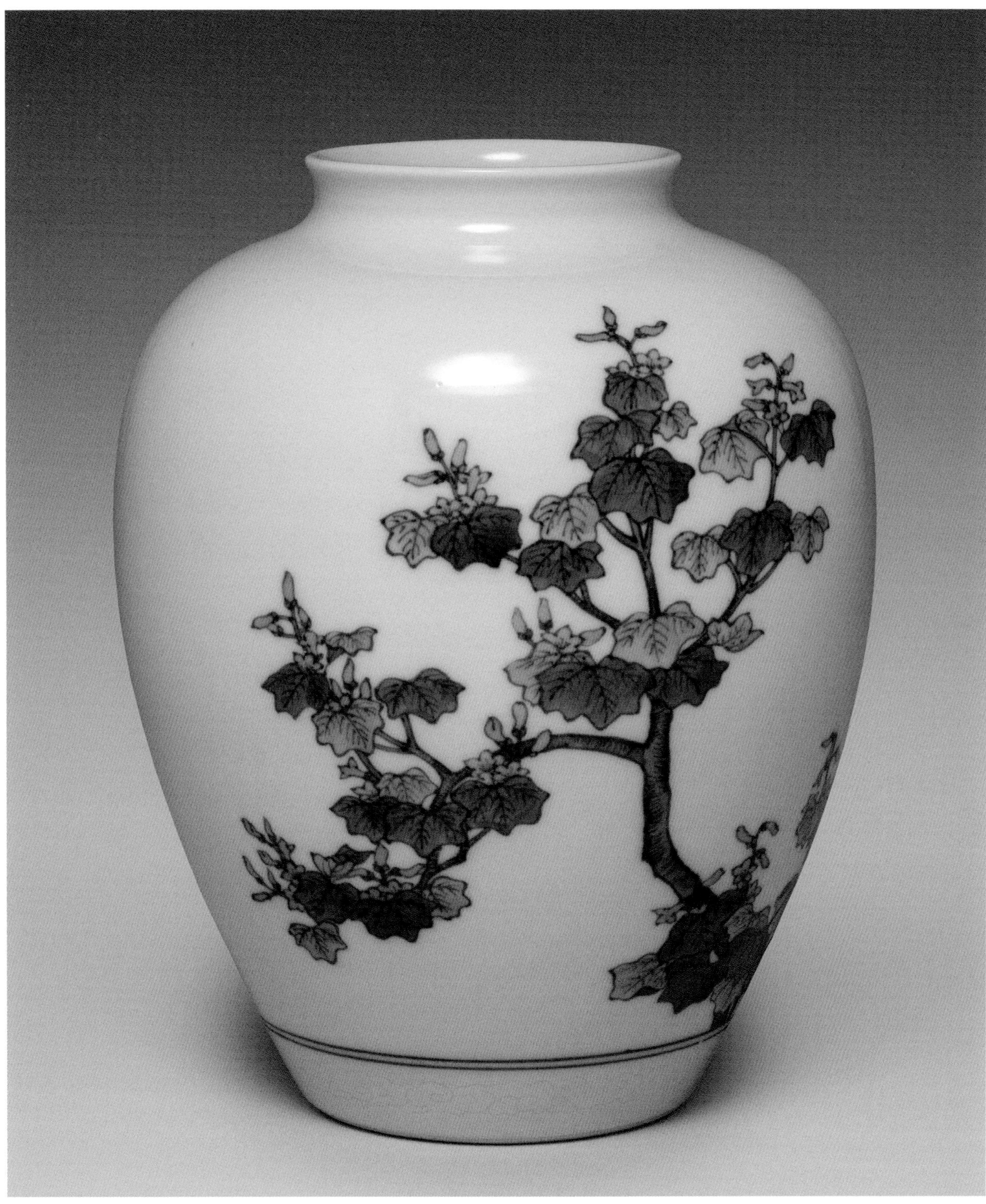

56 VASE WITH PHEASANTS IN LANDSCAPE, 1900–14

Porcelain with molded and carved design, underglaze color, and cream glaze
H. 39 cm, diam. 28.5 cm
Lent by the James and Christine Heusinger Collection

Like the design of *Flower Vase with Phoenix in Paulownia* (see [55]), the pair of pheasants in a dramatic landscape setting on this vase was created by adding clay to the surface of the clay body and then molding and carving it. Here, instead of a typical white clay, Yohei III has used an ivory clay. He then added gradated pink around the complex design, which with its multitude of cherry blossoms must have been painstaking to mask with precision. For the birds' eyes, he added a touch of yellow. He then fired the vase with an all-over translucent cream glaze. The resulting *kanpakuji* piece is one in which an academic subject long favored by painters of the Kano school for screen and sliding door paintings in important buildings, that of impressively sized birds within a scene of precipitous, angled rock faces and twisting trees, is made soft and ethereal while retaining a sense of gravitas.

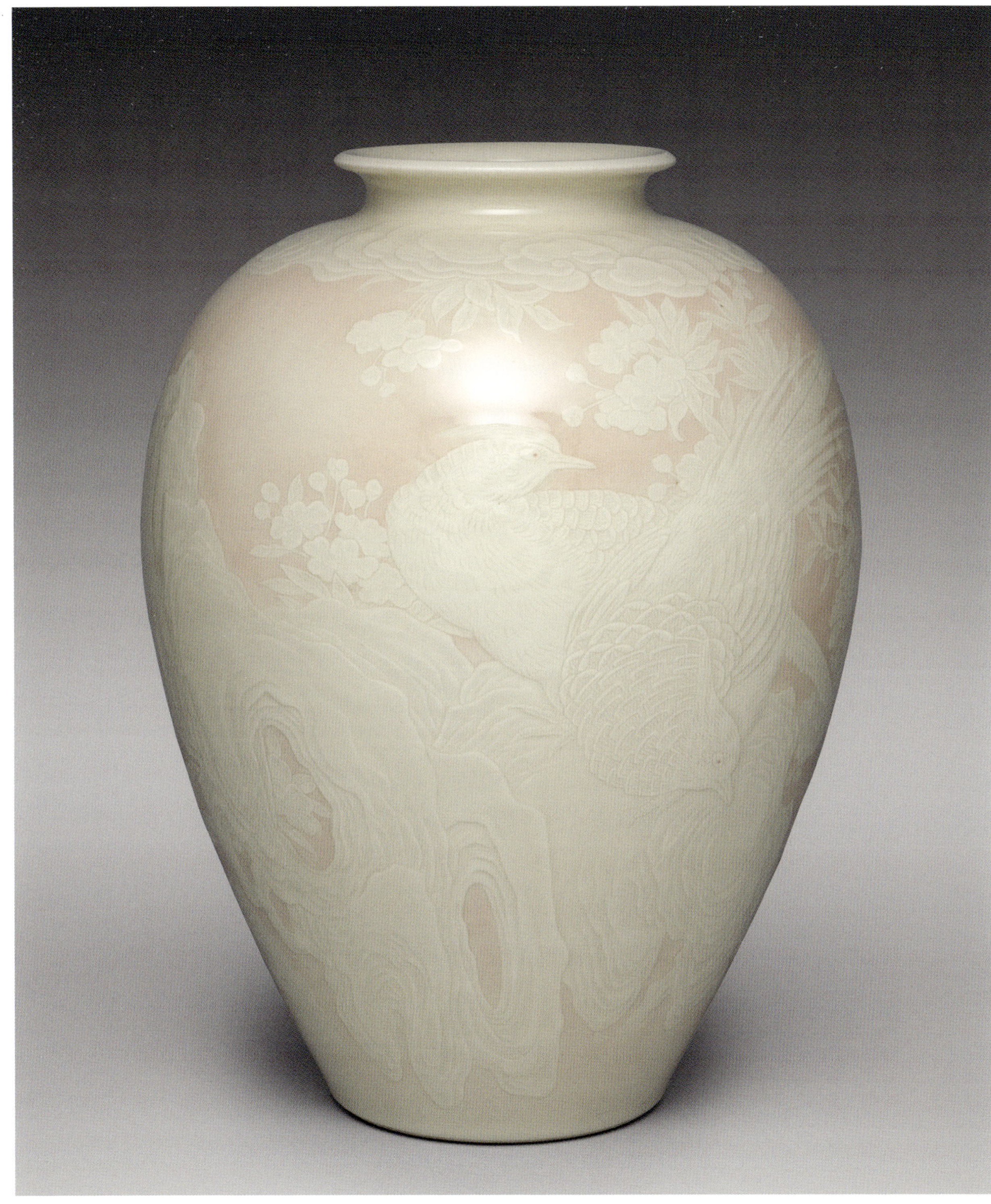

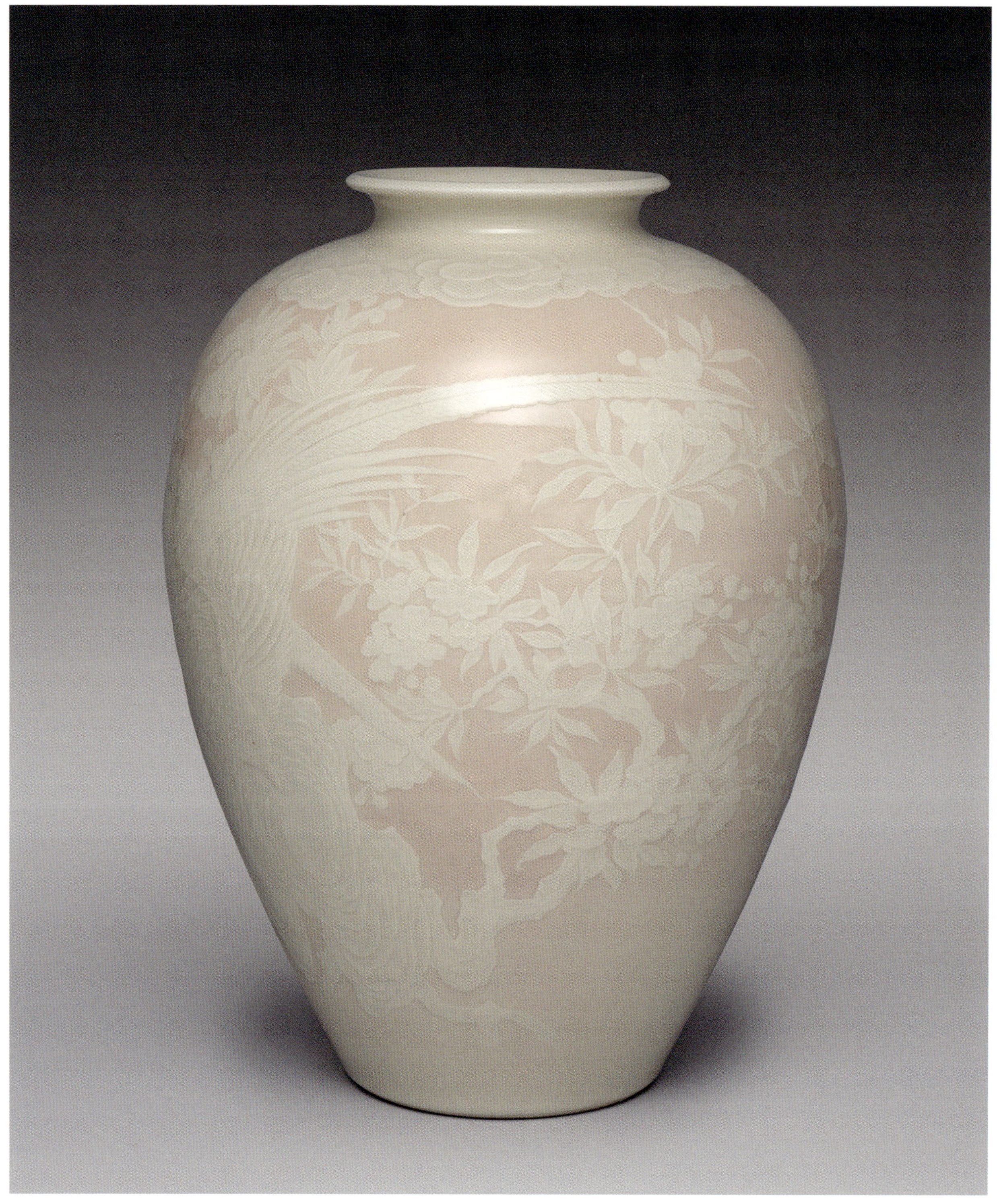

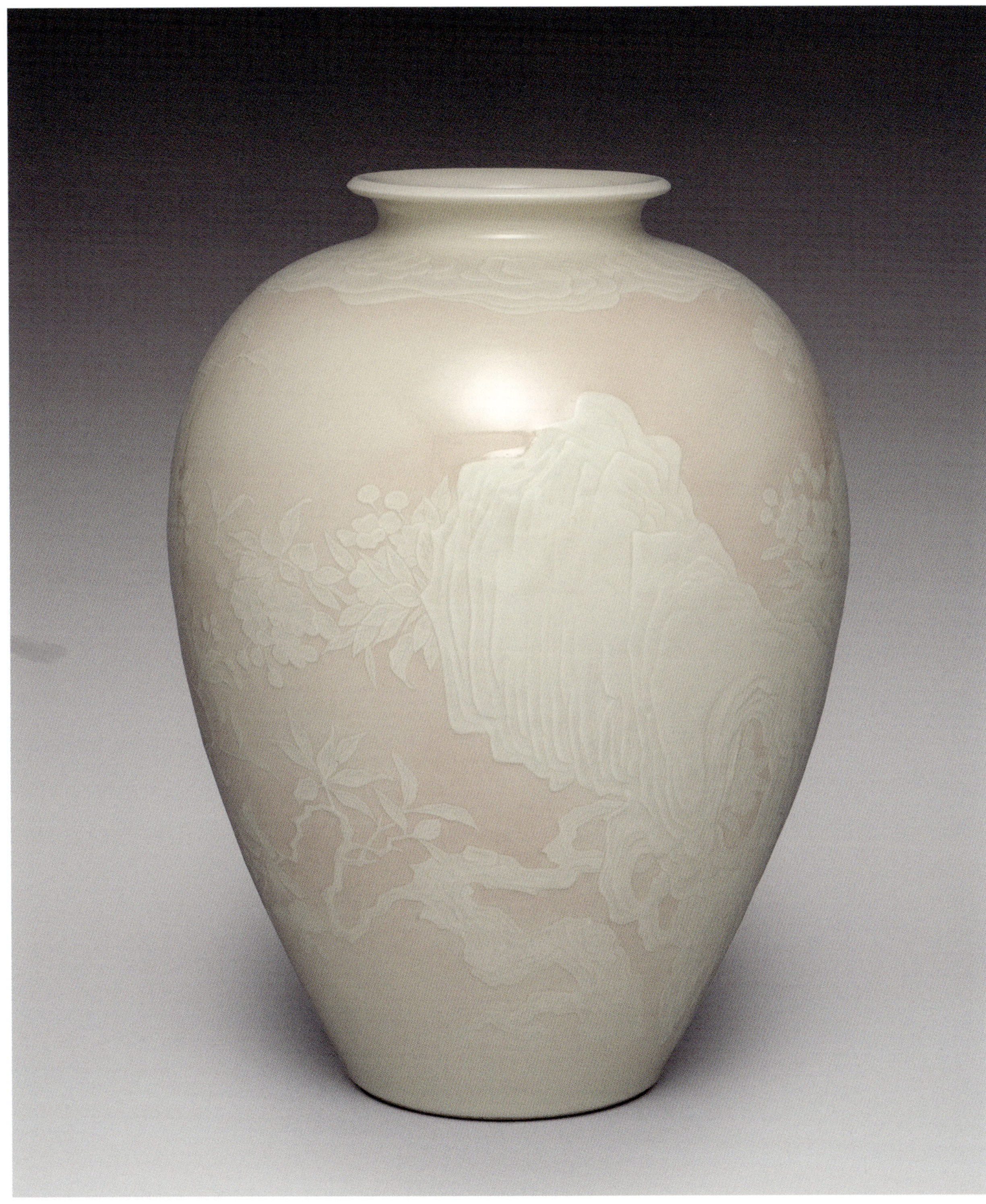

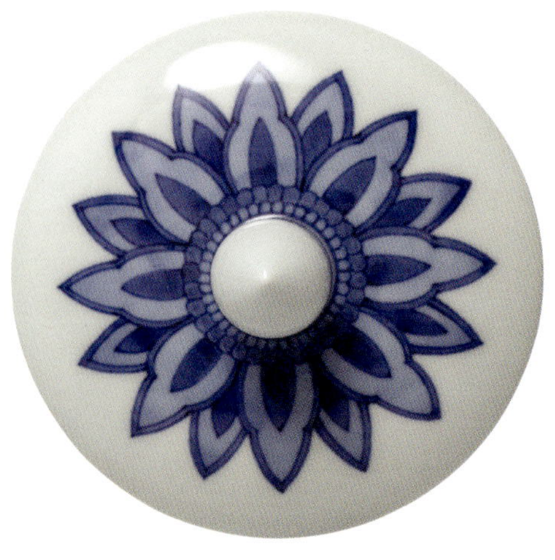

57 LIDDED JAR WITH PEONIES, 1897–1912

Porcelain with molded and carved design and underglaze color
H. 27 cm, diam. 26.4 cm
2022.200

The petals of the large, white peonies on this jar were made by applying molded clay to the body and incising the clay with lines for definition. The flowers' centers were then painted with yellow, along with the leaves in cobalt blue line and wash. A subtle blue gradation was also added all around the flowers using a masking method. The lid, with its treasured jewel-shaped finial, was also decorated with foliate motifs in underglaze cobalt blue. Finally, a transparent glaze was applied over the entire body of both the jar and lid. It is a special demonstration of Yohei III's use of precision and control to create a completely balanced composition.

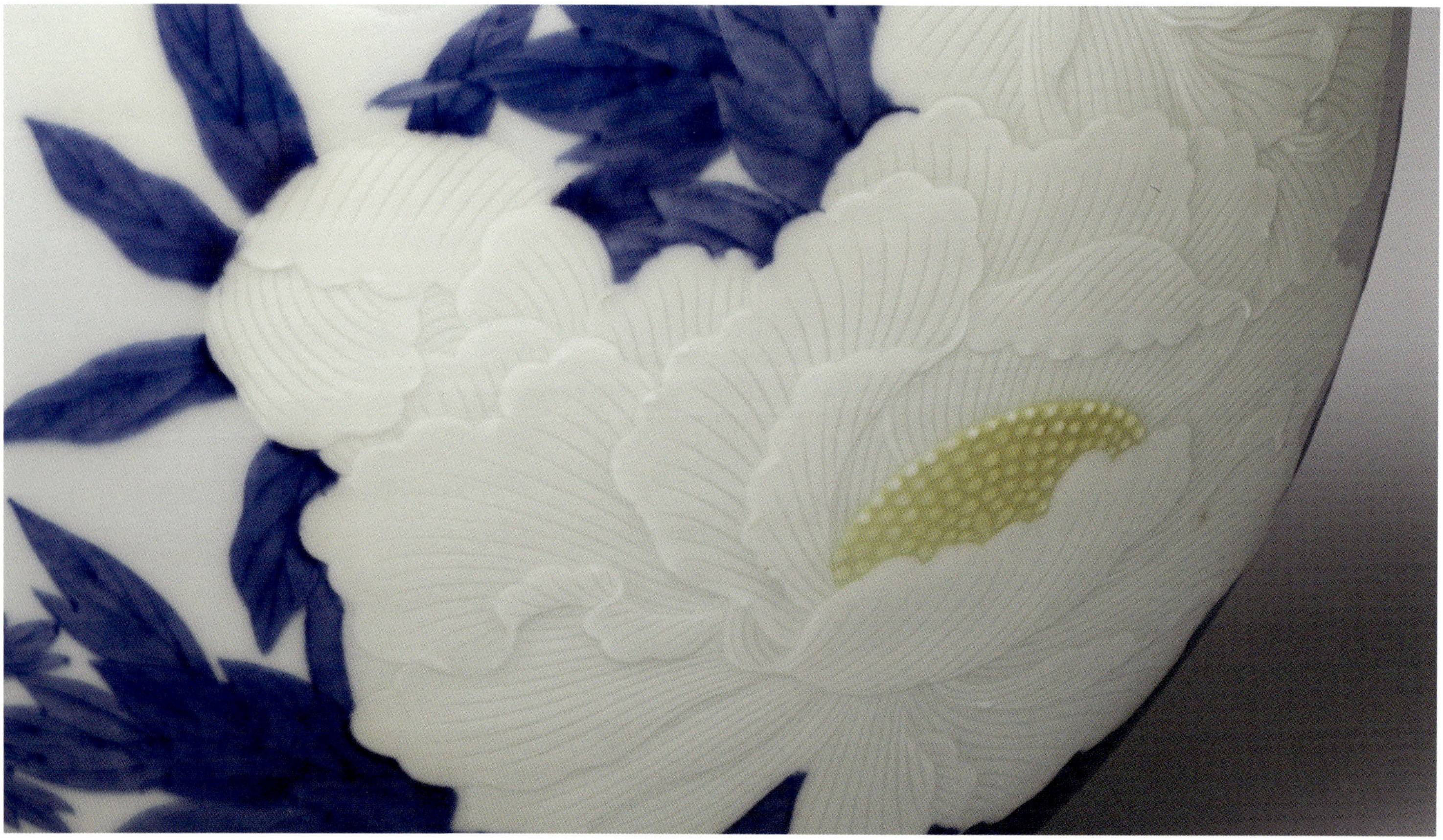

Detail of [57]

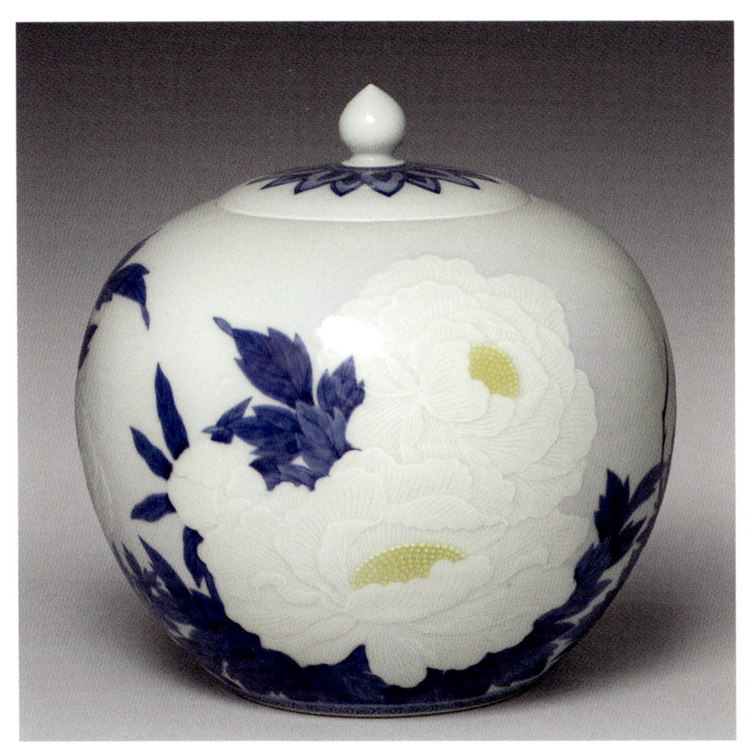
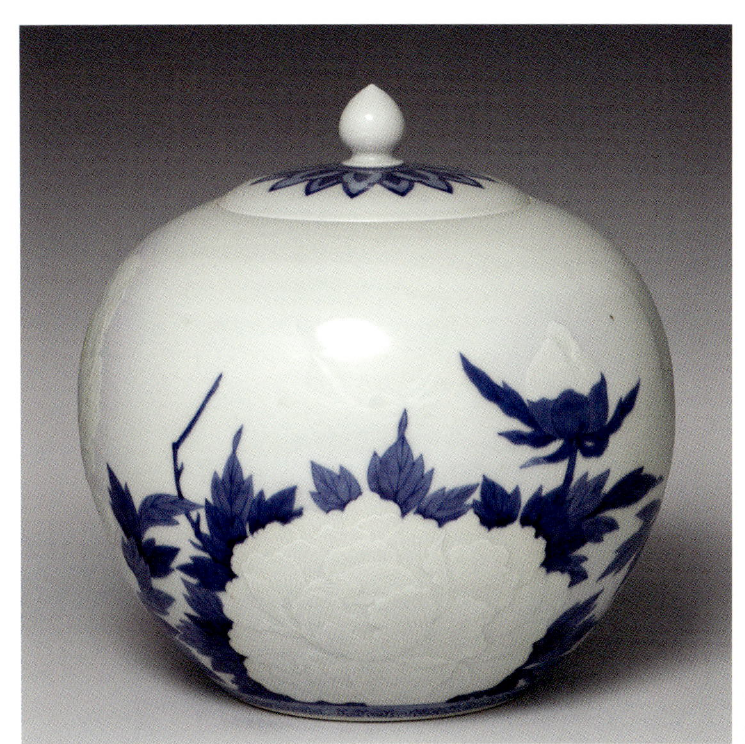
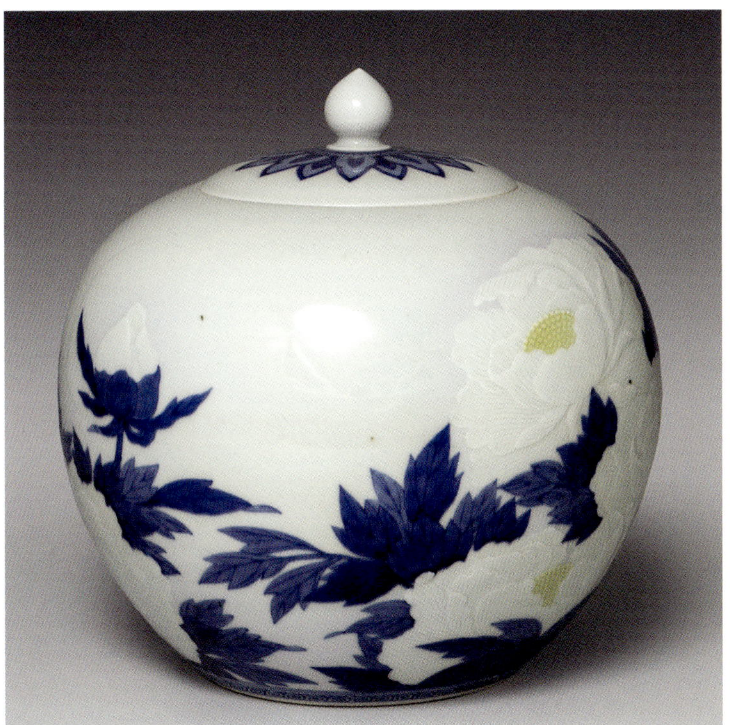
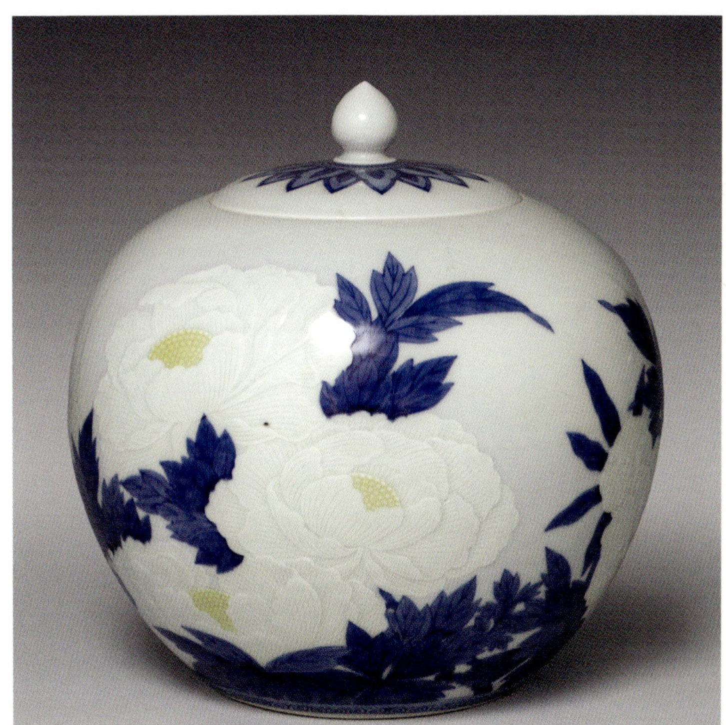

SEIFŪ YOHEI IV

58 TEACUPS WITH CHINESE LANDSCAPES, 1914–46

Eleven from a set of twelve cups; porcelain with underglaze blue
Each: h. 4 cm, diam. 6.6 cm
2022.202

Originally from a set of twelve, each of these eleven *sencha* teacups has a different landscape wrapped around the body, giving individual cups their own engaging narrative. These paintings are comfortingly familiar in their formulaic qualities, known to any casual fan of ink painting; they are also enjoyable in the way the narratives are revealed as one manipulates the cups. They would be perfect as conversation pieces for a tea gathering. Four of the cups focus on travelers

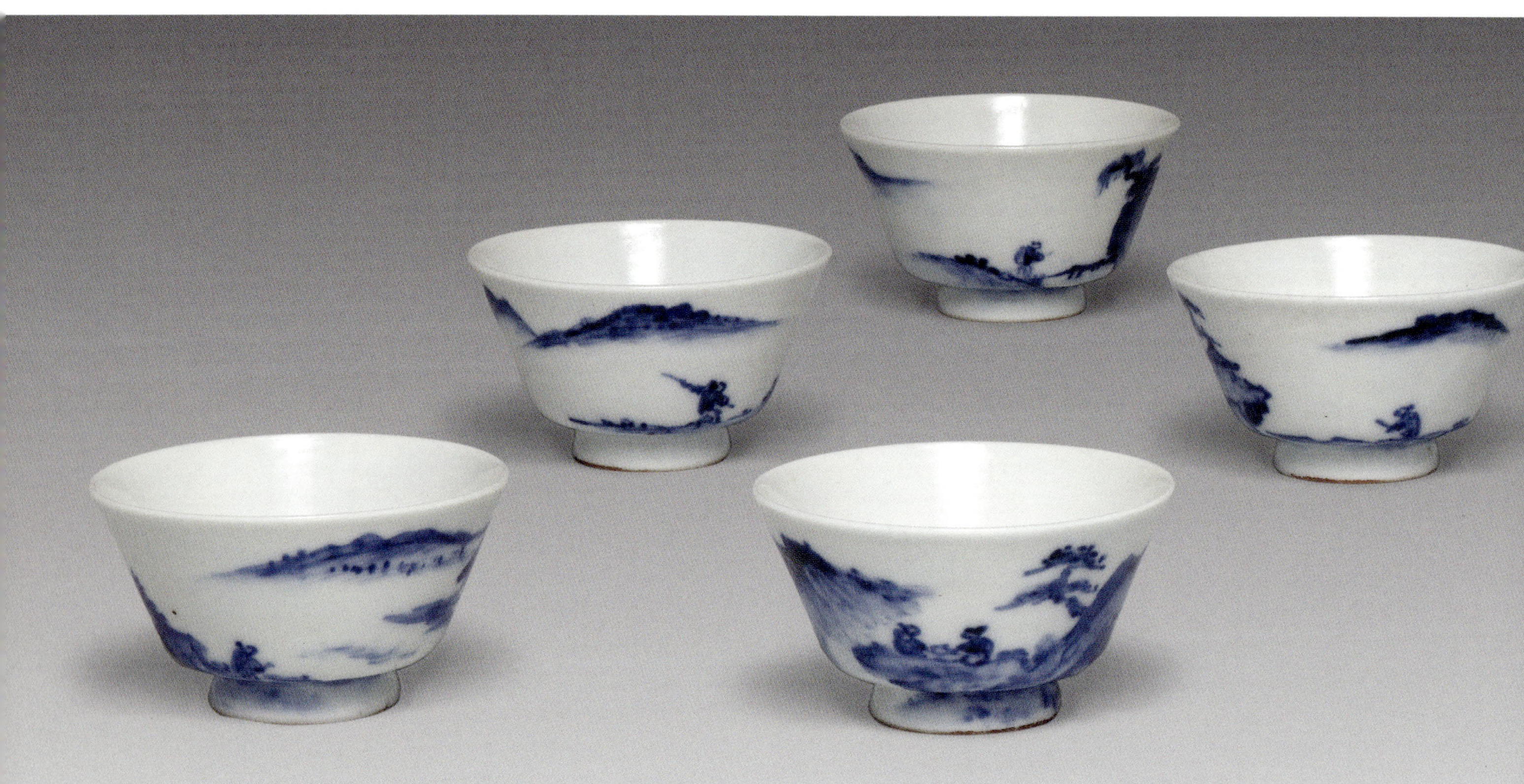

approaching residences. Two have a person crossing a bridge as their central motif: one man has a backpack, and the other, a cloth-wrapped bundle hanging from a pole slung over his shoulder. Another cup depicts a pair of friends gathered together on rock platforms. A single cup shows a man carrying a furled banner toward a pavilion. The remaining three cups feature people riding in boats: two have literati passengers, and the third is occupied by a fisherman. Seifū Yohei IV's training as a painter with Tanomura Shōsai (1847–1909), an adoptive son of Tanomura Chokunyū, his father's painting teacher, is evident in the details of the tiny worlds created on the cups.

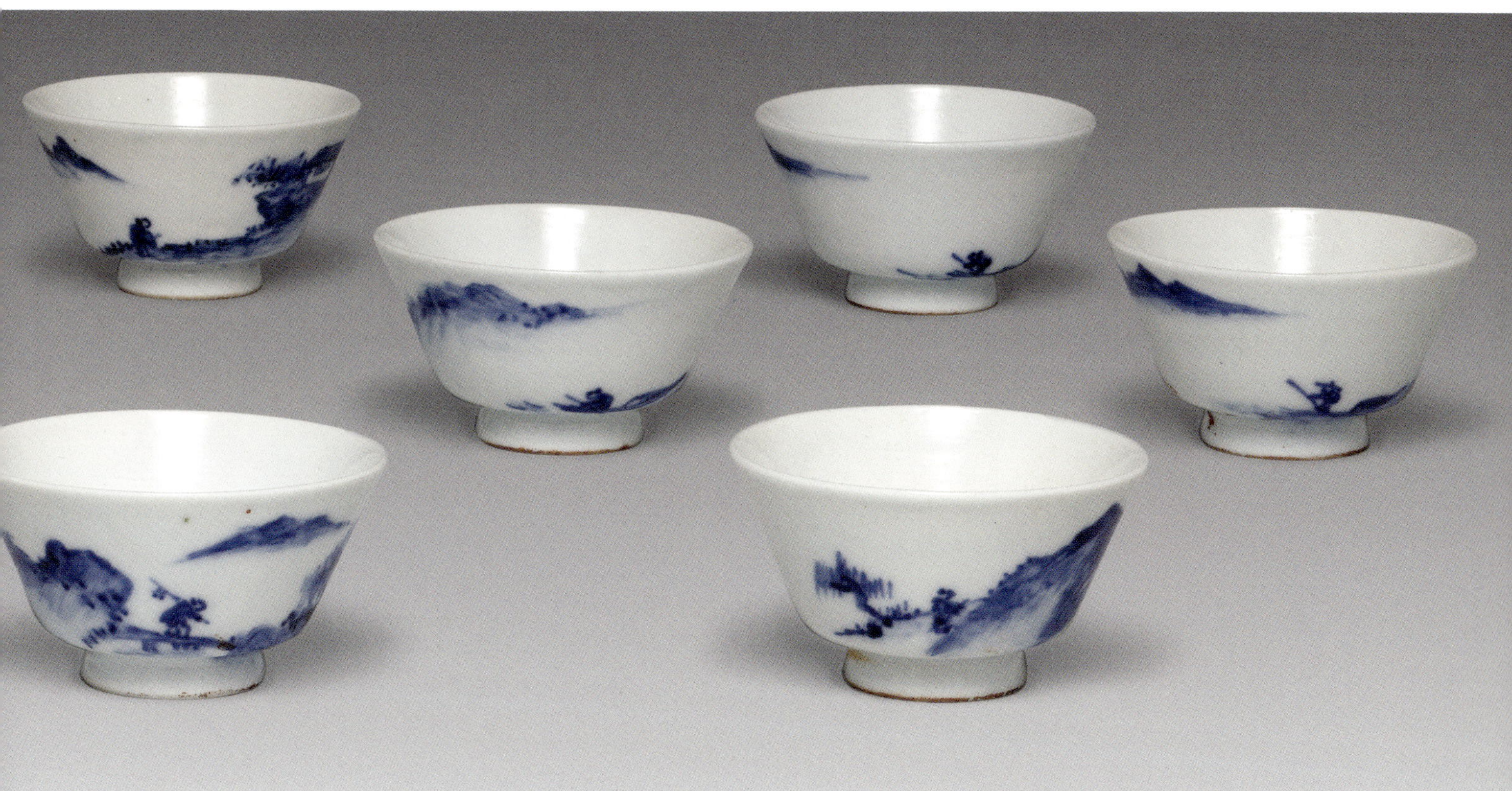

59 TEAPOT WITH MOUNTAIN CHERRY BLOSSOMS, 1914–46

Porcelain with underglaze blue
H. with lid 8 cm, w. with handle 10 cm, diam. 8 cm
2022.201

This teapot with mountain cherry blossom motifs has its design in underglaze cobalt blue. It runs over both the pear-shaped body and the recessed lid, with its pointed, jewel-shaped handle. There is a faint bluish-green tint to the glaze. The mark impressed into the base of this work appears to be one used by Yohei III. However, the box inscription is brushed in a hand matching that of Yohei IV, and while the seal on the lid is one often used by Yohei III, that next to the signature on the back of the lid is one generally used by Yohei IV. The signature, too, resembles others belonging to Yohei IV. As the design, technique, and object named on the box accurately describe the contents, it seems unlikely, but not impossible, that it is mismatched. There are many cases in which Yohei III works are contained in boxes with inscriptions, seals, and a signature by Yohei IV. However, in such examples, Yohei IV clearly identifies himself as authenticating the work of his father and often includes his father's Imperial Household Artist seal. This may be an example of a transitional piece in which Yohei IV has used his father's mark on the base of his own work.

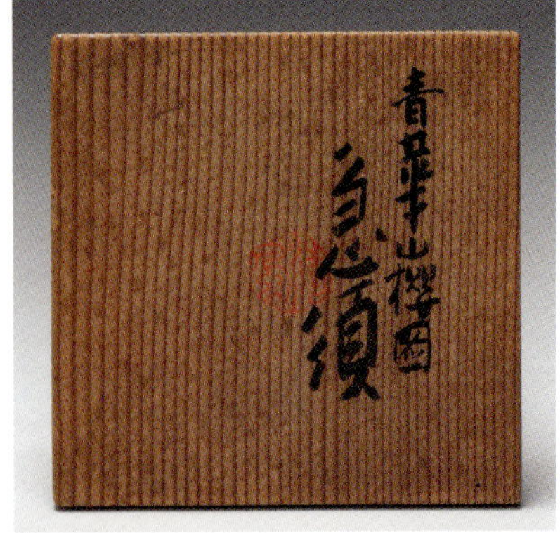

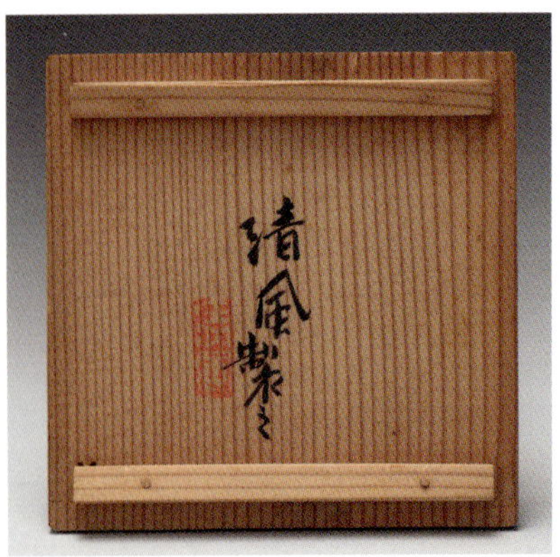

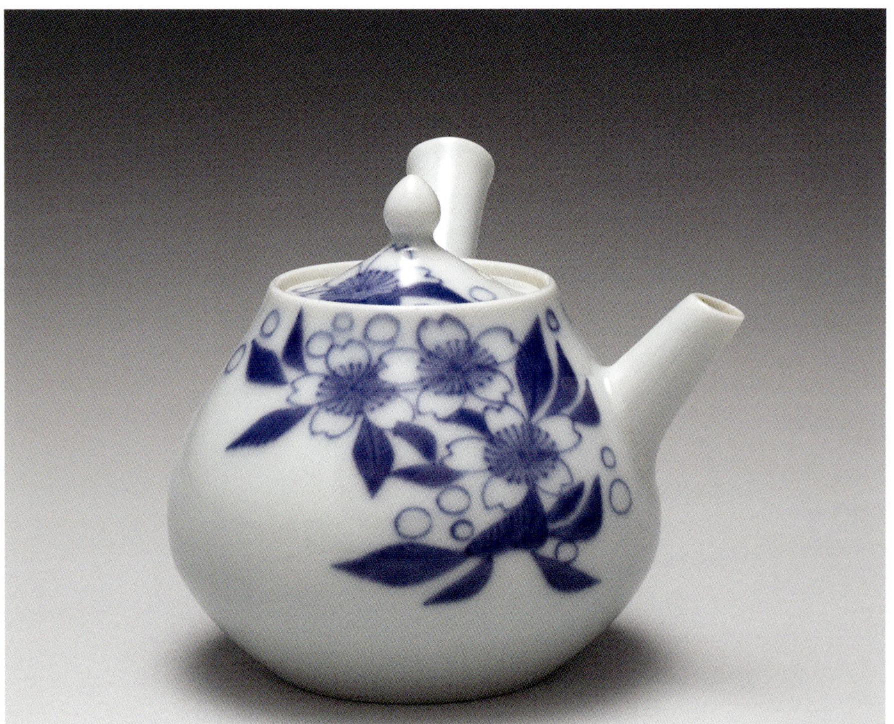

60 TEAPOT WITH BAMBOO, 1914–46

Porcelain with molded decoration, underglaze blue, and metal handles
H. with handle 16 cm, w. with spout 14.5 cm
2022.203

This teapot has a well-balanced design of bamboo in underglaze blue and *nyoi* staff-head motifs applied to both sides at the shoulder.

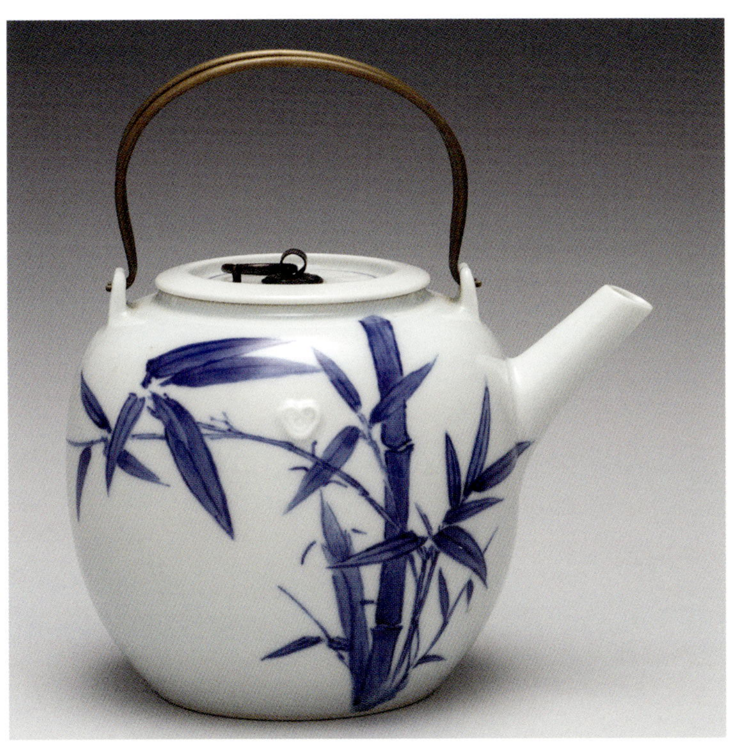

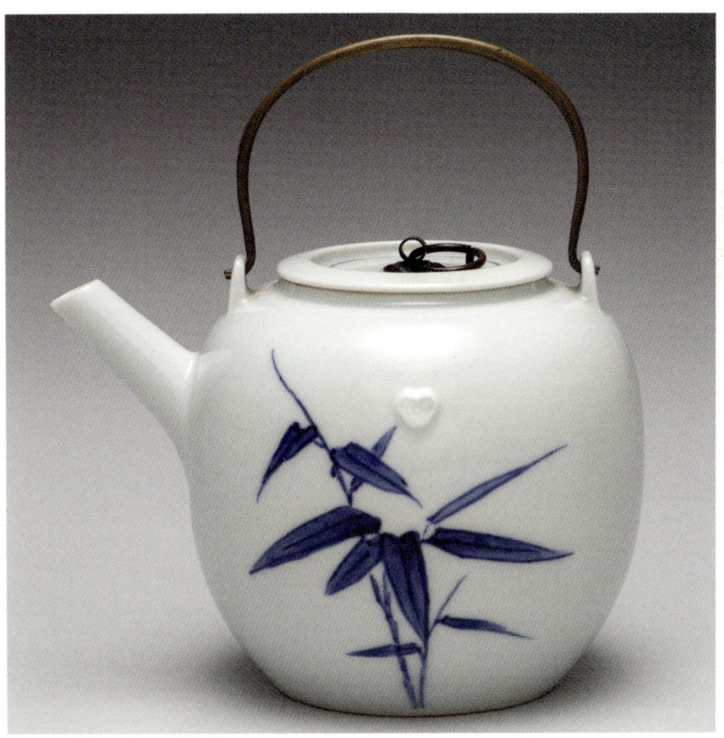

61 INCENSE BURNER WITH PEONY AND CLOUD, 1914–46

Porcelain with molded and incised design, pale pink glaze, and floral openwork silver lid
H. with lid 12.9 cm, diam. 13.5 cm
2022.204

Yohei IV's incense burner has a scrolling floral pattern of peonies and *nyoi* staff-head forms around the body and a band of clouds around the collar. These are done in low relief, with incised lines marking the details in the flower petals and leaves. The silver lid has a proliferation of flowers, including lily, peony, and a variety of chrysanthemums. The box lid identifies the subtle pink over an ivory body as "dawn's light[–glazed] porcelain" (*shokōji*). After he became an Artist of the Imperial Household, Yohei III created a number of glaze and clay combinations with what would have been considered Japan-focused names to be in alignment with his position as an artist representing the nation.[1] Among them was a glaze called "dawn's light pale [pink] color" (*akebonoiro tansai*), which he invented in 1895. It is possible that this incense burner is an example with this glaze, despite the slightly different name given on the box. While the name alludes to the Land of the Rising Sun, an epithet for Japan, the burner's motifs remain very much drawn from the Chinese repertoire.

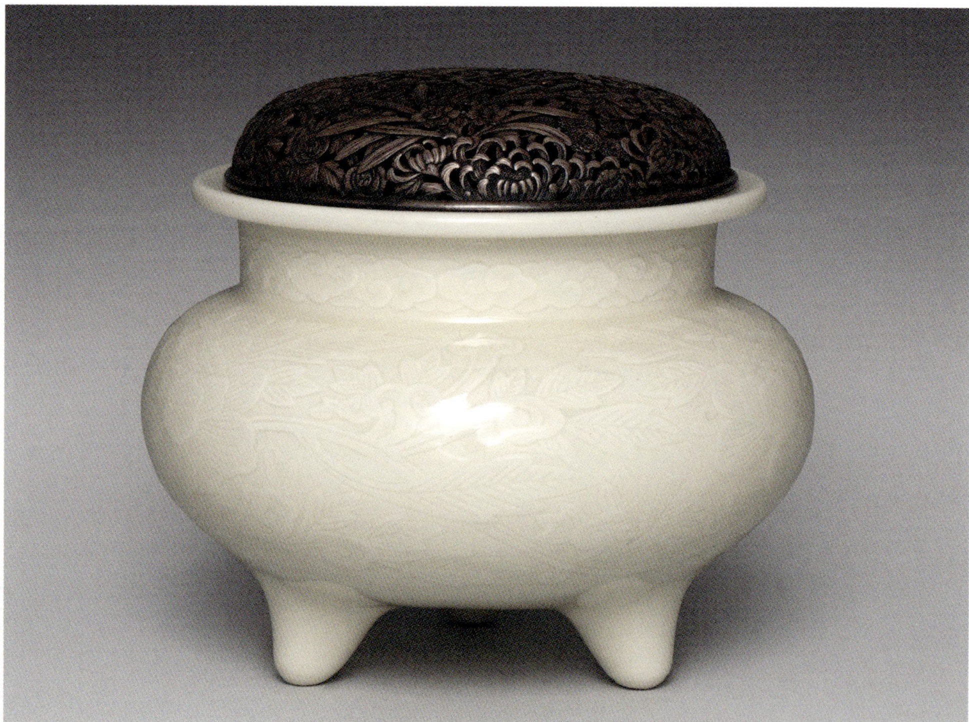

1. Maezaki, "Qing-Style Porcelain," 232.

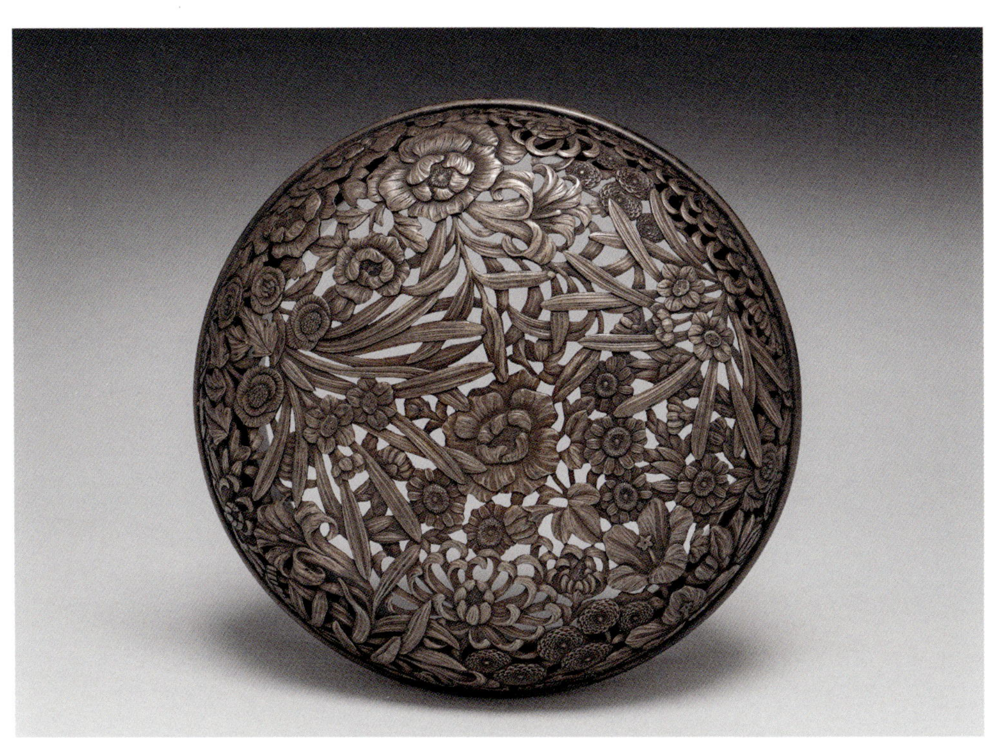

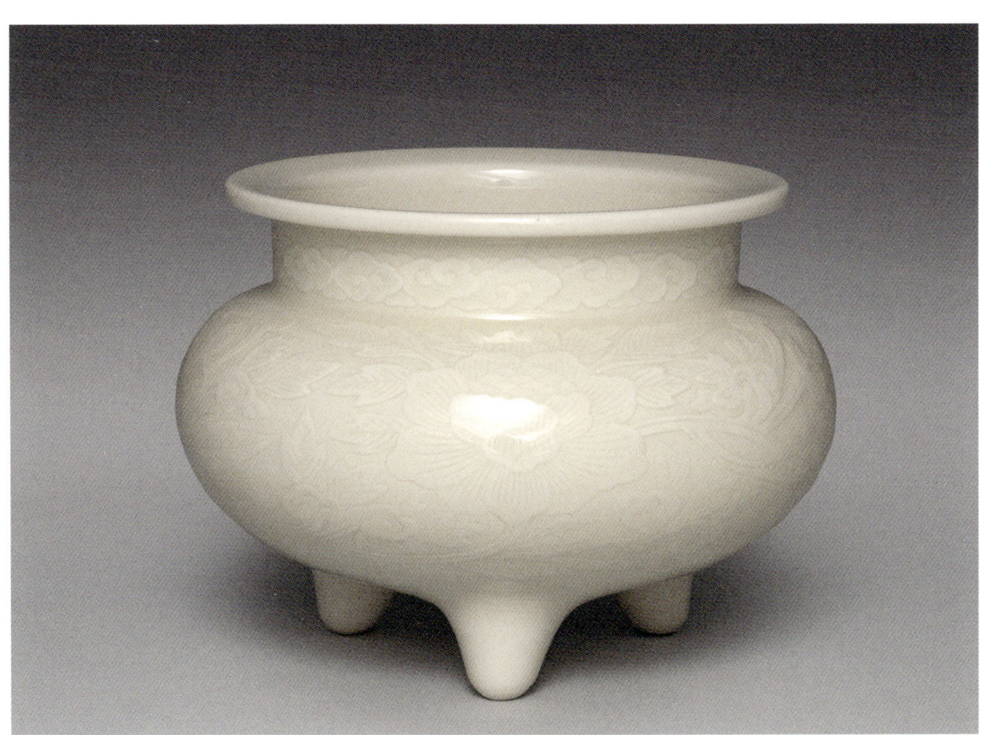

62 FLOWER VASE WITH CHRYSANTHEMUMS, 1914–46

Porcelain with molded and carved design, underglaze pink, and cream glaze
H. 28.6 cm, diam. 15.2 cm
2022.205

In creating this *kanpakuji* vase, Yohei IV has applied his father's signature creamy translucent glaze in combination with underglaze pink gradation surrounding motifs in low relief over an ivory clay body. This method was used to achieve the creamy white of the stalks, leaves, buds, and flowers of the elaborate design of chrysanthemum flowers in diverse stages of bloom.

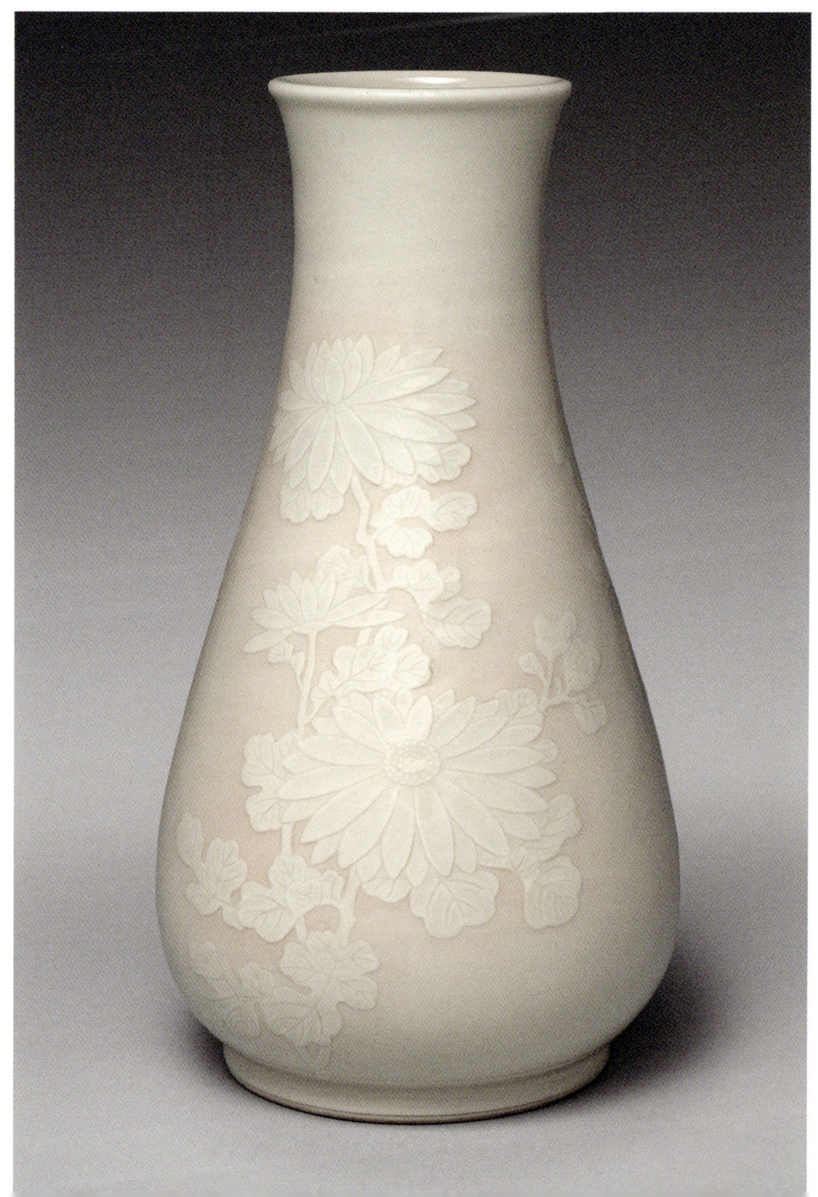

63 SWEETS BOWL WITH CHRYSANTHEMUMS, 1914–46

Porcelain with molded and carved design, underglaze color, and cream glaze
H. 8.5 cm, diam. 18.5 cm
2022.207

64 SWEETS BOWL WITH CHRYSANTHEMUMS, 1914–46

Porcelain with molded and carved design, underglaze color, and cream glaze
H. 8.5 cm, diam. 18.5 cm
2022.206

Sweets bowls hold the confections enjoyed when drinking tea. These two bowls offer an important lesson in appreciating Yohei IV's ceramic practice, for while they have the same design and shape and are made with the same materials, the execution of the pieces makes them entirely different upon close inspection, thereby demonstrating the range of possible production results from a single template. Each bowl has the same composition of two different types of chrysanthemum flowers, one with long, slim, knife-like petals and the other with short, rounded, multilayered petals, shown running around its surface in low relief. The centers of the flowers are painted with yellow under the glaze.

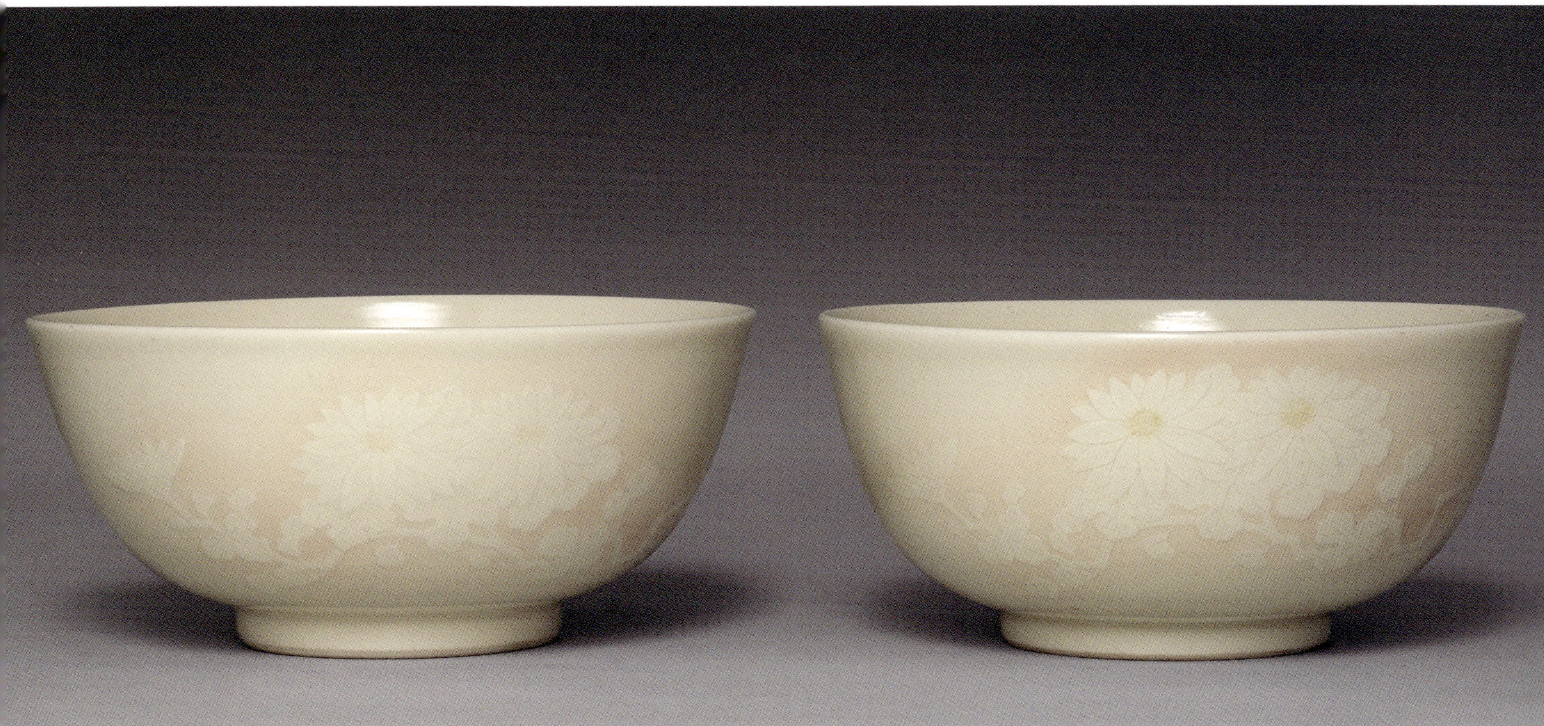

[63] [64]

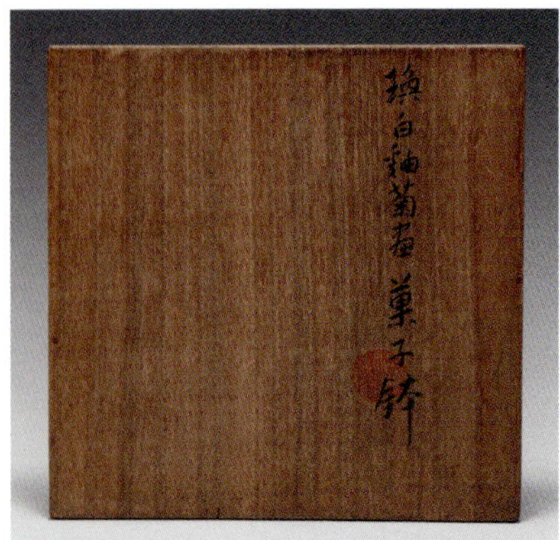

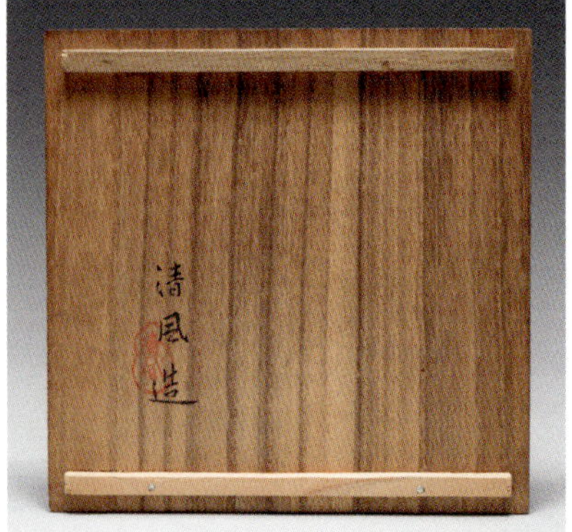

[64]

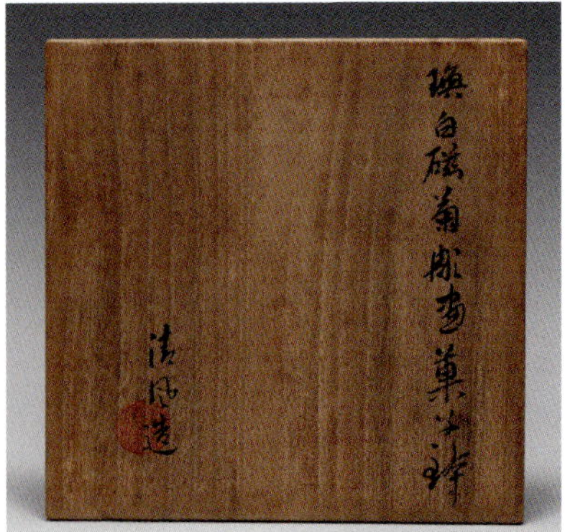

[63]

Yohei III formulated a number of new underglaze colors during his career, and this is likely one of them. For both bowls here, Yohei IV used his father's *kanpakuji* formula, with underglaze pink for the gradated wash of color surrounding the flowers.

The storage box lids provide abbreviated descriptions of the complex processes used in the surface decorations—one identifies the bowl inside as "Sweets dish with picture of chrysanthemum in *kanpakuyū*," while the other goes a bit further with "Sweets dish with carved picture of chrysanthemum in *kanpakuji*." The box for the latter bowl has Yohei IV's signature on the lid's exterior, along with a seal reading "Seizan Seifū" 成山清風. The ink inscriptions are done in an elegant semiformal calligraphy. The box lid for the former bowl has on its exterior the same seal, which includes Yohei IV's style name, but no signature. Instead, a signature is found on the interior of the box lid, accompanied by another seal, this time a gourd-shaped seal reading "Seifū." The ink inscriptions are in a mode closer to formal script.

Of the two bowls, it is this one, with the signature on the inside of the box lid, that stands out for a distinctively bubble-filled glaze with a heavier pink effect, as well as more noticeable yellow at the flowers' centers and deeper carving in the relief decoration [64]. The other bowl is more subtle and smooth in both the effect of the glaze and the execution of the relief [63]. In addition, the designs themselves are applied in different locations. On the more subtle bowl, they are centered on the body between rim and foot, while on the one with stronger color and more deeply carved relief, one design has crept much closer to the rim. A closer look at the delineation of the flower petals reveals that the designs differ at times with respect to which petals appear in front or behind others. The centers of the bases of both bowls are incised with "Seifū" in a manner matching many other works by Yohei IV, although there are slight differences. As one might expect from the other differences in the bowls, the characters on the base of the subtle bowl are gentler, finishing in a tapering out of the strokes, while those on the bold bowl end in triangular pinheads.

55 BOWL WITH CHRYSANTHEMUMS, 1914–46

Stoneware with underglaze iron oxide and crackled glaze
H. 7.9 cm, diam. 18 cm
2022.208

The chrysanthemums in underglaze iron oxide of this Kyoto-ware bowl have a casual feel, which is emphasized by its shape. When held, the bowl's slightly ridged body would gently massage one's palms, contributing to the sensory, tactile experience of the piece and possibly generating a sense of comfort and ease. The inside of the box lid has a seal indicating that the bowl was included in a renewal opening of the gallery Manjudō in Tokyo.

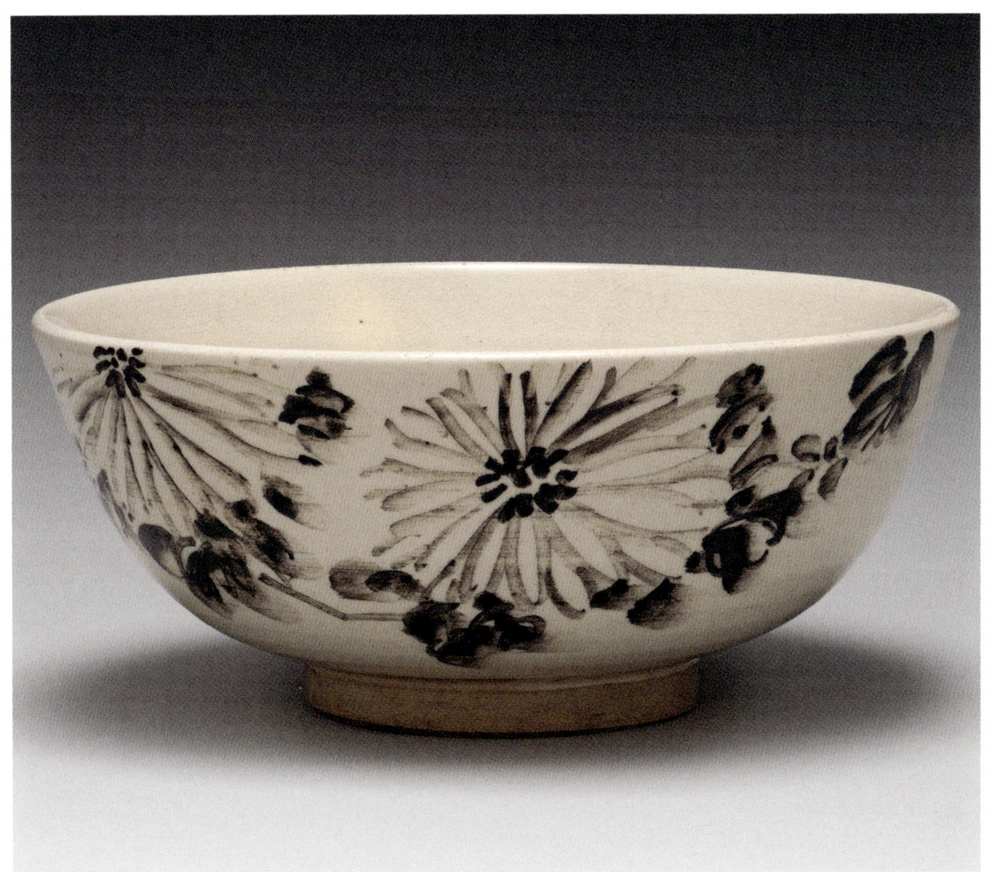

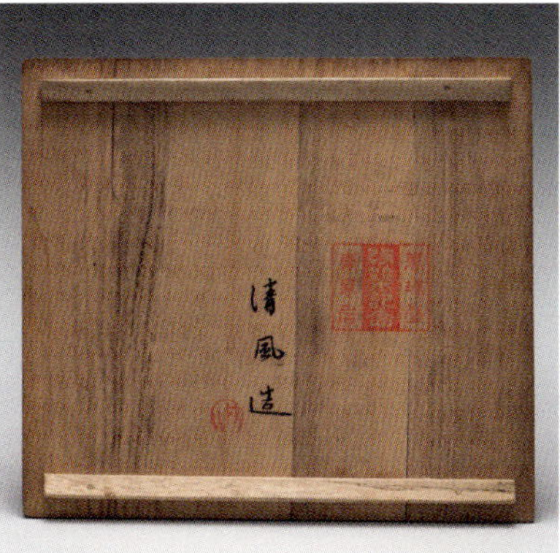

66 BOWL WITH OLD PINE AND POEM, 1914–46

Porcelain with carved design and cream glaze
H. 8 cm, diam. 19.1 cm
2022.209

A grand, aged pine is carved into the body of this bowl. The inscription on the reverse side explains the tree's presence. It is an altered version of two lines from a poem by Li Jiao (646?–715?) called "Pine." Li Jiao was a senior government official who had a tumultuous career under the reign of Wu Zetian (r. 690–705), as well as those of her sons and grandson, during the Tang dynasty (618–907). Although little known today, his work was read in Japan during the Heian (794–1185) and Kamakura periods (1185–1333). An anthology containing his poems, which was lost in China, was passed down across the generations in Japan. The translation of the inscription is as follows (the original characters, written and read from right to left, are shown below from left to right):

> *The crane nests in the mastwood tree,*
> *the wind flicks at its peaceful branches.*
> 鶴樹君子樹風拂太平枝

The mastwood is a pine-like evergreen, and the crane sheltering there is protected from the wind. In the original poem, the characters before "branches" (枝) are rather 大夫, meaning "high official." This is likely a reference to the title bestowed upon a pine tree by the emperor Qin Shi Huang (r. 221–210 BCE) in thanks for its protection when a fierce rain fell as he ascended Mt. Tai to pay his obeisance to the heavens.

Detail of [66]

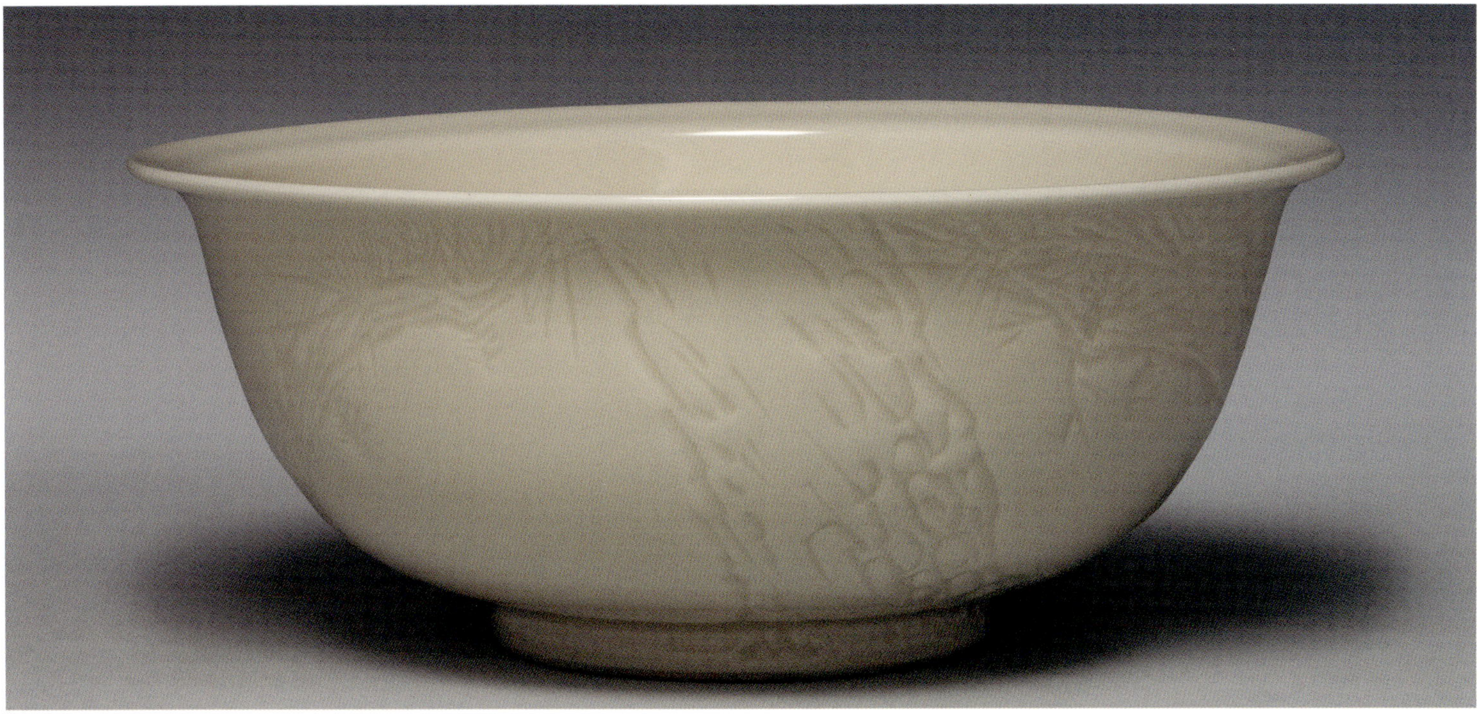

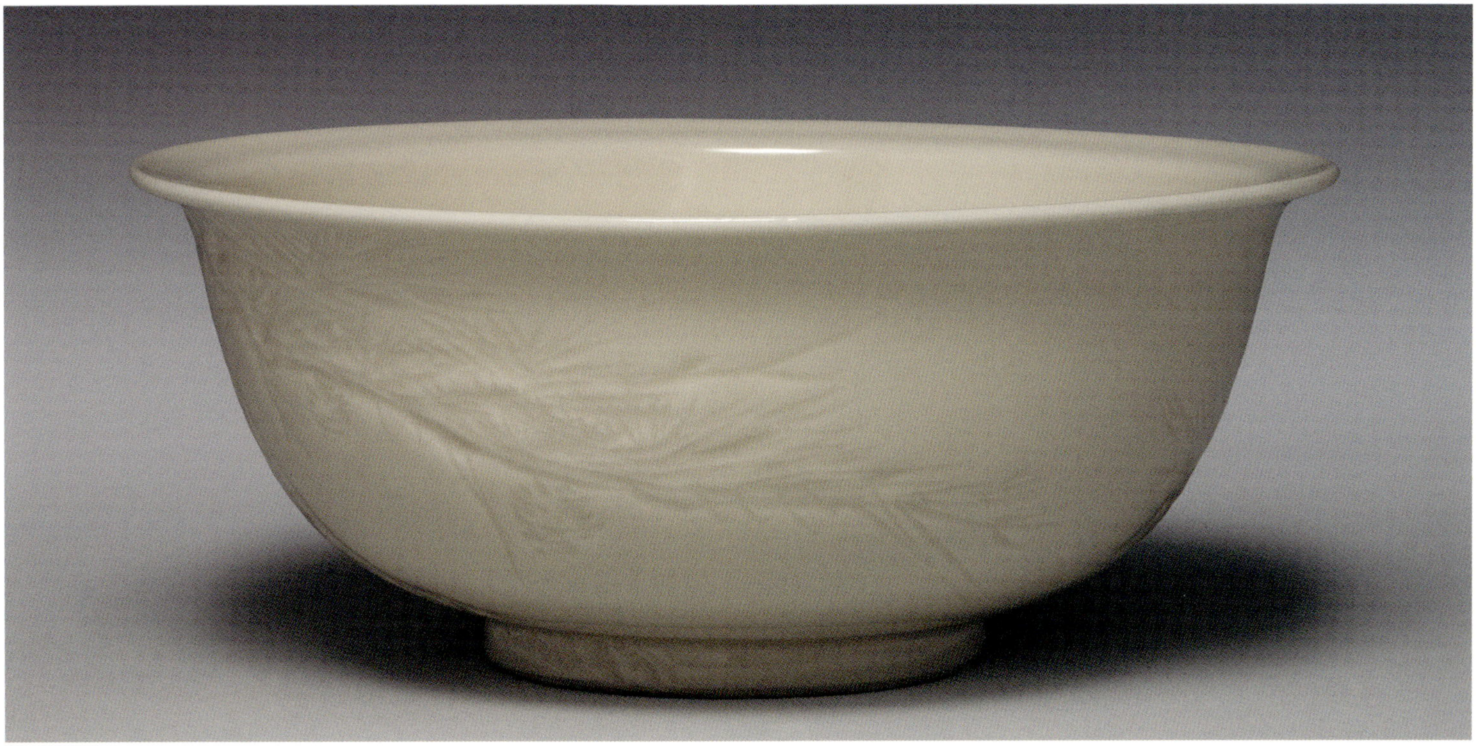

67 SINGLE STEM VASE, 1914–46

Porcelain with molded designs and copper red glaze
H. 17.1 cm, diam. 9.5 cm
2022.210

This vase has lion heads for "ears." It is copper red in color at the top and becomes purple closer to the bottom, not unlike a Chinese transformation or flambé glaze with mottling and dripping of the glaze. The lip of the vase and much of the lion-head designs remain white. On the box lid, the color of the glaze is called *shinsha*, which is often glossed as copper red or oxblood, or sometimes cinnabar. Here, it is meant to refer to a Qing-dynasty glazing technique developed in an effort to reproduce a red glaze used during the reign of the Xuande emperor (r. 1426–1435) of the Ming dynasty.

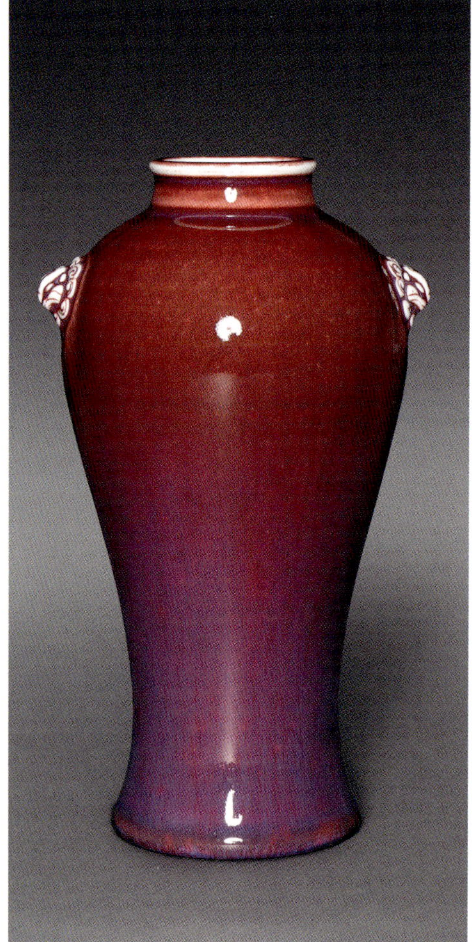

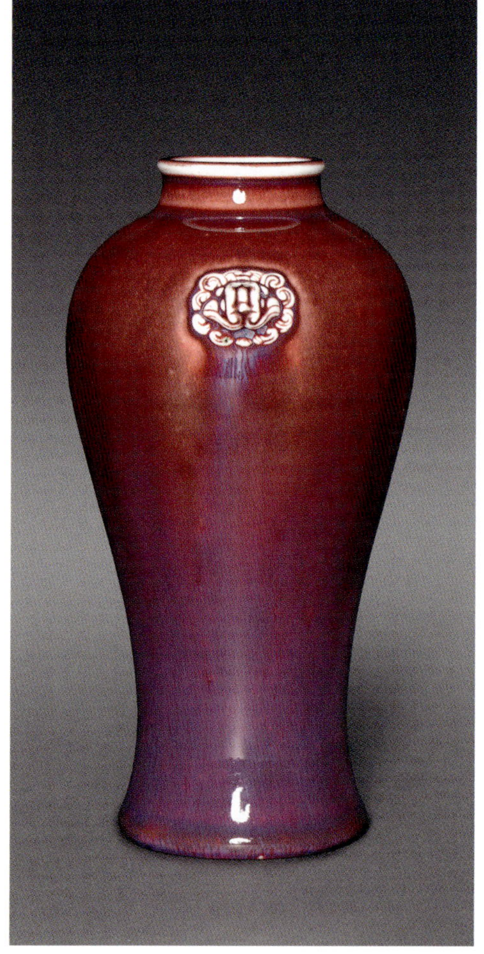

168 VASE WITH PLUM BLOSSOMS, 1914–46

Porcelain with molded and carved design and blue glaze
H. 32.9 cm, diam 23.1 cm
2022.211

The dense, all-over pattern of flowering plum, or prunus, branches on this vase resembles Japanese textile patterns. The trunks and forward-facing blossoms anchor the design, which is also filled with thinner branches and flowers ranging from round bud to full bloom, with the occasional flower facing upward or downward. As they might in a textile design, the trunks run in alternate directions up and down the surface. At the foot is a classic running design of spirals and at the neck, a collar of clouds. Although the vase has unfortunately lost its box, the glaze color is probably "water color" (*mizusai*). The visual effect is like that of a silk brocade, in which the pattern takes a supporting role to the color.

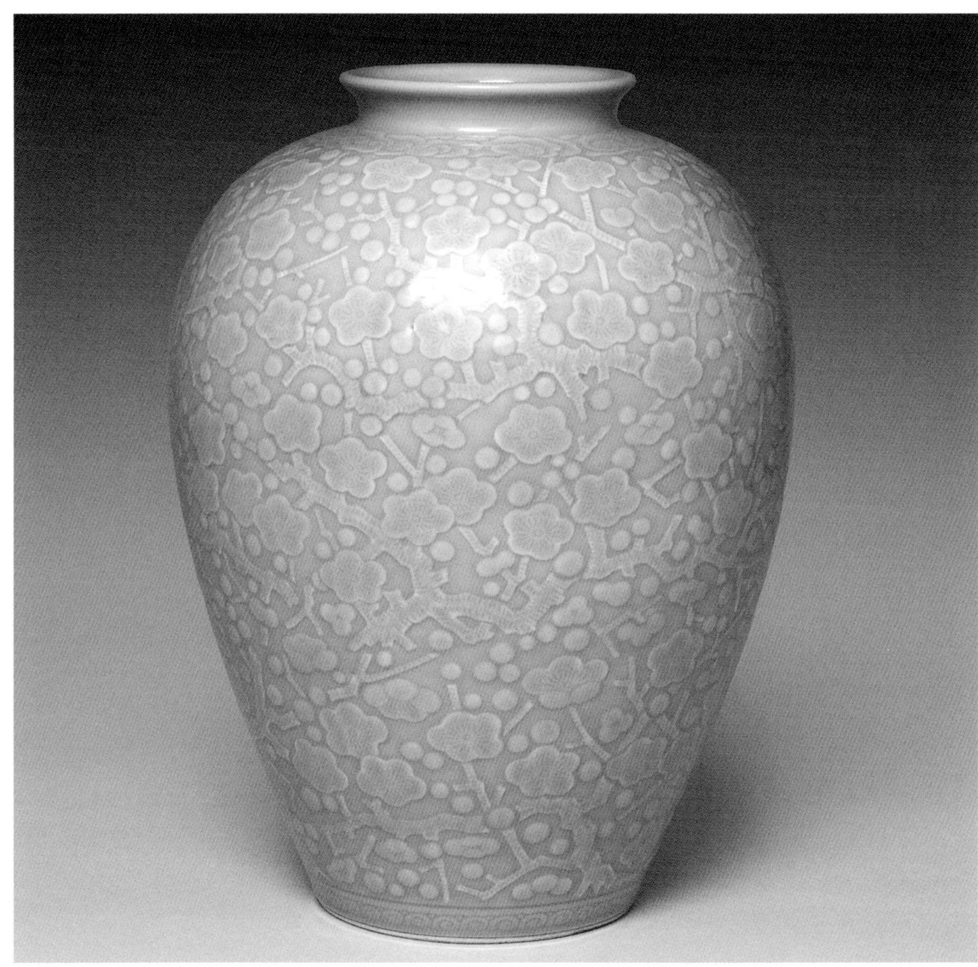

69 **WATER CONTAINER WITH SHELL AND SEAWEED, 1914–46**
Porcelain with molded design, underglaze blue, blue glaze, and lacquered wood lid
H with lid. 16.5 cm, diam. 14 cm
2022.212

70 **DISHES WITH SHELLS, 1914–46**
Set of five dishes; porcelain with molded design, iron oxide, and blue glaze
Each: h. 2.5 cm, diam. 12.1 cm
2022.213

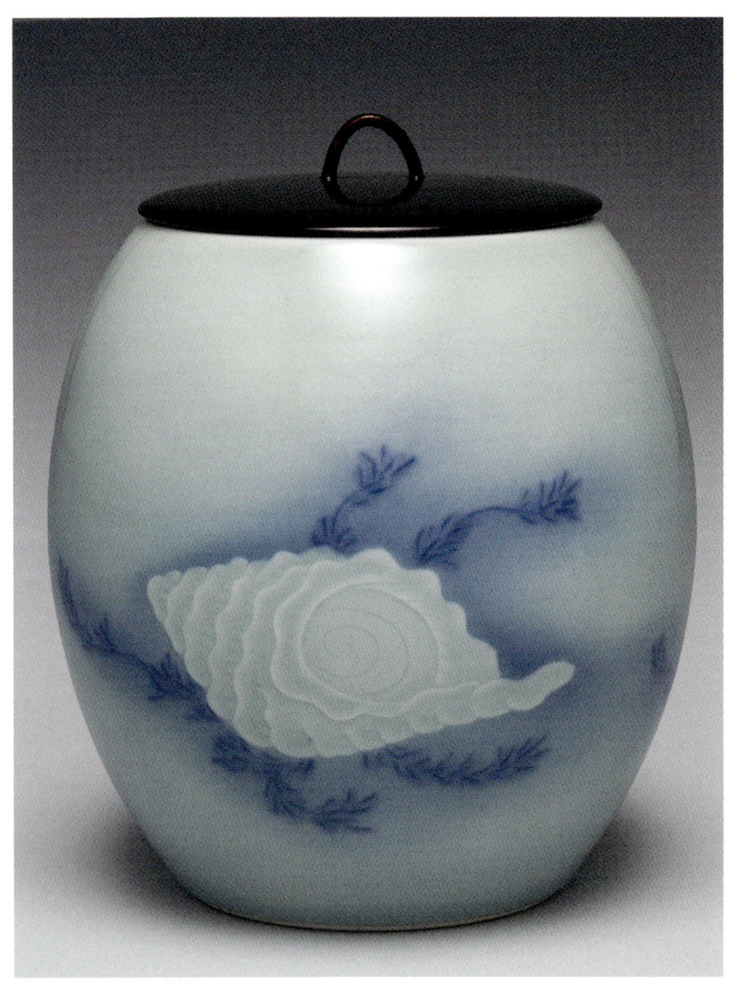

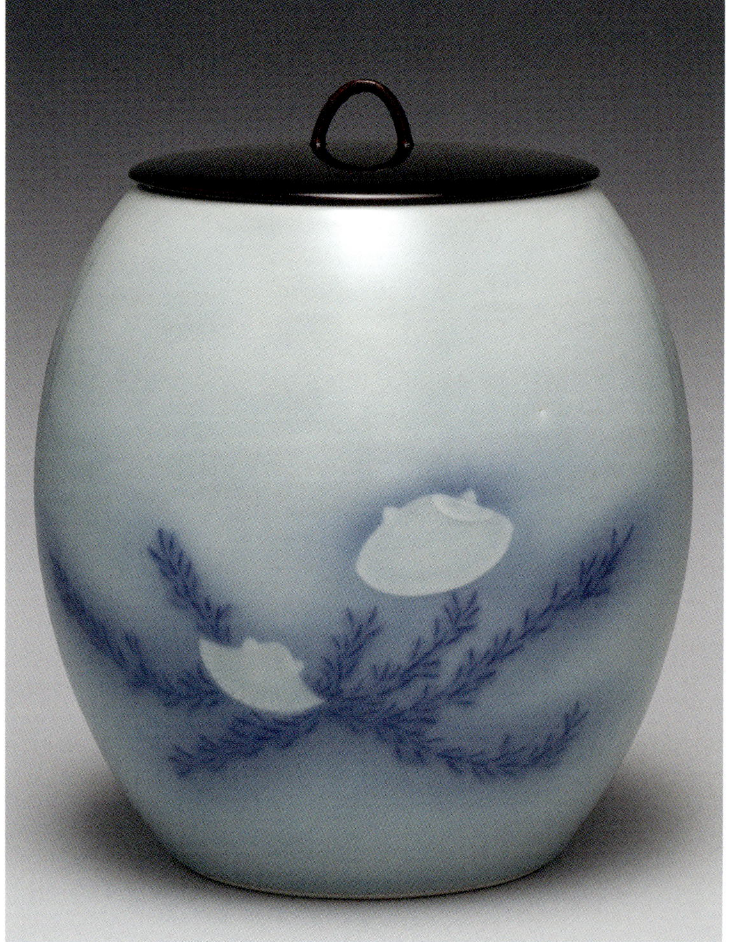

[69]

Yohei IV chose an aquatic theme for this *mizusashi* and did a variation on it in a set of five *mukōzuke*. For the *mizusashi*, he applied clay to the surface and molded the shape of a large conch on one side and, on the other, a clam and a scallop. The finer details he incised into the surface of his low-relief shapes. He then painted seaweed as though it were coming out from behind the sea creatures, and he further set off the animals using a masking technique with a gradated blue surround. Finally, he applied a translucent blue glaze identified on the box as *mizusai* over the entire body of the vessel. The resulting effect is that one imagines having descended through the water to the ocean floor.

For the side dishes, Yohei added an iron oxide rim and skipped the underglaze blue, instead using a more concentrated blue glaze on both the interior and exterior. The glaze, named on the box lid, is his father's "evening moon" (*tsukiyoi*) color. The conch, again in relief, takes up the entire bottom of the dish. Up the sides are two snails on one end and on the other a scallop. These are less finely articulated than the shells on the water container, resulting in a boldly graphic, less realistic effect.

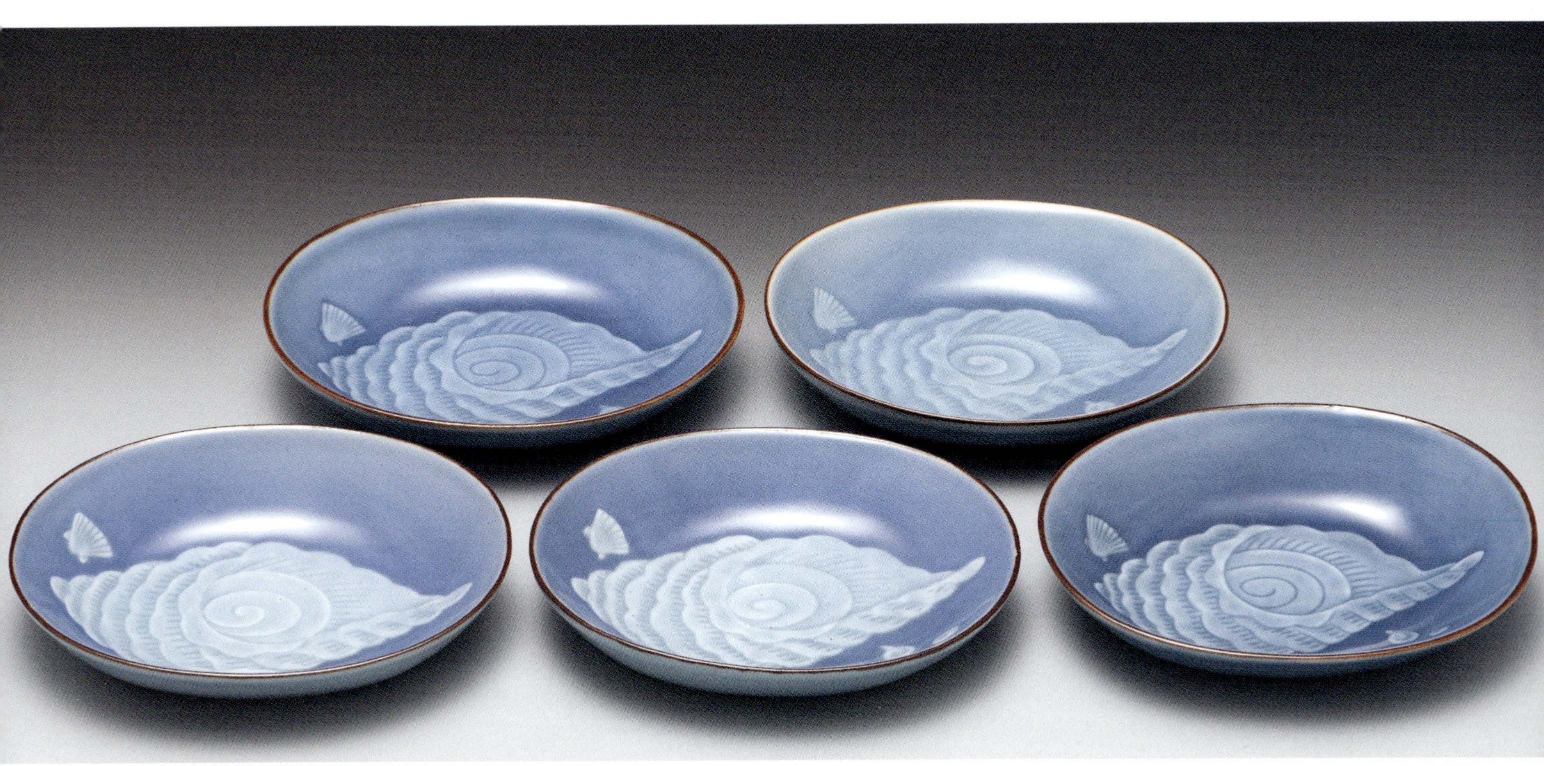

[70]

71 DISHES WITH FLOWERS, 1914–46

Set of five dishes; porcelain with underglaze yellow and blue glaze
Each: h. 4 cm, diam. 10.2 cm
2022.214

One can imagine a cool summer breeze when looking upon this set of dishes, each shaped with a crenulated mouth and glazed with blue. Around the rim and into the basin, the bowls have low-relief designs of flowers with underglaze yellow petals; their leaves and stems show white through the glaze. On each dish, the design continues over the rim onto one side.

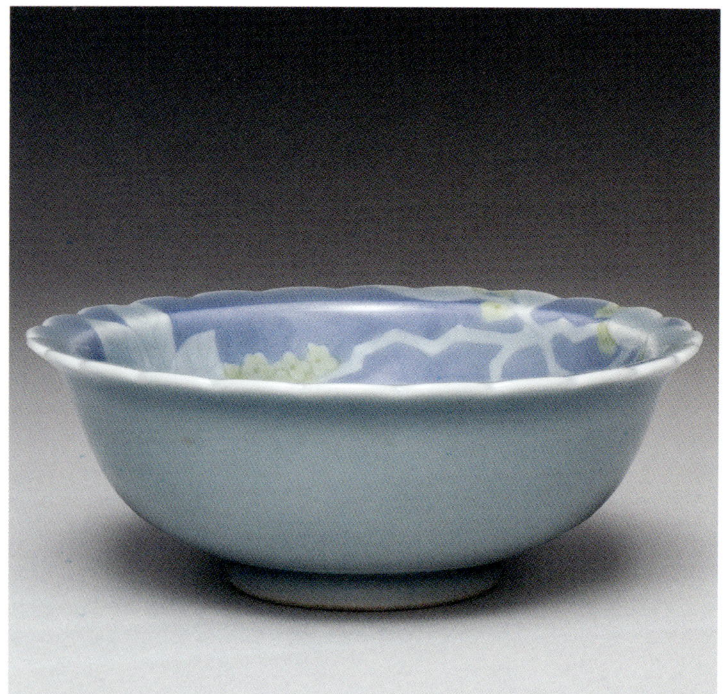

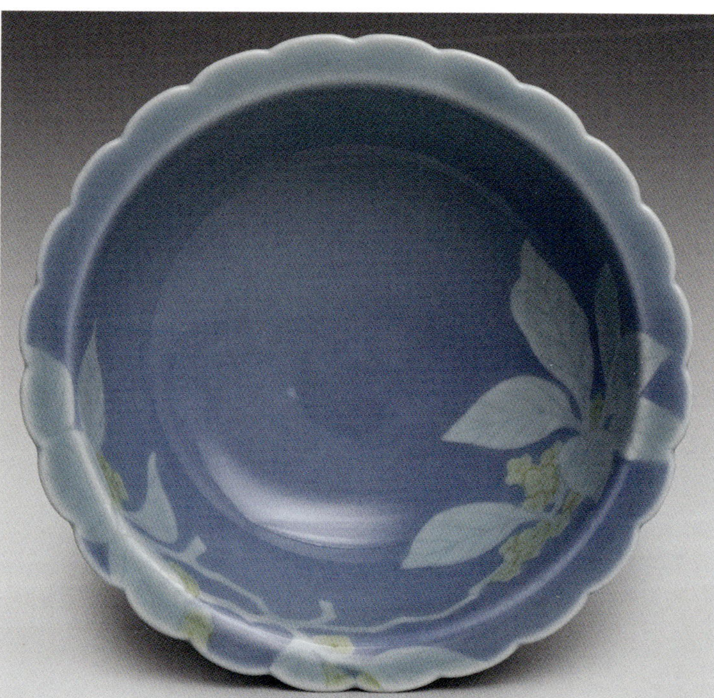

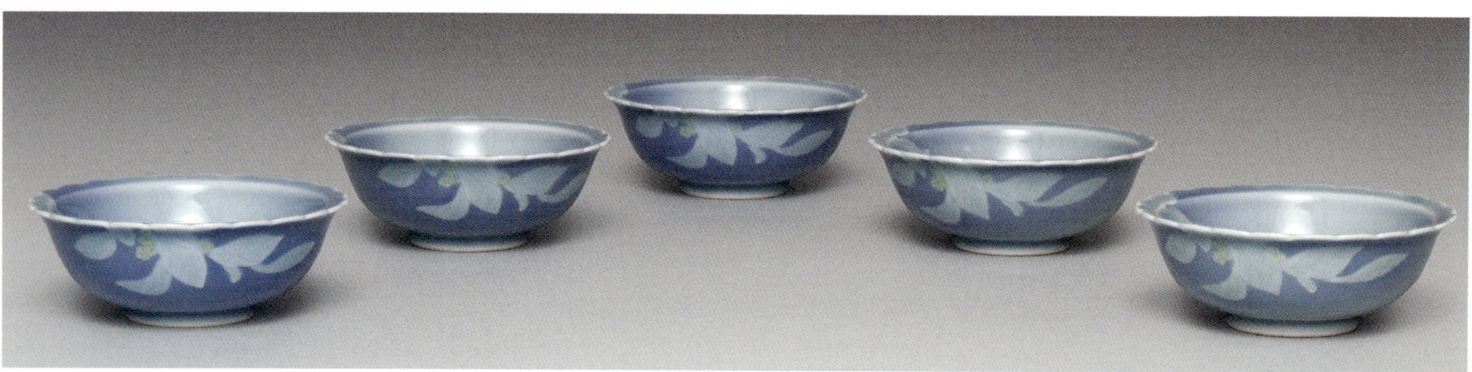

72 SWEETS BOWL WITH PLUM TREE, 1914–46

Porcelain with underglaze color and blue glaze
H. 11.5 cm, diam. 21.5 cm
2022.242

In this sweets bowl, Yohei IV combines ink painting techniques with advanced glazing techniques. He has painted the gnarled boughs of a plum tree in iron oxide on the surface of the bowl. The tree's blossoms are made slightly in relief by a build-up of slip. Their centers are painted with yellow. All of this is under a blue glaze that his father developed in 1893 and named "evening moon" (*tsukiyoi*). Before applying the glaze, he would have covered the blossoms with paper so that they remained white. It appears that after applying the *tsukiyoi* glaze, he then went back over the design with iron oxide to add luster and dimensionality to the branches before applying a transparent glaze.

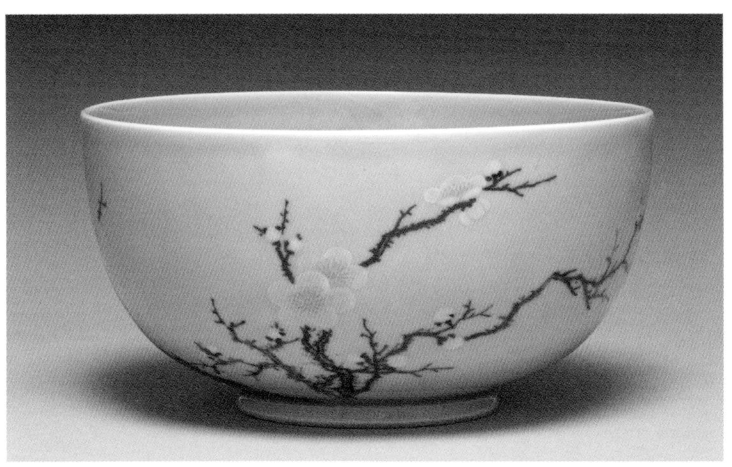

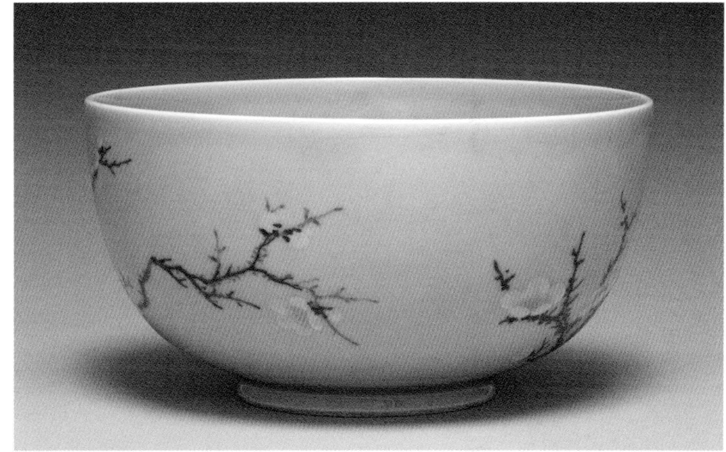

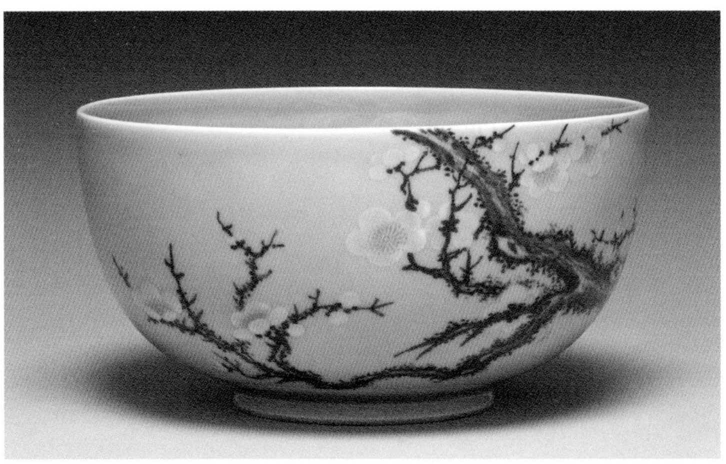

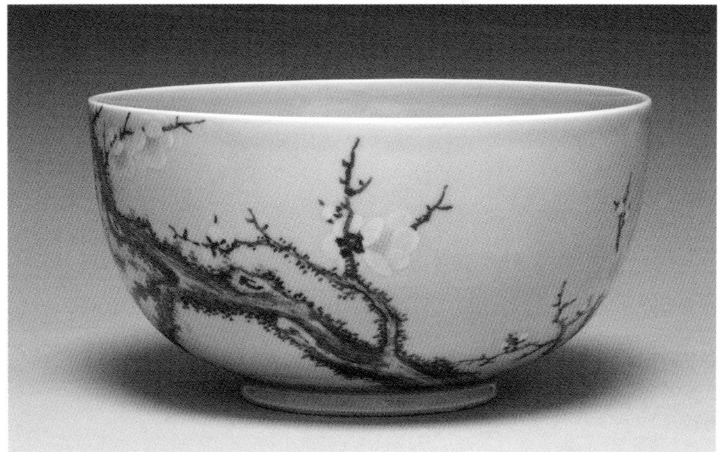

73 **SWEETS BOWL, 1914–46**
Porcelain with red glaze
H. 9 cm, diam. 19 cm
2022.215

74 **CUPS, 1914–46**
Set of five cups; porcelain with yellow glaze
Each: h. 6.5 cm, diam. 9 cm
2022.217

75 **SAKE POURERS, 1914–46**
Porcelain with yellow glaze and bamboo lid handles
Each: h. 13 cm, diam. 5.5 cm
2022.216

76 **CHRYSANTHEMUM-SHAPED DISH, 1914–46**
Porcelain with molded design and yellow glaze
H. 2.5 cm, diam. 12.7 cm
2022.218

Like his father, Yohei IV also produced works with red or yellow monochrome glazes. His red coral-glazed sweets bowl with white interior is an example of the former. His yellow-glazed works here include a set of five drinking cups, a pair of sake pourers, and a sweets bowl molded into the shape of a chrysanthemum.

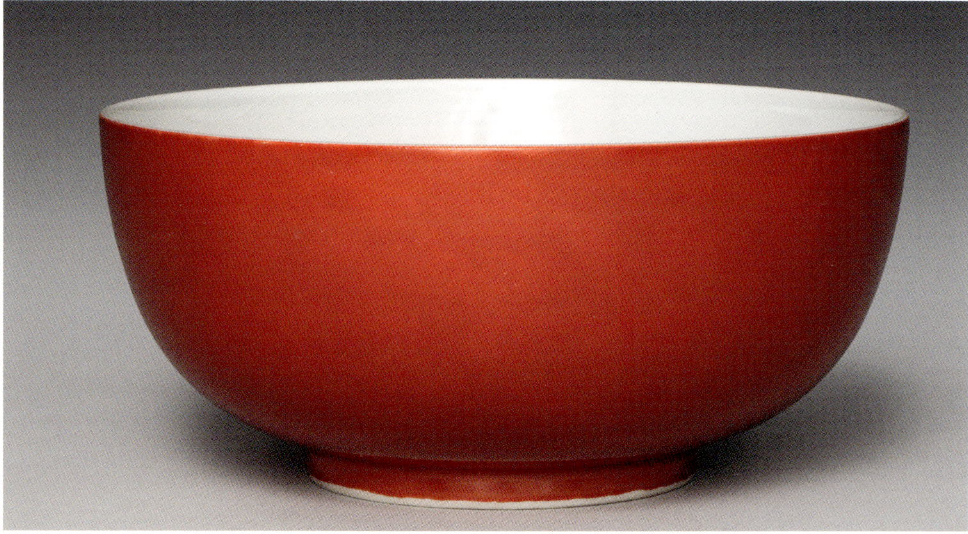

[73]

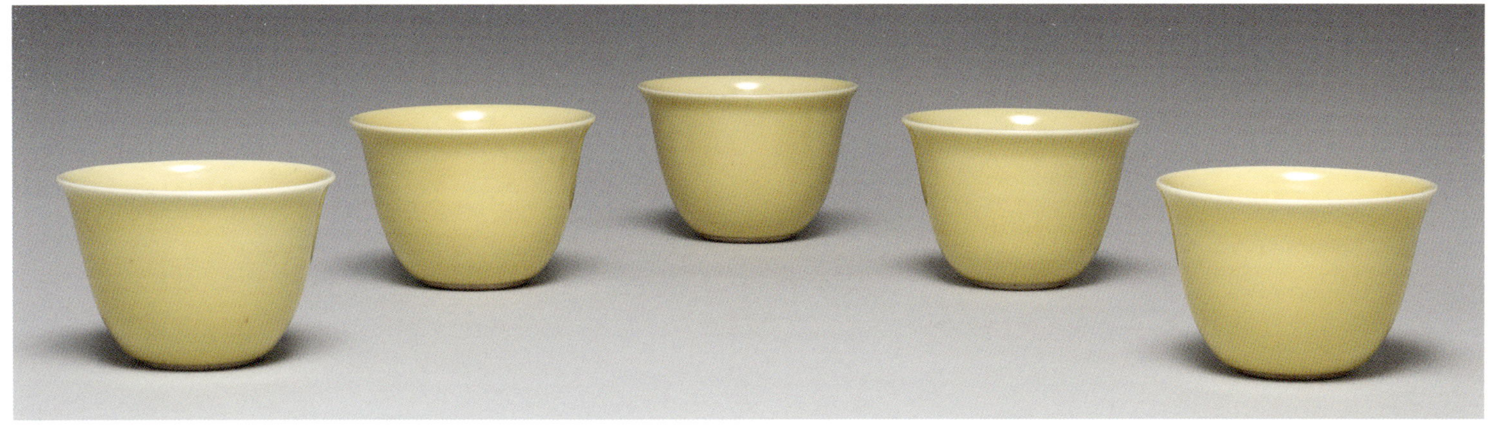

[74]

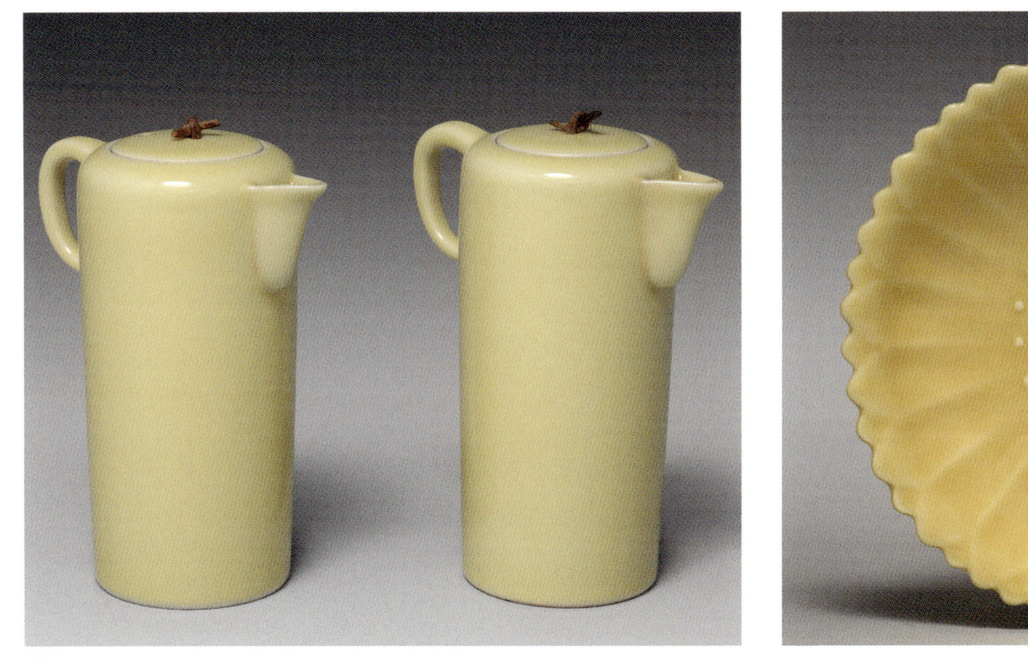

[75]

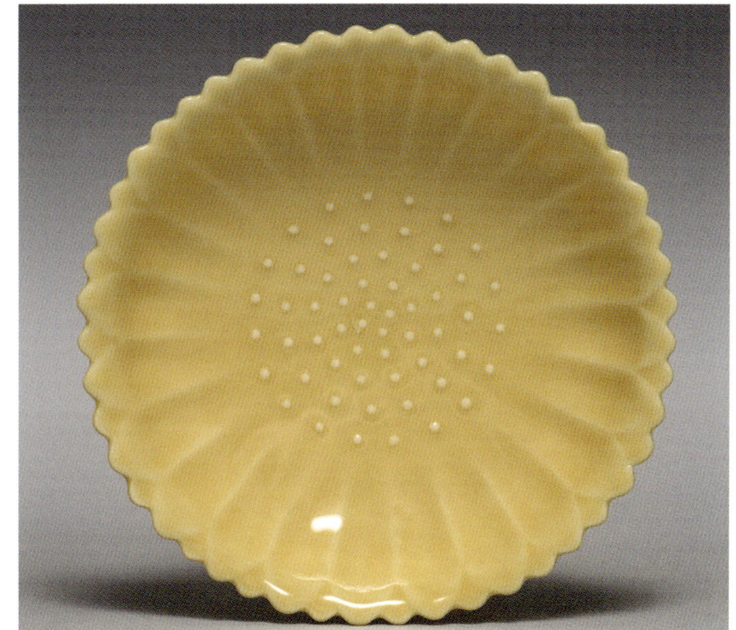

[76]

77 RINSING BOWLS, 1960–91

Pair of bowls; porcelain with underglaze blue and overglaze color enamel
Each: 9 cm, diam. 13.5 cm
2022.219

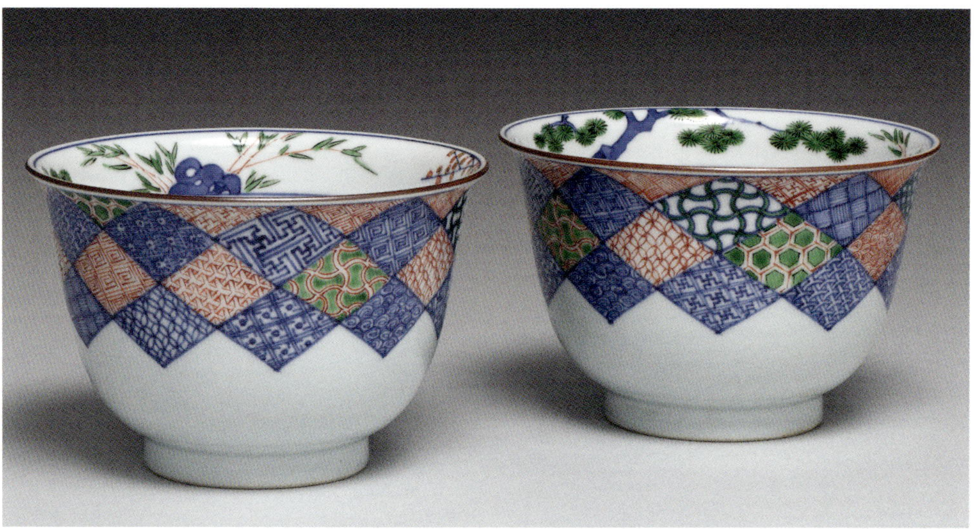

Bowls for rinsing serving cups, especially sake cups, on the fly are called *haisen*. This matching pair has a Three Friends of Winter theme below the rim on the inside. In Japan, this motif of pine, bamboo, and plum, or prunus, remains a very popular one in lacquer and textile design. Underglaze blue is used to paint the twisted trunk of the plum, the leaning trunk of the pine, and the garden rock in front of the bamboo. In addition, the pinwheel pine needles are in black on green, as are the bamboo leaves. The stalks and fresh sprouts of bamboo are done in red. Over the underglaze blue, plum branches and flowers are painted in a combination of red outline with wash and yellow. On their exteriors, the bowls have a diamond pattern in underglaze blue as well as red and green overglaze enamels. Within the individual lozenges are a variety of patterns. Some are painted only in blue or red, while others combine one of the two with green. Given their very festive pattern and color, it is a reasonable hypothesis that they were intended for use at New Year's celebrations. Although for much of his life, circumstances prevented him from producing such works, Yohei V did eventually create some ceramics close to the spirit of those made by earlier generations of the Seifū studio.

78 INCENSE BURNER WITH BIRDS IN FLIGHT, 1930s–90s

Porcelain with incised design, cream glaze, and rosewood cover
H. with lid 10 cm, diam. 8 cm
2022.221

79 SEAL INK BOX WITH SNAIL, 1930s–90s

Porcelain with molded and carved design, underglaze iron oxide, and green glaze
H. 3 cm, diam. 10.4 cm
2022.222

80 RABBIT WITH JEWEL, 1930s–90s

Porcelain sculpture with underglaze pink and cream glaze
H. 16 cm, w. 9 cm, d. 12.5 cm
2022.220

These three pieces by Shinkai Kunitarō 新開邦太郎, who took the artist style name Kanzan 寛山, are exemplars of his cute design sense and keen interest in birds, insects, and animals as subject matter. The incense burner here has on its rosewood cover an incised pattern of birds in flight and swirling clouds, and

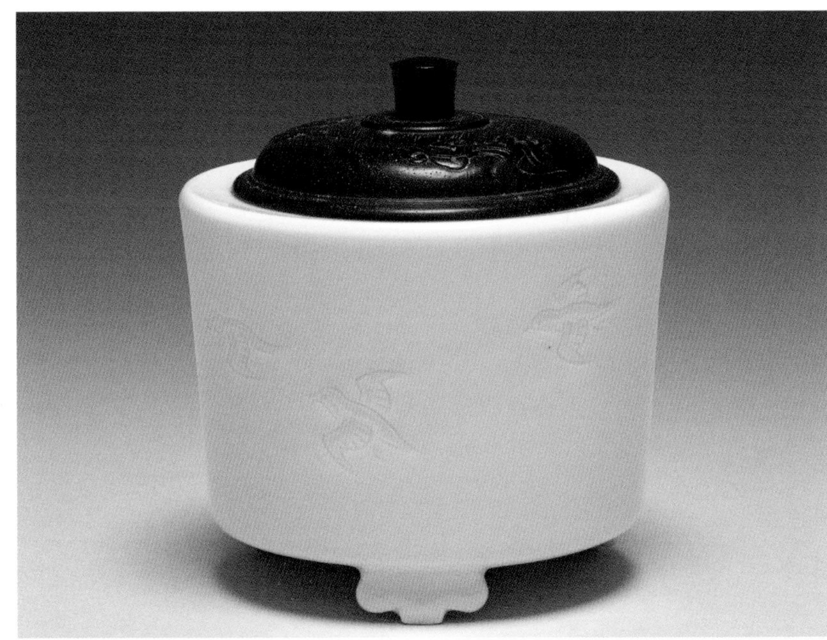

[78]

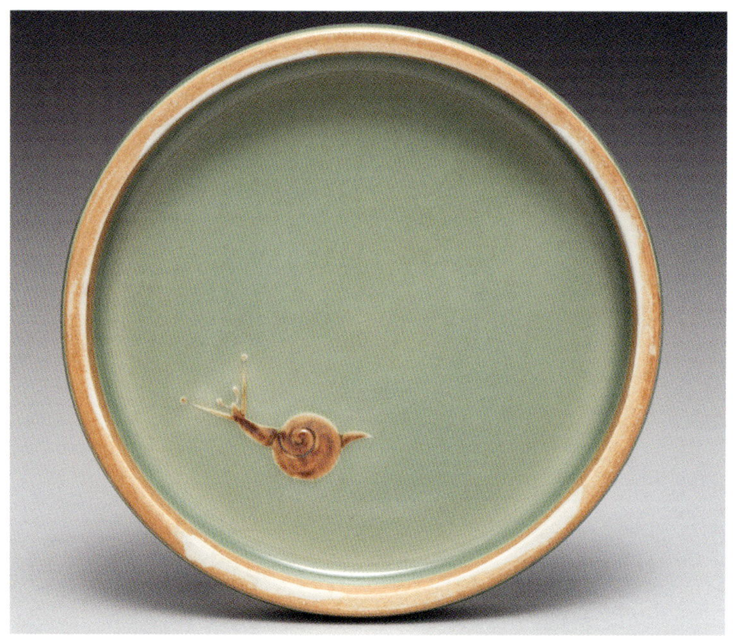

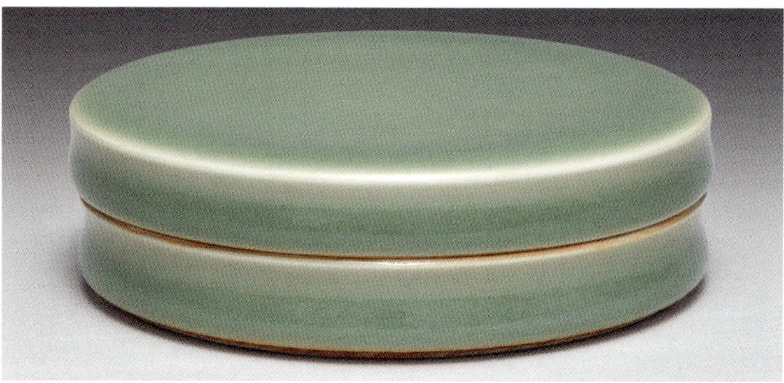

[79]

his seal ink box opens to reveal a diminutive snail in an orange hue. His rabbit, which is entirely cream colored but for touches of deep pink for the eyes, is meant for display at New Year's in the Year of the Rabbit. The animal looks up while holding a treasured jewel, which is banded to indicate that it is tricolored. On the box lid for the incense burner, Shinkai identifies his work as *taihakuji*, and on the inside of the lid, his seal identifies him as a member of the Seifū studio. Seifū Yohei III was the artist's grandfather, and Yohei IV was his uncle and the older brother of his father, who specialized in throwing ceramics on the wheel.[1] Shinkai studied ceramics with Yohei IV and attended the Kyoto City School of Fine and Decorative Arts, where he studied design and painting on the advice of his father, for in the world of the ceramics studio, those who applied designs and paintings

1. A most helpful biographical resource for Shinkai Kanzan is a blog post: "Gendai tōgei 41 (Shinkai Kanzan)."

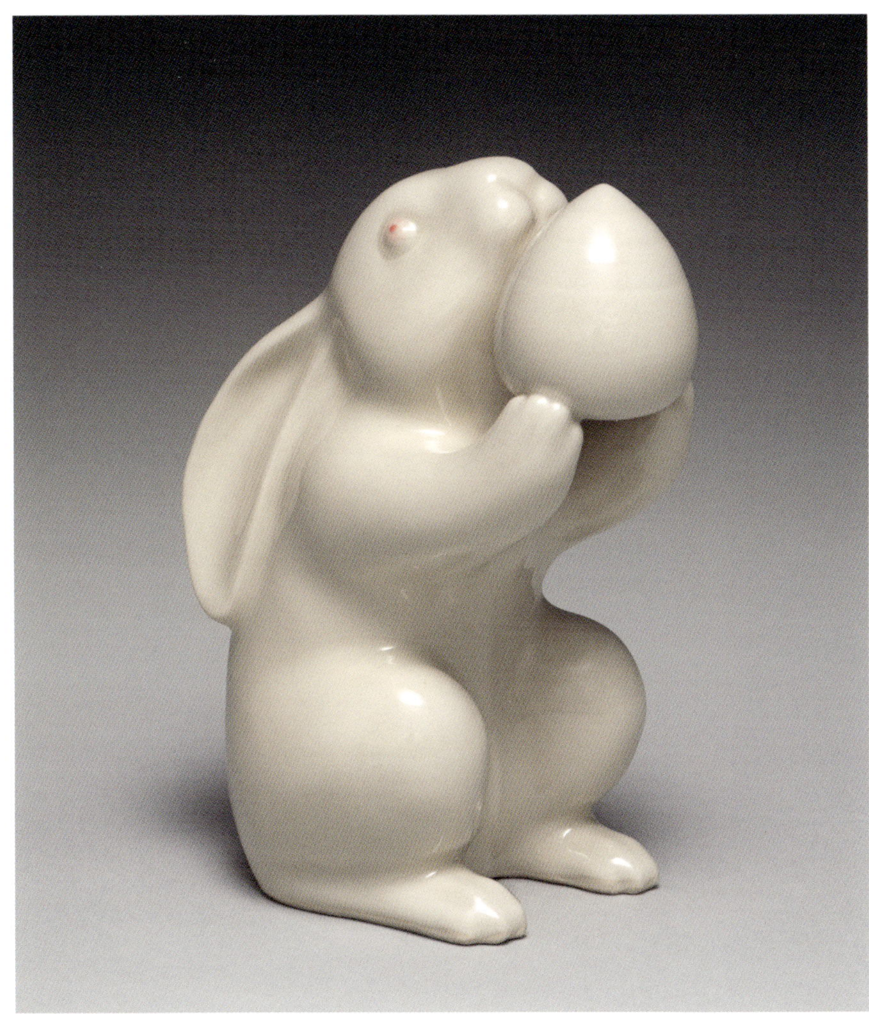
[80]

had a more elevated status than those who worked the wheel. In 1930, the year of his graduation, he first exhibited in the 11th Imperial Exhibition. From 1932, he went on to receive additional ceramics training from Kiyomizu Rokubei VI (1901–1980) after joining the ceramics society of Rokubei VI's father, Kiyomizu Rokubei V (1875–1959). After World War II, he reinvented himself and exhibited extensively in national-level exhibitions, garnering numerous prizes. He later served as a jurist or committee member for many of the same shows. In 1989, he was awarded the Kyoto Prefecture Culture Award for Lifetime Achievement and remained active on the board of the Japan Fine Arts Exhibition, or Nitten, as late as 1992.

CHINESE FORMS

SEIFŪ YOHEI III

81 **GU-SHAPED VASE, 1912–14**
Porcelain with crackled glaze
H. 27.9 cm, diam. of top 14.6 cm
2022.223

82 **GU-SHAPED VASE, 1893–97**
Porcelain with molded and carved design and cherry blossom glaze
H. 31.1 cm, diam of top 13.5 cm
2022.224

83 **TONG-SHAPED VASE WITH BAND OF CLOUD, 1893–1914**
Porcelain with green glaze and molded and carved design
H. 26.7 cm, diam. 11.4 cm
2022.225

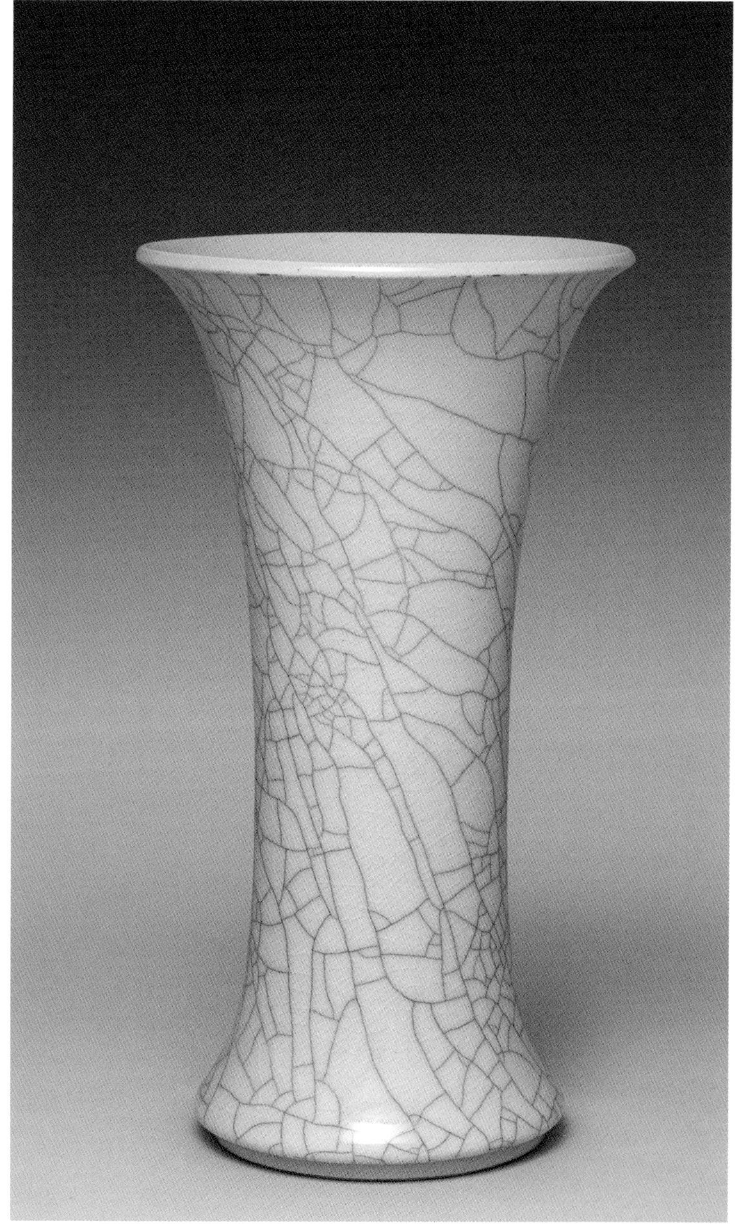

[81]

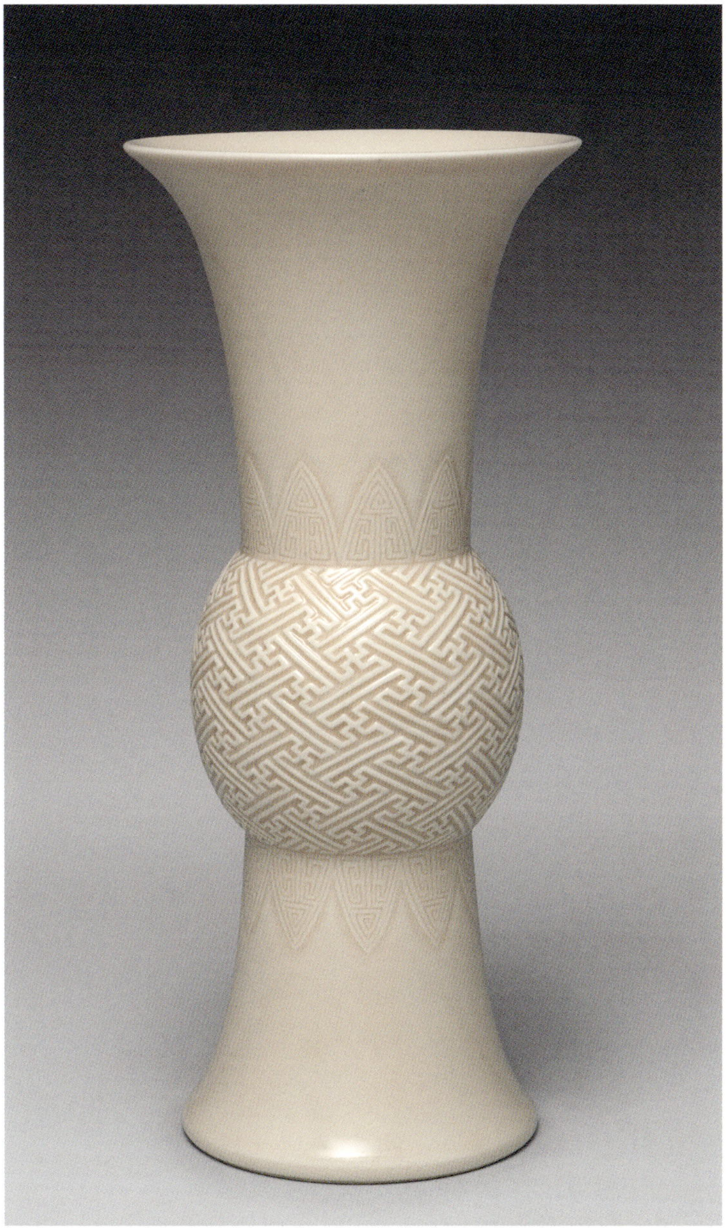

[82]

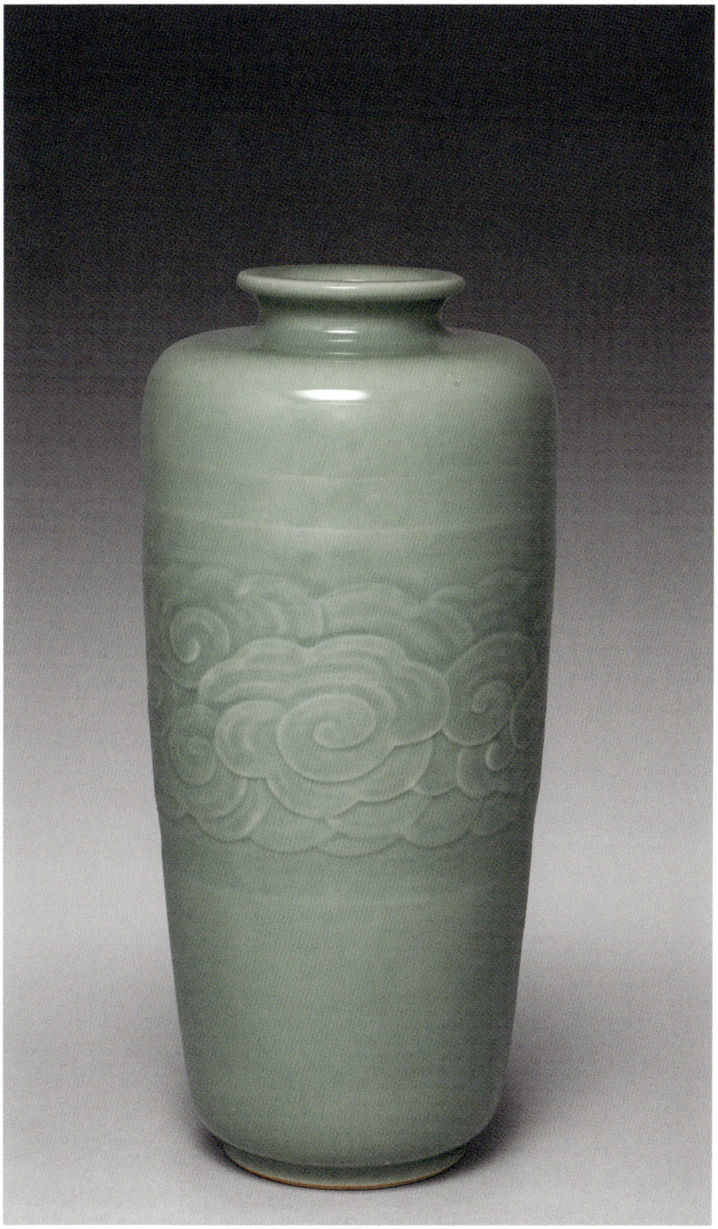

[83]

84 **HU-SHAPED VASE WITH HANDLES, 1914–46**
Porcelain with molded and carved design and green glaze
H. 31 cm, diam. 21.5 cm
2022.226

85 **GUAN-SHAPED VASE WITH FLORAL SCROLL, 1914–46**
Porcelain with molded and carved design and cream glaze
H. 25.7 cm, diam. 24.2 cm
2022.227

86 **TONG-SHAPED VASE WITH FLOWERS AND GRASSES, 1914–46**
Porcelain with molded and carved design and green glaze
H. 31.5 cm, diam. 12 cm
2022.228

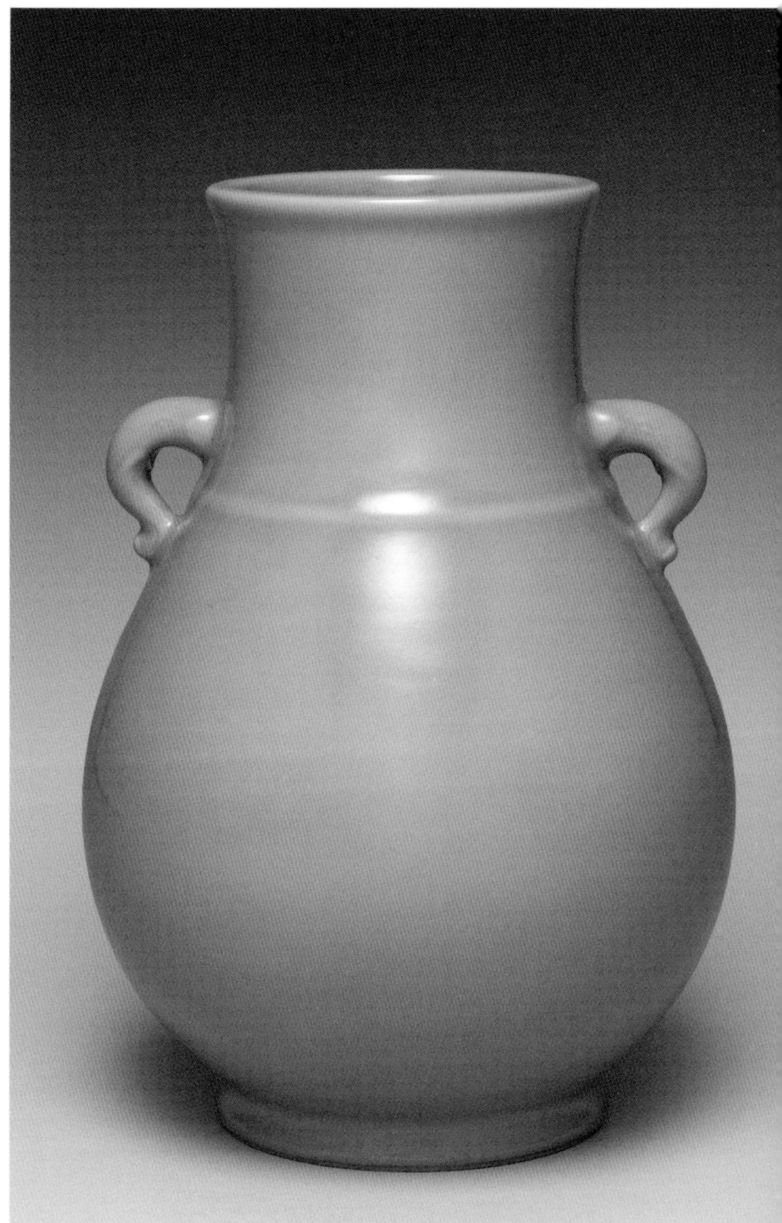

[84]

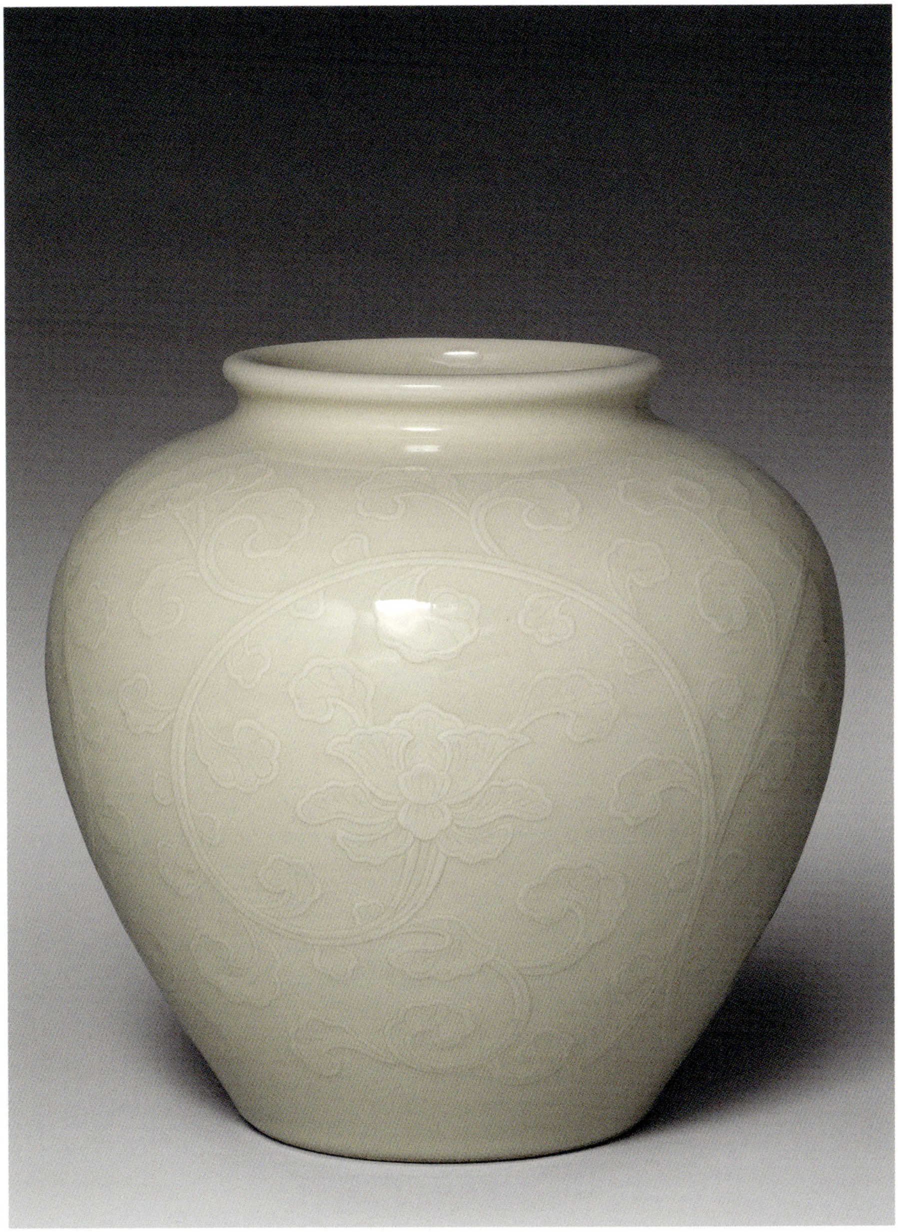

[85]

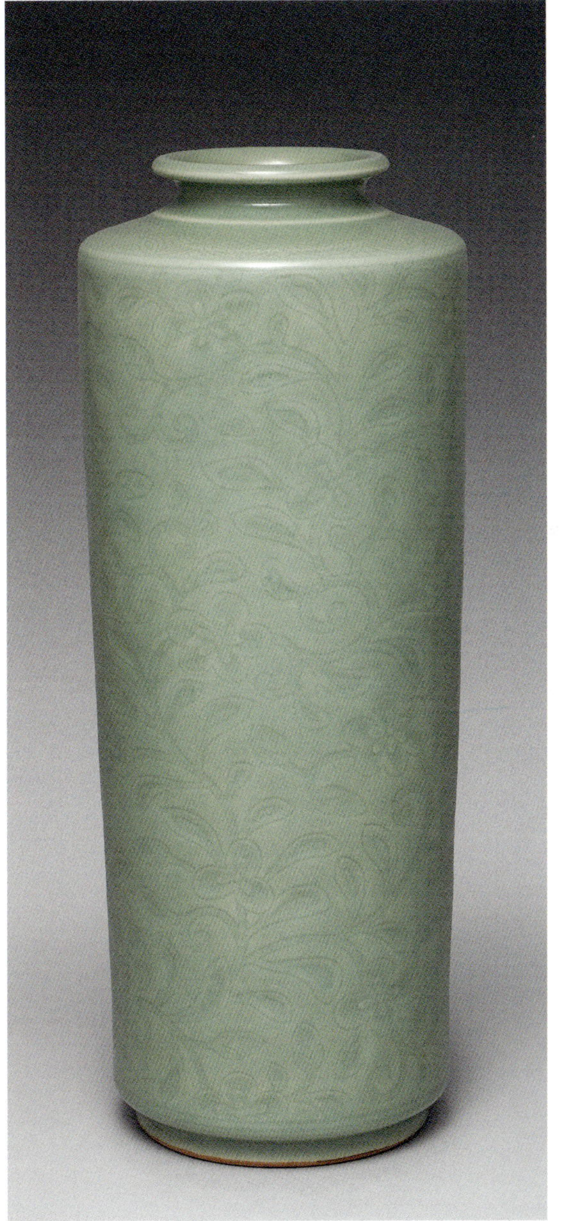

[86]

Many of the vases created by Yohei III and IV were made with reference to and in emulation of Chinese ceramics in both form and glazing. One of the most recognizable vessel types is the *guping*, or *kobin* in Japanese. These are relatively slender cylinders that flare at both the mouth and foot. They often have orbs or drum-like forms partway up the vessel. Generally called "beakers" in English, *gu* appeared as early as the Neolithic period (c. 8000–2000 BCE) in China. Originally made of clay and then of cast bronze during the Shang dynasty (c. 1600–c. 1046 BCE), they were used as wine vessels and in ritual settings. Like many other bronze vessel types, they were reproduced in porcelain in later centuries as part of antiquarian movements; these later versions were used as vases. Those copied by the Seifū studio likely included Qing-dynasty examples, some of which are rather wide relative to classical examples. One of the *gu*-shaped vases here [81], by Yohei III, has a cracked-ice glaze, which was once customarily called Ge (J. Ka), after the kiln where it purportedly originated during the Southern Song dynasty (1127–1279). The glaze's double-crackle pattern, featuring both deeper and shallower cracks, is called "gold threads and iron lines." Widely spaced deeper cracks characterize Guan (J. Kan) ware, first made in Hangzhou in Zhejiang Province during the Southern Song dynasty and later copied. The effect was enhanced here by coating the vessel with ink or another stain, which was allowed to seep into the cracks before the surface was wiped clean. The other *gu*-shaped vase by Yohei III here has "cherry blossom glaze" (*ōkayū*), according to its box [82]. There is record of Yohei III having invented a glaze he called "cherry blossom" in 1890. The vase also has a dramatic molded and carved geometric pattern on the orb at its middle, as well as sharp molded and carved petal designs above and below this bulging form. Of the two vases, this one more immediately calls to mind ancient bronzes. It is signed on the base "Made by Seifū of Great Japan." A label affixed to the side of the box gives a sense of how previous owners conceived of the piece. Although the label is partially abraded, one can make out the character *nezu* 鼠, used in the names of numerous light pinks, from Naniwa pink (Osaka pink) to Miyako pink (Kyoto, or capital, pink). Also legible is the phrase *hakugōrai*, a broad term that can describe a shade of white associated with ceramics discovered in Korean tombs, but often applied to other ceramics of similar coloration, many from Chinese kilns, including Ding (J. Tei) ware of the Northern Song dynasty.

The Seifū studio was also inspired by later Chinese copies of two other archaic vessel types, the *hu* (J. *ko*) and *guan* (J. *kan*). In simple terms, in their original contexts, the *hu* and *guan* were storage jars that also appeared in ritual contexts. One example of a *hu*-form vase by Yohei IV has a green glaze and handles in the shape of an elephant head (see detail of [84]). The details of the elephant heads are quite easy to miss, but a close look reveals that each has carved eyes with pupils defined, tiny ears and tusks in very low relief, and a curved trunk with the end curled up. This sort of container is even known as the "elephant ear" type. The only other decorative element on the vase's pear-shaped body is a raised cord-like band around the shoulders. A hefty *guan*-shaped vase by Yohei IV [85] has a floral scrolling pattern known in Japanese as *karakusa*, or "Chinese grasses." The flowers are generally identified as lotus or peony. According to the box lid, the vase is a *kanpakuji* work. This flower vase might alternately be categorized as having the form of what is called a *shukaiko* in Japan, or a large vessel for holding wine. *Shukaiko* were created as early as the latter part of the Kamakura period after Yuan-dynasty examples.

The vessel type called *tongping*, pronounced *tōbin* in Japanese, is tall and cylindrical, like the thick length of bamboo referenced in the shape of the ideograph *tong* 筒. Unlike the ancient *gu*, *hu*, and *guan*, this form did not emerge in China until the Ming dynasty, and many such vases date to the early Qing dynasty. Two green-glazed vases, one by Yohei III [83] and the other by Yohei IV [86], are interpretations of this form. Yohei III's version has slightly hunched shoulders and is somewhat wider at the top below the small neck and lip. Yohei IV's vase is more angular. The wide rack of molded cloud encircling the Yohei III vase rises subtly from very low relief banding above and below it, accentuating the vessel's rounded edges and complementing the form. In contrast, the all-over flower vine pattern on the body and "seven treasures" pattern at the collar of the vase by Yohei IV evokes a garment's cuffed sleeve, like the common English appellation for this type of vessel—"sleeve vase."

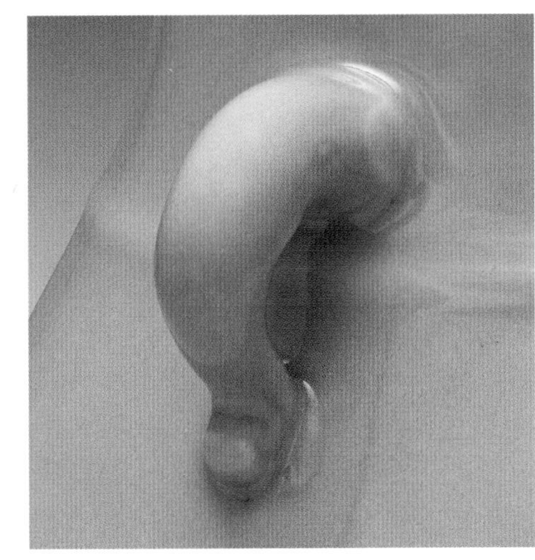

Detail of [84]

87 PRUNUS VASE WITH AMARANTHUS, 1914–46

Porcelain with yellow glaze, overglaze color enamel, and gold
H. 29.8 cm, diam. 11.4 cm
2022.229

88 GU-SHAPED VASE WITH PATINA, 1914–46

Porcelain with overglaze color enamel
H. 31.2 cm, diam. 16.5 cm
2022.230

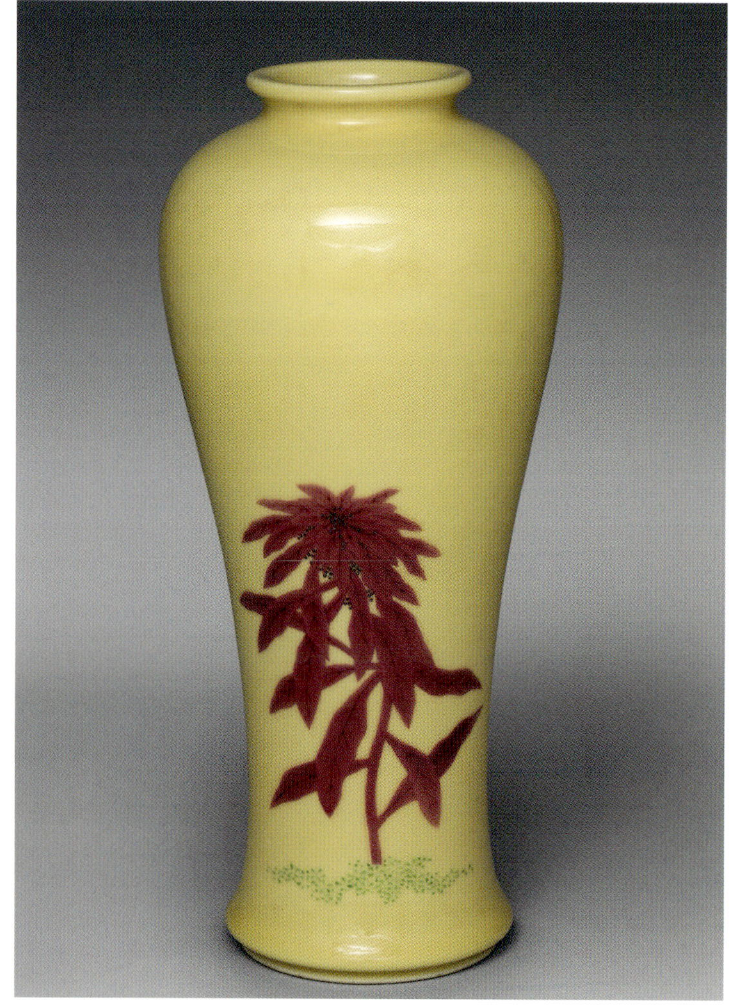

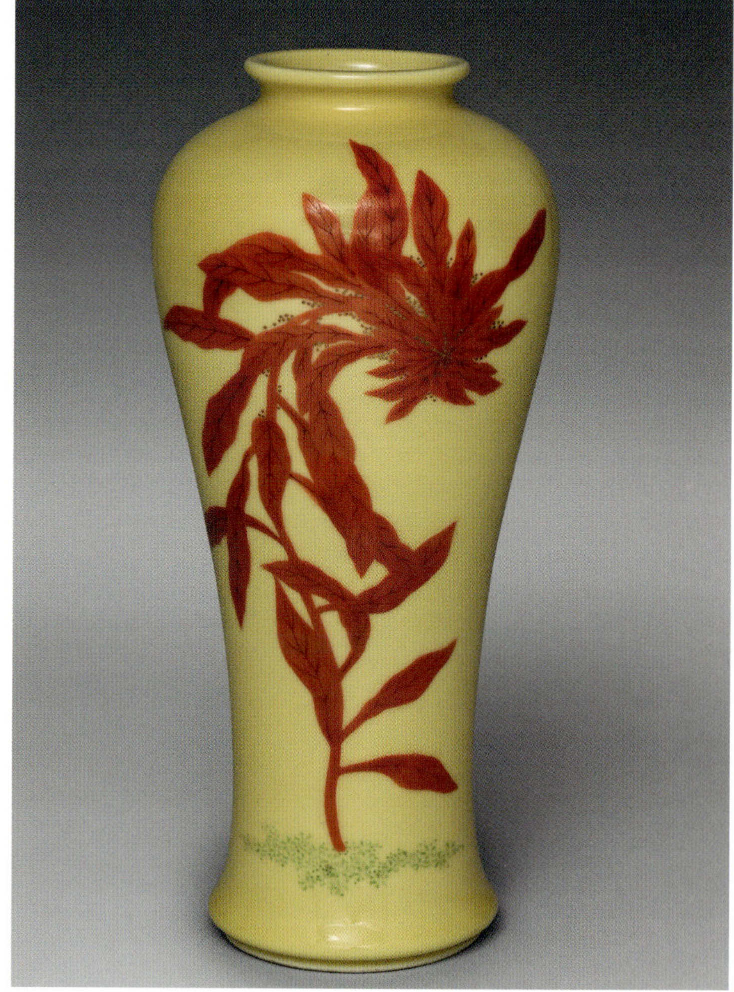

[87]

Yohei IV's interest in bold, colorful designs is on full display in these two vases. The one shaped like a "prunus vase," or *meiping* (J. *meipin*), has two colors of amaranthus on a yellow ground [87].[1] It follows a design appearing on a sleeve-shaped vase by Yohei III (fig. 44). Yohei IV uses bright spring-green dots of overglaze enamel to suggest a ground plane in his yellow environment; he also uses red and magenta accented with wild gold cascades of dots for two plants he places on opposite sides of the vase, one much larger than the other. In Yohei III's version, the body of the vessel is white, and the foliage of one plant is red with carefully painted veins in gold, while another plant strategically positioned behind it has a deep rust color, again carefully detailed in gold. In a sense, Yohei IV has deconstructed his father's logical, balanced design and re-presented it as an emotive,

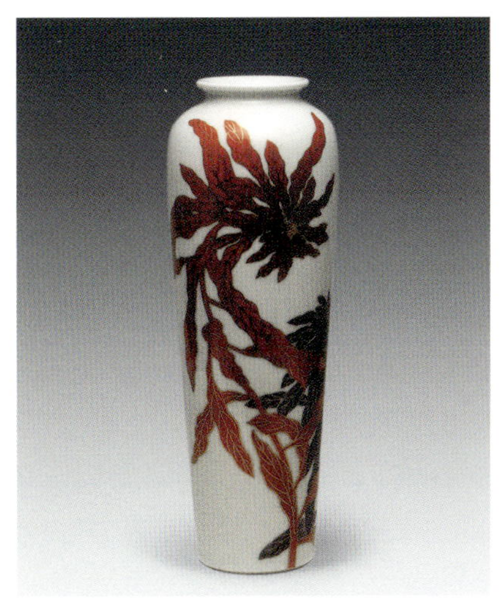

Figure 44. *Vase with Amaranthus*, 1893–1914. Seifū Yohei III. Porcelain with overglaze color enamel and gold; h. 29.8 cm, diam. 11.4 cm. Private collection

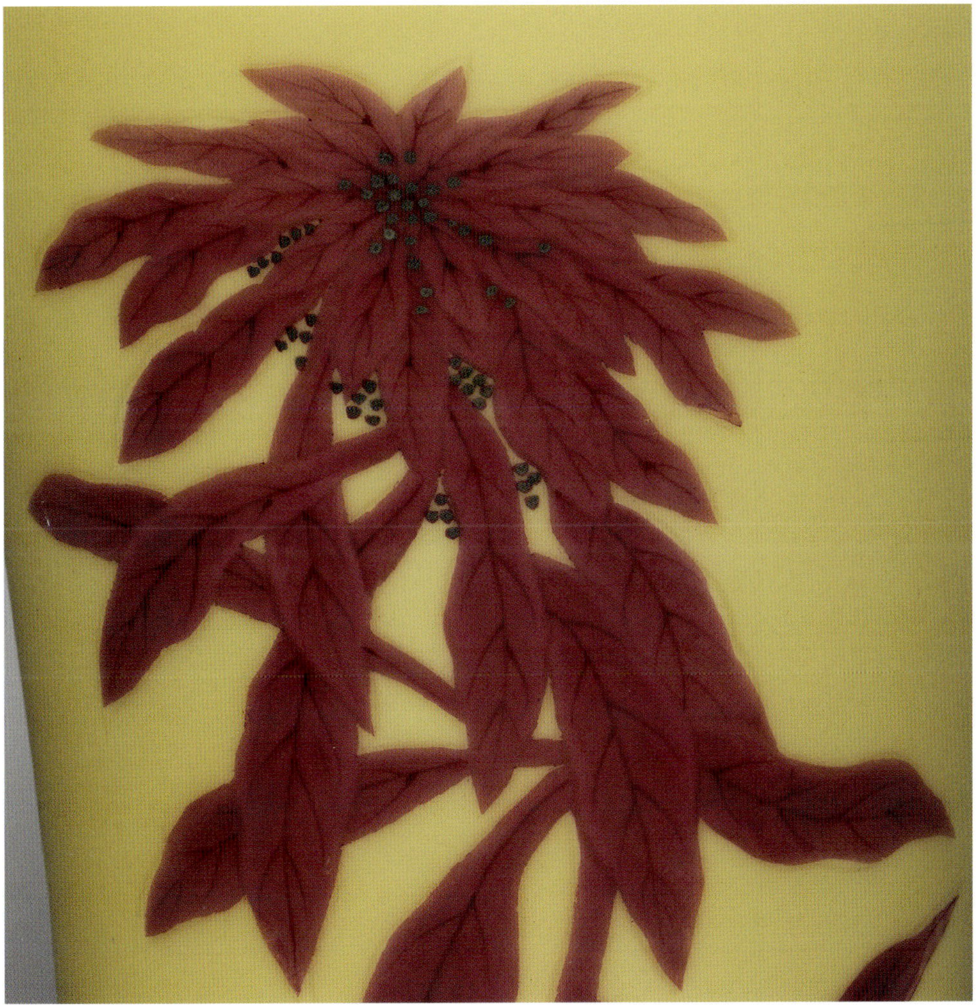

Detail of [87]

1. Inscriptions on the lids of the outer and inner boxes and on a paper affixed to the side of the vase's outer box refer to the plant as *yunraikō* (C. *yanlaihon*). This term is an alternate for *gen* or *hiyu* (C. *xian*). Both may be translated as amaranthus. In Japan, there is also the word *hageitō*, or "leaf[–variety] cockscomb." The amaranthus family includes the *Celosia* genus of plants, among which is the cockscomb (*Celosia cristata*). The plants on this vase, however, more closely resemble the plumed celosia (*Celosia plumosa*). The genus name derives from the ancient Greek term κήλεος meaning "burning." The paper label on the side of the outer box also has a seal that reads "Kept by Watanabe" 渡邊所蔵.

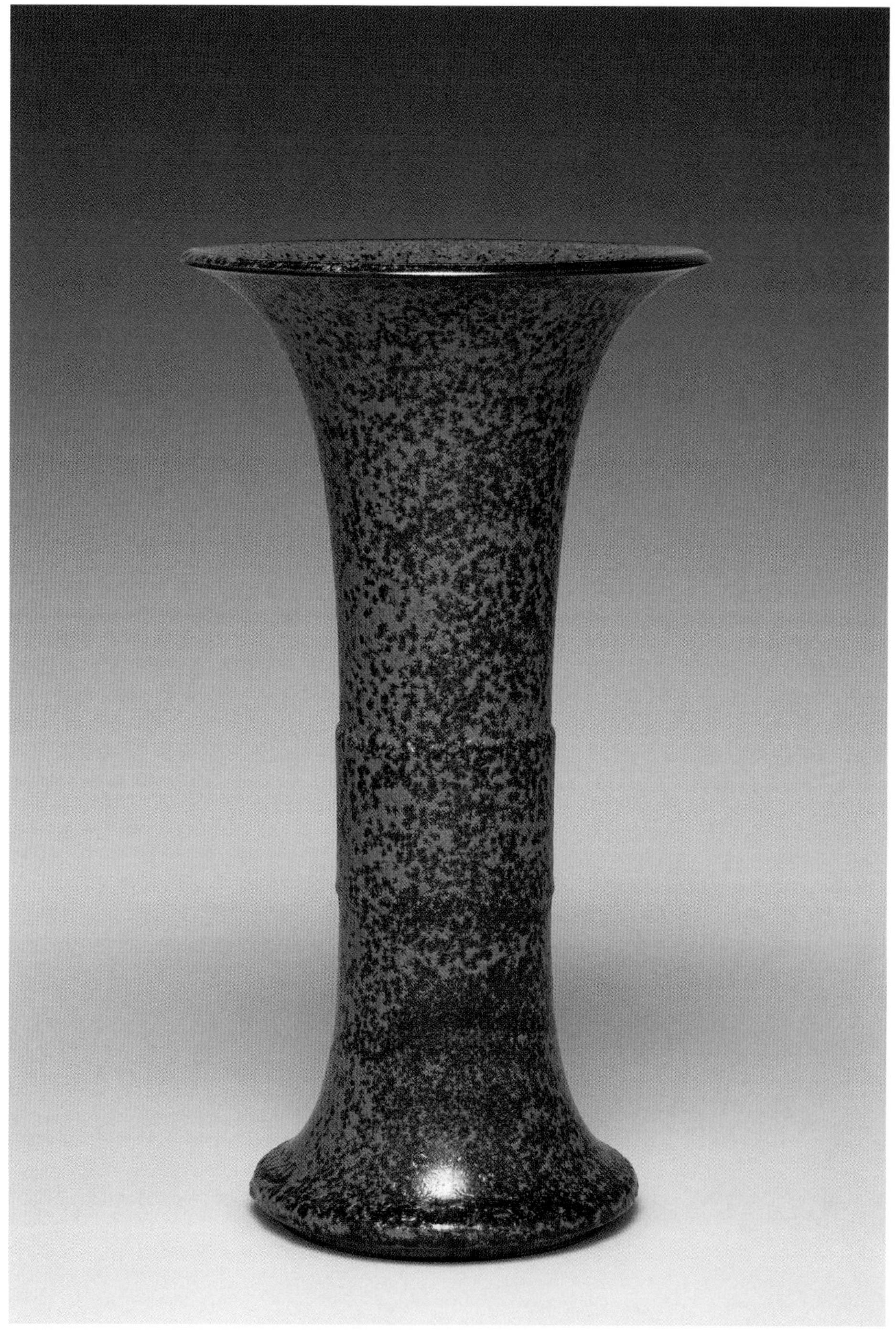

[88]

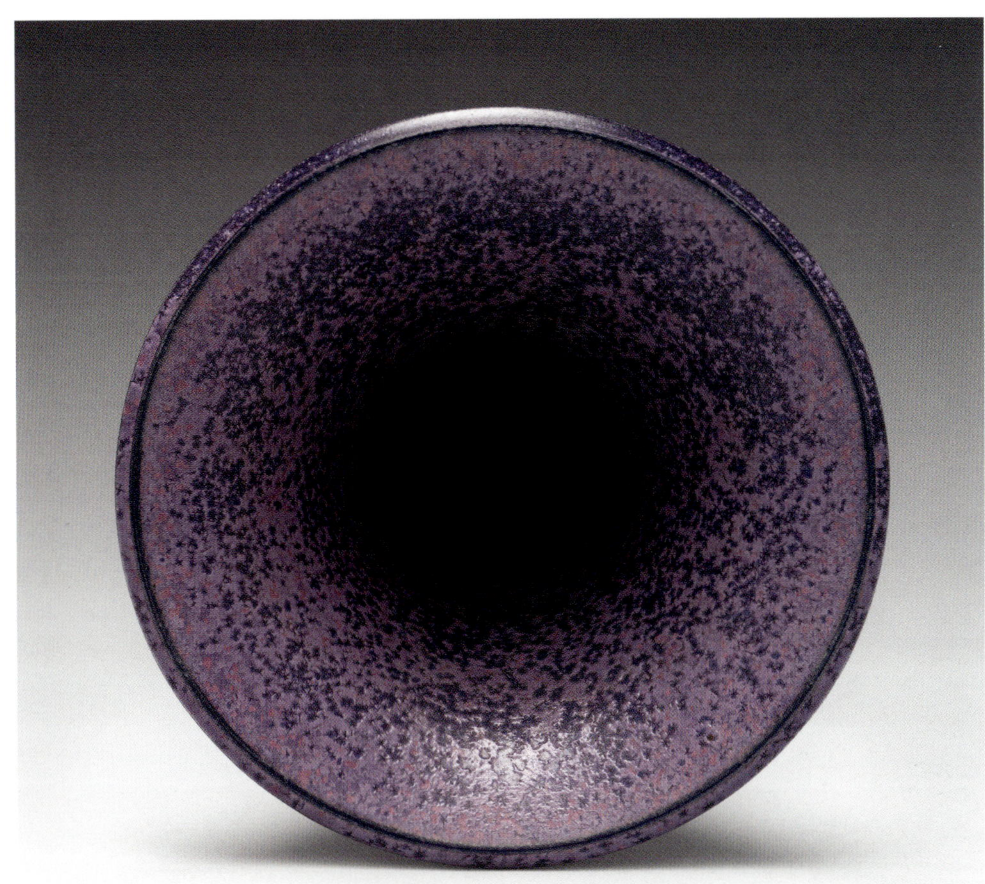

lightheartedly chaotic one that sates the appetite for instant gratification, much as his father's creation rewards the pursuit of elegance. In his purple *gu*-shaped vase [88], Yohei IV not only exhibits his penchant for bold colors but also shows off a complex surface that suggests the patina on an ancient bronze. The body of the vase is a dark, greenish blue over which there is a thick application of color. While the predominant overlaid color is lavender purple, salmon pink and cornflower blue appear in places along with myriad nearly black forms, perhaps floating dandelion seeds or tiny flowers, scattered over the surface. The glaze recalls in some respects a Chinese glaze named "snowflake blue," or *xuehualan* (J. *sekka'ai*), a low-fired lead-fluxed glaze.

SEIFŪ YOHEI III

89 **DINING BOWL, 1912–14**
Porcelain with green glaze
H. 9 cm, diam. 18.5 cm
2022.231

90 **SWEETS BOWL, 1893–1914**
Porcelain with green glaze
H. 10.5 cm, diam. 21 cm
2022.232

91 **FLOWER VASE, 1912–14**
Porcelain with green glaze
H. 35.5 cm, diam. 16.5 cm
2022.233

92 **FLOWER VASE WITH BUTTERFLIES, 1907–14**
Porcelain with carved and molded designs and green glaze
H. 35.5 cm, diam. 16 cm
2022.234

SEIFŪ YOHEI IV

93 **VASE WITH BAMBOO JOINTS, 1914–46**
Porcelain with molded design and green glaze
H. 30.5 cm, diam. 15.2 cm
2022.235

The Yohei III dining bowl here with an everted rim [89] has a glaze identified in its box lid inscription as *hisoku* (C. *mise*), or "mysterious color." This name typically refers specifically to a type of high-quality, green-glazed ceramic produced in the ninth and tenth centuries at the Yue kilns in China's Zhejiang Province as tribute ware for the imperial family. Similarly, the box for this sweets bowl [90] has an attestation by Yohei IV that it is a work by Yohei III and in the *hisokuyō* (C. *mise yao*), or "mysterious color ware," style. In fact, as actual examples of *mise* ware were unknown in Yohei III's time, he would have associated the color with the green-glazed ceramics of kilns at Longquan, also in Zhejiang Province,

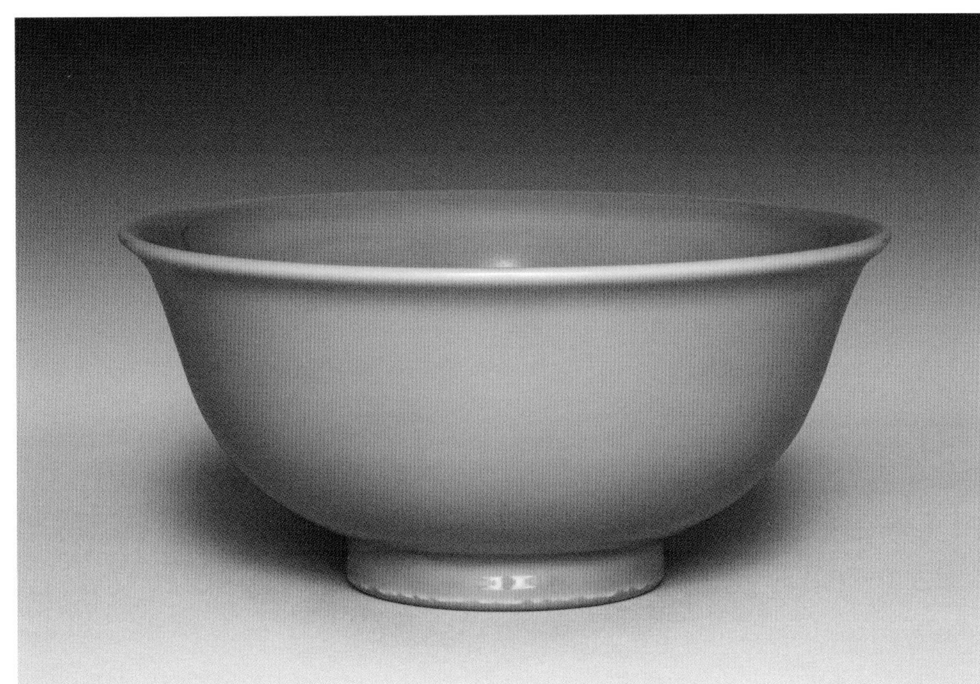

[89]

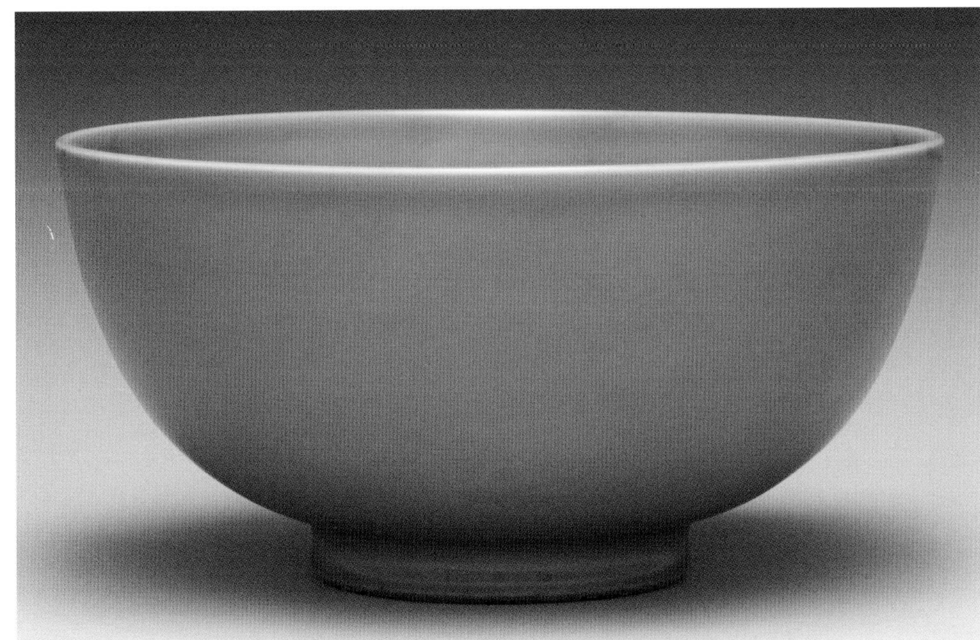

[90]

produced during the Yuan dynasty.[1] Also identified on their boxes as *hisoku* are two flower vases, each with a tall, slightly flared foot and bulbous body with a slimmer neck. One of them is completely undecorated but for the glaze [91]. Its box lid has a red seal with a flower on it, a rather unusual feature also seen on the box for the green-glazed water container that belonged to the Hosokawa family (see [53]). The other vase has two pairs of butterflies forming low-relief roundels, one on each side [92]. The butterflies face each other, one positioned above and the other below, their antennae curling up to a centrally placed floral motif. In the spaces between the pairs of insects, additional raised floral designs are set within vine-like extensions reminiscent of open metalwork banners and

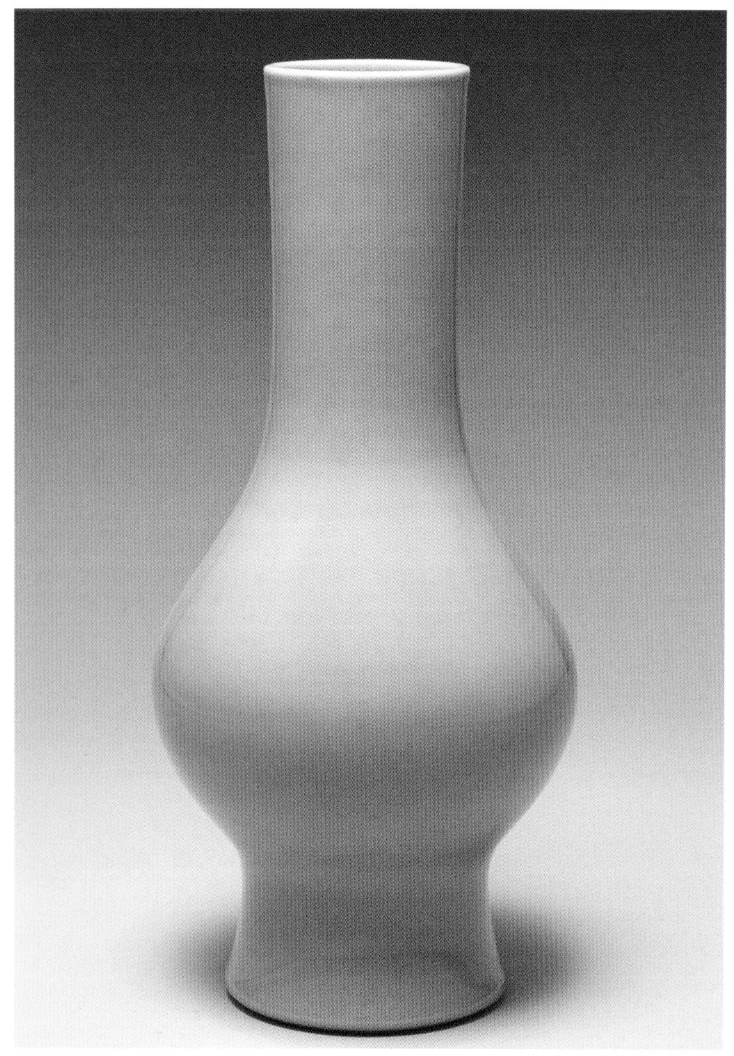

[91]

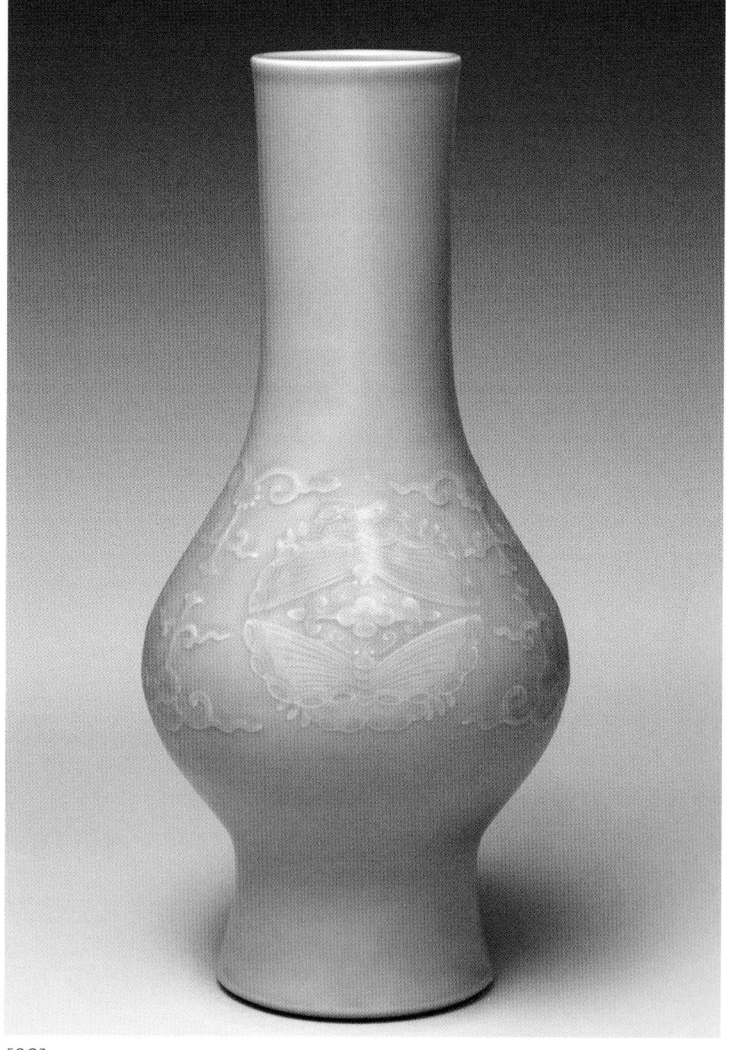

[92]

canopy adornments in Buddhist temples. The lip and the foot of the vase remain white, and the thinning of the green glaze within the higher-relief portions of the body decoration accentuates the designs. This work, like the sweets bowl, has a box lid attribution to Yohei III by Yohei IV. His inscription is dated to the autumn of 1919. Yohei IV's *Vase with Bamboo Joints* [93], another example of *hisoku* glazing, has a shape often seen in pairs of bronze flower vases placed to either side of Buddhist altars before sculptural icons. While the term *hisoku* indicates a more specific green color than *seiji*, a more general word for green-glazed porcelain, there is still some range in the actual color of the glaze, as evidenced by the pieces grouped together here.

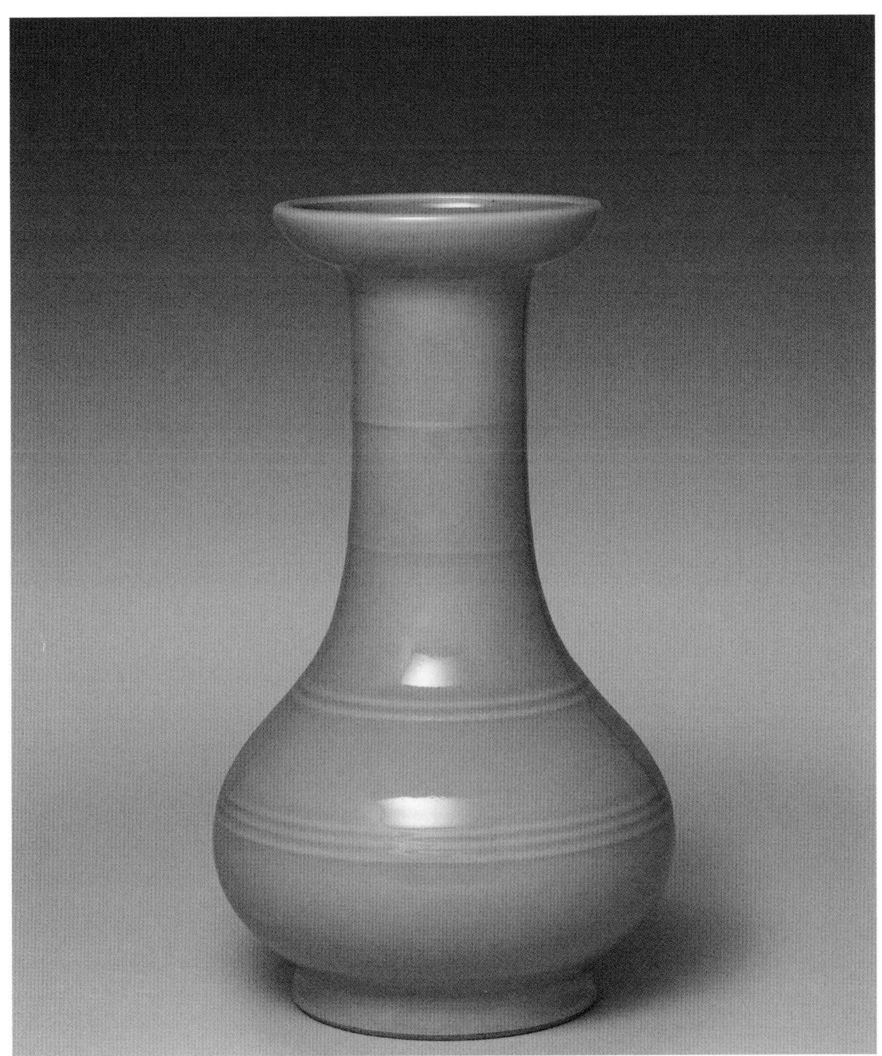

[93]

1. See Maezaki, "Qing-Style Porcelain," 55–56; Maezaki, *Botsugo hyakunen*, 34.

SEIFŪ YOHEI III

94 VASE WITH DRAGON ROUNDELS, 1900–14

Porcelain with molded and carved design and purple glaze
H. 15 cm, diam. 10 cm
2022.236

Each side of this lavender-colored vase is nearly covered with a low-relief design of a four-clawed dragon curled around a flaming jewel. The box lid carries an attestation by Yohei IV that the vase was produced by his predecessor, and the signature on the base is one Yohei III used later in his career. The lid also makes reference to Jun (J. Kin) ware, which was made in numerous kilns in what is now Yuzhou or Yuxian in Henan Province, China, during the Northern Song dynasty. Some Jun wares had an opalescent purple glaze, which was clearly the inspiration for the color seen on this vase.

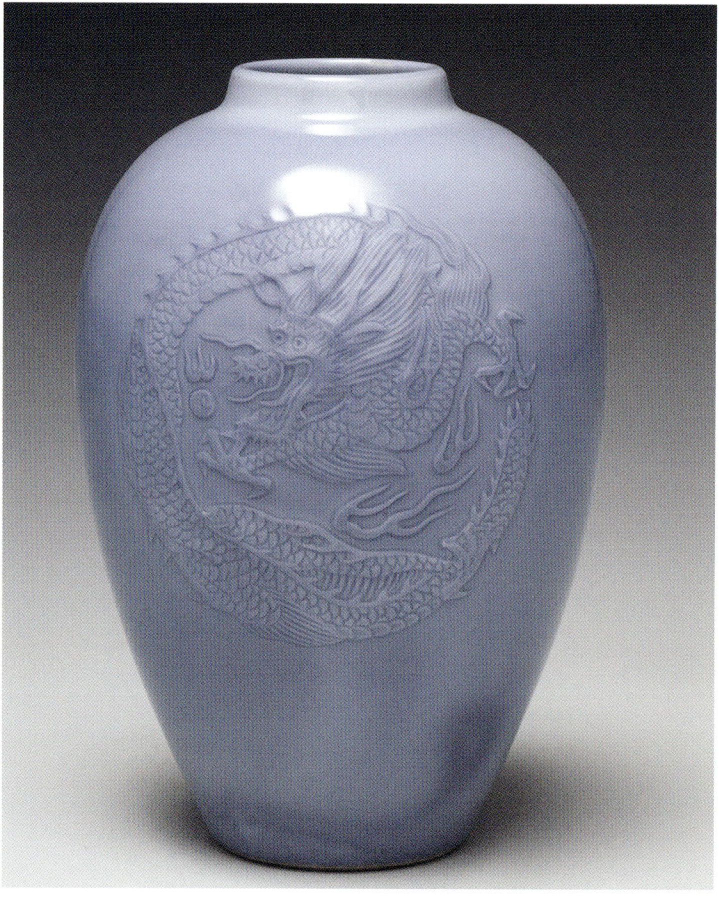

95 BOWL WITH DRAGON ROUNDELS, 1897–1914

Porcelain with underglaze blue and yellow glaze
H. 8.1 cm, diam. 18.2 cm
2022.237

While this bowl has no box, it is attributed to Yohei III based in part on the style of the signature on its base. Below the rim, the bowl's interior has a ring of clouds in underglaze blue. On the outside, bright yellow is combined with roundels of dragons capturing flaming jewels, painted under the glaze in blue, while the inside has a single dragon roundel in underglaze blue against a white ground. The work's bold decorative scheme is more in keeping with what might be expected from the high-output studio of Miyagawa Kōzan in Yokohama, whose products were designed for mass appeal. A similar bowl is in the collection of the Museum of Ceramic Art, Hyōgo.

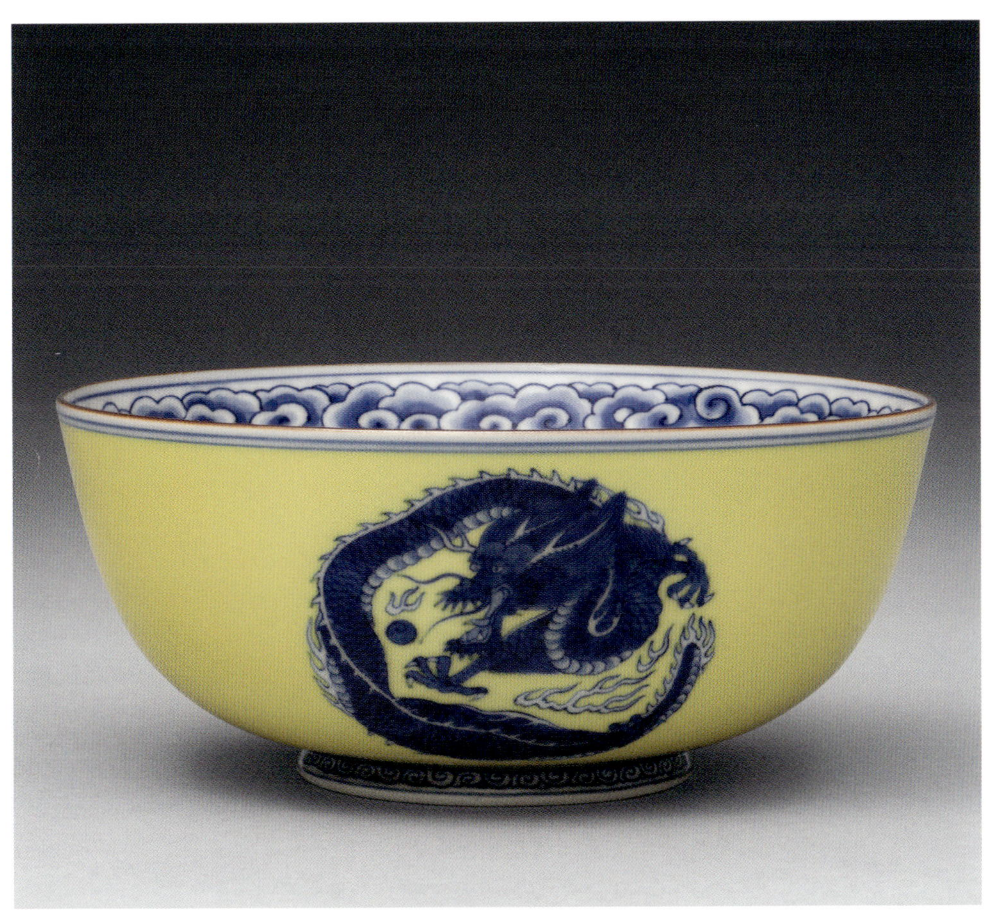

96 BOWL WITH DRAGONS CHASING FLAMING JEWELS, 1893–97

Porcelain with molded and carved design and cream glaze
H. 9.5 cm, diam. 18.6 cm
2022.238

The decoration of this large bowl, described as a *donburi* on one side of its box, is executed entirely in molded and carved relief under a creamy, pink-tinged translucent glaze. The main motif is a pair of four-clawed dragons pursuing flaming jewels. As is standard for this design, the beasts are surrounded by wisps of cloud, and a foliate pattern runs around the bottom of the basin. A geometric pattern circles the exterior of the footring. The white-on-white design makes the bowl subtle and elegant.

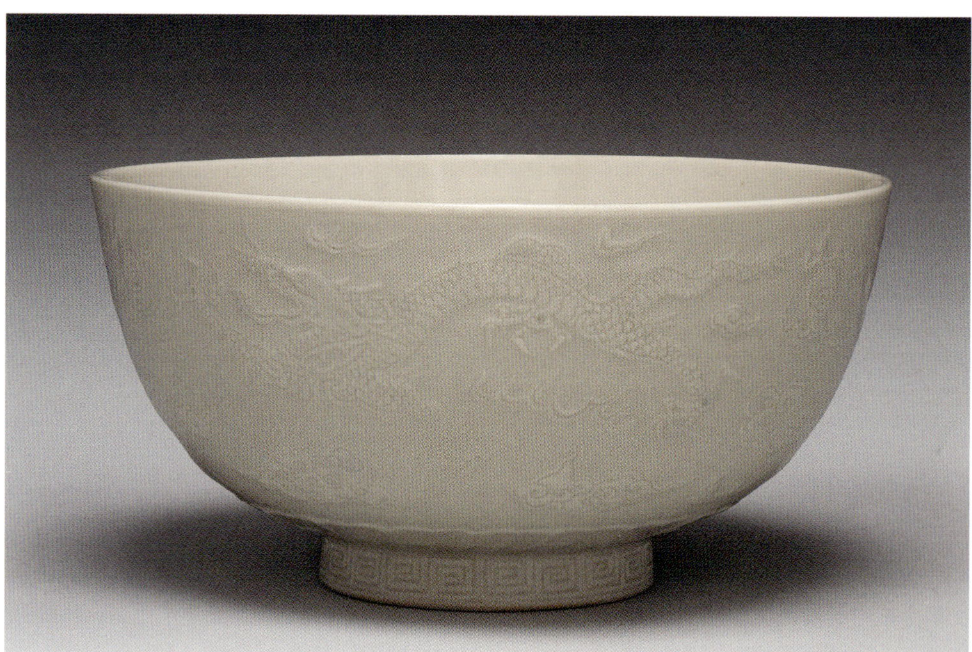

97 SAKE CUPS WITH DRAGONS, 1893–1914

Set of six sake cups; porcelain with underglaze blue and iron oxide rims
Each: h. 5 cm, diam. 4.5 cm
2022.239

Each of these sake cups pictures two backward-looking dragons. The highly stylized creatures resemble jade carvings.

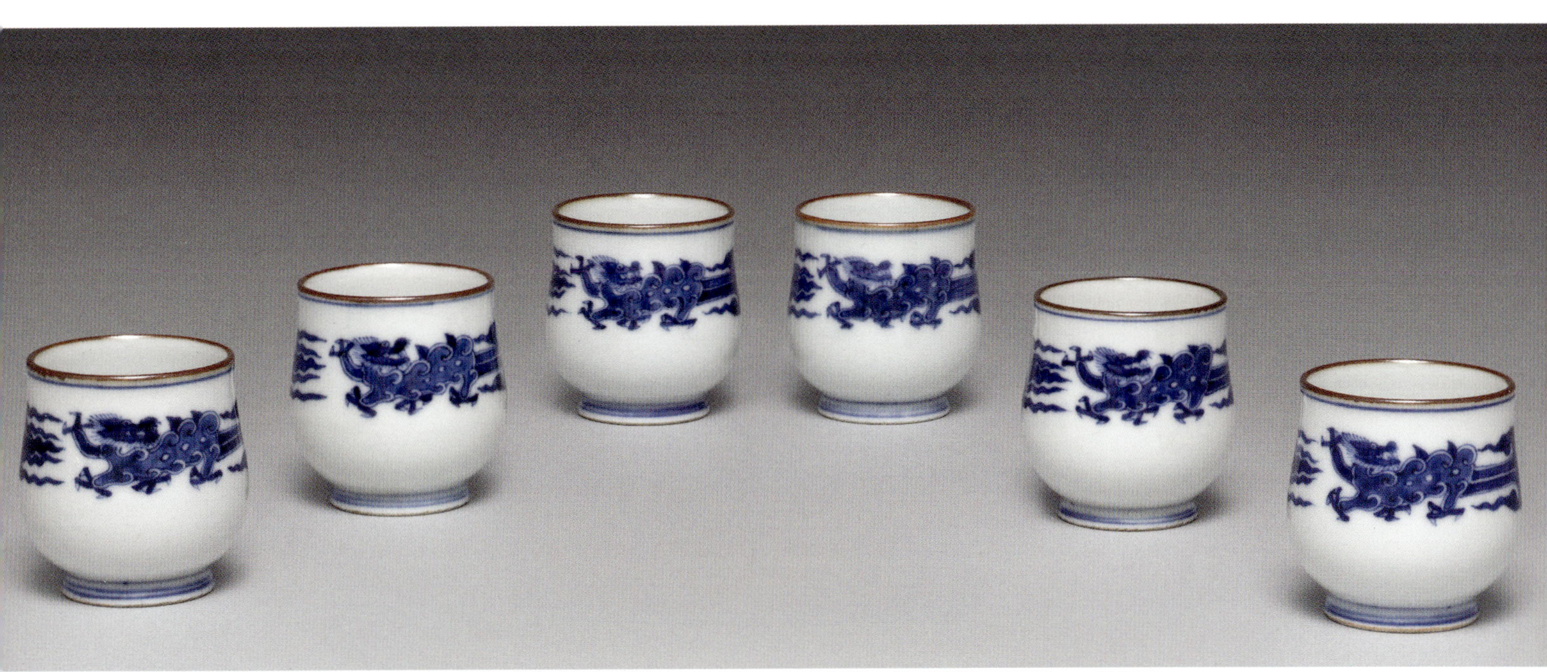

98 DISH WITH CARP IN WAVES, 1893–1914

Porcelain with incised designs, iron oxide, and red glaze
H. 3.5 cm, diam. 16 cm
2022.240

The exterior of this low, wide dish with flared foot is covered with a red coral glaze. Its interior is white with incised designs, and the rim is decorated with brown iron oxide. The primary design occupies the flat bottom of the bowl and is bound within a single band. It is of a carp swimming vigorously against roiling waves with frothy crests moving in multiple directions; the water just above the fish's head is beginning to form a whirlpool. A closer look at the fish's face reveals that it somewhat resembles that of a dragon. It is possible that the motif is meant to be a carp who jumps over the waterfall and transforms into a dragon, who flies into the sky. The iconography symbolizes the transformative experience of striving to one's utmost and achieving the impossible against tough odds. Originating in China, the narrative's visual representation as well as its meaning crossed the ocean to Japan, where it often appeared on items gifted to those celebrating pivotal successes in life, such as obtaining elevated status in one's work or graduating from an academic program. The design is completed with three abstract flowers, each represented with five circles ringing a central circle, from which leafy tendrils stretch in both directions along the top of the inside of the bowl.

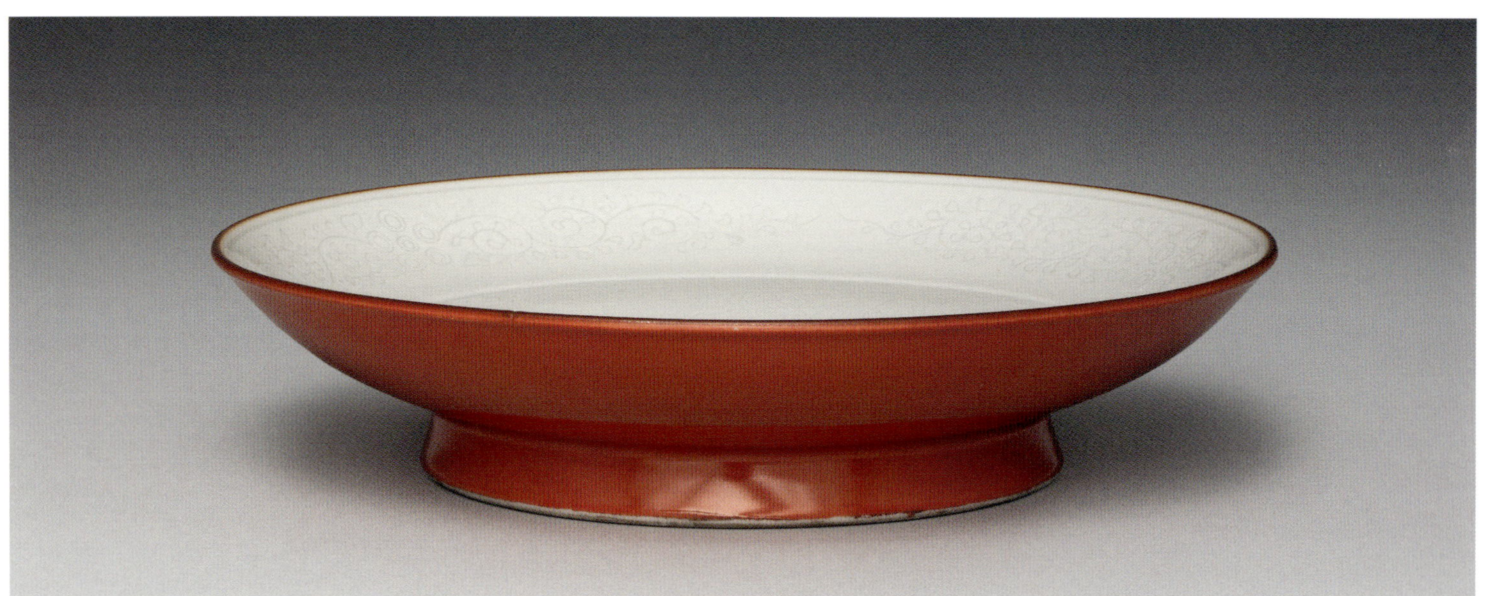

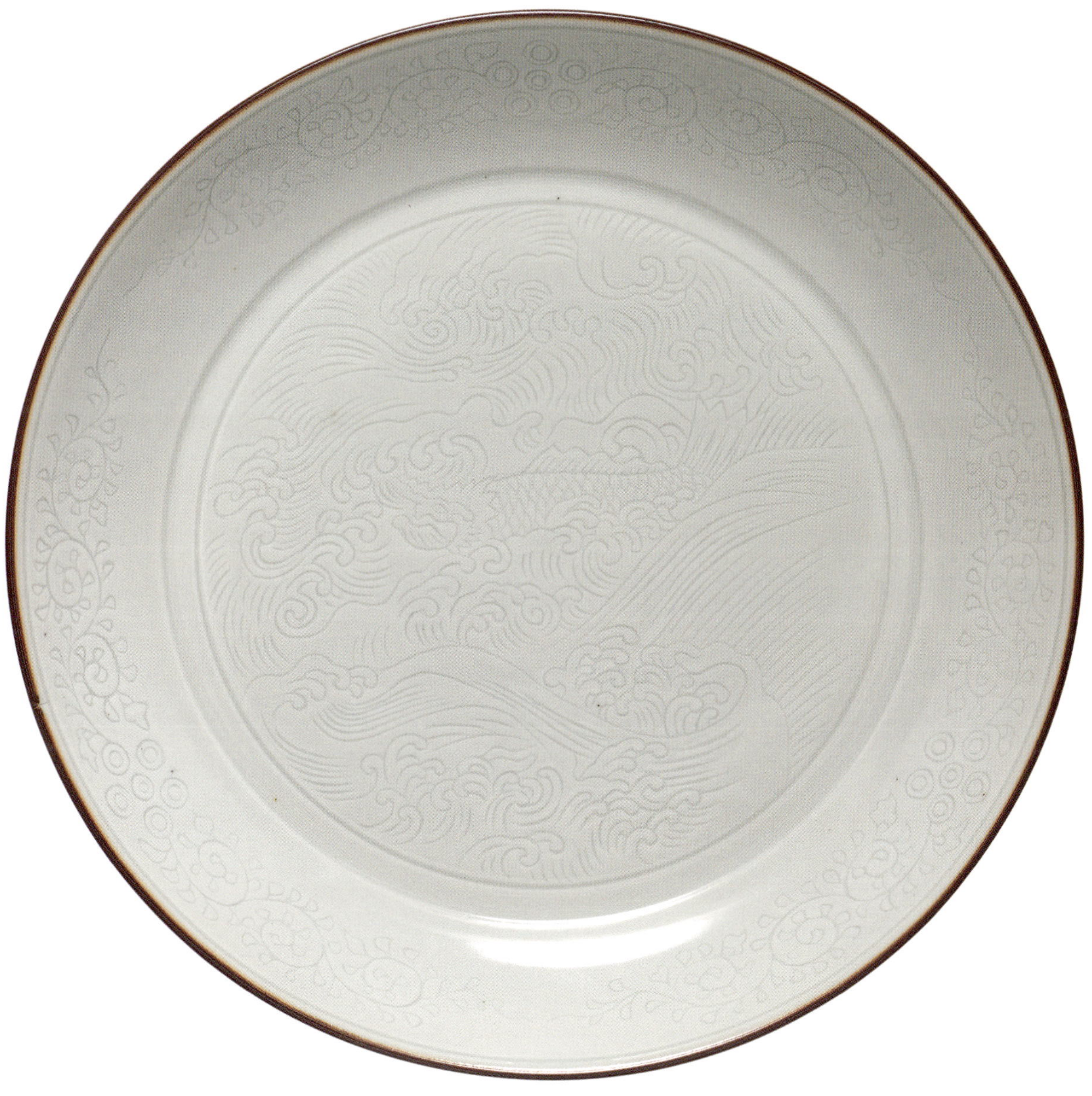

99 BOWL WITH NUMINOUS FUNGI AND *KIRIN*, 1893–1900

Porcelain with cobalt blue glaze, overglaze color enamel, and silver painting overlay
H. 8.3 cm, diam. 18.3 cm
2022.241

The complex design of this bowl is also technically sophisticated in its execution. On the interior, Yohei III has placed a mythical beast called a *kirin* (C. *qilin*) within a double-banded circle painted in cobalt blue under the glaze. Around the interior of the mouth, bordered at top and bottom with underglaze blue under a brown iron oxide painted rim, he has painted a continuous coin pattern with a red wash and green color enamels. The pattern is further defined and embellished with black iron outlining the green- and gold-painted diamonds over the diluted red. The inside is otherwise left white. On the exterior, the body has a dark blue glaze and an overlaid silver design of *reishi* with incised lines for detail.

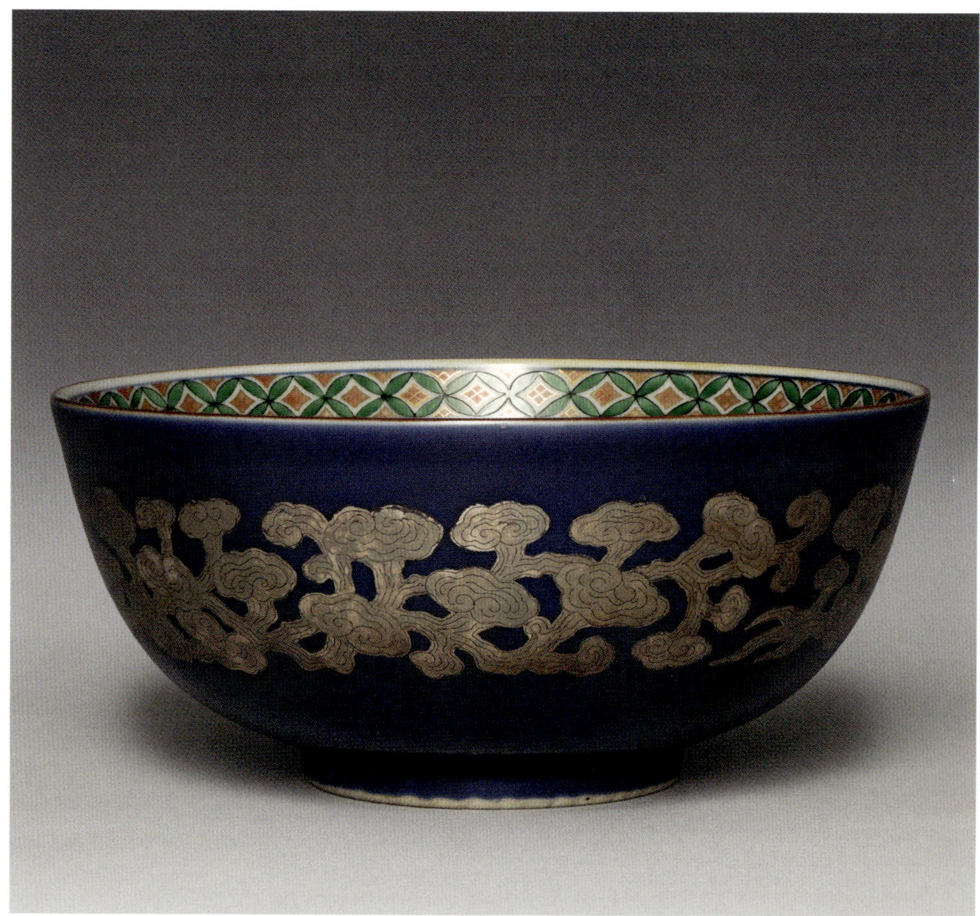

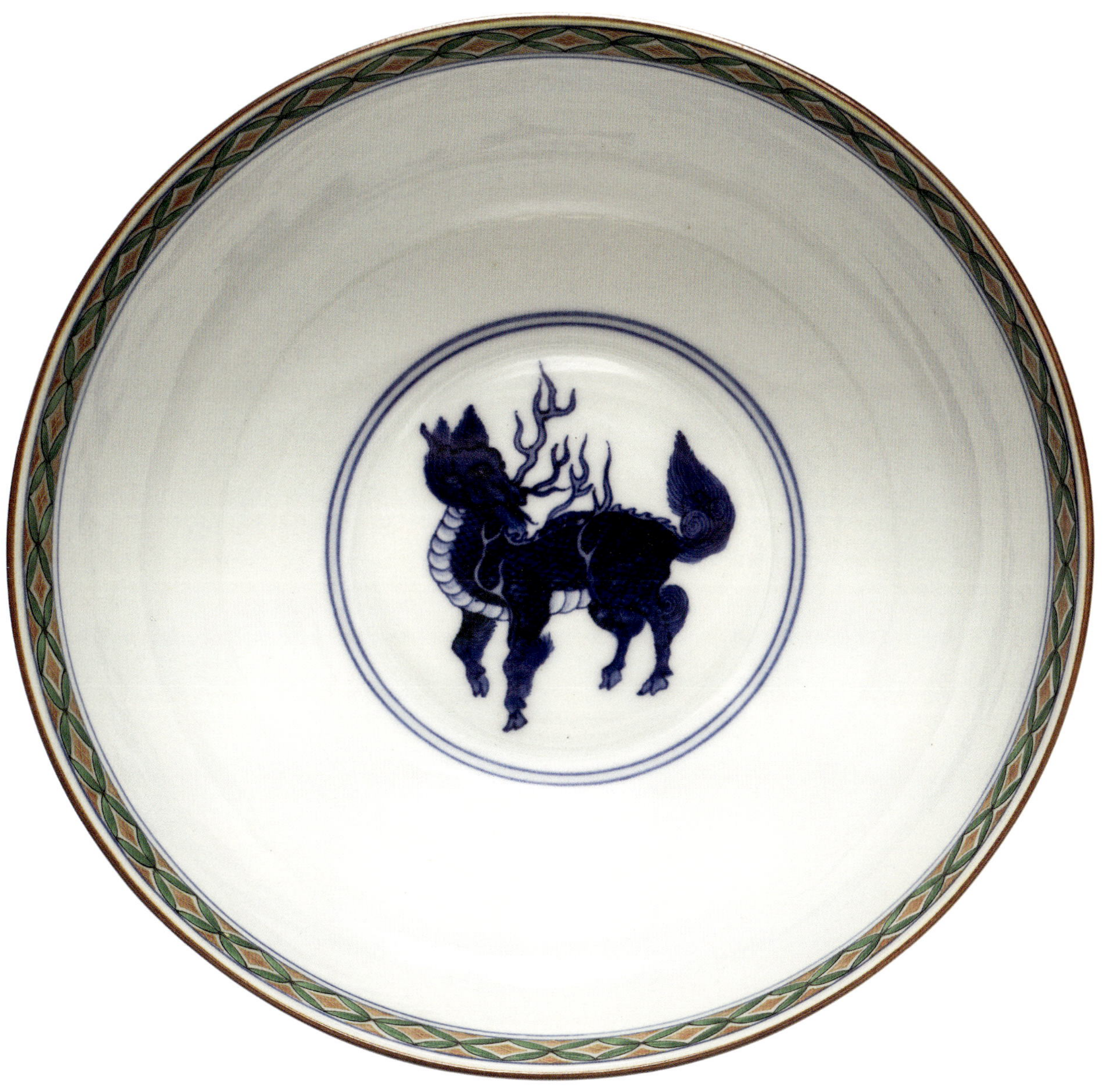

100 BOWL WITH AUSPICIOUS IDEOGRAPHS AND FLORAL MOTIFS, 1600S

Ming dynasty (1368–1644)
Stoneware with overglaze color enamel
H. 9 cm, diam. 21.5 cm
2022.243

As part of their work, members of the Seifū studio, and Yohei III in particular, engaged in the viewing and appreciation of Chinese ceramics. While they were not authenticators, they would have been familiar with imported examples of Chinese stoneware and porcelain through tea gatherings, meetings with their elite clients, exhibitions, and other opportunities to see and study actual pieces from the mainland. This object and its box may be a reflection of Yohei III's experiences of this kind. The bowl itself is slightly misshapen and roughly glazed with overglaze color enamels in red and green. Flanked by floral motifs, four Chinese characters brushed in red appear in roundels: 長命富貴. Meaning, respectively, longevity, life, prosperity, and status, they are pronounced together in Japanese as the phrase *chōmeifūki*, or "live long and prosper." Additional loosely painted foliate designs in red and green circle the area above the foot and inside of the bowl. It is a relatively simple piece made by someone who was likely capable of much finer, more precise work but who could also do completely passable wares on short order. Of greater interest is the storage box lid for this piece. It has an

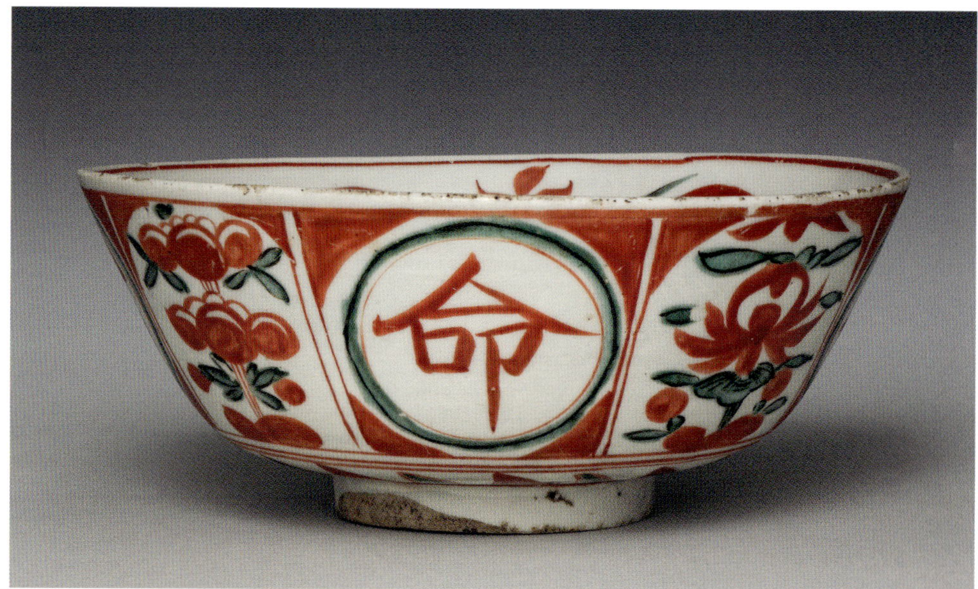

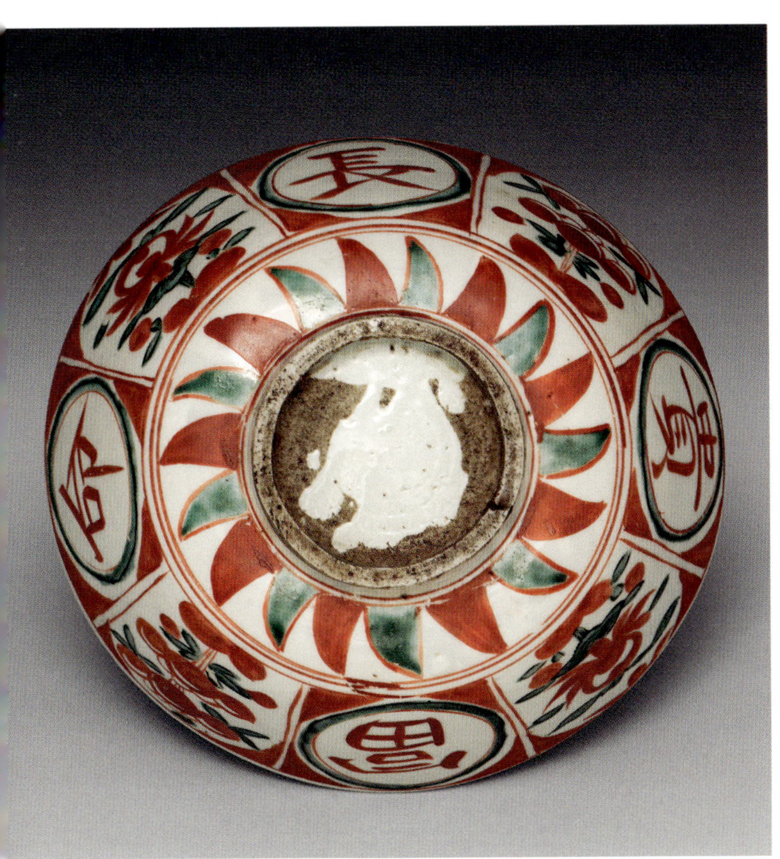

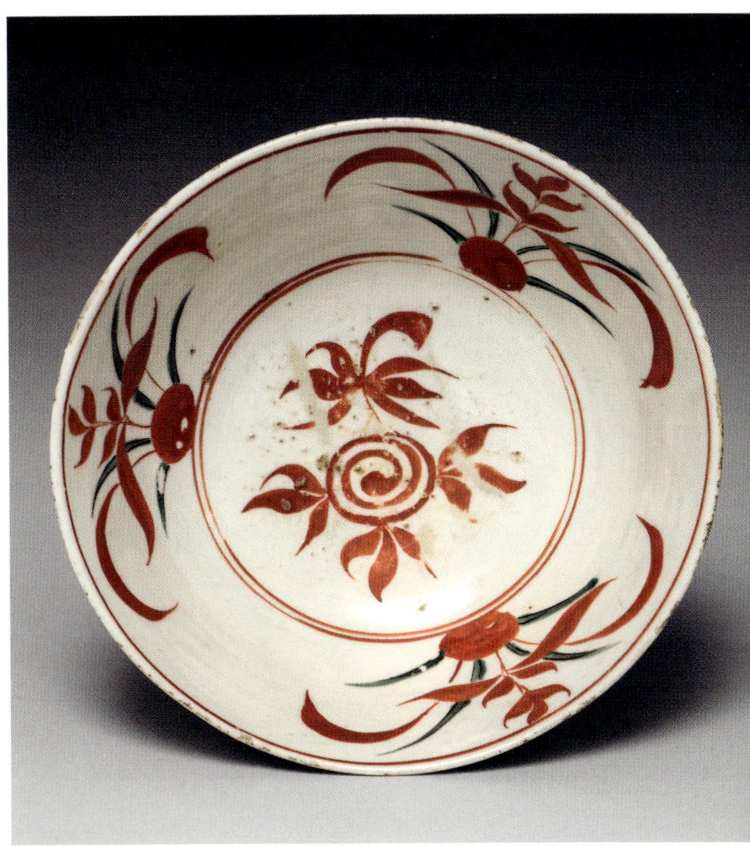

inscription by Yohei III, with his seal, declaring it to be a "sweets dish from southern China with color images." On the reverse of the lid, Yohei has written his name and placed his Imperial Household Artist seal, but instead of writing "made by," he wrote "saw this [ceramic]." To the left of this is another inscription in a different hand, stating that the piece is a work from southern China with red-painted designs, produced at the very end of the Ming dynasty. It is signed "Kushi Takushin" 久志卓真, along with his seal. Kushi Takushin (1898–1973) was a Japanese musician and music critic, as well as an antiques researcher and authenticator. He was especially interested in Ming-dynasty Chinese ceramics and wrote extensively on Chinese, Japanese, and Korean ceramics. Originally from Hokkaido, he was active in Kyoto and began collecting art at a young age. Both he and Yohei appreciated and commented upon the bowl, and perhaps they both owned it.

APPENDIX
SEALS AND SIGNATURES

Object signatures and marks are indicated as follows: a "painted signature" is the artist's signature; a "painted mark" uses standardized characters; an "incised mark" is carved with standardized characters; a "relief mark" has raised characters that stick up from the surrounding clay; and an "indented mark" has characters that depress into the clay.

Box seals, whether relief or intaglio, are listed simply as box seals. If Yohei IV has used a box seal to authenticate a Yohei III work, it is noted as "IV on III." Box signatures are not listed. Seizan seals and Imperial Household Artist seals and inscriptions are presented separately. A bold catalogue number indicates the object/box whose signature/mark/seal is pictured.

Seifū Yohei I

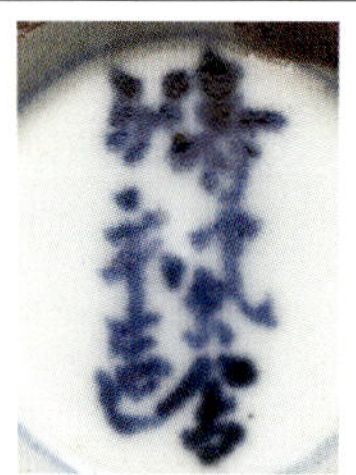

Painted signature
Seifū sha Yohei zō
清風舎与平造
[1]

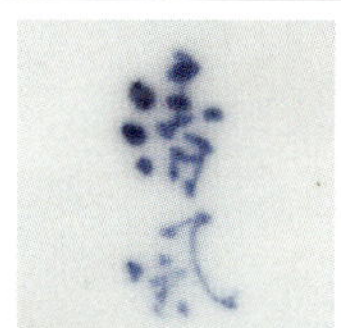

Painted signature 2
Seifū 清風
[2]

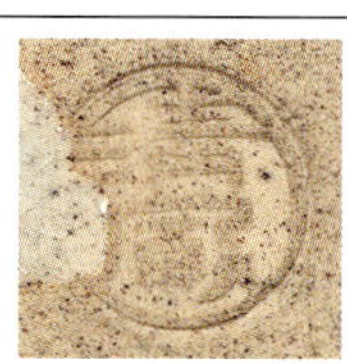

Relief mark 1
Seifū 清風
[3]

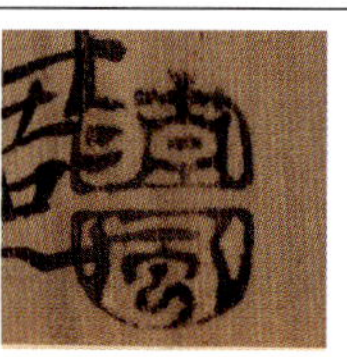

Box seal 1
Seifū 清風
[2]

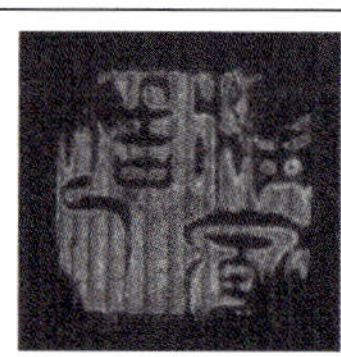

Box seal 2
Seifū zō 清風造
[3]

Box seal 3
Seifū Yohei 清風與平
[3]

Seifū Yohei II

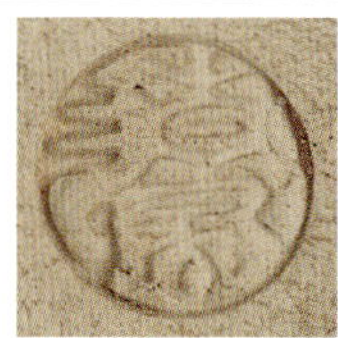

Relief mark 1
Seifū 清風
[5]

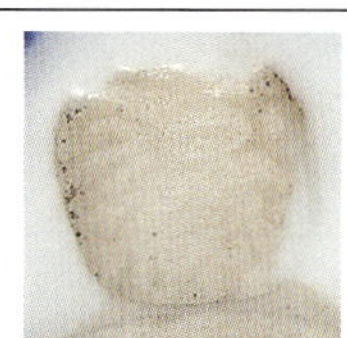

Relief mark 2
Seifū 清風
[4]

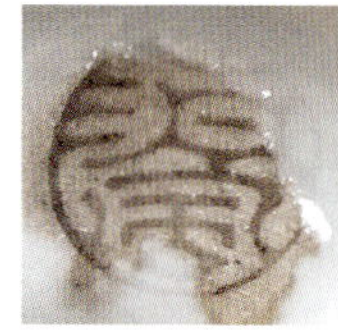

Indented mark 1
Seifū 清風
[4]

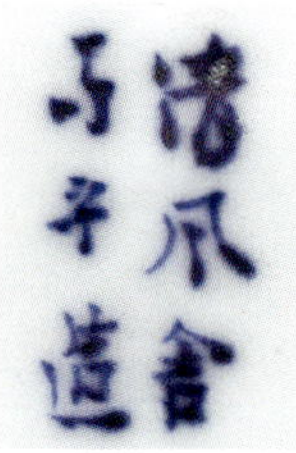

Painted signature 1
Seifū sha Yohei zō
清風舎与平造
[6]

Box seal 1
Seifū no saku
清風之作
[5]

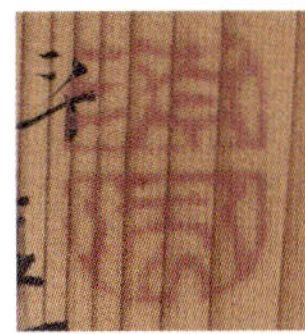

Box seal 2
Seifū 清風
[4]

Box seal 3
Seifū zō 清風造
[4]
[6]
[7]

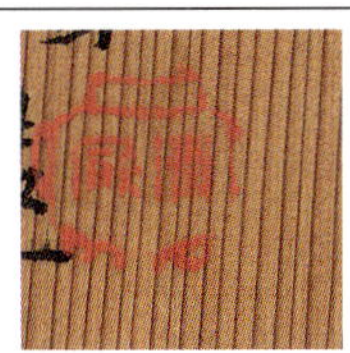

Box seal 4
Seifū 清風
[5]
[6]
[7]

Seifū Yohei III

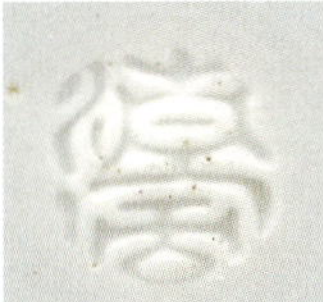

Indented mark 1
Seifū 清風
[43]
[50]

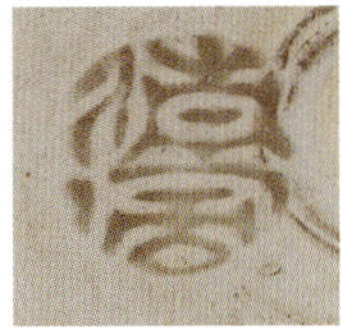

Indented mark 2
Seifū 清風
[18]
[21]
[22]
[23]
[27]
[30]
[46]
[59]
[90]
[98]

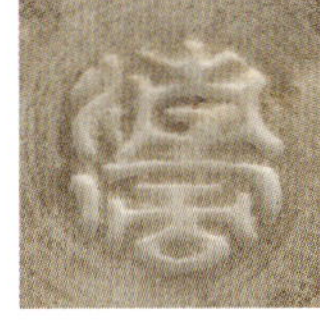

Relief mark 1
Seifū 清風
[36]

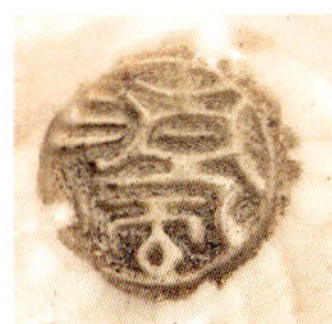

Relief mark 2
Seifū 清風
[40]

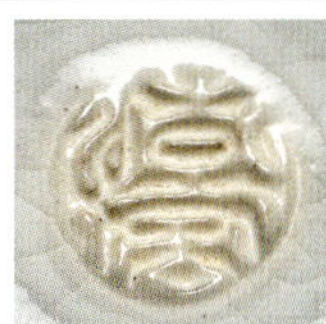

Indented mark 3
Seifū 清風
[45]

Indented mark 4
Seifū 清風
[29]

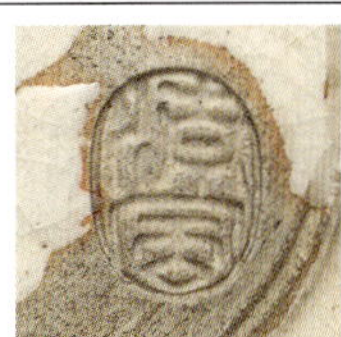

Indented mark 5
Seifū 清風
[31]
[38]

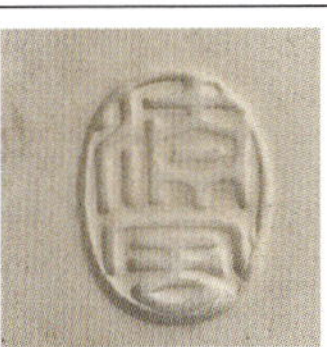

Indented mark 6
Seifū 清風
[28]
[32]
[34]
[35]

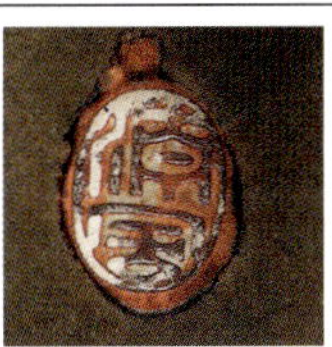

Relief mark 3
Seifū 清風
[33]
[39]

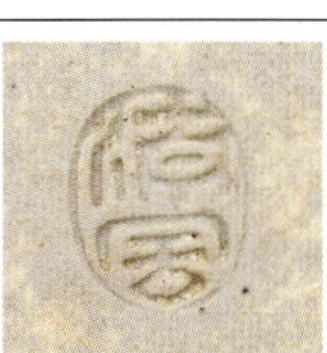

Indented mark 7
Seifū 清風
[49]

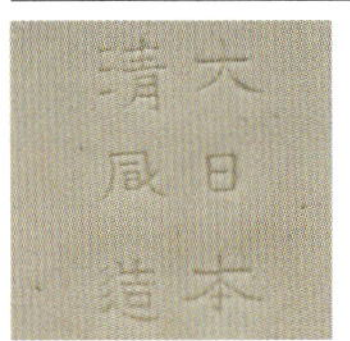

Incised mark 1
Dai Nihon Seifū zō
大日本清風造
[82]

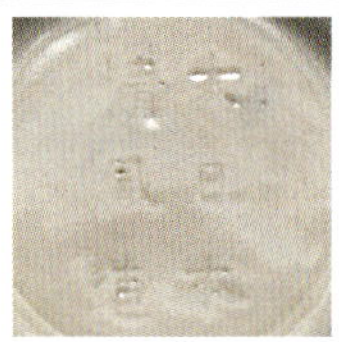

Incised mark 2
Dai Nihon Seifū zō
大日本清風造
[96]

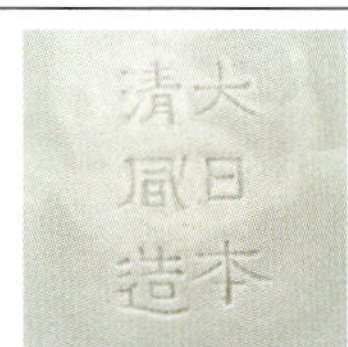

Incised mark 3
Dai Nihon Seifū zō
大日本清風造
[57]

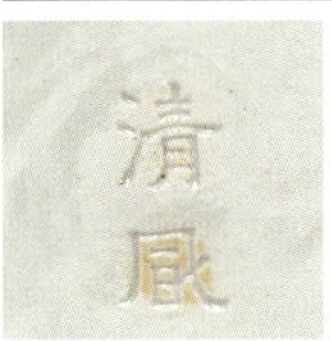

Incised mark 1
Seifū 清風
[99]

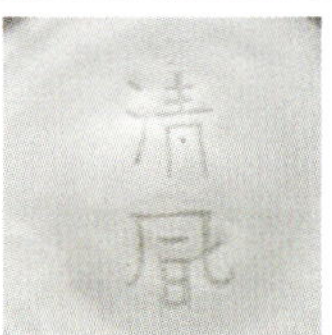

Incised mark 2
Seifū 清風
[12]

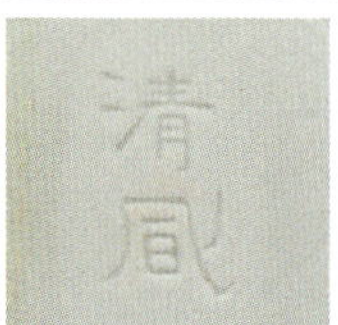

Incised mark 3
Seifū 清風
[55]

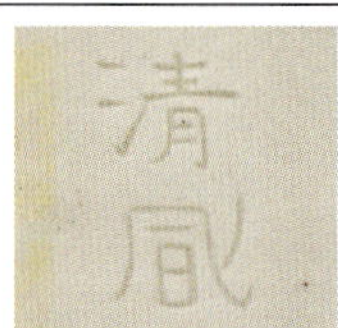

Incised mark 4
Seifū 清風
[54]

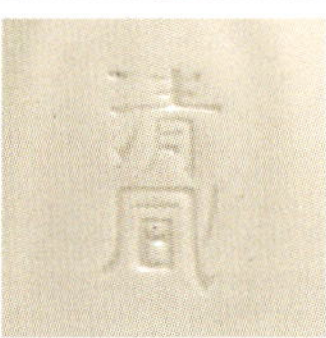

Incised mark 5
Seifū 清風
[51]

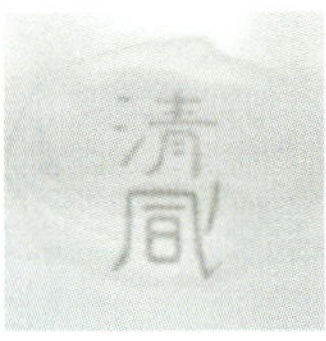

Incised mark 6
Seifū 清風
[24]

Incised mark 7
Seifū 清風
[20]

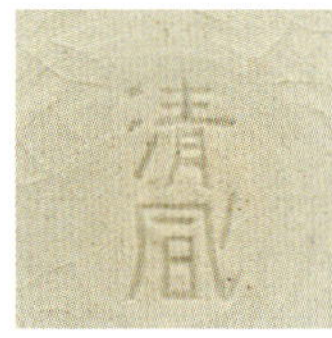

Incised mark 8
Seifū 清風
[81]

Incised mark 9
Seifū 清風
[26]

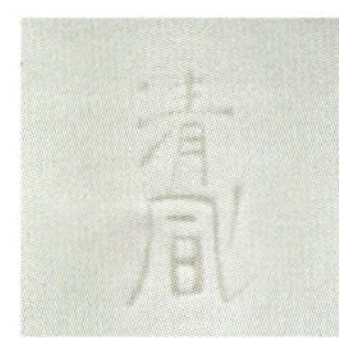

Incised mark 10
Seifū 清風
[48]

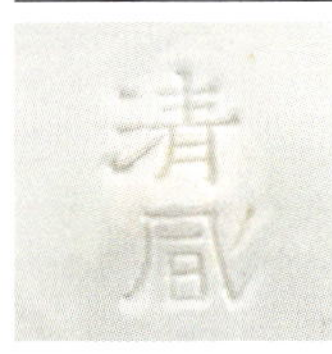

Incised mark 11
Seifū 清風
[95]

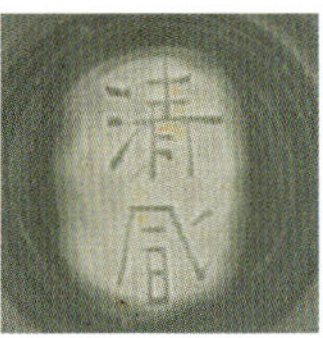

Incised mark 12
Seifū 清風
[91]

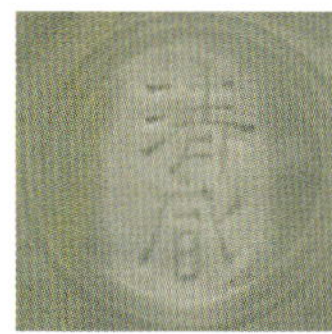

Incised mark 13
Seifū 清風
[53]

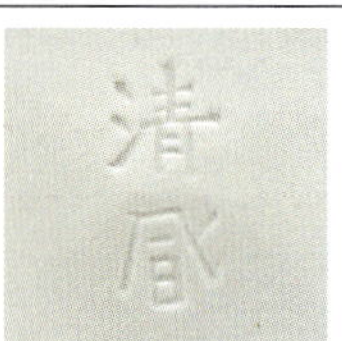

Incised mark 14
Seifū 清風
[11]

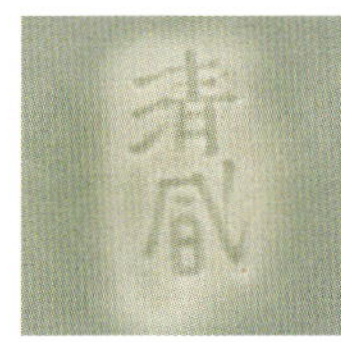

Incised mark 15
Seifū 清風
[83]

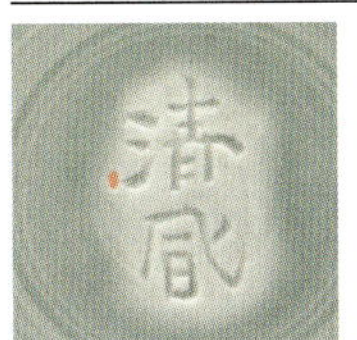

Incised mark 16
Seifū 清風
[92]

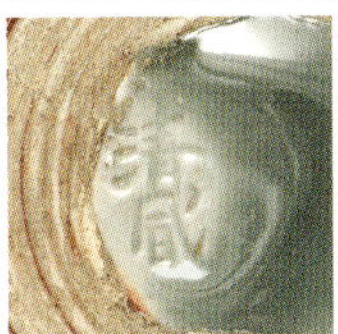

Incised mark 17
Seifū 清風
[89]

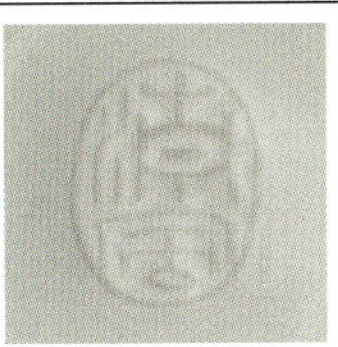

Incised mark 18
Seifū 清風
[19]

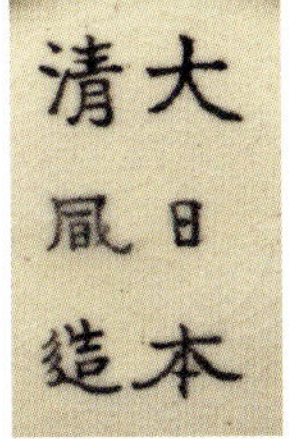

Painted mark 1
Dai Nihon Seifū zō
大日本清風造
[52]

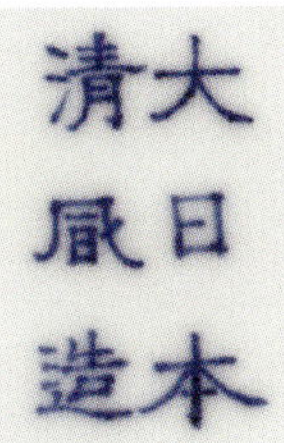

Painted mark 2
Dai Nihon Seifū zō
大日本清風造
[13]

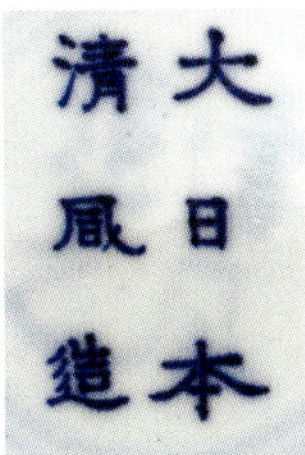

Painted mark 3
Dai Nihon Seifū zō
大日本清風造
[41]

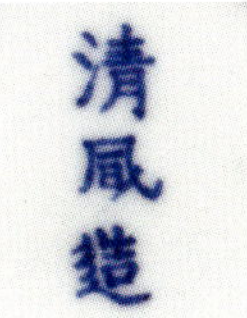

Painted mark 4
Seifū zō 清風造
[25]

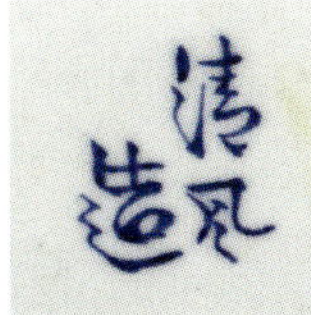

Painted signature 1
Seifū zō 清風造
[14]

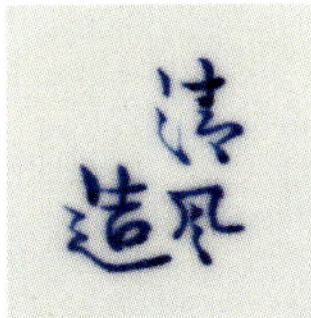

Painted signature 2
Seifū zō 清風造
[15]

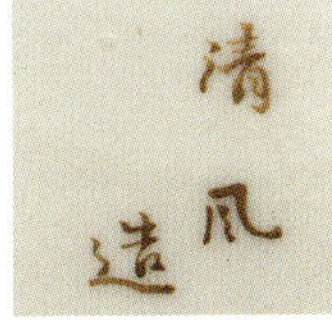

Painted signature 3
Seifū zō 清風造
[7] (III on II ?)

Painting seal 1
Chōshōkayu Seifū
長松下有清風
[8]

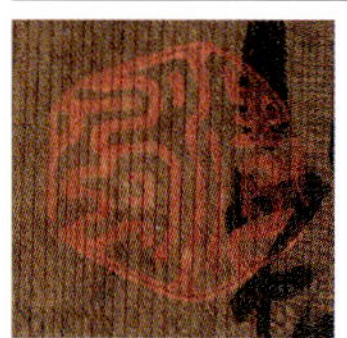

Box seal 1
Seifū 清風
[12]
[13]
[17]
[28]
[29]
[31]
[33]
[34]
[39]
[47]
[50]
[55]
[59] (III or IV)
[81]
[82]
[96]
[99]
[100]

Box seal 2
Seifū 清風
[43]

Box seal 3
Seifū 清風
[9]
[13]
[17]
[28]
[29]
[34]
[36]
[43]
[99]

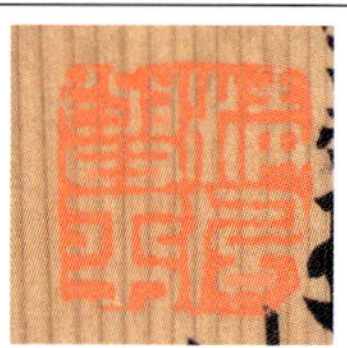

Box seal 4
Seifū Yohei 清風與平
[14]
[25]
[31]
[41]
[82]
[96]

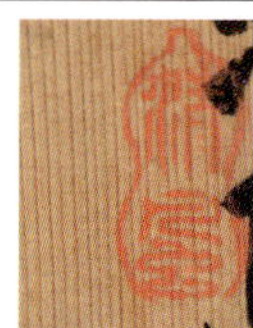

Box seal 5
Seifū 清風
[33]
[41]
[55]

Box seal 6
Seifū 清風
[38]

Box seal 7
Kinsei gyokushin
金聲玉振
[16]
[24]
[26]
[27]
[37]
[43]
[48]
[51]
[57]
[60] (IV)
[72] (IV)
[83]

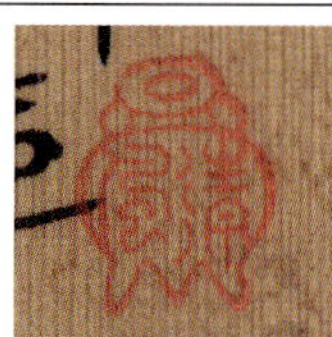

Box seal 8
Seifū 清風
[15]
[25]
[40]
[62] (IV)

Seifū Yohei IV

Incised mark 1
Seifū 清風
[73]

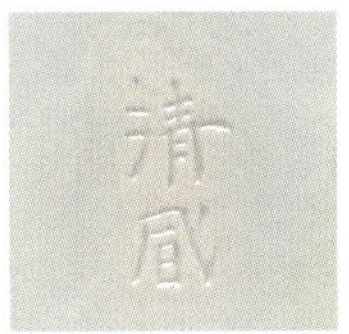

Incised mark 2
Seifū 清風
[72]

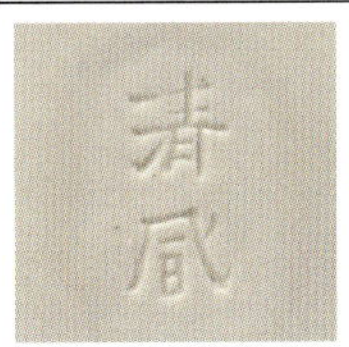

Incised mark 3
Seifū 清風
[62]

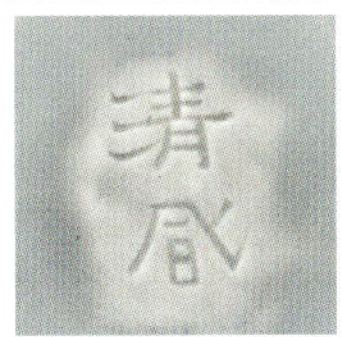

Incised mark 4
Seifū 清風
[68]

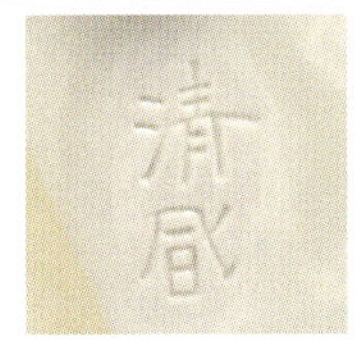

Incised mark 5
Seifū 清風
[61]

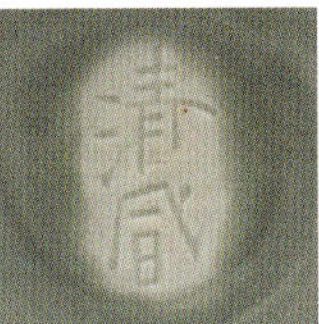

Incised mark 6
Seifū 清風
[86]

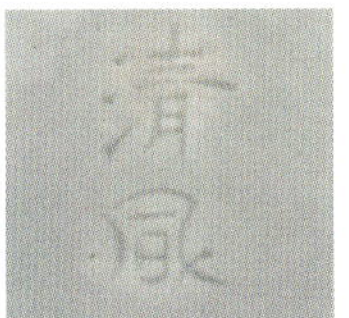

Incised mark 7
Seifū 清風
[63]
[64]
[67]
[69]
[85]
[87]
[88]

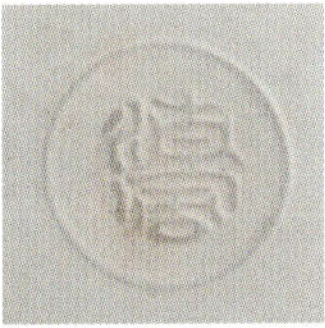

Indented mark 1
Seifū 清風
[10] (III)
[26] (box inscriptions in hand of III)
[60]

Indented mark 2
Seifū 清風
[70]

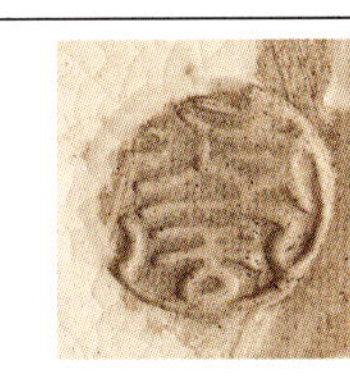

Indented mark 3
Seifū 清風
[55]
[71]
[74]

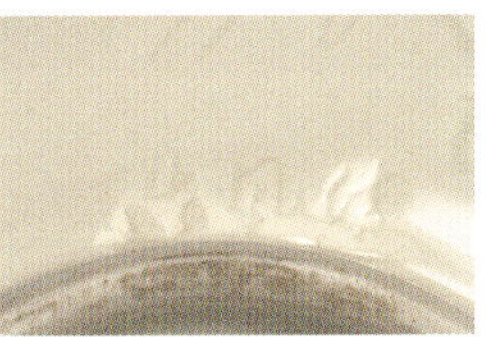

Incised signature 1
Seifū zō 清風造
[66]

Box seal 1
Seifū rojin 清風盧人
[20] (IV on III)
[52] (IV on III)
[74]
[76]

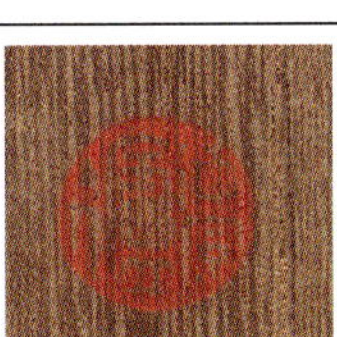

Box seal 2
Seifū rojin 清風盧人
[73]

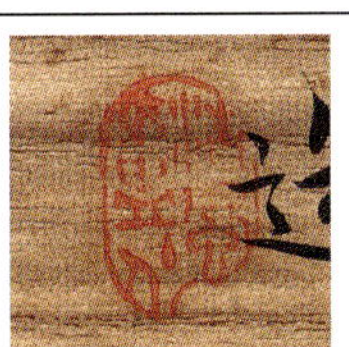

Box seal 3
Seifū rojin 清風盧人
[58]
[67]
[71]

Box seal 4
Seifū 清風
[86]

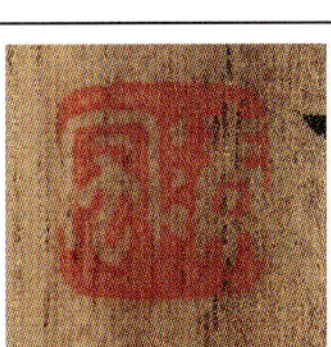

Box seal 5
Seifū 清風
[76]

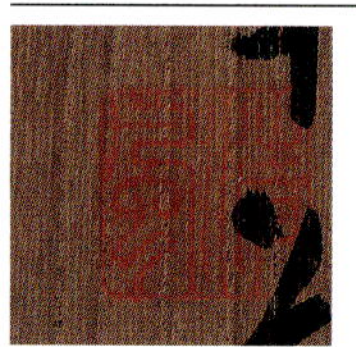

Box seal 6
Seifū 清風
[62]

Box seal 7
Seifū 清風
[66]
[69]
[77] (V)
[84]
[88]
[93]

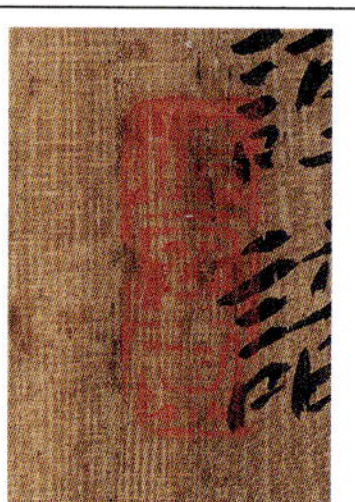

Box seal 8
Seifū ro 清風盧
[98] (IV on III)

Box seal 9
Seifū 清風
[61]

Box seal 10
Seifū 清風
[8] (IV on III)
[11] (IV on III)
[53] (IV on III)
[59]
[60]
[72]
[89] (IV on III)
[91] (IV on III)

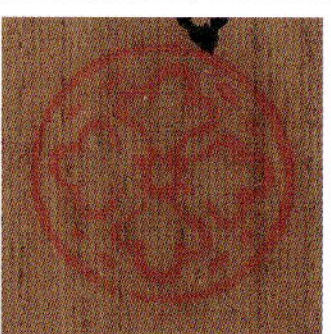

Box seal 11
Flower
[53] (IV on III)
[91] (III)

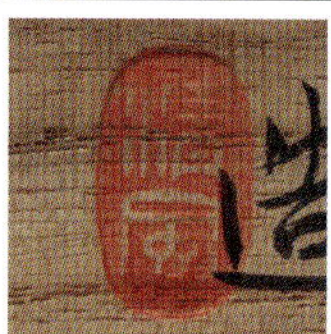

Box seal 12
Seifū 清風
[75]

Box seal 13
Seifū Yohei 清風與平
[87]

Box seal 14
Seifū 清風
[65]
[85]
[98] (IV on III)

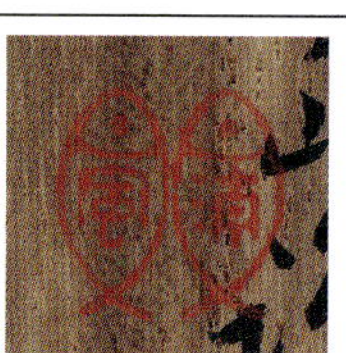

Box seal 15
Seifū 清風
[35] (IV on III)

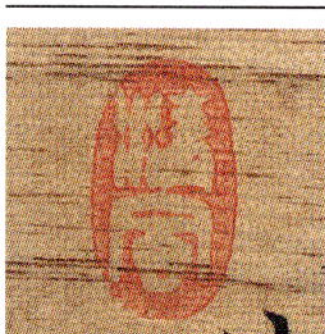

Box seal 16
Seifū 清風
[70]

Box seal 17
Seifū 清風
[45] (IV on III)

Seifū Yohei III
Seizan box seal

Box seal
Seizan 晟山
[9]
[19]
[21]
[22]
[23]
[30]
[36]
[40]
[42]

Seifū Yohei IV
Seizan Seifū box seal,
Seizan box seals

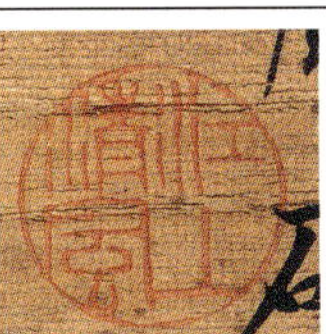

Box seal
Seizan Seifū 成山清風
[61]
[63]
[64]
[66]
[69]
[70]
[75]
[77] (V)
[84]
[88]
[93]
[94] (IV on III)

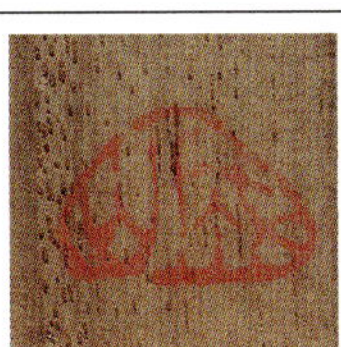

Box seal 1
Seizan 成山
[86]

Box seal 2
Seizan 成山
[65]
[67]
[74]
[85]
[87]

Box seal 3
Seizan 成山
[71]
[73]

Imperial Household Artist

Box seal 1
Teishitsu gigei'in
帝室技芸員
[8] (IV on III)
[11] (IV on III)
[12]
[19]
[21]
[22]
[23]
[24]
[27]
[30]
[35] (IV on III)
[42]
[45] (IV on III)
[47]
[48]
[50]
[51]
[52] (IV on III)
[53] (IV on III)
[57]
[81]
[83]
[89]
[90] (IV on III)
[91]
[92] (IV on III)
[100]

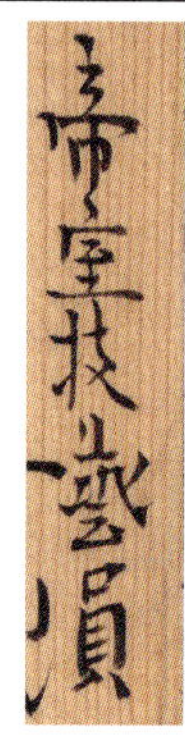

Box inscription 1
Teishitsu gigei'in
帝室技芸員
[82]

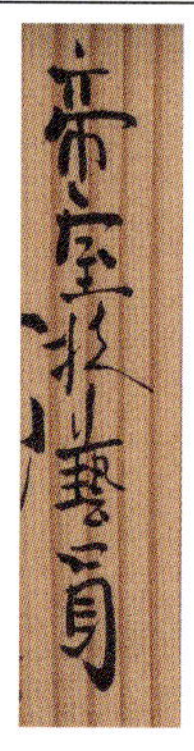

Box inscription 2
Teishitsu gigei'in
帝室技芸員
[33]

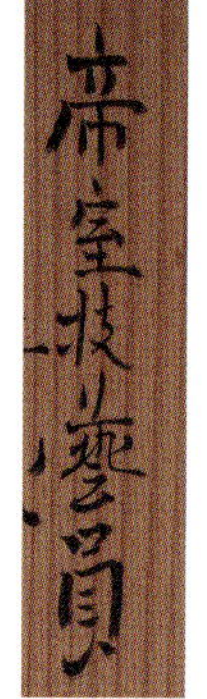

Box inscription 3
Teishitsu gigei'in
帝室技芸員
[13]

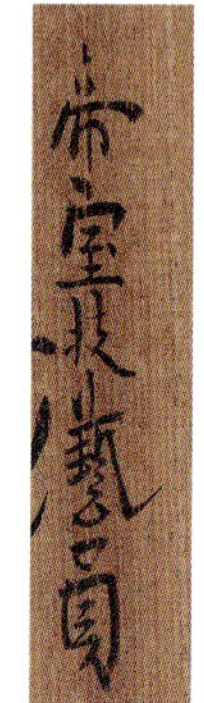

Box inscription 4
Teishitsu gigei'in
帝室技芸員
[51]

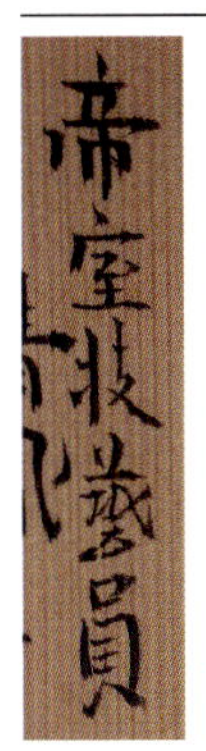

Box inscription 5
Teishitsu gigei'in
帝室技芸員
[**31**]

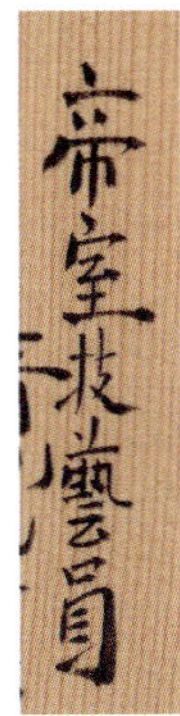

Box inscription 6
Teishitsu gigei'in
帝室技芸員
[**43**]

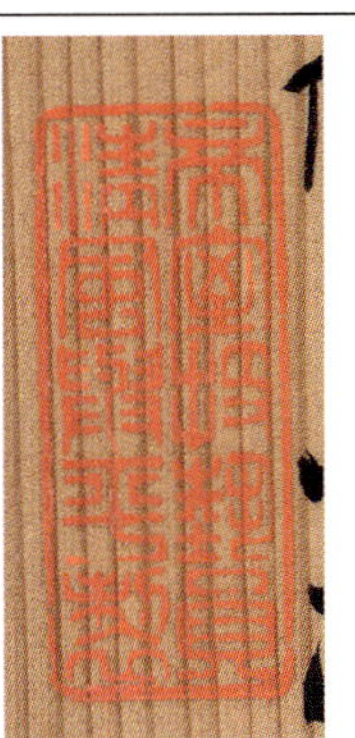

Box seal 2
Teishitsu gigei'in Seifū Yohei zō
帝室技芸員清風與平造
[8]
[26]
[**37**]

Seifū Yohei V

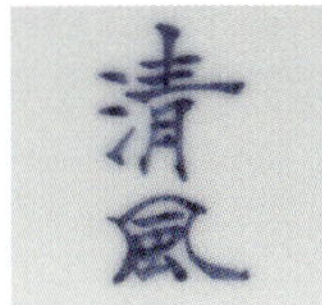

Painted mark
Seifū 清風
[**77**]

Shinkai Kanzan

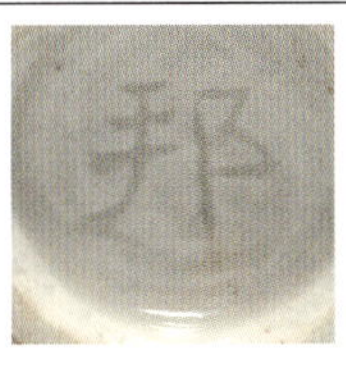

Incised mark
Kuni 邦
[**78**]

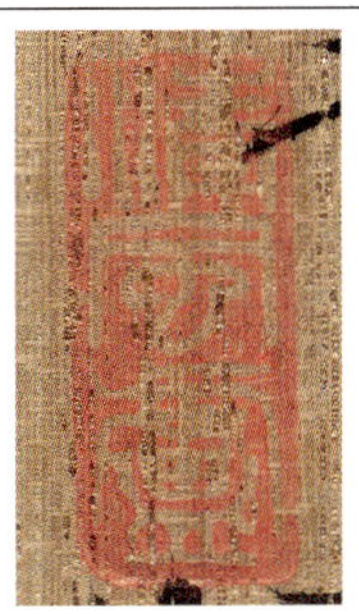

Box seal 1
Seifū ro 清風盧
[**78**]

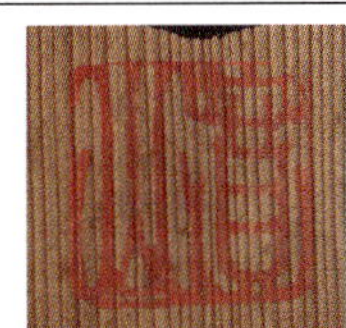

Box seal 2
Kanzan 寛山
[78]
[**80**]

CONCORDANCE OF TERMS

Glosses are provided for key Seifū studio names and terms.

akebonoiro tansai	曙色淡彩	"dawn's light pale [pink] color"
Aoki Mokubei	青木木米	
Arita	有田	
Awata	粟田	
Bai Juyi	白居易	
Baisaō	売茶翁	
bunjincha	文人茶	
bunjinga	文人画	
chanoyu	茶湯	
chayōji	茶葉磁	"tea leaf [color–glazed] porcelain"
Chōjirō	長次郎	
chōshi	銚子	
Daikokuten	大黒天	
Dehua	徳化	
Ding	定	
donburi	丼	
Edo	江戸	
Eiraku Hozen	永樂保全	
fūmon	風門	
ganraikō	鳫来紅	
Ge	哥	
gen (or *hiyu*)	莧	
gohon	御本	
gosu	呉州・呉須	
gosu aka-e	呉須赤絵	
gu	觚	
Guan	官	
gyokuro	玉露	
hageitō	葉鶏頭	
haisen	杯洗	
hakugōrai	白高麗	"Korean white [cream-colored]" ware
Heian	平安	
hiire	火入	
hisokuji	秘色磁	C. *mise ci*; "mysterious color [green] porcelain"

hisokuyō	秘色窯	C. *mise yao*; "mysterious color [green] ware"
hōhin	泡瓶	
hōka	法花	C. *fahua*
Hon'ami Kōetsu	本阿弥光悦	
hongama kōtekiji	本窯璜玓磁	high-fired "lustrous yellow[–glazed] porcelain"
Hosokawa	細川	
hu	壺	
hyakka nishiki	百花錦	"hundred-flower brocade"; multicolor enamel
hyakurō	百老	
hyōretsu	氷裂	"cracked-ice" glaze pattern
Ike Taiga	池大雅	
iro-e	色絵	
Itō Hirobumi	伊藤博文	
Jiangnan	江南	
Jiangsu	江蘇	
Jingdezhen	景徳鎮	
jisaiga	磁彩画	
Jun	均・鈞	
Kagetsuan	花月菴	
Kakiemon	柿右衛門	
Kangxi	康熙	
kanpakuji	瑍白磁	"bright-jewel white porcelain"; abbreviation of *kanpakuji tankōyū*
kanpakuji tankōyū	瑍白磁淡紅釉	"bright-jewel white porcelain with light crimson glaze"; ivory-colored porcelain with translucent cream-colored glaze over ivory-colored low-relief clay designs, surrounded by underglaze gradated pink glaze
kanpakuyū	瑍白釉	"bright-jewel white glaze"; abbreviation of *kanpakuji tankōyū*
karakusa	唐草	
kashibachi	菓子鉢	
Katō Tamikichi	加藤民吉	
Kimura Kenkadō	木村兼葭堂	
kinrande	金欄手	
kinutayū	砧釉	"mallet glaze"; blue-green glaze
kirin	麒麟	C. *qilin*

Kiyomizu Gojōzaka	清水五条坂	
Kiyomizu Miyo	清水みよ	wife of Yohei II
Kiyomizu Rokubei	清水六兵衛	
Kiyomizu Shichibei	清水七兵衛	
Kiyomizuyaki	清水焼	
kōchi	交趾	
kōgō	香合	
kōhakuji	臭珀磁	"lustrous pearl[–glazed ivory] porcelain"
kōro	香炉	
kōyū	紅釉	crimson glaze
kumihimo	組紐	
Kushi Takushin	久志卓真	
kyokusai	旭彩	"morning sun color" pink and yellow glaze
kyūsu	急須	
Li Jiao	李嶠	
Longquan	龍泉	
Lu Tong	盧仝	
Maeda Handen (Chōdō)	前田半田 (暢堂)	
Manchu	満洲	
manji	卍	
Maruyama	円山	
Matsumoto Masaaki	松本雅亮	original name of Yohei VI
meiping	梅瓶	
Ming	明	
Miura Chikusen	三浦竹泉	
Miyagawa (Makuzu) Kōzan	宮川(真葛)香山	
miyako	都	
mizuiroyū	水色釉	"water-colored [blue] glaze"
mizusai	水彩	"water color" [blue] glaze
mizusashi	水指	
Mt. Penglai	蓬莱仙	J. Mt. Hōrai
mukōzuke	向付	
myōhei	茗瓶	
Nabeshima	鍋島	

Nagasaki	長崎	
Nagatani Sōen	永谷宗円	
Nakayoshi	仲吉	
namakoyū	海鼠釉	"sea cucumber [dappled blue] glaze"
nanga	南画	
Naniwa	難波	
Natsume Sōseki	夏目漱石	
nezu	鼠	
Nihonbashi	日本橋	
Nin'ami Dōhachi	仁阿弥道八	
Nishimura Zengorō	西村善五郎	
Nonomura Ninsei	野々村仁清	
Nōtomi Kaijirō	納富介次郎	
nyoi	如意	C. *ruyi*
Ōbaku	黄檗	C. Huangbo
Ogata Kenzan	尾形乾山	
Ogata Kōrin	尾形光琳	
Okada Heikichi	岡田平吉	original name of Yohei III
Okada Ryōhei	岡田良平	father of Yohei III
Okada Seizō	岡田誠三	grandson of Yohei III
ōkayū	櫻華釉	"cherry blossom glaze"
Okuda Eisen	奥田穎川	
Ōshio	大塩	
Qianlong	乾隆	
Qing	清	
Qin Shi Huang	秦始皇	
Qiwan chage	七椀茶歌	J. *Shichiwan chaka*
Raku	楽	
reishi	霊芝	C. *lingzhi*
rōkanji	琅玕磁	dark green glazed porcelain
ruiza	擂座	
rusu mōyō	留守模様	
ryōro	涼炉	
Sagami	相模	

sangōyū	珊瑚釉	coral red glaze
Satō	佐藤	
Satsuma	薩摩	
Seifū Kuma	清風くま	wife of Yohei III
Seifū Yohei	清風與(与)平	name used by the Seifū studio
seiji	青磁	green-glazed porcelain/stoneware; celadon
seika	青華(青花)	underglaze blue
Seizan	靖山	style name of Yohei III while assisting Baikei
	晟山	style name of Yohei III
	成山	style name of Yohei IV
	清山	style name of Yohei III during Shinkai period
sekkashiki	雪花式	snowflake (lit. snow flower)-shaped
sencha	煎茶	
Shigaraki	信楽	
Shinkai Kanzan (Kunitarō)	新開寛山 (邦太郎)	nephew of Yohei IV; Shinkai also used by Yohei III as family name during interim period before taking Seifū name
shinsha	辰砂	red glaze (copper red, oxblood)
shōchikubai	松竹梅	
shoki Imari	初期伊万里	
shokōji	曙光磁	"dawn's light[–glazed] porcelain"
shukaiko	酒海壷	
sometsuke	染付	underglaze blue
Song	宗	
suichū	水注	
taihakuji	太白磁	"great white porcelain"; ivory-colored porcelain with cream glaze
Takahashi Dōhachi	高橋道八	
Takahashi Yoshio (Sōan)	高橋義雄(箒庵)	
takatsuki	高月	
Tang	唐	
Tanomura Chikuden	田能村竹田	
Tanomura Chokunyū	田能村直入	
Tanomura Shōsai	田能村小斎	
teishitsu gigei'in	帝室技芸員	Imperial Household Artist
tenmoku	天目	C. Tianmu

tenseiji	天青磁	“heavenly blue[–glazed] porcelain”
tōchō	豆碟	
tōgosu	唐呉須	
Tomioka Tessai	富岡鉄斎	
tomobako	共箱	
tongping	筒瓶	J. *tōbin*
Tsukinowa Yūsen	月之輪涌泉	
tsukiyoi	月宵	“evening moon [blue]” glaze
Ueda Akinari	上田秋成	
Utagawa Hiroshige	歌川広重	
wucai	五彩	J. *gosai*
Wu Zetian	武則天	
Xiao and Xiang	瀟湘	
Xuande	宣徳	
xuehualan	雪花藍	J. *sekka'ai*; “snowflake blue” glaze
Yamamoto Shōseidō	山本昇盛堂	
Yinyuan Longqi	隠元隆琦	J. Ingen Ryūki
Yongzheng	雍正	
Yosa Buson	与謝蕪村	
Yuan	元	
yuzamashi	湯冷	
Zhangzhou	漳州	
Zhejiang	浙江	
Zhuang Zhou	莊周	
Zhuangzi	莊子	

BIBLIOGRAPHY

Addiss, Stephen. *The World of Kameda Bōsai: The Calligraphy, Poetry, Painting and Artistic Circle of a Japanese Literatus*. New Orleans: New Orleans Museum of Art; Lawrence: University Press of Kansas, 1984.

Barnes, Laurie E. *High Tea: Glorious Manifestations East and West*. West Palm Beach, FL: Norton Museum of Art, 2014.

Bonhams. "Fine Chinese Art: Live Auction 8 November 2018, 10:30 GMT, London." https://www.bonhams.com/auction/24596/fine-chinese-art/.

Dai Sankai Naikoku Kangyō Hakurankai Jimukyoku [Third National Industrial Exhibition Office]. "Meiji nijūsannen dai sankai naikoku kangyō hakurankai shinsa hōkoku: Daiyonrui: Tōjiki" [Review of the 1890 Third National Industrial Exhibition: Section 4: Ceramics]. In vol. 116 of *Meiji zenki sangyō hattatsushi shiryō: Kangyō hakurankai shiryō* [Documents related to the development of industry in the early Meiji period: Industrial exhibition materials], edited by Meiji Bunken Shiryō Kankōkai [Meiji Historical Documents Publishing Association], 153–56. Tokyo: Meiji Bunken Shiryō Kankōkai, 1974. Originally published in 1891.

"Gendai tōgei 41 (Shinkai Kanzan)" [Contemporary ceramics 41 (Shinkai Kanzan)]. *Wa!katta tōgei (Meisōgama)* [Wow, I got it! Ceramic art (Meisōgama)] (blog), February 8, 2012. https://blog.goo.ne.jp/meisogama-ita/e/3aea587e624ea002ab2f43ef9884df5f.

Graham, Patricia J. *Tea of the Sages: The Art of Sencha*. Honolulu: University of Hawai'i Press, 1998.

Honey, William Bowyer. *The Ceramic Art of China and Other Countries of the Far East*. London: Faber & Faber; Hyperion Press, 1945.

Hur, Nam-lin. "Korean Tea Bowls (Kōrai chawan) and Japanese Wabicha: A Story of Acculturation in Premodern Northeast Asia." *Korean Studies*, no. 39 (2015): 1–22.

Jahn, Gisela. *Meiji Ceramics: The Art of Japanese Export Porcelain and Satsuma Ware 1868–1912*. Translated and edited by Michael Foster. Stuttgart: Arnoldsche Art Publishers, 2004.

Krahl, Regina, and Jessica Harrison-Hall. *Chinese Ceramics: Highlights of the Percival David Collection*. London: British Museum Press, 2009.

Kuroda Yuzuru (Tengai). *Ikka issairoku* [Biographical anthology of famous people], 181–84. Tokyo: Kokusho Kankōkai, 1920.

———. "Seifū Yohei-shi" [Mr. Seifū Yohei]. In vol. 1 of *Meika rekihōroku* [Interviews with famous artisans], 25–45. Kyoto: printed by the author, 1899.

Kyōto Bijutsu Kyōkai [Kyoto Art Society], ed. "Teishitsu gigei'in Seifū Yohei shi ri-reki" [Biography of Mr. Seifū Yohei, Imperial Household Artist]. *Kyōto Bijutsu Kyōkai Zasshi* [Journal of Kyoto Art Association], no. 17 (1893): 13–22.

Kyoto Prefecture, ed. *Tōjiki setsu* [Report on ceramics]. Vol. 2. Kyoto Prefecture, 1872. Kyoto Prefectural Library and Archives.

Maezaki, Shinya, ed. *Botsugo hyakunen: Ōshio ga unda kyōyaki no meikō, sandai Seifū Yohei* [One hundred years after his death: Seifū Yohei III, the renowned Kyoto ware craftsman to whom Ōshio gave birth]. Tokyo: Kyacchibōru, 2014.

———. "Kindai tōji to tokkyo seido; Seifū Yohei-ke kara mita 'utsushi' o meguru Kyōyaki no jūkyū seiki" [Early modern ceramics and the patent system: Nineteenth-century Kyoto ware and the issue of "copying" as seen from the perspective of the Seifū Yohei family]. In *Utsushi no chikara: Sōzō to keishō no matorikkusu* [The power of copying: The matrix of creation and continuity], edited by Arata Shimao, Princess Akiko of Mikasa, and Kameda Kazuko, chap. 3. Kyoto: Shibunkaku, 2013.

———. "Naturalism in Meiji-Period Ceramics: Basin with a Crab by Miyagawa Kōzan I (1842–1916)." *Andon*, no. 99 (April 2015): 33–41.

———. "Qing-Style Porcelain in Meiji Japan: The Ceramic Art of Seifū Yohei III." PhD dissertation, School of Oriental and African Studies, University of London, 2009. https://doi.org/10.25501/SOAS.00029585.

Mashimizu Zōroku II. *Kokon kyōgama deichū kanwa* [Idle talks about Kyoto kilns old and new]. Kyoto: Nagasawa Kinkōdō, 1935.

Nomura Museum and Aichi Prefectural Ceramics Archives. *Katamono kōgō banzuke no sekai: chajin no asobigokoro: Nomura bijutsukan kaikan sanjisshūnen kinen tokubetsuten* [The world of the battle of incense burners from molds and the playfulness of tea practitioners: Special exhibition commemorating thirty years since the opening of Nomura Museum]. Kyoto: Nomura

Bunka Zaidan; Seto: Aichi-ken Tōji Shiryōkan, 2013.

Ōe Yoshihide. “Yūsen to Seifū Yohei no kōryū” [The friendship between Yūsen and Seifū Yohei]. In *Tsukinowa Yūsen, Heian Kōzan* [Tsukinowa Yūsen and Heian Kōzan], edited by Kindai Bonsai Henshūbu [Modern Bonsai Editorial Department], 125–27. Kyoto: Kindai Shuppan, 2016.

Ohki Sadako, with a contribution from Takeshi Watanabe. *Tea Culture of Japan*. New Haven, CT: Yale University Art Gallery, 2009.

Okada Seizō. *Jibun ningen* [Self human]. Tokyo: Chūō Kōronsha, 1977.

Okamoto Takashi. “Sandai Seifū Yohei ni tsuite (3): 1900-nen Pari Bankoku Hakurankai shuppinsaku o megutte” [On Seifū Yohei III (3): Works submitted to the 1900 Paris Exposition]. *Sannomaru Shozōkan nenpō, kiyō* [Sannomaru Shozōkan annual report and journal], no. 14 (2007): 47–54.

Osaka Museum of History. *Kimura Kenkadō: Naniwa chi no kyojin; Tokubetsuten botsugo 200-nen kinen* [Kimura Kenkadō: Intellectual giant of Naniwa; Special exhibition commemorating his 200th memorial anniversary]. Kyoto: Shibunkaku, 2003.

Ōshio Kōminkan Kyōdoshi Henshū Iinkai [Ōshio Community Center Local History Committee], ed. *Ōshio ni ikiru hitobito: Kyōdoshi* [The people living in Ōshio: A local history]. Himeji: Ōshio Kōminkan Kyōdoshi Henshū Iinkai, 1995.

Pitelka, Morgan. *Handmade Culture: Raku Potters, Patrons, and Tea Practitioners in Japan.* Honolulu: University of Hawai‘i Press, 2005.

Rousmaniere, Nicole Coolidge. *Vessels of Influence: China and the Rebirth of Porcelain in Medieval and Early Modern Japan.* London: Bloomsbury Academic, 2012.

Scidmore, Eliza Ruhamah. “The Porcelain-Artists of Japan.” *Harper's Weekly* 42, no. 2144 (1898): 83–88.

Seki Kazuo. *Kyoto Ceramist Seifū Yohei III: The Brilliance of the Meiji Era; Beginning of the Modern Ceramic Age.* Tokyo: Sōjusha Bijutsu Shuppan, 2012.

———. *Sandai Seifū Yohei: Meiji no kagayaki, kindai tōgei no hajimari* [Seifū Yohei III: Meiji brilliance and the start of modern ceramics]. Tokyo: Sōjusha Bijutsu Shuppan, 2012.

Shin'ei Takesato, ed. *Toki no kaze: Ōshio daiichi tochi kukaku seiri jigyō kankō kinenshi* [The wind of time: In commemoration of completion of the Ōshio No. 1 land readjustment project]. Himeji: Himeji-shi Ōshio Daiichi Tochi Kukaku Seiri Kumiai, 1992.

Shirahara, Yukiko. *Japan Envisions the West: 16th–19th Century Japanese Art from Kobe City Museum.* Seattle: Seattle Art Museum, 2007.

Takahashi Yoshio (Sōan). *Kinsei dōgu idōshi* [History of the transition of tea wares]. Tokyo: Ariake Shobō, 1936.

Tanomura Chokunyū. *Seiwan chakai zuroku* [Illustrated record of the Azure Bay Tea Gathering]. Vol. 3, *Jin* [People]. Naniwa: printed by the author, 1863. National Diet Library Digital Collections.

Ueda Akinari. *Seifū sagen* [Trifling stories of pure wind]. In vol. 2 of *Ueda Akinari zenshū* [The complete works of Ueda Akinari], edited by Kokusho Kankōkai, 479–502. Tokyo: Kokusho Kankōkai, 1918.

Watanabe Shun. “Kyōyaki to sono meikō ni tsuite” [On Kyoto ware and its craftsmen]. *Toshi to geijutsu* [City and art], no. 205 (1930): 15–20.

Watanabe, Takeshi. “From Korea to Japan and Back Again: One Hundred Years of Japanese Tea Culture through Five Bowls, 1550–1650.” In “Japanese Art at Yale,” edited by Sadako Ohki and Melanie B. D. Klein. *Yale University Art Gallery Bulletin* (2007): 82–99.

Zhuang Zhou. *Chuang Tzu: Basic Writings.* Translated by Burton Watson. New York: Columbia University Press, 1964.

INDEX

Page numbers in *italics* refer to illustrations.

THE CLEVELAND MUSEUM OF ART BOARD OF TRUSTEES